IMAGES OF AFRICA

D1563035

IMAGES OF AFRICA
Stereotypes & Realities

Edited by Daniel M. Mengara

Preface by Molefi Kete Asante

Contributors

Martin Bernal

Miriam Dow
Buluda Itandala
Janet S. McIntosh
Mahamadou Diallo
Kristof Haavik
Mongi Bahloul
Jonhattan Gosnell
Valerie Orlando
Jeannette Eileen Jones

John Gruesser
Victoria Ramirez
Jessica Levin
Martha Grise
Jean Muteba Rahier
Bill Gaudelli
Augustine Okereke
David Pattison
Sharmila Sen

Africa World Press, Inc.

P.O. Box 1892
Trenton, NJ 08607

P.O. Box 48
Asmara, ERITREA

Africa World Press, Inc.

P.O. Box 1892   P.O. Box 48
Trenton, NJ 08607   Asmara, ERITREA

Cover design: Ashraful Haq

Library of Congress Cataloging -in-Publication Data

Images of Africa : stereotypes and realities / edited by Daniel M. Mengara.
    p.   cm.
  Includes bibliographical references and index.
  ISBN 0-86543-906-0 – ISBN 0-86543-907-9 (pbk.)
    1. Stereotype (Psychology)--Africa. 2. Africa--Public opinion. 3. Africa--In mass media. 4. Africa--In literature. 5. Africa--Foreign relations. 6. Public opinion--Europe. I. Mengara, Daniel M., 1967-

HM1096.I42 2000
306'.096–dc21

00-048521

Dedication

I dedicate this book to:

My parents, Pierre Minko and Akui Assogo who are back there in Minvoul, Gabon. They have always been so supportive of me. I know this endeavor will make them proud.

My wife, Sylvie.

My children, Pierre and Melanie.

My brother, Ndong Minko

My African extended family: my aunt, Eyang Assogo, her children (my brothers according to Fang traditions), Ze Ondo, Obame Ondo, Mba Ondo, Mbolo Ondo, Ella Ondo, Zong Ondo and all their children, including the whole Essangwame clan in the village of Mekaga, Minvoul, Gabon, where I was born 33 years ago.

All the Africanists seeking to bring some light into the darkness with which Africa was covered.

Contents

Jean Muteba Rahier, *Florida International University*, "(US-Centered Afrocentric Imaginations of Africa: L.H. Clegg's *When Black Men Ruled the World*, and Eddie Murphy's *Coming to America*" 261

Acknowledgement

I would, first and foremost, like to express my greatest gratitude to Professor Victoria Larson to whom I am deeply indebted in relation to this volume. We began this book project together, but Professor Larson could not continue due to her being overwhelmed by other professional engagements.

My gratitude also goes to all those who, at Montclair State University, helped me with the SORAC 98 International Conference. It is thanks to this conference and to the exceptional quality of the papers presented that I was able to engage in the putting together of this volume. In particular, I would like to thank all those who, at Montclair State University, played an important role in making SORAC 98 possible: the French Department, for their warm support, Tim Renner and Sally Garson of the Institute for the Humanities for helping to sponsor and organize the conference, the Global Education Center for generously issuing the grant that helped to finance SORAC 98, SORAC Executive Board members Victoria Larson, Leslie Wilson and Adele McCollum for helping with advice, planning and assistance, and our student assistants Paul Emile Stephan Simon and Benjamin Lociano.

My thanks also go to all those who closely or remotely contributed to the editing of this volume, including all the authors who submitted their essays for publication in the current book. Special acknowledgements should go to *Life* Magazine for authorizing reproduction of the photos of Albert Schweitzer and his Lambaréné Hospital in Gabon (pp. 239 and 243), and to the University Press of Kentucky for allowing John Gruesser to reproduce parts of his book in his article included in this volume.

Thanks to all for giving Africa an additional and powerful voice through this exceptionally informative volume.

Preface

Molefi Kete Asante
Temple University

At the top of the twentieth century Africa remains the most misunderstood of continents, crippled in our imagination by images rooted in the minds of imperial Europeans who attempted to shape and invent an Africa useful to their political ambitions. With the publication of *Images of Africa: Stereotypes and Realities* edited by Daniel M. Mengara we have a volume that seeks to provide a more rounded view of the continent.

Mengara has organized a well-qualified group of scholars to present images of Africa from antiquity to the present, from literary visions to political reconstructions, and from education to medicine. Discovering an accomplished cadre of authors willing to engage in rational discourse on the nature of the African continent and then bringing them together in such a work is a feat of no small undertaking.

The book is rationally constructed in seven parts: Ancient European Perceptions of Africa, Western Imperial Ideology in Theory and Practice, Africa, Orientalism and the West, Africa in the Americas, Media-ting Africa, Feminism and Women in Africa, and African Literatures: Text and Pre-Text. Of course, Mengara has utilized his own personal gifts as a literary theorist and critic to position the authors in this volume according to their intellectual, rhetorical, and aesthetic significance. The presence of Martin Bernal as the cornerstone author for the first part is quite significant and rather impressive. Having secured Bernal for the section on Ancient European Perceptions of

Africa, Mengara succeeded in placing his volume in the forefront of those interested in serious discourse on the role of Africa in the world. There are other brilliant thinkers in this volume and most of the pieces hold together quite well. Of course, there are uneven parts as one will find in any volume of collected works.

In many ways the authors in this volume point to Europe's intervention in Africa as the beginning of the most nefarious images. An Africa invented for European purposes could no longer serve the interest of its own people. Taken off of its political, economic, and cultural terms Africa became an object to be used, abused, and then shoved to the historical curb. It was not without background that Hegel wrote in 1828, "Let us forget Africa, for it is no part of human history." By the 19th century the images of Africa were already tattered and torn by Europe's handling of the information about the lands that had been conquered, colonized, and Christianized. Unable to escape the constant and prolific barrage of imperial European writing about Africa, the people of Africa became, for the rest of the world, nothing more than the "bearers of burdens" for Europe.

Rather than argue about the meaning of Europe in Africa, the authors in this volume by Mengara have spent considerable time and energy trying to demonstrate that Africa remains its own continent through all of the haze of European intervention. Of course, some nations and cultures of Africa have survived and prospered better than others. The verdict on the continent can neither be given today nor tomorrow, but must await a future time when an Afrocentric Africa, aware of itself in a self conscious way, will step back on the world stage with its own gifts, however evolved, shaped, and altered by experience and history, to claim what was lost.

It is impossible to appreciate the full extent of the stereotypes that have been portrayed about Africa without some historical knowledge. Happily for the reader, the authors of this volume have provided the reader with ample information to cover those areas that are not well discussed in contemporary literature, e.g., the German massacre of the Herero ethnic group in Namibia. Those who approach African studies without the necessary historical depth will find the chapters in this book helpful. I believe that Professor Mengara's critical insight and keen sense of propriety have given us ample opportunity to declare that the images of Africa will not remain forever locked in the negative chambers of the past.

This book will be consulted by scholars and lay people in many fields but most importantly by those in African Studies, African literature, African American Studies, and history. *Images of Africa: Stereotypes and Realities* speaks to the possibilities of an Africa that is freed of the imposition of others and consequently an Africa that could rise at any occasion. I am excited by all the uses that could be made of the works that appear in this expertly edited and well written volume.

Molefi Kete Asante
Limon, Costa Rica
September 2000

Introduction
White Eyes, Dark Reflections[1]

Daniel M. Mengara
Montclair State University

Africa has indeed come a long way since the first European set foot on the continent several centuries ago. The colonial encounter between Europe and Africa has, over the span of the more than 500 years of common history that they now share, led not only to the enslavement of the African negro for the purposes of economic capitalism, but also to the construction of racial and cultural stereotypes that have seen in Africans only the embodiment of primitivism, chaos, and sexual lust, among other negative characterizations (Davidson 1970; Scholefield, 1975; Sala-Molins, 1992). Africa has also been seen as a land of despotic civilizations with no legacy of those democratic principles that have been so dear to the West's self-image.[2]

In precolonial[3] times western historical knowledge of sub-Saharan Africa was in fact very limited. Although the ancient Greeks had heard of Ethiopia, land of the blacks, earlier acquaintance with Africa, above all as it applies to Africa below Egypt, was mostly limited to the mythical accounts to be found in the works of such ancient Greek writers as Homer (e.g., *The Odyssey*, set down in writing around 750BC) or Herodotus (e.g., *Histories*, 430-420BC). In spite of the fact that knowledge of North Africa and of the area that ancient Greeks knew as Ethiopia became more material in later centuries due to the major invasions that brought the Assyrians, the Greeks, the Persians, the Ptolemies, and the Romans, among others, to this northern part, a better awareness of Africa beyond its primal Egyptian legacy was not achieved until the Arab penetrations of the seventh and eighth centuries AD. These Arab conquests led to the establishment of more elaborate trade routes that, from then on, enabled commercial links—most of which were based on the slave, gold and ivory trade—between sub-Saharan Africa and the outside world along the east coast and across the Sahel Corridor. They also brought to the world the first modern accounts of Sub-Saharan Africa by eye-witnesses such as Ibn Battuta whose 14th century writings and testimonies have been very helpful in reconstructing some aspects of Africa's pre-European history (Hamdun and King, 1994).

It was not, however, until the arrival of the first European explorers in the 15th century that acquaintance with sub-Saharan Africa found its most concrete expression. Contrary to popular belief, which often holds that not much was known of the interior of Africa before the great explorations and "discoveries" of the 18th and 19th centuries, I would rather assert that the consequences of the encounter between Europe and Africa very early on left no part of Africa unstirred. In fact, it can even be said that, by the 17th century—and certainly due to the intensification of the trans-Atlantic slave trade—almost all of Africa's hinterland had had contacts of some sort, either directly or indirectly, with the outside world (McEvedy 1995: 80). But such contacts also culminated in the subsequent centuries, above all in the 18th and 19th centuries, with the categorizing and labeling that eventually led to what Mudimbe calls "the invention of Africa" (1988), that is, the systematic and systemic manufacturing of a continent on the basis of the Aristotelian paradigms of superiority versus inferiority, civilized versus uncivilized, among other epithets. It is also around this very time that concepts of color as distinctive determinants of racial categorization and classification found their most vivid expression within the western establishment (Bernal, 1987). The Berlin Conference of 1885 that signalled the "scramble" for the formal territorial ownership of the whole of Africa by individual empires was thus to be seen as the predictable outcome of 1) the European empires' long attested desire to own portions of the world as a way of signifying their hegemonic grandeur, 2) the transfer of their secular European rivalries onto virgin grounds where imperial wars could be indirectly fought, and last but not least, 3) a capitalist fervor that the colonial "discoveries" of rich lands in Africa and the Americas, the slave trade and the development of commerce with the eastern and middle eastern worlds had helped to trigger.

However, in order for the colonial process to appear acceptable to the European mind, it had to be justified. Such a justification could be validated only if the lands to be conquered and the peoples who inhabited them were expropriated[4] of their own identities and constructed in the western mind as objects of devastation, ignorance and primitivism that needed to be saved by the West. This process of expropriation, that is, of construction, of invention of a European-made Africa as Mudimbe (1988) would put it, took about five centuries—from the Portuguese arrivals in the 15th century to the Berlin conference of the 19th. These five centuries quickly became centuries of all-around explorations and expropriations during which missionaries and other tycoons undertook to re-map, re-shape, re-name Africa according to a European view of the world.

This process of expropriation could be seen as one by which Africa's *identities* as plurally defined by indigenous Africans themselves were progressively replaced with a single monolithic *African identity* as specifically reformulated by the European empires. Thus, territories that were once defined by the individual ethnicities (*identities*) that inhabited them were now conglomerated, amalgamated and reshaped into artificial nations—with *one national identity.* Territories with such names as Rhodesia brought foreign designations to local areas. Nature itself was not spared. Lakes took on such European names as Lake Victoria, and the African names by which some features of indigenous landscape were known prior to the European penetrations fell into oblivion.

One of the factors that can help to explain the re-shaping, re-naming and re-mapping of the African continent could be found in the necessity for Europe to recreate a new home for itself in Africa. For this to happen, it had to Europeanize the black continent and make it an extension of itself. Expropriating the continent of its African identities therefore meant, concurrently, an imposition of a European identity over the African infrastructure[5]. African identities thus had to be suppressed and reformulated to fit the western model of civilization.

In order to have a better idea of how important it was for the European conqueror to export himself to the deemed "virgin" lands of Africa, it suffices to take a look at the motivations of Cecil Rhodes in Southern Africa. Approbatory analogies, implicit and explicit, between Rhodes' scramble for Africa, and the imperial conquests made by the Greeks and Romans are endemic, not only in the older, adulatory, and indeed almost cringing biographies of Rhodes, to which genre Baker's book, *Cecil Rhodes by his Architect* (1938), for example, belongs, but also in modern, ostensibly more objective biographies such as Robert Rotberg's *The Founder: Cecil Rhodes and the Pursuit of Power*.[6] It appears that Rhodes himself had a vision of his empire in Southern Africa as a new Roman Empire and of himself as a Roman emperor[7]. Baker, his architect, tells us, for example, that Rhodes

> was fond of turning over the pages of a book containing photographs of busts of the Roman emperors and, coming to that of Titus, I have heard him say, 'He has a fine forehead,' as his hand passed over his own. Was he thinking perhaps of one of his marked texts of Marcus Aurelius, 'Take care always to remember that you are a Roman. Have a care you are not too much a Caesar?'"[8]

In so doing, Rhodes participated, we suggest, in a vision of the British empire that was endemic among nineteenth-century British imperialists and that was instrumental to the acquisition and/or administration of the British empire in all parts of the world. In fact, only in the matter of motivation does the British empire differ from its Roman predecessor according to writers that at the turn of the century elaborated the analogy between modern British imperialism and ancient Roman imperialism.[9] Whereas, it is asserted, the Romans conquered merely for their own self interest, the British, it is claimed, conquered for the good of others or, as Cecil Rhodes put it so bluntly in his *Confession of Faith* (Flint: 1974):

I contend that we are the finest race in the world and that the more of the world we inhabit the better it is for the human race ...Africa is still lying ready for us – it is our duty to take it! (Flint: 248-250)

Even if Rhodes's visions reflected a particularly British view of the imperial process, he nevertheless stands as an embodiment of a manner of thinking that was general throughout imperial Europe as competition for Africa grew harsher during the centuries of the scramble (18 and 19th mostly).

But there was more. For the imperial process to be effective, the knowledge that Africans had of themselves and of their own environment also had to be obliterated. Thus, the various "discoveries" of peoples, lands, mountains and rivers were presented by the various explorers as happening for the *first time* thanks to *them* and owing to their unfaltering courage. The Africans who lived around those areas and who had names for all of those paradoxically newly "discovered" things were seen as invisible presences whose knowledge of the existence of these things did not count. Also, despite the fact that all the European explorers (Livingston, Speke, Stanley and many others) who traveled across and throughout Africa used native informants who usually took them to those "undiscovered" places, native knowledge was not considered valuable. The basic assumption in the European mind was therefore that the acquaintance that the natives had with their environments did not exceed the confines of their tribal dwellings: beyond these territorial delimitations, there was only darkness.[10]

It is in this context that Sala-Molins, in his *Les misères des lumières: sous la raison, l'outrage* (1992, The Miseries of the Enlightenment: Beneath Reason, the Outrage), contends that it is an act of deliberate cleansing of historical realities that Enlightenment thinkers should be read and credited with high intellectual standards without any mention of their less admirable positions on matters of colonization and enslavement of the Africans. Sala-Molins argues that the Enlightenment period was in itself a period of intellectual expansionism and therefore cannot be dissociated from the colonial enterprise and its slavery-based imperialism. As a consequence, most contemporary images of Africa may be said to have reached a formative peak during and after the Enlightenment period in Europe, where great thinkers such as Hobbes, Montesquieu, Condorcet, Hegel, Hume and later Victor Hugo, to mention a few, did not hesitate to formulate racist theories about Africans as primitive peoples who:

1.   had no history; therefore, they could not claim to know themselves and had to be told who they were by Europeans.
2.   were cultural children shaped by sexual lust, immorality and degeneration.
3.   could not rule themselves because of their primitive irresponsibility; therefore, they needed enlightened masters to show them the ways of superior civilization and deliver them from ignorance.
4.   could not claim ownership of Africa, or even of their lands since they were incapable of cultivating and managing them.
5.   had no right to human justice, being sub-humans as they were.
6.   had no religion and therefore needed the light of Christianity if they were to be freed from their chaotic state of nature and from animism.

As Sala-Molins argues, then, these judgments formulated by European thinkers on the human inadequacy of black Africans since the beginnings of the colonial era acquired, in the 17th, 18th and 19th centuries, several functions:

1.   justification of territorial occupation in Africa
2.   justification of the enslavement of Africans
3.   fabrication of multifarious images of Africa that would permanently justify its violent exploitation and enslavement on the basis of the God-given right to conquer those who need God's salvation and the light of Christian "humanism."

In fact, the Bible itself had long been at the root of imperialism. In Deuteronomy (7: 1-3), for instance, it is said:

When the Lord your God brings you into the land which you are entering to occupy and drives out many nations before you (...), when the Lord delivers them into your power and you defeat them, you must put them to death (...). (...) you must not intermarry with them, neither giving your daughters to their sons nor taking their daughters for your sons.

The spirit of conquest is also present in Western philosophical thinking as can be seen through the writings of Aristotle, doyen of western philosophy, who declares:

For that some should rule and others be ruled is a thing not only necessary, but expedient; from the hour of their birth, some are marked out for subjection, others for rule (...). (...) The rule of the inferior is always hurtful. The same holds good of animals in relation to men; for tame animals have a better nature than wild, and all tame animals are better off when they are ruled by man; for then, they are preserved. Again, the male is by nature superior, and the female inferior; and the one rules, and the other is ruled; this principle, of necessity, extends to all mankind (Aristotle, *The Politics*, I.v.2, Jowett's translation).

Aristotle, that is, western philosophy itself, when it comes to sociopolitical organizations, is clear: there must be rulers and ruled, slaves and masters, superior beings and inferior beings, for the world to function properly. Only those who are marked to be strong and civilized from birth, deserve to rule. By ruling the inferior, and by imposing on them the rule of "civilization," the strong are saving the "uncivilized" from extinction and self-destruction. The impact of ancient Greek philosophy on western history and thinking in general therefore helps to explain the imperialist surges and urges that have gripped the west throughout most of its history, urges that became even more poignant during the Enlightenment period and beyond.

Indeed, European colonial and commercial imperialism—based, unlike African cultures, on the high valuation of land ownership and the private good—implied expansion; but such an expansion could only occur in a context of forceful impositions on cultures not prepared for the armies and centralized power structures that made expansion by the European monarchies possible. In fact, if anything is to explain the reasons why, beyond the absence of any material proof of "civilization" (for instance, a writing system, vestiges of ancient civilizations as seen in Greek art, Egyptian and Aztec pyramids, Eastern sciences, monumental architecture, among others), the peoples of sub-Saharan Africa were categorized at the very bottom of humanity (Davidson, 1970 & 1991; Scholefield, 1975; Mudimbe, 1988), this is certainly to be found in the way their decentralized structures of sociopolitical organization and absence of private land-ownership were perceived. By this perception—typified, for example, by the teleological theories of the Swiss antiquarian Johann Bachofen (1815-1887)—"progress" was conceived only in terms of an evolution away from common land ownership (accompanied inevitably, in this view, by sexual promiscuity, female power, and natural chaos) towards private ownership of land (accompanied by the "western virtues" of good agricultural practice, monogamy, and patriarchy). Such a view of progress was conditioned by multifarious stereotypes which, century after century, came to deform, invalidate and misconstruct the African universe, burying it under layers of historical fallacies that explorers, missionaries and 18th-century scholars and thinkers consecrated as historical truths in their attempts to denigrate the non-west in general, and Africa in particular.[11] At the same time, they undertook to elevate western civilization to a level of specificity and superiority that sought to recognize none of the contributions from a non-western world forcefully reduced to a simple existentialism that equated primitivism with evil and animality (Bernal 1987; Mudimbe 1988).

Clearly, the Africa that we know or hear about today is, essentially, a European-made Africa. It is a world almost totally manufactured in image, molded into postcolonial[12] chaos and dependence, and conditioned to be permanently perceived as a continent where nothing works because of the inherently chaotic, despotic and uncivilized nature of its peoples (Christopher, 1984; Eboussi-Boulaga, 1981). However, such a perception of Africa is itself inherently misleading because totally inaccurate in its portrayal of the specific values and traits of civilization that typify the African universe. In present-day Africa, one finds, not one type of society, but hundreds, all intertwined into an undecipherable bulk of traditional alliances and ethnicities upon which artificial, European-manufactured nationalities were imposed. When dealing with Africa, western as well as (conditioned) African scholars have not always attempted to decipher this sociocultural *imbroglio* and have thus perpetuated inherited perspectives and stereotypes which have now become the "natural skin" of a whole continent and its peoples. This perpetuation of historical fallacies inevitably poses a serious threat to Africa's ability to redefine itself, because little that is "known" about Africa today originates from Africans themselves. Since the very beginnings of European colonial expansion, works claiming to be anthropological had been published by questionable missionaries, explorers and administrators[13] who, in order to justify their conquest of the continent, *had to* present the continent as a land of civilizational devastation that needed European enlightenment if it were to be saved from its spiritual obscurity and its continental darkness (Deschamps, 1971; Sévry, 1991).

Among the most nefarious legacies of Europe's presence in Africa, one finds such socio-cultural traits as:

1) **Central authority, despotism and dictatorship**: according to such scholars as Mengara and Larson (2001) and Ayittey (1991), strong central and monarchical authority of the western or Arab kind, which tends to concentrate enormous powers in the hands of an individual ruler, was absent in Africa prior to Arab and European penetrations. On the basis of observations of Western civilizations from ancient times to the present, Mengara and Larson (2001) were able to conclude that, in fact, the West never invented democracy, but, rather, "stole" it from Africa.[14] Thus, the introduction and transfer into Africa of ways of ruling that were individual rather than communal, and the post-independence machinations that led the crumbling colonial empires to transfer power to African puppets who would continue to secure their capitalist interests, paved the way for the despotic and dictatorial regimes that epitomize Africa today.

2) **Tribalism and warfare spirit**: because of the European empires' need to secure territories in Africa, division of tribal groups was often used as a means of controlling the various in-

digenous forces. Some of the earliest examples of such strategies could be seen in the Portuguese manipulations of the Kongo kingdom rulers in the 15th and 16th centuries. Such manipulations, as could be expected, led to internal conflicts that eventually led to the kingdom's downfall (Hilton, 1985). Also, the artificial borders that resulted from the carving up of Africa into territories whose configurations did not take into account the ethnic make-up of the continent led to perpetual internal tensions among the various ethnic groups that were now forced to share the same country. The genocidal wars between the Hutus and the Tutsis in Rwanda certainly stem from such arbitrary regroupings of peoples with distinct cultural backgrounds.

3) **Political instability, mismanagement and economic bankruptcy**: according to McNamara (1989), the fact that Africans were almost never associated with the management of their territories under colonial rule helps to explain why they were basically unprepared to rule over new artificial nationalities that required of them that they manage not only economic systems to which they had not had the time to adapt, but also political and governmental systems that were often alien to the indigenous ones. Another factor that was to add to the postcolonial political instability in Africa was that groups used to being ruled only by their own were now forced to be ruled by ethnicities with whom they had little in common. In such a context, the preservation of power was going to be dependent upon the implementation by the (precariously) ruling group of strategies of survival that would often involve military dictatorship, corruption and the despotic manipulation of internal politics.

4) **Economic and political dependence**: indeed, the fact that the colonizer did not, in a calculated and purposeful move, involve natives in the management of their own lands, resulted in a general state of African unpreparedness at the time of their independence. The former colonizer had, by this method, simply paved the way for his own return to Africa as a neo-colonizer. In other words, the European empires, when granting "offered" independences to Africans, knew they would still be needed for a while by countries that were now dependent upon western economic systems which they were not yet prepared to manage. In addition, in a global context where economic dependence neces-

sarily meant political dependence, the former empires had en-sured themselves of the full cooperation, loyalty and ready avail-ability of their dependent African nations in matters of world politics and economics.

Of course, Africans themselves have their share of responsi-bility in this equation too. Taking inspiration from their former colonial masters, they diligently sought to imitate them, bor-rowing and perpetuating the same despotic laws and methods of governing that the Europeans had used to maintain Africans un-der firm control: a strong police force or military, the harnessing of the freedom of expression, unlawful and arbitrary arrests of political activists or opponents, general abuses of human rights, etc. As a result, they reproduced a bastardized model of socio-political, cultural and economic organization that is neither Afri-can nor western. Because of the particular circumstances of its history and the failed syncretisms that western values and Afri-can values have produced therein, the African continent south of the Sahara has been able to offer to the mirror of the world only a pale reflection of its true self: it has become the epitome of cor-ruption, mismanagement, despotism, ethnic warfare, disease, economic and political irresponsibility, and societal failure.

Some forty years after African independences, one is forced to note that Africa has not yet come to terms with the experience of colonization. The meeting of African and European cultures has, for centuries, produced a bastardized—not totally African and not totally European—culture on the African continent and the effects of this bastardization are still felt today. Indeed, Afri-can intellectuals have in the past attempted to address the issue of African identity(ies). From the 1930's to the 1960's, and later, figures such as Léopold Sédar Senghor, Kwame Nkrumah, Chinua Achebe, Ngugi wa Thiong'o and many others undertook to redefine African identity through political/literary movements such as Negritude and Pan-Africanism, among others, that sought to give to the black man and woman a sense of direction and specificity that would revive in them the pride of being black that had been crushed by the European colonialists. At the scien-tific and scholarly level, Cheick Anta Diop's anthropological and historical research opened the way for new possibilities of per-ceiving Africa's contributions to human history. In the African diaspora, the works of earlier Negritude scholars such as Aimé Césaire, Frantz Fanon, or of America's Harlem renaissance writers such as W.E.B. Du Bois and Langston Hughes, among others, have been echoed by modern intellectual movements such as Afrocentricity (or Afrocentrism), a movement that has been popularized in North America by such scholars as George G. M. James, ben-Jochannan, and Molefi Asante, to mention a few.[15] Western scholars themselves have also started to re-visit their notions of Africa. For instance, in *Black Athena*, the first volume of which was published in 1987, Martin Bernal posited a theory that revolutionized classical history because it saw Africa as being at the root of Greek civilization, that is, of western civilization itself.

All of these endeavours have resulted in a process of historical and cultural palimpsesting[16] that has sought to rewrite, over the more and more blurred text of European perceptions, things African from an African(ist) perspective. However, these identity reconstruction efforts at the historical and cultural levels have remained in sharp contrast with the images continually displayed by current events in Africa: Africa still stands today as a poverty-stricken, war-devastated, disease-full, corrupt and despotic continent due to the mismanagement and cleptocracy of an old generation of leaders that had been left or placed in power to serve the needs of both their former colonial masters and themselves

While the deconstruction of Africa's European-made identity has been relatively successful at an intellectual and historical level, the reconstruction of Africa's identities from a practical, cultural and contemporary point of view does not seem very promising due to the too many interests—both national and international—that have been exploiting and ransacking the continent since the very day when the first European set foot on the continent some 500 years ago. The reconstruction of Africa's future will therefore be achieved only when the systems left in place by the colonial establishment and what the Africans themselves have done with their own countries are deconstructed. It is in this context of the deconstruction of Africa's European-made past that this volume sets itself.

This book stems from a conference entitled "Images of Africa: Stereotypes and Realities" organized by the editor of this volume during the Fall semester of 1998. The conference featured some 140 speakers from 17 countries in Africa, Europe and North America. Its object was a re-exploration of African history that would enable a better understanding of the African continent through a revisitation of the various western-made stereotypes that have come to define the African world as we "know" it today. The rationale was therefore to show that Africa had a history of its own prior to European invasions, and that this history had been hijacked by the West for the purposes of colonization and world supremacy. Because people do not often see Africa as a continent whose historical course was deviated by the imposition, upon it, of European models of civilization, it was important that they understood, through a book exclusively consecrated to this end, that Africa as it stands today is in fact Africa as shaped by European colonialists. In other words, there is a huge blank gap of about 500 years from the time when the first Europeans set foot on the continent separating pre-European Africa from the African independences, a gap so enormous that it represents not only 500 years of invisibility, but also 500 years of an imposed loss of historical memory. Thus, Africa's history and contributions to human civilization cannot be fully understood and appreciated without a thorough exploration of its European legacy and the peeling away of this legacy in order to reveal the true essence of the African world.

This book is all the more important because Africa is now poised over a significantly symbolic line, a line that represents the continent's crossing over from its European-made past to the third millennium of, hopefully, an African-made future. This volume therefore aims to contribute in several respects to a recovery of this lost African memory by offering insights into how and why it was lost. As such, this collective endeavor certainly has a significant role to play in the Afrocentrism vs. Aryanism[17] debates that currently permeate the academic world, debates that Martin Bernal's *Black Athena* has helped to rekindle since its publication in 1987. However, unlike Bernal's masterpiece whose focus is primarily on the impact of Africa's Egypt on the civilizations around the Mediterranean, our volume concentrates on the whole of Africa, from North to South, and from ancient to colonial to modern times. Because of its comprehensive nature, it is our conviction that the reader of this book will not only find in it the kind of intellectual stimulation that will bring closure to often unanswered questions, but also help to unveil the still "dark continent" and bring it into the sun of world recognition.

Part I of this volume, entitled "Ancient European Perceptions of Africa," contains a new article by Martin Bernal who, in his "European Images of Africa - Tale of Two Names: Ethiop and N...," will investigate the issues revolving around the word "nigger" and its ancient and modern origins (which Bernal controversially places in Africa itself). Miriam Dow offers a post-colonial reading of ancient texts in her "Menelaos, the Cyclopes, and Eurybates: a Post-Colonial Reading of Homer," and Buluda Itandala explores the various "European Images of Africa from Early Times to the Eighteenth Century."

Part II deals more specifically with "Western Imperial Ideology in Theory and Practice," and features articles that provide insights into the various motives that led the European colonists to conquer Africa. This subject is tackled in "Strategic Amnesia: Versions of Vasco da Gama on the Kenya Coast" (Janet S. McIntosh), "Literature of Empire and the African Environment" (Mahamadou Diallo), and "From Crusades to Colonies: Africa in French Literature" (Kristof Haavik).

In Part III, "Africa, Orientalism and the West," Mongi Bahloul, Jonathan Gosnell and Valerie Orlando examine issues pertaining to "The North-African Motif in Early American Fiction," the "Mediterranean Waterways, Extended Borders and Colonial Mappings: French Images of North Africa," and "Transposing the Political and the Aesthetical: Eugene Fromentin's Contributions to Oriental Stereotypes of North Africa," respectively.

Part IV proposes to look at the perceptions and transpositions of "Africa in the Americas." Jeannette Eileen Jones explores twentieth-century museum (re)constructions of Africa in her article entitled "'In Brightest Africa': Naturalistic Constructions of Africa in the American Museum of Natural History, 1910-1936," while John Gruesser and Victoria Ramirez respectively approach race and class issues in "From Race to Class:

The African American Response to the Italo-Ethiopian War," and "The Herero in the Harz: Pynchon's Re-Presentation of Race Relations in *Gravity's Rainbow.*"

Because one cannot address contemporary images of Africa without looking at the way the media have participated in the stereotypical portrayal of what many still consider the dark continent,[18] Part V seeks to look at the way in which the media has been "Media-ting Africa." Here, Jessica Levin analyses press coverage in "In the Heart of Sickness: A Life Portrait of Dr. Albert Schweitzer," while Martha Grise examines television coverage in "'Scarred for Life?' Representations of Africa and Female Genital Cutting on American Television News Magazines." Jean Muteba Rahier, in a controversial article that looks at African-American portrayals of Africa in film and cinema, tackles the "(US-Centered Afrocentric Imaginations of Africa: L.H. Clegg's *When Black Men Ruled the World,* and Eddie Murphy's *Coming to America.*"

Part VI focuses on another important aspect of African cultures, especially as it relates to "Feminism and Women in Africa." Thus, Daniel M. Mengara offers insights into the "Perceptions of African Feminism: A Socio-Historical Perspective," while more contemporary issues that affect the lives of women in Africa, particularly in Kenya, are analyzed by Bill Gaudelli in "African Women: Educational Opportunities and the Dynamics of Change."

A volume such as this one cannot be complete without a section on African literatures. As a result, Part VII explores the various socio-literary responses that African authors have provided to various colonial (mis)depictions of Africa and Africans. Thus, proceeding from the point of view of "African Literatures: Text and Pre-text," Augustine Okereke discusses some of these responses in his article entitled "Once Upon A Time... Representations, Misrepresentations and Rehabilitations in African Literatures." David Pattison and Sharmila Sen, on the other hand, respectively look at the subversive textuality inherent in the works of Dambudzo Merechera in "'Oxford, Black Oxford': Dambudzo Merechera and the Last Colony in Africa," and the complexities of African societies' puzzling theatricality in "Playing Africa: The Fictions of Ferdinand Oyono."

As the reader engages in this exploration of the stereotypes and realities of Africa, let him or her be mindful of the dictum of the former president of Malawi, Dr. Hastings Kamuzu Banda, who once said, in reference to those who claimed to have discovered Africa that: "[t]here was nothing to discover, we were here all the time" (McLynn 1993: ix). This thought remains true today.

Notes

[1] Parts of this introduction contains sections of text that will appear in a larger piece entitled "Africa and the Invention of Democracy". This piece will be published in Malinda Smith's *Globalizing Africa* (forthcoming in 2001). Both articles are themselves adapted and contain text from a book manuscript by this author currently in progress called *Africa and the Invention of Democracy*.

[2] Note that Mary Lefkowitz's double rebuttal (*Black Athena Revisited*, 1996; *Not Out of Africa*, 1997) of Martin Bernal's *Black Athena* (1987) aims precisely at asserting the so-called preponderance of western civilization over all others. In this battle of histories, scholars such as Lefkowitz see Africa mostly as a continent that never could have produced civilizations sophisticated enough to influence the course of western history and thinking.

[3] In this paper, the term "precolonial" is used to refer to the state of sub-Saharan Africa prior to both Arab and European invasions.

[4] I use this term to refer to the process of alteration of African identities, a process which left the indigenous peoples psychologically vanquished into a belief in their inferiority. This process is also one that built the whole perception of African around the "negative." By so doing, the Europeans who visited or wrote about Africa progressively reformulated the essence of the African world, thus limiting its presentation only to those "dark" aspects that were going to become the image by which Africa would be permanently known to the outside world.

[5] I define the term "African infrastructure" as all the values of civilization proper to the African world(s) prior to foreign invasions (Arab or European).

[6] OUP, 1988

[7] Although Greece was probably more highly esteemed than Rome in the nineteenth century, ultimately it was the Roman imperial example rather than the Athenian one that was important for nineteenth-century British imperial ideology. The short-lived nature of the Athenian empire and its precipitous end generally made the Roman empire a more comfortable source of parallels for the British empire. Analogies between the Athenian empire and the British were made at times of anxiety and in war it was the behavior of Greek heroes

that came to mind. But most were agreed with Gilbert Murray that "at home England is Greek. In the empire she is Roman."

[8] Baker, p. 133.

[9] See for instance *Ancient and Modern Imperialism* published in 1910 by Earl Cromer, British administrator in and virtual ruler of Egypt from 1877 and also a Greek scholar, also Sir C. P. Lucas' *Greater Rome and Greater Britain* (1912), and Viscount Bryce's *The Ancient Roman Empire and the British Empire in India* (1914).

[10] This is what, for instance, I derive from McLynn's book (McLynn, 1993: ix). Pakenham's *The Scramble for Africa* (1991) also provides an extensive account of the various European ideologies behind the scramble, ideologies that were often aimed at "saving" Africa not only from its ignorance of itself, but also from its self-destructive chaos.

[11] This trend has continued well into the 20th century where everything that would look like a sign of "civilization" is explained only in terms of borrowing, owing to the assumption that nothing "civilized" could have originated in Africa. Theories such as Davidson's (1970; 1991) explanation of the origin of the African Iron Age, Sagan's (1983) denial of the possible African origin of agriculture or astronomy, and Tempels's (1962; 1979) explanation of Bantu philosophy have all denied Africa's possible independent discovery of civilization. For them, Africa took everything "civilized" from Egypt, the Arabs or Europe, or even from the Martians as Däniken suggested (see Mudimbe 1988: 15). See also Davidson's strange explanation on how black Africans may have borrowed the cult of the ram from ancient Egypt. Yet, as Davidson himself shows, ancient Egyptians venerated sub-Saharan Africa as "God's land" (1970). Could Egyptians not have possibly borrowed this cult from black Africa, then?

[12] Based on Ashcroft, *et al.* (1989), and Mengara (1996), the term "postcolonial" is hereby defined as all the continuities and discontinuites triggered in the colonized world from the very moment of colonization up to the present. Thus, post-independence to us is not equivalent to postcoloniality; rather, post-independence is itself a result and part of the postcolonial condition, among other aspects. The guiding principle in this interpretation is that the events and changes that were set in motion by colonial contacts left an indelible mark on, at least, the colonized societies, and as a result, things could never be the same again for them, either before or after factual independence. In addition, because the effects of colonization are still felt today in the colonized world, independence did not mean a total suppression or disappearance of these effects after the departure of the imperial powers. The very notion of neocolonialism itself explains it all. All of these events and periods are therefore part of the postcolonial condition.

[13] This is what, according to Killam (1997), had led Chinua Achebe to write such novels as *Things Fall Apart* (1958) and *Arrow of God* (1964). He wanted to respond to what he believed were the misrepresentations of the African universe by the various missionaries and explorers who had contributed to building Africa into a "dark continent."

[14] This suggestion was made in an article entitled "Africa and the Invention of Democracy." (Mengara and Larson, 2001). I am currently working on a book manuscript that will help to expand the theory much more explicitly than was done in the limited context of this article.

[15] For a good historical exploration of the Afrocentrist movement and its origins, see Howe (1998).

[16] I coined this term from the word "palimpsest" as used in Chantal Zabus's excellent book, *The African Palimpsest: Indigenization of Language in the West African Europhone Novel* (1991). Zabus's masterful critique of African Europhone literature defines this literature as one in which authors are seeking to indigenize western cultural influences through literary and artistic strategies aimed at giving an African "flavor" to their works. This process of re-writing issues relating to African cultures, the author argues, calls to mind the idea of the palimpsest which, in crude terms, represents a document whose original text has been erased so that a new text could be written over it. The "palimpsesting" process therefore entails the "re-writing" of African history from an African(ist) perspective.

[17] Martin Bernal states that his "two volumes are concerned with two models of Greek history: one viewing Greece as essentially European or Aryan, and the other seeing it as Levantine, on the periphery of the Egyptian and Semitic cultural area. I call them the 'Aryan' and the 'Ancient' models" (Bernal 1987: 1). Thus, Aryanism, in the context of the current debates, may be defined as the scholarly position that not only views Ancient Greece as both Aryan and European as Bernal puts it, but that also takes stock of the Greek heritage, purifies it of any influence from Africa or Asia, and uses this miraculous purity to assert the supremacy and superiority of western civilization over all others. On the other hand, Afrocentrism stands as a position that seeks to revise such exclusive views of history and that promotes recognition of the often ignored African contributions to human civilization.

[18] See for example the title and contents of Franck McLynn's book, *Hearts of Darkness* (1993)

Works Cited

Achebe, Chinua. *Things Fall Apart*. London: Heinemann, 1958.
_____. *Arrow of God*. London: Heinemann, 1964.
Ashcroft, Bill, *et al*. *The Empire Writes Back: Theory and Practice in Post-Colonial Literatures*. London: Routledge, 1989.
Ayittey, Georges B. N. *Indigenous African Institutions*. Dobbs Ferry, NY: Transnational Publishers, 1991.

Baker, Herbert. 1938 (2nd ed). *Cecil Rhodes, by his architect, Herbert Baker*. Freeport, N.Y., Books for Libraries Press, 1969.

Bernal, Martin. *Black Athena:The Afroasiatic Roots of Classical Civilization. Vol. I: The Fabrication of Ancient Greece, 1785-1985*. New Brunswick, NJ: Rutgers UP, 1987.

Christopher, A. J. *Colonial Africa*. Totowa (NJ): Barnes and Noble, 1984.

Davidson, Basil. *The Lost Cities of Africa*. 1959. Boston: Little, Brown and Company, 1970.

_____. *African Civilizations Revisited*. Trenton (N.J.): Africa World Press, 1991.

Deschamps, H. *Histoire de la traite des noirs de l'antiquité à nos jours*. Paris: Fayard, 1971.

Eboussi-Boulaga, F. *Christianisme sans fétiche: révélation et domination*. Paris: Présence Africaine, 1981.

Flint, John. *Cecil Rhodes*. Boston and Toronto: Little, Brown & Co., 1974.

Hamdun, Said, and Noël King. *Ibn Battuta in Black Africa*. 1975. Princeton: Markus Wiener Publishers, 1994.

Hilton, Anne. *The Kingdom of Kongo*. Oxford (ENG.): Clarendon Press, 1985.

Howe, Stephen. *Afrocentrism: Mythical Pasts and Imagined Homes*. London: Verso, 1998.

Killam, G. D. "Chinua Achebe." *African Writers*. Ed. C. Brian Cox. New York: Charles Scribner's Sons, 1997: 15-35.

Lefkowitz, Mary R., and Guy MacLean Rogers, eds. *Black Athena Revisited*. Chapel Hill: U of Northern California Press, 1996.

Lefkowitz, Mary R. *Not Out of Africa: How Afrocentrism Became an Excuse to Teach Myth as History*. 1996. New York: Basic Books, 1997.

McEvedy, Colin. *The Penguin Atlas of African History*. 1980. London: Penguin Books, 1995.

McLynn, Frank. 1992. *Hearts of Darkness: the European Exploration of Africa*. New York: Carroll & Graf Publishers, 1993.

McNamara, Francis Terry. *France in Black Africa.* Washington (DC): National Defense University, 1989.

Mengara, Daniel M. "Postcolonialism, Third-Worldism and the Issue of Exclusive Terminologies in Postcolonial Theory and Criticism." *Commonwealth* 18, 2 (1996): 36-45.

Mengara, Daniel, and Victoria Larson. "Africa and the Invention of Democracy." Forthcoming in *Globalizing Africa,* Edited by Malinda Smith. Trenton, N.J.: Africa World Press, 2001 (tentative date).

Mudimbe, V. Y. *The Invention of Africa. Gnosis, Philosophy, and the Order of Knowledge.* Bloomington, IN: Indiana UP, 1988.

Pakenham, Thomas. *The Scramble for Africa: White Man's Conquest of the Dark Continent from 1876 to 1912.* New York: Avion Books, 1991.

Rotberg, Robert. *The Founder: Cecil Rhodes and the Pursuit of Power.* New York: Oxford UP, 1988.

Sagan, C. *Broca's Brain: Reflections on the Romance of Science.* New York: Ballantine Books, 1983.

Sala-Molins, Louis. *Les misères des Lumières: sous la raison, l'outrage.* Paris: Laffont, 1992.

Scholefield, Alan. *The dark kingdoms: the impact of white civilization on three great African monarchies.* New York: Morrow, 1975.

Sévry, Jean. *Chaka, Empereur des Zoulous: histoire, mythes et légendes.* Paris: L'Harmattan, 1991.

Tempels, P. *Notre Rencontre I.* Léopoldville (Kinshasa, Zaire): Centre d'Etudes Pastorales, 1962.

_____. *Philosophie bantu.* Kinshasa: Faculté de Théologie Catholique, 1979.

Zabus, Chantal. *The African Palimpsest: Indigenization of Language in the West African Europhone Novel.* Amsterdam: Editions Rodopi B. V., 1991.

PART I
Ancient European Perceptions of Africa

European Images of Africa - Tale of Two Names: Ethiopia and N----

Martin Bernal
Cornell University

Ethiopia

In the seventeenth, eighteenth and nineteenth centuries, when European respect for "Negroes" or "Niggers" plummeted with their need to justify race-based slavery, the reputation of Ethiopia remained relatively high. This positive image of Ethiopia among Europeans has gone through three stages: the Classical and Biblical picture of Ethiopians as handsome and morally superior beings; Ethiopia as the Medieval Christian land of Prester John beyond Islam, which could come to the rescue of European Christendom; and the Modern independent country that defeated the Italians and simply by this fact could not be seen as typically African.[1]

The Classical and Biblical

Iconography clearly shows that Blacks with "African" features existed around the Mediterranean during the Bronze Age.[2] The Greek word Aithiops, "burnt face," is first attested in Mycenaean texts of the fourteenth or thirteenth centuries BCE, with the personal name Ai_3-ti-jo-qo.

One of the earliest Greek poems--now lost-- was called *Aithiopis,* and concerned Memnôn, king of the Ethiopians. Its date is uncertain but the story of the "the most beautiful," noble, and brave Ethiopian prince who marched to Troy's rescue and died there heroically was known by the earliest Greek poets whose works survive, Hesiod and Homer, who lived in the tenth or ninth centuries BCE.[3] There is some confusion as to whether Memnôn was an Asian "Ethiopian" or an African one but he was certainly Black.[4]

Memnôn was not the only Ethiopian to play a prominent role in the Homeric epics. In the first book of the *Iliad* (I.423-424), Zeus goes with the other gods to feast with "the blameless Ethiopians." The *Odyssey* opens with Poseidon visiting them (I.22-24).[5] For Homer and presumably other Greeks of his time, the Ethiopians were a particularly virtuous people with close associations with the gods.

These passages cannot be entirely explained away as mere literary tropes designed either to get the parental gods out of the way in order to have some excitement, or to pose distant utopias used to reproach their own societies, although these were certainly aspects of such idealization. The basis in fact was that civilized states really existed to the south of Egypt and were inhabited by Black people unconquered by Persian Greeks and Romans.

Later writers like the historian Herodotus in the fifth century BCE and Diodorus Siculus in the first century of that era, also expressed admiration for the Ethiopians. Herodotus described them as "the tallest and the most beautiful people in the world" (III.20). According to Diodorus Siculus (III.2-3) the Ethiopians were autochthonous and had been created by sunlight (This is the origin of Afrocentrist image of Africans as "sun people"). Diodorus also stated that Egypt was a colony of Ethiopia. If Egypt was the gift of the Nile Ethiopia was the giver of the Nile. This statement leads us to the more general and vexed question of the identity of the *Aithiopes* or "Ethiopians" in modern terms. Frank Snowden has argued forcefully that the term did not merely mean dark or black skinned but was restricted to "Negroes" or the European stereotype of West Africans. As he puts it, "*all* Ethiopians were black or dark *but not all peoples* described as black or dark were designated as Ethiopians." [his italics].[6] While this is undoubtedly true, his scheme presents a number of problems. The most notable of these is that the statement does not deal with the fact that Greeks frequently saw two sets of Ethiopians. As Homer put it at the beginning of the *Odyssey* (I.22-25), the Ethiopians:

> are sundered in twain, the furthermost of men, some where Hyperion sets and some where he rises.

Herodotus (VII.71) spells out where the latter came from:

> The Eastern Ethiopians--for there were two sorts of Ethiopians in the army--served with the Indians. These were just like the southern Ethiopians except for their language and their hair: their hair is straight, while that of the Ethiopians of Libya is the crispest and curliest in the world.[7]

The fact is that the term *aithiops* was as uncertain in classical antiquity "Black" is today. At times it was restricted to the European stereotype of West Africans. At other times, however, *aithiops* was also used much more broadly to include any people substantially darker than the Greeks and Romans themselves.

Greek writers tended to think of "Ethiopia" as the kingdoms of Napata and Meroe in the upper Nile.[8] However, the name later became attached to the region we now call Ethiopia. Ethiopians today see their country as the continuation of the powerful kingdom of Axum that flourished at the southern end of the Red Sea from the middle of the first millennium BCE to the eighth century CE. However, Greek versions of inscriptions made by the pagan kings of Axum use the term "Ethiopia" to describe only one of their territories. In versions of the inscriptions in the classical Ethiopian language of Ge'ez, the name is rendered as "*Ḥabäsät*." Like "Ethiopia," the name Ḥabäsät appears to have been very ancient, as it is found in Egyptian texts from the 15th century BCE rendered as "*Ḫbstïw*," inhabitants of the Holy Land of Punt, up the Red Sea from Egypt.[9] Thus the alternation of the Greek name Ethiopia and the local term *Ḥabäsät* from which the name Abyssinia derived has existed at least since the fourth century CE.

Once Aksum converted to Christianity under King Ezana in the early fourth century CE, Greek writers associated the Christian kingdom with the biblical Ethiopia. What is more, the translation of the Bible into the classical Ethiopian language of Ge'ez merely transcribed the Greek name *Aitiyopia*. Apparently, this word was used by later Aksumite rulers to refer to their own kingdom as a whole. The usage can be confirmed in the *Kebra Nagast*, "Glory of Kings," a book written in the thirteenth century CE setting out the legends of the new dynasty's descent from Menelik, son of Solomon and the

Queen of Sheba. From then on national rulers described themselves as kings of Ethiopia and the association was taken on as the royal title.[10]

Ḥabäsät has not disappeared either. For Mohammed and the first califs, the Arabic al Ḥabaša was an honorable title for Ethiopia, but with the rise of Islamic racism in the eighth century and punning with the word "ḥabaṣ", "mixed", Ḥabaša became a pejorative term for peoples of the horn of Africa who were neither Black nor Arab in the eyes of southwest Asian Muslims. Nevertheless the Amharic form Habäša has remained the term of self-definition among Highland Ethiopians. In European languages, Abyssinia, lacking the etymological blackness of Ethiopia, became a name suggesting an Oriental not an African country and, therefore, was used by authors in a racist environment who wished to praise the country.

The N--- Word

It is a strange coincidence that the Latin *niger,* from which we derive "negro" and "nigger," should be the same as Niger, the major river of West Africa. The most likely connection between the two would appear to be that the river name came from the Latin color *niger* because "black" people lived along its banks. In fact, a neat parallel for this connection can be found in the toponym "Sudan," which comes from the Arabic *Bilād as Sūdān*, "Land of the Blacks." A derivation of the Latin word from the river name would appear much less likely. This, however, is precisely what I do want to propose, that is to say, I maintain that there is a connection between the color and the river name, but that the Latin *niger* comes from the Sahara and not vice versa. Specifically, I believe that *niger* comes from the skin color of the people of Niger rather than that the place name originates from the color term.

Lexicography

The root (n)gr has two semantic fields in West Semitic. One of these, which appears in Ugaritic and four times in Punic inscriptions as well as in New Hebrew, is a loan word from the Sumerian *nan-gar* and the Akkadian *naggâru* "carpenter."[11] The latter is not, however, attested in the Bible, where, *ngr* is restricted to what appears to be a derivative of a root, grr, single or doubled, "throat" with connotations of "swallow." The Arabic *ğarā* means "flow" or "stream" and in the Bible, the general meaning of the *ngr* or *nigir*, appears to be within the semantic field of a liquid--usually water-- that gushes out or falls down, usually onto the ground and is lost.

Geography

Many place-names containing *gr(r)* or *ngr* can be found both in the Arabian desert and the Sahara. The standard explanation for the many toponyms: Ghor, Gher, Ghir and Ghar as well as Niger, Nigir and Nigris, mentioned by Classical writers, is simply that they derive from the Berber word for water.[12] No doubt all of these toponyms are connected with water. Furthermore, *'ger* with the prefix n- "of" does exist in Tamashek, the Berber language of the Tuaregs, found in Tassili n'ajjer, "Plateau of Rivers," famous for its rock paintings.[13] This hypothesis, however, does not explain the Ger(r) and Nagar place names in southwest Asia where Berber has never been spoken and the fact that the alternation *ger/niger* meaning "streams" or more precisely "oases" is found in Hebrew and Arabic.

Possibly *(n)gr* could be common to Semitic and Berber, as both are Afroasiatic languages. More likely, however, the Berber *gher* is one of its many loan-words from Phoenician and *n'gher* simply coincided with the Canaanite *niger*. Speakers of Berber and Northwest Semitic were in contact with each other in the Maghreb from at least 900 BCE to 700 CE. The most plausible explanation for the classical place-names is that *ger* and *niger* were relatively common terms for "oases" and "rivers that disappear(into the sand)" and that Greek and Roman geographers learnt them from Phoenician speakers, who lived on the African coast but traded someway into the desert. Athenaeus' story (II.44.e) of the Carthaginian Mago who crossed the waterless desert three times is impossible in some of its details but there is no reason to deny that expeditions of this type took place.

Herodotus (II.32) described a journey made by some coastal Libyans or specifically Nasamonians:

> The story then was that the young men, sent off by their companions on their travels with a good supply of food and water, passed through the inhabited parts of the coun-

try to the region of wild beasts and then came to the desert, which they proceeded to cross in a westerly direction. After traveling for many days over the sand they saw some trees growing on a level spot; they approached and began to pick the fruit which the trees bore, and while they were doing so were attacked by some little men-of less than middle height who seized them and carried them off. The speech of these dwarfs was unintelligible, nor could they understand the Nasamonians. They took their captives through a vast tract of marshy country and beyond it came to a town, all the inhabitants of which were of the same small stature, and all black. A great river with crocodiles in it flowed from west to east.

Herodotus accepted the view of the Ammonian king Etearchus, who told him the story that this river was a source of the Nile. This version did not disappear even though that of the source in the "Mountains of the Moon" in East Africa was probably more popular. In any event, the view that the Nile rose in the Morrocan Atlas mountains was repeated by many later writers.[14] The known melting of the snows of the Atlas being given as the explanation for the Nile flood.

Most modern scholars, however, have associated Herodotus' river with the Gers and Nigers of Pliny and Ptolemy and to have assumed that the river was the modern Niger, which is indeed "A great river with crocodiles in it [that flows inexplicably not towards the ocean but]...from west to east."[15]

Ethnography

The place names Ger and Niger were also applied to peoples. The Garamantes, whose capital was called Garama, were based on the present Wadi al Agial in the Fezzan. They practiced agriculture but were also prosperous traders and famous charioteers. In his studies of the Garamantes, Charles Daniels plausibly supposed that they were Berber speakers and that their physical remains reveal a population that was "North African, negroid and hybrid."[16] Pietro Laureano a specialist in deserts and their irrigation, sees the Garamantes as the probable antecedents of the modern Touareg.[17] Herodotus refers to their using four-horse chariots to hunt Troglodotai Aithiopes The specific troglodytes referred to were probably related to the Teda, a people who still use caves as refuges in the Tibesti

Mountains in Northern Chad. The fact that they speak a Nilo-Saharan language would explain why Herodotus' Afroasiatic speaking informants described them "as speaking a language like no other and squeaking like bats."[18]

In any event, the Garamantes seem to have been less dark than Herodotus' "Ethiopians." As mentioned above, classical writings on the Sahara refer to a people known variously as Nigretae, Nigritai or Nigretes. These names were associated with the river Niger, wherever that was placed. Even this is probably too specific. They seem to have been simply the people of the *niggårôt*, oases and rivers of the central and southern Sahara.[19]

The connection of Nigr- with distant desert regions appears later in Pliny's description-- which even he admits to be fantastic--of the "Nigroe" on the banks of the Upper Nile [which for him could have been south of the Sahara] whose king had one eye in his forehead (VI.30). By the first century CE, however, his choice of name may well have been influenced, if not determined, by the Latin word *niger* itself.

Nbty, Napata and Nabataeans.

The name Nigretai, is attested not merely in Latin but in Greek, which had no word *niger*. The hypothesis that Nigret- was originally simply a Phoenician name for the "men of the oases" is strengthened by some Asiatic, Egyptian and Libyan parallels. The G(h)errae, described by classical authors, were traders and raiders in the deserts of Eastern Arabia. Presumably they took their name from the cities called Gerra.[20] There are analogies for this. Since the Middle Kingdom in early second millennium BCE, one of the more frequently used Egyptian terms for "barbarians" was Wh̩ɜtyw "people of the Wh̩ɜt," "oasis region." Much later, there are references to the Napatans, inhabitants of Upper Nubia and the surrounding deserts.

Now let us turn to southwest Asia and the Semitic root *nbṭ*... The Nabataeans or *Nbṭw* who lived in the northern Arabian desert derived their name from *nbṭ* found in the Sabaean *nbṭ*--"dig a well"--and the Arabic *nabaṭa* "well out, gush out, stream forth."[21] In Islamic times, the root was also used in the western Sahara. Early Arab geographers referred to a people there interchangeably as >*Anbiṭ* or >*Aswad*, "Blacks." The modern historian John Wansbrough explains that >Anbiṭ was not used in reference to pigmentation but to the occupation of agriculturalist.[22] Thus it is likely that here too, the root *nbṭ* was used to describe the inhabitants of the oases, but the parallel suggests that a significant number of them were black.

The western Sahara was the region where the classical authors reported the presence of Nigretai. In the first century CE Strabo--presumably basing his statement on earlier sources--wrote that the Nigretai were neighbors of the Pharusai in a region that seems to have been that of the modern Mauritania. According to Strabo (CXVII.33-37), the two peoples, riding horses--with bladders tied to their girths, so that they could cross the desert--and chariots with scythes attached to their wheels, had raided and destroyed 300 Tyrian (Phoenician) cities on the coast, apparently that of Morocco.

Strabo claimed that the Nigritai lived to the West of the Ethiopians. Pliny on the other hand maintained that they were the westernmost Ethiopians (V.43). If these two were uncertain, so too are modern physical anthropologists. Some hold that as the Sahara expanded and contracted it acted as a pump causing population admixture, others that the peoples of the inland Maghreb represent a survival of undifferentiated population before the division into Africans and "Caucasians."[23] Whatever the cause, and the two are perfectly compatible, rock paintings in the Tassili Massif and elsewhere, dating back to the fourth and fifth millennia BCE, as well as human remains from that period and later, indicate that the inhabitants of the Sahara were mixed in appearance, but predominantly black, some "negroid," others not.[24] Many are strikingly similar to the Fulani, who live around the southern rim of the Sahara today.[25] Indeed, some anthropologists have even claimed to see similarities between a scene in one of the paintings and a contemporary Fulani initiation ceremony.[26]

The Fulani today are classified by physical anthropologists along with the Nuer, Shilluk and Tutsi as "elongated Africans" tall with thin facial features. Unlike the other Sudanic peoples, however, the Fulani have a relatively light skin. And in this respect, they seem to differ from the people portrayed in the Saharan rock paintings who appear considerably darker.[27] The latter seem closer to the typical Sudanic Africans and have a blue-black pigmentation, darker than that of the peoples living further south. This type is predominant among the Haratîn found in the central Saharan oases today, who are plausibly thought to be the descendants of the original Saharans of the early Holocene.[28]

The few early physical remains from the Sahara tend to indicate a rather heavier physical type with wider nasal passages, suggesting contact with or derivation from people from the forests to the south.[29] The consensus among physical anthropologists is that the "elongated African" type developed in the Sudanic region to adapt to the intense dry heat and exposure to the sun in the savanna and desert rim.[30]

In any event, the inhabitants of the Central Sahara have tended to be very dark though with varied heights, weights and physiognomies. This would seem to fit with the ancient writers' references to "Ethiopians" there.

The situation on the northern rim of the Sahara during classical times was more complicated. Even so, despite the variation in their actual color and pigmentation, the Nigretai whether Western Ethiopians or their neighbors and allies were seen by the inhabitants of the coastal Maghreb as Blacks.

Niger as a Color.

According to the lexicographers of Latin A. Ernout and A. Meillet, "Sauf pour 'rouge' les noms de couleurs ne sont d'ordinaire pas Indo-européens." They wrote this in the entry for "albus." Under "niger" they concluded: "Étymologie inconnue. Du reste, il n'y a pas d'adjectif indo-européen commun attesté pour 'noir."[31]

Certainly neither *ater* nor *niger,* the most frequent Latin words covered by the English "black" has a known Indo-European derivation and the latter is only found in Latin.[32] Both words are old and appear in the works of Ennius in the third century BCE. In the early period, however, *ater* was much more common. In his *Étude sur les termes de couleur dans la langue Latine,* Jacques André made a fascinating comparison between the semantic fields of the two words. Before about 100 BCE, *ater* was the opposite of *albus.* The pair were simply "black" and "white" without any reference to luminosity. *Ater* was the word for "shade" and "darkness" with somber and sinister connotations. The opposite of *niger* was *candidus,* "glowing white." Where *ater* was matte, *niger* was brilliant. According to André: "*Niger* est un noir brillant doué de la beauté de son éclat."[33] In this early period, *niger* was used to describe such southern products as ebony. Sometimes it connoted a violet tinge and was the color of mulberries and dark wine.[34] Although at this time nothing shows it was used to describe men and women, this luminous color would fit well with that of the people of the central and south Sahara and hence the coastal stereotype of the Nigritai. Thus, a derivation of *niger* from Nigritai--and of the latter from *niggârôt* and *ngr*--fits very well, in terms of both phonetics and semantics.

The thorough study of possible Semitic loans in Latin was not acceptable during the nineteenth and twentieth centuries. I am convinced, however, that it will prove very rewarding in the near future. Phoenicians were present in the Central Mediterranean at least from the early tenth century BCE.[35] There is also strong evidence of Phoenician involvement in the earliest Roman cult.[36] The three alliances between Carthaginians and Romans after 509, the year after the Etruscan kings had been driven out, indicate considerable official and popular contact between the two peoples and their allies.[37] It is also likely that there was a "colony" of Phoenicians in Rome from the seventh century BCE and it is possible that this was continuous until the attested presence of a Punic, Canaanite speaking population in Rome in the early second.[38] Later still, Rome colonized the west Phoenician world. Given all this, it would be amazing if West Semitic had not made substantial loans into Latin. This failure to investigate can be explained very easily in terms of the sociology of knowledge.[39]

Even today there are scattered concessions of individual loans: *mapalia*, "hut," *mappa*, "napkin," and interestingly, *ave*. Given the lack of Indo-European roots for colors, it would not be surprising to find that some of these too come from Semitic. Looked at in Indo-European terms the relationship between the Greek *malakhe* and the Latin *malua* is puzzling. Both mean "mallow" and "mauve," but though roughly similar, their phonetics have a curious discrepancy. Generally both are admitted to come from a Mediterranean language.[40] The simplest explanation is that the Greek word was borrowed from West Semitic before the merger of *ḫ>ḥ* in Canaanite and the Latin after it had taken place, from the form preserved in Hebrew. An even more exact parallel, though into a different language, is the derivation of the Later Greek μαῦρος, the word for "black" that displaced all others. It comes partly from the Classical ἀμαυρός--"dim" or "faint"--but also from

Μαῦροι, the Moors or inhabitants of Mauritania. All in all, nothing is anomalous in the hypothesis that *niger* was borrowed from a Punic proper name.[41]

The mode of transmission from Punic into Latin is much less clear. In this sense, the absence of **ngr* from West Phoenician is not surprising given the extremely limited and repetitive corpus of Punic inscriptions. Nevertheless, the word could plausibly have been used on the coast of the Maghreb as a general term for Black people. It is also possible --though less likely--that Romans took the ethnic name as a general term to describe the Blacks in Carthaginian armies. The attestation of *niger* in Ennius' works makes it impossible for this to have happened as late as Hannibal's invasion of Italy in the second.

During the first century BCE, the popularity of the more vivid word crushed *ater*. *Niger* became the standard Latin word for "black" with all its connotations.[42] As such, it passed on to the Romance languages as the Old French *nigre, negre, neire* and *noir*; the Spanish and Portuguese *negro*, and the Italian *nero*. It is possible but unlikely that any sense of the specific original meaning of "Black People" survived.

Return to Ethiopia

In the seventh and eighth centuries CE, Islam tore the heart out of the Christian world, leaving only peripheral fragments beyond Muslim rule: the truncated Byzantine Empire; Roman Catholic western Europe, north of the Pyrenees, groups of Nestorians in Central Asia and India; Nubia which had been converted to Christianity in the sixth century and Ethiopia. Aksum was landlocked by the Muslims who occupied the Dahlac islands and denied any possibility of restoring Aksumite sea power. The Muslims, however, made no attempt to conquer the African side of the Axumite Empire. The religious reason for this restraint came from the Prophet's early friendly associations with Christian Ethiopia, but there were also practical reasons for leaving Ethiopia alone: the difficulties in conquering it and the advantage of keeping a non-Muslim reservoir of slaves in the Horn of Africa. Thus, Ethiopia became the one exception to the Islamic dichotomy of the peaceful world of Islam, "Dar al Islam," and the violent non-Islamic sphere, "Dar al Harb," against which Jihads should be conducted. At a state to state level there was generally mutual respect between the two entities even during most of the Crusades.

During the twelfth century, however, the kings of the Zagwe dynasty in Ethiopia contacted with crusaders in Jerusalem. These connections helped foster the myth of an African Prester John, the Christian Priest King beyond Islam who would rescue European Christendom. Generally, Christians, like Jews, had visualized the Messiah as coming from the East. The Persian Cyrus was the first man to be called the Messiah. In the thirteenth century, many Christians pinned their hopes on the Mongols who were attacking Islam from the East. In the mid and late twelfth century, however, their attention was focused on "the Indies," which generally referred to lands bordering on the Indian Ocean, including Ethiopia.[43] And there was a strong tradition that located the base of Prester John's kingdom in Ethiopia. In fact the Zagwe kings of Ethiopia were also priests with the title "Jan". The most notable of this dynasty was Lalibela, who, before he came to power, spent twenty years in Jerusalem. On his return, he built a Jerusalem of his own, the extraordinary city of rock-hewn churches at his capital of Roha, which was later given his name, Lalibela. During this period and with the restoration of the Solomonic Dynasty in the 13th and 14th centuries, Christians were impressed, and the Moslem rulers of Egypt were frightened, by what they saw as the military power of the kings of Ethiopia and by the possibility that they could divert the Nile.

Interest in the Black Christians of Ethiopia beyond Islam continued in Medieval and Renaissance Europe. It is clear that while the fifteenth century Portuguese were eager to round Africa to reach the wealth of the Asiatic Indies, they were also deeply concerned with Ethiopia. They sent spies through Islamic territory to establish contact and their vicious and tragic dealings with Congo in the sixteenth century can be seen too as an attempt to establish an Christian Ethiopia of their own.

At the end of that century, Islamic relations with Ethiopia broke down. This was at least in part because of the Reconquista in Spain and the subsequent Christian attacks on the Maghreb. In the long term, however, the Portuguese severance of the connections between its two centers in south-west and southeast Asia struck an even more fundamental blow at the Islamic world. In this atmosphere an attack on the Ethiopian Empire by Ahmed Gragn the Emir of Harar became a

Jihad, which with some Turkish help, very nearly destroyed Christian Ethiopia and has remained a trauma among Ethiopian Christians ever since. The centrality of Ethiopia to Portuguese overseas concerns in the sixteenth century is shown by the campaign to aid the Ethiopian Emperor that was led by Vasco Da Gama's son Christoforo. Da Gama was killed but his troops played a significant role in reestablishing Christian rule.

For the next century, Portuguese priests and Ethiopian emperors enjoyed close relations. However Portuguese attempts to bring the Ethiopian church under the Bishop of Rome caused a reaction that led to their expulsion by the emperor Fasilidas in the mid seventeenth century. Before that, Portuguese priests had made generally favorable, and on the whole accurate, reports of Ethiopia which were widely circulated in Europe. The most famous of these by Jeronimo Lobo was translated into French in 1728, and into English by Samuel Johnson in 1733.[44] Dr. Johnson was a conservative in English politics and this stance included a hatred of "trade" and particularly of West Indian planters. He systematically provoked the latter by asserting that his Black servant Francis Barber was the most intelligent person he knew and once toasted an Oxford audience to "the next insurrection of the negroes in the West Indies." He also continued his interest in Ethiopia and one of his best known works, a play entitled "Prince of Abissinia" or "Rasselas was published in 1759.[45] At the end of his life in the 1780s, he led the barrage of criticism against James Bruce on the latter's return from Africa.

Bruce was a Scottish nobleman and intrepid explorer who spent many years in the 1770s exploring Egypt and Ethiopia. His ostensible mission was to discover the source of the (Blue) Nile. Since Jeronimo Lobo maintained that he had already found it over a century earlier, Bruce saw himself in competition with the Portuguese priest. The Presbyterian Bruce's unfair criticisms of the Catholic Lobo led to Johnson's even more unfair condemnation of Bruce's reports, which have later proved to be essentially correct. Bruce also had more mystical researches in mind and he believed that the source of the Nile was in many ways the source of civilization. We shall return to this idea later.

N... Once More.

In some ways, Medieval Europeans had a remarkably

vague sense of ethnography. The outstanding example is Wolfram von Eschenbach's noble infidel King Feirefiz, who was pied black and white like a magpie.[46] British pub signs for "the Turk's Head" still portray a West African. With much less inaccuracy, the patron saint of soldiers and in particular of the Teutonic Knights, was St. Maurice, a soldier from Upper Egypt of the third century CE, who was always portrayed as a "negro."[47] Furthermore, when precision was needed, a vocabulary was available. The names Moor and Saracen were frequently used interchangeably. On the other hand, they could be employed to distinguish between Maghrebi Berbers and Arabs. Moreover, despite the absence of any clear difference in pigmentation, the "Moors" were definitely seen as darker. In England, "Moor" or "Blackamoor" remained an alternative name for Black Africans until the ninteenth century.

As mentioned above, in Old French many different forms of the Latin *niger* existed. In the *Chanson de Roland,* composed about 1100 CE, before crusader contact with Ethiopia, the name *Nigres* was used to describe a particularly evil infidel people. The image may have drawn specifically from the Almohads, Berbers from what is now southern Mauritania, just to the north of Senegal, whose invasion saved Islamic Spain in the late eleventh century. However, the tone of the passage also indicates a more general connection between Black, the Christian color of sin and infidelity. It is possible that the use of Nigres shows continuity in the special sense of *niger* and its descendents as referring to an African people but it is more likely that it was simply a reflex from the general sense "Black."[48] In other contexts, particularly after there was European knowledge of Ethiopia "negro" was used positively. *The Catalan Atlas* of 1375 contains the portrait of a splendid Black king holding a golden nugget with the inscription: "This negro lord is Mussa Mally (Mansa Musa king of Mali), *Senyor de los negros de Guineia.*"[49]

Within a hundred years, however, a new and indelible aspect was added to the word. During the middle of the fifteenth century, when Portuguese explorers, or rather exploiters, needed to distinguish the Moors or Moroccans, who had crossbows and arquebuses, from the people south of the Senegal river, who lacked these and, therefore, could be kidnapped and enslaved. The latter were called "Negros." Thus, unlike the name "Ethiopian" which has generally retained some semblance of dignity, from this point on, "Negro" was associated not merely with Africans south of the Sahara but with chattel slavery.[50] It was also seen by Europeans as the epitome of ugliness and evil.

The facts that Iberians dominated the slave trade until the late sixteenth century, that Portuguese formed the linguistic basis for the creole used in the slave trade, and Spanish owned many of the early Caribbean plantations, *negro* was introduced or reintroduced into French as *nègre* and into the Dutch and German as *neger*. This term was also used in English. The "gallant Elizabethan seadog," Sir John Hawkins pioneered the English slave trade in the 1560s. In the following decades, there are attestations of the Iberian "negro" as well as "neger," "neager," "neeger" and "niger."[51]

With the establishment of race-based slavery in the second half of the seventeenth century, "negro" and "niger" became synonomous with "slave." Interestingly, the earliest attestation of the n-word with a double g only comes--not in English but in Scots--in the late eighteenth century. By this time the identification of blackness with slavery was complete. Paradoxically, the word appears in the works of Robert Burns, who composed a moving poem against the evils of slavery.[52] Elsewhere in his *Disputation* he wrote: "How graceless Ham leugh at his Dad, which made Canaan a nigger."

Ethiopia Once Again

James Bruce was in France in the 1780s, just before the revolution. Earlier in the decade the Scottish explorer had claimed that he had seen many traces of the most ancient Egyptians having been linked to Ethiopians and that the city of Thebes had been founded by them.[53]

Bruce was in most respects extremely reactionary. He believed in the positive effects of slavery. In the intellectual ferment of the 1780s, however, he opened the way to a new and very radical historical scheme.

Charles François Dupuis and Constantine Chasseboeuf dit Volney

We should now turn to Egypt. St. Clair Drake claimed that the new confident identification of Ancient Egypt with all Africans evident in David Walker's famous *Appeal To the Coloured Citizens of the World: but in particular, and very expressly to those of the United States of America* (1829), came from "the findings of some French Egyptologists."[54] The term "Egyptologist" is somewhat misleading because for this period it immediately suggests Champollion. However, while not altogether clear on the issue, Champollion denied that the head of the Sphinx and hence the ancient Egyptians as a whole were "negro."[55] As someone living before the fall of the Ancient Model, Champollion had of course no doubt that Greece derived its civilization from Egypt.[56]

The men who established the idea that the ancient Egyptians were Black Africans were Charles François Dupuis and Constantine Chasseboeuf dit Volney. Dupuis was a scholar of antiquity and a scientist who had invented semaphore. His major publication was a multi-volume work entitled *Origine de tous les Cultes.* The volumes' chief purpose was to deconstruct Christianity, which he saw as based on mistaken interpretations of ancient allegory which itself largely derived from science. For Dupuis the origin of all religions was Egypt and he further cited Lucian (pseudo) Philopatris who stated that astronomy, which for Dupuis was the source of all science and religion came from the South of Egypt.[57]

As a Girondist, Dupuis was initially at least, an ardent revolutionary. He was also the chief organizer of the very Egyptian festivals of Reason in France. He probably saw the view that science or the core of civilization arose in Black Africa as a powerful argument in favor of the abolition of slavery, but I have not so far been able to find this expressed in his works. Nevertheless, a conversation with Dupuis inspired Volney to write *The Ruins of Empires,* first published in 1793. This included near its beginning the famous passage:

> There a people, now forgotten, discovered, while others were still barbarians, the elements of the arts and sciences. A race of men now rejected from society for their *sable skin and frizzled hair,* founded on the study of the laws of nature, those civil and religious systems which still govern the universe.[58]

Volney's explicit statement of the Blackness of Egypt, and his linking a Negro origin of Western civilization to Abolitionism, formed an important radical strand of opinion in the movement that insisted upon intellectual equality between Blacks and Whites. In France the great abolitionist Abbé Grégoire, in his book *An Enquiry Concerning and Moral Faculties, and Literature of Negroes,* devoted the first chapter to Volney's arguments emphasizing that the Ancient Egyptians were "negroes" and concludes:

> Without ascribing to Egypt the greatest degree of human knowledge, all antiquity decides in favour of those who consider it as a celebrated school, from which proceeded many of the venerable and learned men of Greece.[59]

Since the work was translated into English in Brooklyn in 1810, it would have been available to educated African Americans.

Northern free Black intellectuals emphasized African Egypt as the fount of civilization, while southern slaves naturally obsessed with slavery and identified with Israel under Egyptian bondage.

Despite the interest in ancient Egypt, African Americans in the nineteenth century were even more concerned with Ethiopia, Ethiopia which was not only admired as the source of Egyptian civilization but respected in its own right. However, as the anthropologist St. Clair Drake pointed out:

> the exact location of Ethiopia prior to the late nineteenth century, was never a matter of much concern to Afro-Americans. Ethiopia was both the name of a place--whose location somewhere in Africa was vague--and a metaphor for a widely scattered diaspora people, as the term "Israel."[60]

By the end of the 19th century, however, educated African Americans were aware of the location and interest soared after the Ethiopian victory over the Italians at Adwa in 1896. Ethiopia's survival from the European "scramble for Africa" provided a symbol of independence for people of African descent throughout the world. Asia had to wait for a similar symbol until the Japanese defeat of Russia in 1904.

At the same time Europeans intellectually bound hand and foot by racism could only explain the Ethiopian victory over an admittedly-minor European power by denying Ethiopia's Africanity. In turn, this victory appears to have provided an important political impetus for the development of the Hamitic theory, which was used to deny the possibility that "true" Africans could create anything that Europeans could see as "civilized."

Conclusion

The clear-cut difference in the reputations of Ethiopians and Negroes established in the eighteenth century had many causes. The positive classical image, and the idea of the Christianity of the Ethiopian empires blended with the new acute racism brought about by race-based slavery. Most slaves held by Europeans were West Africans and, therefore, N... was identified with slaves and not merely associated with Blackness but with West African features. Ethiopians, while Black to the European eye, frequently have East African features, which can resemble those of many non-African peoples.

Having made this distinction I must end by deconstructing it. Racists--a term that should be restricted to whites--neglect such subtleties. For them all people of African descent are N's and should be treated with contempt and barbarity. In 1997, the skinhead killers in Portland, Oregon, were not deterred by the fact that their victim Mulugeta Seraw was an Ethiopian.

Notes

[1] For a survey of these images, see John Sorenson, *Imagining Ethiopia: Struggles for History and Identity in the Horn of Africa.* New Brunswick N.J.: Rutgers University Press, 1993: 21-37.

[2] S. Marinatos, "An African in Thera," *Analekta Archaiologika Athenôn* 2 (1969): 374-375 and "Ethnic Problems Raised by Recent Discoveries on Thera," in R. A. Crossland and A. Birchall, eds., *Bronze Age Migrations in the Aegean.* London: Duckworth, 1973: 199-201. See also V. Karageorghis, *Blacks in Ancient Cypriot Art,* Houston: Menil Foundation, 1988: 7-15.

[3] For this dating see Martin Bernal, *Black Athena: The Afroasiatic Roots of Classical Civilization. Vol. I. The Fabrication of Ancient Greece 1785-1985.* New Brunswick, NJ: Rutgers UP, 1987: 86-88.

[4] Frank Snowden, *Blacks in Antiquity: Ethiopians in the Greco-Roman Experience.* Cambridge Mass. and London: Harvard University Press. 1970, pp.151-152 and Martin Bernal, *Black Athena: The Afroasiatic Roots of Classical Civilization.* Vol. II. New Brunswick, NJ: Rutgers UP, 1991, pp. 258-260.

[5] Martin Bernal, *Black Athena: The Afroasiatic Roots of Classical Civilization. Vol. I.* New Brunswick, NJ: Rutgers UP, 1987: 22-24.

[6] Frank Snowden, "Response," *Arethusa* 26, 3 (1993): 319-327, esp. p.320.

[7] Herodotus, VII, 70 Trans. A. de Sélincourt, *Herodotus: The Histories, sp.* 468.

[8] Strabo, 18 and Plutarch, *De Iside,* para 13.

[9] See Jean Doresse, *Historie Sommaire de la corne orientale de l'Afrique.* Paris: Geutner, 1971: 55-56.

[10] See Bahry Zewde, *History of Modern Ethiopia 1855-1974.* Addis Ababa, Ethiopia: Eastern African Studies, and Nairobi, Kenya: Nairobi University Press and Heinemann Kenya, 1992: 1.

[11] See Richard S. Tomback, *A Comparative Semitic Lexicon of the Phoenician and Punic Languages.* Society of Biblical Literature Dissertation Series. No.32. Missoula Mont.: Scholars Press, 1978. The Semitic root *gr* found in the Semitic equivalent of "a saw" raises the possibility that the Sumerian comes from Akkadian rather than the other way around.

[12] Münzer, "Niger," in Pauly-Wissowa-Kroll, *Realencyclopedie der classischen Altertumswissenschaft* 83 vols., 1894-, vol. XVII, cols. 190-200: 197. See also Charles Joseph Tissot, *Géographie comparée de la province Romaine d'Afrique.* Vol. I. Paris: Imprimerie Nationale, 1884: 97; S. Gsell, *Histoire ancienne de l'Afrique du Nord.* 8 vols. Paris: Hachette, 1914-1928, I. 316 and R.C.C. Law, "North Africa in the Period of Phoenician and Greek Colonization, *c.* 800 to 323 BC." in vol. II of *Cambridge History of Africa: From 500 B.C. to A.D. 1050,* London: Cambridge University Press, 1978: 143, n. 3.

[13] See J. M. Cortade, *Lexique Français Touareg,* Paris: 1968 and Henri Lhote, *The Search for the Tassili Frescoes.* A. M. Broderick, trans. New York: Dutton, 1959: 40.

[14] Pliny *Nat. Hist.* V.296; VI. 35; Strabo XVII.3, 4; Diodorus, I.37; Cass. Dio, LXXV, 15; and the Arab Edrisi, I.206.

[15] For a list of these scholars, see Alan B. Lloyd, *Herodotus Book II: Commentary 1-98.* Leiden: Brill, 1976: 138.

[16] See Charles Daniels, *The Garamantes of Southern Libya.* Stoughton, Wisconsin and Harrow: Oleander, 1975. Also S.O.Y Keita, "Studies of Ancient Crania From Northern Africa," *American Journal of Physical Anthropology* 83 (1990): 35-48, p.37

[17] Pietro Laureano, *La Piramede Rovesiata: Il modello dell' oasi per il pianeta Terra.* Torino: Bollati Boringhieri, 1995: 52.

[18] Herodotus IV. 183. Trans. de Sélincourt, p.332. See also Roger Blench, "Ethnographic and Linguistic Evidence for the Prehistory of African Ruminant Livestock Horses and Ponies" pp.71-103 in T. Shaw *et al.*, ed. *The Archaeology of Africa.* London: Routledge, 1993: 92.

[19] Conceivably, there was a *nisba* form **Niggerôty* meaning precisely people of the oases, but, it is normal in Canaanite to place the gentilic *-y* on the singular forms of dual or plural place names. See Cyrus Gordon, *Ugaritic Textbook.* Rome: Pontifical Biblical Institute, 1965: 62.

[20] See Geoffrey Bibby, *Looking for Dilmun,* Harmondsworth: Penguin, 1972: 318 and 330.

[21] It has been widely suggested that these were the same as the *Nabaitai* living in the Syrian desert referred to in Assyrian sources of the seventh century BCE. However, Eph'al, (*The Ancient Arabs,* 221-223), however, is not convinced because of the distinction between the ṭ and the *t.* He now sees this distinction as reinforced by the discovery of the name *Nbyt* on a sixth century CE inscription from the Jebel Ghunaiym in an ancient Arabic dialect. I am not so tolerant of coincidences, that two peoples in the same ecological zone should have such similar names seems highly implausible. The Greek νάφθα probably derives from *nbṭ.* Pliny (2.235) described *naphtha, ita appelatur circa Babylonem et in Austacenis Parthiae profluens bituminis liquidi modo.* Although the second place name reinforces the supposition that it derives from the Avestan *napta* and the hypothetical Iranian **nafta,* "wet". The Semitic *nabaṭa,* "issue forth," fits better in both its phonetics and its semantics.

[22] John Wansbrough, "Africa and Arab Geographers," pp.89-101 in David Dalby Comp. *Language and History in Africa: A Volume of Collected Papers Presented to the London Seminar on Language and History in Africa, Held in the School of Oriental and African Studies, 1967-69.* New York: Africana, 1970: 91.

[23] Personal communication Shomarka Keita 1/21/97

[24] This type is described by J. Hiernaux in *The People of Africa,* New York: Scribners, 1975: 127-139. Alfred Muzzolini consistently tries to play down the number of "Negroid" types drawn on the rock paintings. He concedes their presence at Tassili but attempts to deny that they were represented in those from Tadrart Acacus some 100 miles to the east (*L'art rupestre prehistoriques des massifs centraux sahariens* Oxford: B.A.R. 1986: 60). Elsewhere (pp. 236 and 252), however, he concedes their presence not only at Tadrart Acacus but in some Garamantes tombs, even further east, pp. 236 and 252.

[25] Lhote, *Tassili,* 81. See also Laureano, *La Piramede Rovesiata,* 1995: 273.

[26] A. Hampate Ba and G, Dieterlein, *Koumen: Texte initiatique des pasteurs Peul.* Paris: Mouton, 1961.

[27] As I have not seen any of the originals, my judgement here is based on the in Lhote's reproductions and those in Fabrizio Mori, *Tadart Acacus: Arte rupestre e cultura del Sahara preistorico.* Torino: Einaudi, 1965.

[28] J. Hiernaux, *The People of Africa,* New York: Scribners, 1975: 127-139 and Keita "Crania," 36.

[29] Marie-Claude Chamla, *Les populations anciennes du Sahara et des régions limitrophes: Étude des restes osseux humain néolthiques et protohistoriques.* Paris: Centre de Recherches anthropologiques, préhistoriques protohistoriques et ethnographiques, 1968. See also M.Henneberg, J. Piontek and J, Strzalko "Biometrical analysis of the early Neolithic human mandible for Nabta Playa (Western Desert of Egypt)," pp. 389-392 in F.

Wendorf and R. Schild (eds.): *Prehistory of the Eastern Sahara*, New York: Academic Press, 1980.

[30] Hiernaux, *People of Africa*, 137. Hiernaux's suggestion that the light and reddish complexion of the Fulani is a climatic adaptation contradicts his conclusion earlier in the book (p. 77) that "skin colour tends to be darker in the savanna than in the forest, in which less sunlight actually reaches the ground."

[31] Jacques André, *Étude sur les termes de couleur dans la langue latine*. Paris: Klinksieck, 1949, and A. Ernout, and A. Meillet, *Dictionnaire Étymologique de la Langue Latine: Histoire des mots*. 4th ed. Paris: Klinksieck, 1985. Ernout, Meillet and André all disregarded, --presumably on phonetic grounds-- the tradition expressed in T. G. Tucker's *A Concise Etymological Dictionary of Latin*, Halle: Niemeyer, 1931. Tucker attempted to preserve the European identity of *niger* by linking it to the Sanskrit *nila* "dark coloured," and the Gothic *nidwa*--"dark."

[32] *Ater* is attested in other Italic languages. Ernout and Meillet concede that any relationship between *ater* and the Irish *ath* "furnace" is dubious

[33] André, *Étude*, 47.

[34] André, *Étude*, 53.

[35] Hans Georg Niemeyer believes that Phoenician colonization was no earlier than the Greek. See his "Les Phéniciens dans l'ouest," *Revue Archéologique* (1988): 201-204. The positivist and minimalist Maria Eugenia Aubet prefers, on archaeological grounds, a date in early ninth century BCE. (*The Phoenicians and the West: Politics, Colonies and Trade*. Cambridge: Cambridge University Press, 1993: 177-184). On the other hand, the *doyen* of Phoenician studies Sabatino Moscati, argues for Canaanite activities in the western Mediterranean in the fourteenth and thirteenth centuries BCE and Phoenician activities in the tenth. See, for instance, his "I Fenici e il mondo Mediterraneo al tempo di Omero," *Rivista di Studi Fenici* 13 (1985): 179-187. Frank Cross, using himself on epigraphic evidence, would even go to the eleventh century, see his "The Early Alphabetic Scripts" in F. Cross, ed. *Symposia: Celebrating the Seventy-fifth Anniversary of the American School of Oriental Research, 1900-1975*. Cambridge Mass.: Harvard University Press, 1979: 97-123. The archaeologist John Boardman sees Phoenician expansion in the Mediterranean as having taken place in the tenth or ninth centuries, "Al Mina and History," *Oxford Journal of Archaeology* 9 (1990): 169-190, esp. p.178.

[36] D. Van Berchen, "Hercule-Melqart à l'Ara Maxima. "*Rendiconti della Pontificia Accademia Romana di Archaologia* serie III, vol. 33 (1959-60): 61-68, and "Sanctuaires d'Hercules-Melqart, Contribution à l'étude de l'expansion phénicienne en Méditeranée," *Syria* 44 (1967): 73-109 and 307-336.

[37] See Polybius, III. 22-25.

[38] R. Rebuffat. "Les Phéniciens à Rome," *Mélanges d'archéologie et d'histoire de l'école française de Rome* 78 (1966): 7-48 For the later date, see Plautus' Poenulus.

[39] See *Black Athena* I. esp. pp. 367-399.

[40] The Italian linguist Vincenzo Cocco indicated that the origin was the Georgian *malokhi* and the Semitic *mlḫ* with the same meaning. Vincenzo Cocco, "D'un' antichissima designazione Mediterranea della 'malva': Preell, μῶλυ 'pianta magica', malva." *Archivio Glottologica Italiano* 40 (1955): 10-28.

[41] The Latin *alba,* Albania "mountain land " and the Greek ἀλφός, "white, leprous" and the Semitic roots *ḥlb* "milk" and *lbn* "white" and snow-capped mountains provide additional parallels. As *ḥlb* is deeply rooted in Afroasiatic, the connection is probably genetic, but the Latin and Greek forms could be the result of loans.

[42] André, *Étude,* p. 53.

[43] See Sorenson, 1993: 23-24.

[44] Joachim Le Grand, *Relation Historique d'Abissinie,* Paris: Gosse & Neaulm, 1728. Samuel Johnson, *A Voyage to Abyssinia,* London: Bettesorth and Hitch, 1733

[45] Not that Johnson completely escaped the prevailing racism of the age. Harold Pagliaro has written a study of the racism involved in Dr Johnson's relationship with his servant Francis Barber. See his "Preface" to H.E. Pagliaro, ed. *Racism in The Eighteenth Century, Studies in Eighteenth-Century Culture,* Cleveland, Ohio, and London: Case Western Reserve University Press, 1973: xv-xviii.

[46] *Parzival,* 15. Von Eschenbach clearly had moral reasons for this description. He began his work with the claim that all men are "motley like a magpie", "Heaven and Hell having equal part in him." This illustrates, the association of the Christian moral color scheme with skin color, and in particular the curious identification of "white" with the pinko-gray complexions among Northern Europeans in early Middle Ages and later.

[47] See St. Clair Drake, *Black Folk Here and There.* 2 vols. Los Angeles: University of California: Center for Afro-American Studies, 1987 and 1990, II, 213-220.

[48] *Laisse,* 237, line 3229. Gérard Brault, *The Song of Roland: An Analytical Editio,* 2 Vols. University Park, Pennsylvania and London: University of Pennsylvania Press, 1978 and 1984, II, *Text,* 197. Brault translates *Nigres* as "negroes." Gérard Moignet in *La Chanson de Roland, Texte Originale et Traduction.* Paris: Bordas, 1989: 231, has *nègres.* The list of peoples in which this description is applied includes a number recognized by their dark colors: Bruns, Blos, Ermins. The vicious "racism" of the text can be seen in other passages, such as those in *Laisse,* 143 and 144.

[49] See Ronald Sanders, *Lost Tribes and Promised Lands: The Origins of American Racism.* Boston and Toronto: Little Brown, 1978, frontispiece and 6.

[50] Richard B. Moore, *The Name "Negro": Its Origin and Evil Use."* Originally published in 1960 reprinted, Baltimore, Md.: Black Classic Press, 1992.

[51] See the *Oxford English Dictionary,* "Negro," and Winthrop Jordan, *White over Black: American Attitudes towards the Negro 1550-1812.* New York and London: Penguin, 1968: 3-20.

[52] "The Slave's Lament" in *Complete Works of Robert Burns.* 6 vols. National Library Edition New York: Bigelow Brown, 1909: 109-110.

[53] See the long note in C. F. Volney, *The Ruins of Empires: English translation of 1804* Baltimore: Black Classic Press reprint, 1991: 16-17.

[54] St Clair Drake, I, p. 131.

[55] See H. Hartleben, *Jean-François Champollion: Sa vie et son oeuvre 1790-1832.* Trans. [into French] D. Meunier. Paris: Pygmalion, 1983: 421.

[56] See for instance Hartleben, 426 and J. Lacouture, *Champollion Une Vie de Lumières,* Paris: Grasset, 1988: 412.

[57] C.F. Dupuis. *Origine de tous les cultes, ou la religion universelle.* 12 vols. Paris: Agasse An III, (1795), vol. 1: p. 73.

[58] Volney, *The Ruins of Empires,* 16-17.

[59] *An Enquiry Concerning and Moral Faculties, and Literature of Negroes.* Paris: 1808, Trans D.B. Warden, Brooklyn: Kirk, 1810: 25.

[60] St Clair Drake, *Black Folk* I: 131.

Menelaos, the Cyclopes, and Eurybates: A Postcolonial Reading of Homer's *Odyssey*

Miriam Dow
The George Washington University

Martin Bernal's monumental *Black Athena: The Afroasiatic Roots of Classical Civilization*--now in the first two volumes (I "The Fabrication of Ancient Greece, 1785-1985," and II "The Archeological and Documentary Evidence"), of the projected four--has already begun a paradigm-shift in several disciplines. But the sociology surrounding his work has obscured some of his principal hypotheses, in the peevish and piecemeal approach of his critics. His over-arching thesis, as the subtitle to the unfortunate title suggests, has to do with a profoundly cosmopolitan cultural exchange prompted by many factors and involving many areas, but getting its original impetus from significant cultural domination over Greece by Egypt in the third millennium BCE, from an Egypto-Semitic colonization of Greece at the beginning of the second millennium BCE under the Hyksos princes of Egypt, and from a second wave of even stronger cultural domination after independence from the colonizing power in the Late Bronze Age, lasting through the Geometric period, the Classical age and down to about 300 BCE. Bernal's scholarship constructs a widely and continuously intertextual ancient Mediterranean.

My paper examines the *Odyssey* of Homer as a postcolonial document, specifically in its construction of Phoenicia and Phoenicians, and most particularly in its construction of Egypt.

Is it possible to see traces of Egypt's being a culture of reference for Greece at some foundational Greek moment? If so, does that inscription reflect the sort of hybridity that results from colonization? After colonization, are there signs of what Gramsci calls domination by consent? Is the difference between the Homeric attitudes to Phoenicia and Egypt revealing in this investigation? My conclusion is that while references to Phoenician cities and other places/cultures reflect a cosmopolitan Mediterranean, the construction of Egypt in the *Odyssey* reflects an entirely different relationship and exceeds what one might call the deference and admiration of a relatively young culture towards a very old one. In not wishing to overstate my claim, I follow Bernal's example in positing what seems more likely: Egypt most likely did colonize Greece at a culturally formative moment and continued to be a culture of reference for the Greeks into the Bronze Age and beyond.

In his revised Ancient Model, Bernal (1991) posits colonization of Greece by fleets (for which there is archaeological evidence) "from Egypt of Egyptians, Syrians or Hyksos" who "established long-lasting heroic dynasties" (II.405). To explain why the resulting civilization was not more overtly Egyptian, Bernal argues by analogy from the Norman Conquest of England, principally achieved by Danes and Norwegians who had first conquered Normandy and made it into an independent duchy. Their military prowess, enhanced by "French and Italian civilian skills" (II.406), made them a sufficiently formidable force to conquer many areas of Europe, England most particularly. There they established a dynasty of some length and changed Anglo-Saxon culture forever, but not by means of Norse culture and languages. French and Latin were the carriers of an altered French feudal system, all of which combined to create the modern English language and culture. While Egyptian and Semitic words and names were current in the Aegean as early as the third millennium BCE, and cultural domination gained momentum during the Hyksos colonization of Greece, Bernal demonstrates that after that period:

> Greek borrowed massively from [Egyptian and Semitic]...languages during the period of Egyptian dominance

of the East Mediterranean in the Late Bronze Age after 1470 BC as well as in the Geometric, Archaic and Classical periods from 950 to 300 BC. Nevertheless, the centuries between 1730 and 1530, which are frequently seen to be the most likely period for the creation of Greek as a language, would seem to be ones when Greece was largely ruled by speakers of West Semitic and Egyptian. There is virtually no doubt that these two languages had high status in the region at that time (II.45).

Bernal's evidence from material culture and language is very persuasive. Particularly interesting to me is the linguistic evidence, such as an Egypto-Phoenician provenance for the Homeric words for "sword" and "dagger," and an Egypto-Greek provenance for "hybris," a word and concept that lies at the core of Greek culture, from Homeric through Classical and Hellenistic times, and continues as a cultural presence in the West. Some names in Homer offer more evidence, "Agamemnon," for example, meaning "Great Memnon," undoubtedly the Memnon who was the Black Egyptian hero from southern upper Egypt and who, if he was a historical figure, preceded Agamemnon by seven hundred years (II.33). "Aigyptios," an Ithakan elder, turns up in the Assembly when Telemachos calls it together. (Bernal does not mention him; perhaps he will appear in Volume III?)

According to Bernal, continued Egyptian cultural dominance after the end of Egyptian colonization can be argued from material culture and linguistics, and has a historical parallel in the relationship between what came to be known as Vietnam and China. In fact, Egyptian cultural influence on Greece in the foundational Greek moment is over-determined; a further analogy of historically peaceful cultural transformation is the millennium-long cultural borrowing from China by Japan, which did not include Chinese conquest.

What traces of either colonization or other kinds of culture contact linger in the *Odyssey*? For the latter there is certainly plenty of evidence; at this remove, the former is more subtle and calls for some outrageousness. Generally, a culture of reference lingers if it is a strong presence at some foundational moment. In our American case, Great Britain is present in the ideological/agentive (the value-laden power structure and its source) in plain view: many of our institutions, for example, are clearly patterned after Britain's. The hegemonic (the "invisible," because absorbed, consented to value-laden power structure) too continues, in naming little girls of all colors and ethnicites "Ashley" or "Brittany," for example, and giving expensive housing developments aspiring to poshness very English-sounding names like "Foxhall Estates," or "King's Arms Cottages". These are just two examples of what Gramsci calls cultural domination by consent. Nor is this kind of cultural hegemony mere nostalgia; descendants of that English culture still dominate politics and business here in America. A careful reading of the *Odyssey*, with Bernal's claims in mind, reveals a Mediterranean intertextuality, both synchronic and diachronic, and most particularly a palimpsest of Egyptian cultural influences.

Many peoples are mentioned in the *Odyssey*, some no longer identifiable, like many of its place names. Egypt is mentioned often, as are Phoenicians, reflecting the historical reality of Egypt as a kingdom and Phoenicia as a string of cities along the coast of modern Lebanon, with Ugarit, Tyre, Sidon, and Biblos being the most famous. Phoenicians come off rather badly in the *Odyssey*, in terms of the Homeric world and its values. The Phoenicians were active traders all over the Mediterranean, with colonies in North Africa and as far west as Spain. The archaic aristocratic circles of the *Odyssey* did not admire trade; piracy was a much more aristocratic means to wealth, as we learn from old Nestor, who reports "cruising after plunder wherever Achilleus led us" (III.106), and from the Sacker of Cities, Odysseus himself. On his way home from Troy, for example, he mentions casually, off-handedly, that he stopped off at the Thracian home of the Kikonians:

> I sacked their city and killed their people, and out of their city taking their wives and many possessions we shared them out, so none might go cheated of his proper portion (IX.40-43).

Odysseus, in other words, does not only sack Troy, but sacks any city in his path, entirely appropriate for the grandson of the noble Autolykos, who "surpassed all men in thievery." On the other hand, when a young man wants to insult and goad Odysseus after the latter has refused to participate in a sporting event, he accuses him of being a merchant, one who is:

> master over mariners who also are men of business, a man who, careful of his cargo and grasping for profits, goes carefully on his way. You do not resemble an athlete (VIII.162-164).

This dreadful insult prompts our heroic pirate to not only join the contest but to win it.

In his second version of his life, the one fabricated for Eumaios, Odysseus tells of living the good life in Egypt when a Phoenician, "well skilled in beguilements, a gnawer at others' goods," persuades Odysseus to accompany him to Phoenicia, with a mind to some business deals in Libya, but really intending to sell him into slavery.

Eumaios, perhaps constructed to be a more reliable witness, a slaveowner's ideal--of noble birth and therefore utterly loyal to his master/owner, with no agenda of his own, one who does not lie--characterizes the Phoenicians in a similar fashion, only more complexly, as "famous seafarers, gnawers at other men's goods," but "with countless pretty things stored in their black ship" (XV.415-416). Eumaios was kidnaped by his Phoenician nanny, who herself had been kidnaped and sold into slavery by pirates from Taphos (western coast of Greece?). But kidnaping the king's son and walking off with some of the plate did not do her any good: there is no honor among these thieving merchants. Her Phoenician compatriots merely push her overboard and sell Eumaios into slavery, to Laertes, Odysseus' father.

That other cruising fortune-hunter, Menelaos, gives Telemachos his most valuable possession, a mixing bowl given him by the king of Sidon, and believed to have been made by Hephaistos, one kind of the "pretty things" fanning out from Phoenician cities across the Mediterranean. In the *Odyssey*, the Phoenicians get around, have at least one noble, generous, or possibly merely politic, king but generally are devious, treacherous traders, exploiting others and even each other. This view is not merely a character-creating device represented by Odysseus, but as echoed by Eumaios may be said to represent the archaic, Homeric opinion. It certainly suggests wide contact between the Greeks and the Phoenicians, and an admiration for at least some Phoenician exports. What it suggests most strongly is the customary aristocratic fear/hatred and/or contempt for trade and merchants, the "othering"of class.

The attitude toward Egypt is entirely different. The ambiguity towards a trading partner whose occupation one scorns but whose goods one covets is entirely absent. The coveted goods "Made in Egypt" have the same cachet as "Made in England" had here until quite recently (and still do, for some). Egypt is also a place to get rich, but in the right way, not by contemptible trade. It is also a source of superior knowledge. The Homeric almost-reverential tone, especially in contrast to the view of Phoenicia, seems more than an attitude of deference one people would have towards another because of the latter's much older and more highly developed civilization.

How would it be helpful to theorize this early "postcolon i-alism" and cultural hegemony? Because the ancient texts focus on the Greek elite, which was most likely complicit in the colonial venture, modern postcolonial theory is not entirely helpful, concerned as it is with the violence of colonization and decolonization, the brutalization of people's cultures, aspects of resistance by the colonized, the double colonization of women and its dilemmas in seeming to offer choices only between patriarchies--one nationalist and the other imposed--, and the combining of capitalism and globalization into a world-wide market economy. This last is perhaps the greatest distinction between ancient colonialisms and European colonialism of the last five hundred years. Instead of merely extracting various forms of tribute and military manpower from colonized countries as was the practice in antiquity, modern European colonial powers restructured their colonies, absorbing their entire economies. As for the status of women, the *Odyssey* makes clear that elite Greek women benefitted from Egyptian colonization, briefly emerging from patriarchal domination, only to disappear into the *gunaikeion* (women's quarters) in the classical period. Not surprisingly, during Greco-Roman domination of Egypt, the status of Egyptian women declined.

Other aspects of current postcolonial   theory seem more
relevant, including the idea of cultural transformation, the idea of
objects of desire originating/residing elsewhere, relationships
articulated in terms of center and margin, and the inscription of
alterity in terms of an unnamed model.

Before applying these postcolonial criteria to the *Odyssey*, I
would like to make an outrageous suggestion, offered in the
semi-ludic spirit of Bernal's self-confessed outrageousness, but
without his solid evidence. My outrageous suggestion is that the
palace scenes in the *Odyssey*, notably those at Sparta and at that
utopian space, Scheria, resemble in tone, constituency, and opulence New Kingdom Egyptian culture much more than they resemble Greek culture. In both palaces royal women are present
and feast with their kings and other aristocrats, eating, drinking,
and talking with the men, very much in line with New Kingdom
palace iconography. Furthermore, Phemios' tale of the adulterous
caper of Ares and Aphrodite is very much in the spirit of New
Kingdom love poetry and its frank celebration of sexual pleasures and its vignettes of mutual seductions amid the luxuries of
fine linen and intoxicating scents.

The former expatriates (in Egypt), travelers, and collectors
of treasures, Menelaos and Helen, are casebook examples of
culturally colonized subjects. The luxuries and other objects of
desire are Phoenician and most particularly Egyptian; the king
and queen are ostentatious "been-tos" with a vengeance. The
center of wealth, opportunity, and magnificence is Egypt, from
which they have retreated to its Greek margins, laden with treasure. The very setting is reminiscent of New Kingdom iconography:

> among them stepped an inspired singer playing his lyre,
> while among the dancers two acrobats led the measures of
> song and dance, revolving among them (IV.17-19).

This elaborate entertainment--on what appears to be an ordinary day--exceeds any other scene of feasting in the *Odyssey*.
Enjoying this spectacle and the food placed before them, Telemachos notes, with awe, "the gleaming of the bronze" and "of

the gold and amber, of silver and ivory" (IV.71-2). Menelaos immediately and proudly identifies these luxuries as imports, brought home in his own ships, by himself, after suffering much and wandering among the Cypriots, Phoenicians, Egyptians, Lybians, Aithiopians. But Menelaos also looks about him lugubriously and remarks that he would give two-thirds of these splendors, if only the Greeks who died at Troy could live again. A barbarous but good-hearted albeit calculating man, Menelaos brought dazzling objects from abroad without acquiring the polish of the ancient civilizations he visited.

A more specific inventory begins with Helen's arrival into the room. She is accompanied by three maids, one of whom brings Helen's silver workbasket, "with wheels underneath, and the edges. . . done in gold," a gift from the wife of Polybos of "Egyptian Thebes, where the greatest number of goods are stored in the houses" (IV.125-132). Menelaos and Helen eagerly imitate Egyptian consumerism, and are very proud of Polybos' gifts, which include two silver bathtubs and a pair of tripods. Luxurious and technologically superior objects, yes; ancient Egyptian ideas of *ma'at*--justice, harmony, royal responsibility--no. If only Odysseus had come home, Menelaos exclaims, "I would have emptied one city for him/out of those that are settled round about and under my lordship" (IV.176-177), a sort of inverted ethnic cleansing in turning out native Spartans to accommodate the loved Ithakan. Or, it is just, perhaps, the hyperbolic boasting of a local chieftain.

Helen seems to have acquired, besides exquisite gadgets, more sophistication in Egypt than Menelaos brought home. After bitter tears for the still-missing Odysseus, Menelaos declares an end to weeping and time for dinner. To make sure things go with a swing, Helen "cast a medicine/of heartease, free of gall, to make one forget all sorrows" into the wine bowls, just one of "the subtle medicines" brought home from Egypt:

> where the fertile earth produces the greatest number of medicines, many good in mixture, many malignant, and every man is a doctor there and more understanding than men elsewhere (IV.229-232).

This homage to the cosmopolitan center from the provincial margins is more significant than the proud consumerism reflected in the objects, objects such as any traveler might bring home from a technologically and culturally more complex civilization.

What ideas traveled from Egypt to Greece? The colonization of Greece by Egypt posited by Bernal gave the Greeks the colonizing gaze, the gaze which the Egyptians must have turned on *them* when they encountered what must have seemed to the Egyptians disorganized, violent, backward tribes, always bickering and fighting each other, illiterate people without a scribal class, without monuments, without geometry, without a divine pharaoh and an imperial hierarchy--the savage other. Odysseus, our cultural icon, learned that colonizing gaze well, the (implied) narrative voice of the *Odyssey* tells us: in Odysseus' description of the Cyclops we have the Magna Carta of colonialism, our complex inheritance from Egypto-Greek antiquity.

Odysseus is drawn to the land of the Cyclops, a place Beth Cohen (1995) describes as "a promising colonial site" (11), by his curiosity. He goes there in his aspect of anthropologist (Odysseus *polutropos*--the many-faceted Odysseus), anthropology being always already the social-scientific arm of imperialism. He wants to

> go and find out about these people, and learn what they are, whether they are savage and violent, and without justice, or hospitable to strangers and with minds that are godly (IX.174-176).

This dichotomy of human possibilities is set up without irony or self-consciousness, immediately after Odysseus remarks casually that he and his men had seized one hundred nine of the Cyclopes' goats for a great barbecue on the beach, washed down with some of the potent wine they had stolen "when [they] stormed the Kikonians' sacred citadel" (IX.165). The paleo-colonizer's hegemonizing gaze tends already to see lazy savages, unable to use their land "properly", to exploit it to the full. Cyclopes "neither plow with their hands nor plant anything," Odysseus observes, but nevertheless "all grows for them," including wheat, barley, grapes. Moreover, they have "no institutions, no meetings for counsels," and live in caves where "each one is the law/for his own wives and children, and cares nothing about the others" (IX.107-115). Very interesting from the man from Ithaka, where the assembly is impotent, as we learn in Book II, although at least one voice there articulates the values of a much older Egypt, as we'll see below. This same man returns to Ithaka and is the law for his wife and child and property, executing the suitors and the betraying slaves--slaves of whom so much grateful loyalty is always expected except in realistic Sparta--without benefit of "institutions" or "meetings for counsels." The unnamed standard applied to the Cyclopes is not Ithakan but Egyptian.

After this prologue, Odysseus approaches the cave of Polyphemos, whom he suspects of being "a monster of a man" (IX.187). Odysseus "had an idea" that he'd encounter a very strong man "with no true knowledge of laws or any good customs," just as the coastal colonized subject looks upon his upcountry counterpart as "bush," before even encountering him. Odysseus and his men admire Polyphemos' husbandry, his generational division of his livestock, the disposition of the milk, whey, and cheese--and the men are all for stealing the lot and getting away. But Odysseus lusts for presents, more booty to justify his long absence and to increase his power and *kleos*--his glorious reputation.

They make sacrifice, eat, wait, and finally watch as Polyphemos returns, arranges his livestock for the night, closes his cave, and, having milked all the animals, sets aside some milk for his supper. His first words are "who are you?" showing his crudity and lack of manners, in which his otherness is encoded. (This crudity is usually more direct, as when the giant says "Fee, fie, fo, fum, I smell the blood of an Englishman," showing very clearly that *he's* no Englishman.) Poseidon's son but no Greek, Polyphemos should have fed them before asking such a personal question. And he's not about to be colonized, or to accept gratefully the ideological yoke, but asks questions that are even more rude, like where they come from and why:

Is it on some business, or are you recklessly roving as pirates

do, when they sail on the salt sea and venture their lives as
they wander, bringing evil to alien people?" (IX.253-255)

The resisting subject offers a totally accurate description and
a moral challenge to the would-be-colonizer, who cannot even
recognize it. Odysseus rises above--or possibly plunges below--
the ethical, and responds by tricking out the destruction of Troy
as an almost holy saga, until very recently the only edition of
Western conquests available. After Odysseus asks for a guest
present in the name of Zeus--here as Zeus Xenios (protector of
strangers)--Polyphemos, savage that he is, reveals his utter indif-
ference to the thieving intruders's gods, and proceeds to eat a pair
of them to show it.

Here we have the first projection of fear of one's own cannibalism extended from one's own cultural community to the other.
Cannibalism is a powerful trope in Greek mythology, starting
with Tantalus (who served his own son to the gods and got the
eternal punishment from which we have a useful adjective and
verb) and his descendants in the story of the over-determined fall
of the house of Atreus, a story in which Atreus, grandson of
Tantalus, serves his brother's children to their father, out of re-
venge. In the grammar of fairy tales and the related genre of the
proto-anthropologizing writings of later explorers and missionaries, the cannibal and other terrifying, taboo-breaking monsters
move out from one's own cultural community in widening con-
centric circles.

Polyphemos is vanquished by means of the imported, the
stolen wine from the sacred citadel of the Kikonians--had no one
warned him to beware of Greeks bearing gifts? Liquor as trope,
as destruction--the liquor that brought such joy to countless
brave new worlds: all that is missing in this early version is the
smallpox and the clap. Polyphemos is vanquished by wine and
his own greed and stupidity, like any lazy savage, because he
fails to see the superiority of one he describes, even after his
blinding, as "a little man, niddering, [cowardly, wretched] fee-
ble..." (IX.515).

The *Odyssey* has absorbed the colonizing gestures and rhetoric well. But it has also absorbed a different ethos, also Egyptian,
but older, still just barely alive but impotent in Ithaka. In Book II

when Telemachos calls the Assembly, the men of Ithaka are cowed by the powerful young suitors--some of them their own sons--and do nothing in response to Telemachos' plea. The aged Mentor is appalled by this reaction, claiming that it is not even the barbarous behavior of the suitors he resents as much as

"...you other people, how you all sit there in silence, and never with an assault of words try to check the suitors, though they are so few, and you so many" (II.239-241).

Mentor holds the bystanders responsible, an ethical level that looks forward to Karl Jaspers' concept of metaphysical guilt, and back to the early Egyptian literature of the third millennium BCE, such as the "Instructions for Merikare." These ancient *nomoi* (unwritten laws and ethical standards) linger in the fading memories of old men.

The *Odyssey* sustains such a reading of early Egyptian influence and the somewhat later influences from the colonizing Hyksos and the cultural climate of the New Kingdom, visible particularly in the Phaiakian court and the status there ascribed to the queen, a most un-Greek status and one approached only by Helen's, because Helen and Menelaos had been Greek expatriates in Egypt for some years. Arete, the Phaiakian queen, we are told by Athene when she is coaching Odysseus, at this moment the helpless refugee, on how to get help in this kindgdom, is the power he should supplicate, not Alkinoos, the king. Alkinoos has given her "such pride of place as no other woman on earth is given," and she not only has the love of her husband and children as we might expect, but also of all the people. The people "look toward her as to a god when they see her," not because of her traditional feminine--and therefore permitted even in Greece-- kindness and goodness, but because "there is no good intelligence that she herself lacks. She dissolves quarrels, even among men, when she favors them" (VII.66-74). This freedom and respect for her mind is unparalleled in a "respectable" Greek woman as constructed in archaic and classical antiquity, and the moment did not last long. The moment was much more Egyptian than it was Greek, and is compatible with Joyce Tyldesley's claim (1994) that the best place to have been a woman in all of antiquity was Egypt.

The *Odyssey* palimpsest bears a later Egyptian imprint, in its claim that Poseidon was away, feasting with the Ethiopians (a statement found in the *Iliad* also; between the two Homeric epics Poseidon, Iris, and Zeus are said to be so feasting, and the Ethiopians are characterized as "blameless"). I wondered about that for decades: what are these Greek deities doing, feasting with Africans, when they never dignify Greeks in the same way? The answer finally appeared in *Blacks in Antiquity*, by Frank Snowden, Jr., published in 1970 but not much discussed or cited. Snowden identifies these Ethiopians with the Nubians that conquered Egypt in 730 BCE and gave Egypt its twenty-fifth dynasty. Snowden--whose book demonstrates an African presence in Greece for a thousand years, in texts and objects, beginning in the seventh century BCE--has some reservations about this influence on Homer because of the dating of Homer's work, but I don't share his scruples, having seen the dating of the writing down of the epics move closer to us by over a hundred years in my lifetime. Scholars cannot agree on the date of the Homeric epics, ranging now from as early as 750 BCE to as late as slightly later than 650 BCE (Cohen, 6-8); when I was an undergraduate, 900 BCE was confidently announced. Snowden feels that pre-25th dynasty stories of "blameless" Africans influenced Homer, but that the 25th dynasty's reputation influenced only Herodotus' view of them. I would like to think it is at least possible that the late, and finally written, version of the epics assimilated the late-breaking news that the new dynasty of Egypt, founded by the black Nubian, Piankhi, was notably righteous. They were reputed, for example, to have eliminated capital punishment and substituted public works for it; criminals were set to work on shoring up the banks of the Nile. They appear to have treated the Egyptian gods and priests with reverence, not attempting to impose their own (Snowden 144-5), both unusual modes for victors, and certainly notable enough to merit inclusion in ever-evolving old Greek epics.

One final interesting piece of evidence for Egyptian influence on the Greeks as inscribed in the *Odyssey* appears in book XIX. Odysseus, disguised as a beggar, is trying to persuade Penelope that he is a reliable informant about the man she has begun to fear is dead, Odysseus himself. She's had many a lying tale from men who've cadged rewards for raising her hopes about Odysseus' return. Now this old beggar claims to have been a Cretan prince in better days, and that he actually entertained Odysseus in his Cretan palace. In that case, Penelope remarks, the old beggar should be able to describe what Odysseus had been wearing. Of course the old beggar can do it, and one better; he adds the following information:

> "Also there was a herald.... who went with him... He was round in the shoulders, black-complexioned, wooly-haired, and had the name Eurybates. Odysseus prized him above his other companions, for their thoughts were in harmony" (XIX.244-248).

If this tale is meant to make the teller credible to Penelope, Eurybates must have started off with Odysseus, from Ithaka. What is the "prized" black man doing there? Is he a descendant of the earlier Egyptian colonists? Of the Hyksos armies? of Sesostris' army? A late interpolation in this polysemous, layered epic, this intertextual cultural product, this postcolonial palimpsest?

Works Cited

Bernal, Martin. *Black Athena: The Afroasiatic Roots of Classical Civilization*. Vol. 2. New Brunswick: Rutgers UP, 1991. 2 vols.

Cohen, Beth. *The Distaff Side: Representing the Female in Homer's Odyssey*. New York: Oxford UP, 1995.

Lattimore, Richmond. *The Odyssey of Homer: A Modern Translation*. New York: Harper and Row, 1965.

Snowden, Frank M, Jr. *Blacks in Antiquity: Ethiopians in Greco-Roman Experience*. Cambridge: Harvard UP, 1970.

Tyldesley, Joyce. *Daughters of Isis: Women of Ancient Egypt*. New York: Penguin Books USA, 1994.

European Images of Africa from Early Times to the Eighteenth Century

A. Buluda Itandala
University of Dar es Salaam, Tanzania

Introduction

Many Europeans and Americans are familiar only with the nineteenth-century European image of Africa as "the dark continent," which was popularized by late nineteenth-century travel literature (Stanley, 1878 and 1890).[1] This image of Africa was, however, partly derived from earlier European images of the continent and partly from nineteenth-century European attitudes and factors. Therefore, in order to understand how this modern European image of Africa came into being in the late nineteenth century, it is necessary to trace the development and nature of earlier European images from earlier European contacts with Africans. This paper intends to do this under four main sub-headings, namely the classical European image of Africans, medieval ideas and concepts on Africa and Africans, the Renaissance view of Africa, and eighteenth-century European racism and Africans.

The Classical European Image of Africans

Among the earliest visitors to Africa were people from the Mediterranean world, namely the Phoenicians, the Greeks and the Romans, some of whom recorded in documents what they saw and heard about the areas they visited. Some of them such as the writers of *The Periplus of the Erythraean Sea* and Plotemy's *Geography* made just brief references on the parts of the continent which they visited and heard about without revealing what or how they felt about the climate and the cultures of the inhabitants of those areas (McCrindle, 1879, freeman-Grenville, 1962: 1-20, Stevens, 1933: 31-109). However, other Greco-Roman writers such as Herodotus, Diodorus, Eratosthenes, Hanno, Strabo, and Pliny appear to have expressed their feelings and prejudices more openly and unhesitatingly on the climate, fauna and cultures of the peoples whom they briefly encountered or heard about (Riad, 1981: 193-98). All these writers were very familiar with the climate, fauna, peoples and cultures of the Mediterranean littoral in North Africa and the Red Sea coast, particularly Egyptian and Carthaginian, which they favourably portrayed apparently because they did not differ very much from their own. But their description of Africans living to the south of Egypt and Carthage, whom they referred to as Libyans and Ethiopians (Rennell, 1800:427-28, Ghent, 1653:116), are generally brief, fragmentary, and "tend consistently to emphasize the strange, the shocking and the degrading qualities of the peoples and cultures they deal with and thus to emphasize the gulf between the [so-called] civilized and the [so-called] primitive worlds", as Katherine George has rightly pointed out (George, 1958: 63). Unable to visit the African interior themselves, these scholars relied on second-hand information which they obtained from local informants in Egypt and other parts of North Africa. Their accounts speak of inner Libya, which was a vague geographical expression signifying what lay beyond the Mediterranean littoral, and of inner Ethiopia, a region lying further south and so named because its inhabitants were more dark-skinned than those of the Sahara or the Mediterranean coast who were then a mixture of black and white. Both inner Libya and Ethiopia were depicted as mysterious regions in which strange human beings and animals intermingled. This negative characterization of Africans and their cultures by classical writers was not only a result of limited data on which it was based but perhaps more particularly a result of deliberate selection of data which harmonized with their biases and prejudices.

These biases and prejudices of ancient classical Greeks and Romans against Africans in general were no doubt caused by their ethnocentrism, a concept which has been defined by R. Preiswerk and D. Perrot as "the attitude of a group which consists of attributing to itself a central position compared to other groups, valuing positively its achievements and particular characteristics, adopting a projective type of behaviour toward out-groups and interpreting the out-group through the in-group's mode of thinking" (Preiswerk and Perrot, 1978: 14). It is, in other words, as William G. Sumner has further explained, the "view of things in which one's own group is the centre of everything, and all others are scaled and rated with reference to it..." and in which each group "nourishes its own pride and vanity, boasts itself superior, exalts its divinities and looks with contempt on outsiders" (Preiswerk and Perrot, 1978: 14).

The ancient Greeks, and later the Roman inheritors of their culture, used also the concepts of civilization and barbarism for distinguishing themselves from the rest of humanity. To them, the peoples of the world were made up of two groups, namely, Greeks (and later Greco-Romans) and others like them, who were civilized, and barbarians, who were uncivilized or primitive. By civilization they meant their urban culture and way of life, which they considered to be more advanced in every respect and therefore superior, while barbarism to them stood for non-Greek or non-Greco-Roman rural culture and way of life, which they considered to represent a low stage of development and therefore inferior.

Armed with these ethnocentric notions about themselves, Greco-Roman scholars who wrote on Africa in classical times have shown by their own testimonies that they regarded Africans living south of the Mediterranean and the Red Sea coasts as the worst kind of barbarians. Herodotus, for example, referred to the people living on the south-western edges of the Libyan desert in one of his writings as wild men and women who lived among dangerous wild animals and strange creatures "without heads" and with "eyes in their breasts" (Rawlinson 1862: 140-41). His accounts resembled Hanno's narrative of his voyage of exploration of the northwest African coast which was full of details about picturesque places, African "savages" and exotic animals (Salama, 1981: 516, Law, 1978: 134, Snowden, Jr., 1970: 106). But of all the classical Greco-

Roman scholars, it was perhaps Plinius the Elder who compiled the most incredible and picturesque details about the African interior. In his book called *Natural History*, he described some Africans as having neither noses nor nostrils, and others having no upper lips or tongues, and others still having only one eye each in their foreheads (Pliny, 1947: 251-53, Jones, 1971: 5-6). These testimonies show clearly that Africans were the worst kind of barbarians apparently because they were entirely different from them in colour, physical features, manners, customs and social organization.

In short, the general classical consensus appears to have been that the peoples living in sub-Saharan Africa lacked not only civilization as Mediterranean Europeans conceived it at that time but also were devoid of every good human attribute. In fact, the most remote among them from the Mediterranean littoral and the Red Sea coast were often denied even the possession of a truly human form and were said to have lived like wild beasts as the statements by Herodotus, Hanno and Plinius testify.

Medieval Ideas and Concepts on Africa and Africans

The classical European image of Africa and its peoples did not end with the fall of the Roman Empire in the fifth century A.D. On the contrary, most of its aspects were retained and passed on to the Middle Ages by Roman and Christian writers of the Dark Ages (400-800). Writers such as Julius Solinus and Cosmas Indicopleustes, for example, presented a Christian view of the world abounding in fabulous stories of strange peoples and animals and Christian legends (McCrindle, 1897: 37-54). This style of writing about Africa and other parts of the non-European world became very characteristic of the Middle Ages, that is the period from about the beginning of the ninth to about the end of the thirteenth century.

The nature of European attitudes on Africa and its peoples in the Middle Ages was determined partly by the limited and indirect nature of contacts which Europe had with most of Africa during this period and partly by the Christian world view which medieval Europeans held. The main factors which led to the establishment of such contacts were the conquest of North Africa and some parts of Southern Europe by Muslim Arabs between the seventh and the twelfth century and the rise and expansion of the trans-Saharan trade between North Africa and the Sudanic Zone (Fisher, 1977: 238-39).[2] The Muslim conquest of North Africa transformed North African communities by converting them to Islam and making them Arabic-speaking. Then by the second half of the eleventh century, a religious-cum-political movement known as Almoravid emerged in the western fringes of the Sahara with the intention of purifying Islam. In its enthusiasm to spread its own brand of Islam, the Almoravid movement invaded and conquered not only the Sudanic Zone in the south, but also the western Maghrib[3] in North Africa (Fisher, 1977: 235-36, Laroui, 1977), and the Iberian peninsula in southwestern Europe. Thus as conquerors of both the Sudanic Zone and the Western Maghrib in Africa and Spain, the Almoravid Muslims provided one of the links between Europe and Sub-Saharan Africa.

Moreover, as a result of the spread of Islam to North Africa and the Sudanic Zone as well as the expansion of the trans-Saharan trade, many people from the Western Sudan were taken to the Maghrib by Berber traders and the Almoravid conquerors as concubines, slaves and soldiers some of whom ended up in Europe. Apparently, the conquests of the Iberian peninsula by Muslim Arab-Berber armies in the eighth and ninth centuries and by the Almoravids in the eleventh century were accomplished with the aid of black African soldiers recruited from the Sahara and the Western Sudanic Zone (Levtzion, 1977: 331-35, Hrbek and Devisse, 1988: 343-66). To distinguish them from Muslim Arabs who were called "Moors" or "Saracens" by Christian Europeans, the Africans were referred to in medieval Europe and subsequently as "Blackmoors" or "Negroes". Debrunner has pointed out that the presence of black African soldiers in the invading Muslim armies in the Iberian peninsula contributed significantly to the defeat of the Christian European warriors because it frightened them very much (Debrunner, 1979: 18).

Besides conquering Spain from North Africa, the Muslim Arabs conquered and controlled the Mediterranean island of Sicily between 827 and 1060 (Fisher, 1977: 241-45, Debrunner, 1979: 18). These Muslims used mainly what are now Tunisia and northern Libya as a springboards for their attack and occupation of the island. As it was the case in their invasion of Spain, the Muslim Arab invaders took Africans with them to Sicily whom they used as concubines, slaves, servants, and soldiers.

Even after the takeover of Sicily by the Normans towards the end of the eleventh century, many Muslim Arabs and Africans resident there remained. It appears that the Norman kings of Sicily obtained gold from the western Sudan and African recruits for their armies (Devisse, 1984: 646-52). This means that the number of Africans steadily increased in Sicily after the Norman takeover. Some of these Africans eventually reached the different Italian city-states such as Genoa, Florence, Venice and Naples where they were employed as retainers, bodyguards, musicians and soldiers by the ruling elites and by commoners.

It is important to note that when Christian Europeans met Africans through the Muslim conquest of the Iberian peninsula and some other parts of Southern Europe between the seventh and the eleventh century, they were already becoming conscious of themselves as a distinct geo-cultural entity which was different from the Muslim invaders whom they referred to as "Moors". But it is not quite clear whether they always distinguished the Africans from the Arabs or not, because in most of the contemporary literature on the subject, the name "Moors" was applied indiscriminately in reference to all Muslims regardless of whether they were Arabs or Africans. There are cases, of course, in which the distinction is made by referring to the Africans as "Blackmoors" or "Negroes", which indicates that medieval Europeans were at least dimly aware that Africans constituted a separate racial group, differing from them and from the Arabs. Their attitudes towards the Africans seem to have been of two kinds. Those who were soldiers among them, as we have already seen, were viewed as dangerous men. This seems to have been the dominant theme in the medieval European mind because their fear of them appears to have led to hatred of them and to equating them with wild beasts and evil. This association of Africans with evil was, no doubt, partly due to the role they played as an instrument of destruction of European culture and religion. Those who were slaves among them, on the other hand, were regarded as inferior beings who could be exploited in all sorts of ways.

I am, therefore, fully in agreement with Hrbek when he says that:

From the European point of view, Africa became identified with the Muslim world as it was from this region that
the main incursions and invasions, but also various influences and ideas, were coming. When more intensive
commercial contacts between the northern and southern
shores of the Mediterranean developed later, Africa,
which the Europeans then came to know, was still Muslim
Africa. It is thus not surprising that Africa was identified
with the arch-enemy of Christianity, and its inhabitants,
irrespective of their colour, were regarded and treated accordingly. The lack in Europe of any direct contacts with
Africa beyond the Muslim sphere must have inevitably led
to the emergence of a very distorted image of the continent and particularly of its black inhabitants (Hrbek,
1988: 19).

However, in contrast to the negative attitudes and prejudices which medieval Europeans acquired about Africa and its
inhabitants through their protracted religious and political
conflicts and commercial relations with Muslim North Africa,
the image of Africa and its peoples which they got through
their peaceful contacts with the Christian kingdom of Ethiopia seems to have been relatively positive. It was the presence
of Ethiopian pilgrims in the "Holy Land" and other parts of
the Mediterranean region such as Syria, the Islands of Cyprus
and Rhodes and the Italian city-states between the eleventh
and fifteenth century which was responsible for the development of this relatively positive image (Tamrat, 1977: 177-
79, Debrunner, 1979: 24-29). These scattered groups of
Ethiopian monks reached Southern Europe via Egypt and Pal-
estine and were responsible for the establishment of cordial
relations between their country and European states. But this
relatively positive medieval European image of Africa was
very fragile and imprecise in Europe north of the Alps because
it was mainly based on assumptions, Christian legends and indirect sources of information.

The Renaissance View of Africans

After the Middle Ages, there were two main ways by
which Europeans established direct contact with Africans.

These were the expansion of Europeans overseas and the presence of some Africans in Europe. After liberating themselves from Muslim Arab control in the thirteenth century, the Portuguese became the first Europeans to establish direct contact with the "land of the blacks" in the Renaissance through explorations and travels overseas. But it was only the coastal areas of West, South and East Africa with which they established contact in the fifteenth century. The rest of the African interior still remained *terra incognita* for several centuries to come.

It is true, of course, that the fifteenth--and sixteenth--century Portuguese explorations and economic activities along the West, South and East African coasts inevitably increased the European knowledge of African geography and peoples and their cultures a little bit. By the end of the fifteenth century, for instance, an outline map of the African continent appeared and tthe monsters, which classical and medieval literature had talked so much about, receded from the frequently visited coasts to the unpenetrated interior as a result of this new knowlege. But being a product of an expanding and aggressive merchant capitalist economy, the early Portuguese observers of African peoples and cultures did not report objectively what they saw and heard about. It appears that their failure to do so was mainly due to their ethnocentrism. To them as it had been the case with classical and medieval writers, this remained a major problem.

It is interesting to note that at a time when slavery was supposed to have disappeared throughout Europe, it was everywhere being replaced by a great liking for the use of Africans as domestic servants, adornment and as playthings in European households from the sixteenth to the eighteenth century, particularly among aristocratic families. Apparently the use of Africans as household servants became so widespread that some people have described it as having become a fashion or fad. No-one who considered himself or herself somebody at that time would have done without such servants because they had become a symbol of prestige (Debrunner, 1979: 97).

The widespread use of Africans as servants made many people aware of their presence throughout Europe. Many European artists had also already begun to paint portraits of these Africans present in Europe from about the beginning of the fifteenth century and continued doing so to the end of the nineteenth century. Most of the representations which these artists made portrayed Africans either as exotic playthings or as comical objects. In other words, Africans in post-medieval European art were made to appear as their masters and the artists wanted them to appear, that is, as stereotypes. A classic example of this type of representation is the painting by the Swedish court painter named D.K. Ehrenstrahl which was painted in 1670 showing an African servant standing in a balcony wearing an oversize dress and surrounded by two monkeys and parrots (Debrunner, 1979: 59-61 and 92-96). Only a few portraits attempted to show Africans realistically. Examples are Albrecht Durer's painting of an African servant girl of 1521 and Gerard Dou's picture of an "African Princess" of between 1613 and 1675, depicting her loneliness and homesickness (Debrunner, 1979: 60-61).

What painters and sculptors did was also done in literature by novelists, poets and playwrights during the same period perhaps even more dramatically. Among the Europeans who revealed their attitudes towards Africans using the literary medium were sixteenth- and seventeenth-century Englishmen. During the Middle Ages, they had no direct contact with Africans yet, but they had probably heard a lot about them from crusaders and merchants returning from the Middle East and Southern Europe where people were already acquainted with them. By the fifteenth and sixteenth centuries their poetry, drama and common speech was already displaying all kinds of negative attitudes towards Africans. Such attitudes appear to have developed before the English people saw any Africans in person. What seems to have made them feel uneasy about Africans even before they set their eyes on them was their dark skin colour. To begin with, medieval Englishmen, as G.K. Hunter has argued, had developed a religious view of the world which in turn led to the emergence of a specific "framework of assumptions" concerning foreigners in general. This means that as Christians who took their religion seriously, medieval Englishmen acquired a "Bible-centred model of the world" with Jerusalem as its centre or focal point (Hunter, 1964: 38). This image of the world was clearly portrayed in the medieval map of the world popularly known as *mappa mundi*. On this map, Jerusalem is shown as the centre of the Christian world because it represents "the natural hub of Christian experience,

which spreads out from this centre to the fringe of circumam-
bient waters...where Pagans live, close to Leviathan... together with Negroes, apes, semi-hominess and others whose
distance from full humanity could be measured by their geographical distance from that area where humanity had been
most fully realized in the life of Christ" (Hunter, 1964:38).
Thus, according to the image conveyed by this map, Africans
and other non-Christian peoples formed part of the strange
world on the fringes of the Christian scheme of things. In
fact, it is interesting to note that Africa was not only shown
as a continent of strange peoples and creatures and many
wonders, but also as the land in the middle of which Hell was
supposed to be located (Hunter, 1964: 39 and 246).

With this image of the world as a Christian entity centring
on Jerusalem, medieval Englishmen seem to have conceived
foreigners in religious terms, that is, as non-Christians and
non-Europeans. This was the case because when Europeans
shared a common Christian experience before the break-up of
Christianity during the Reformation in the sixteenth century,
the idea of foreignness among them was apparently not explicit. After the Reformation, however, national cleavages are
said to have emerged which claimed to represent what were
considered to be better religious and national traditions and
interests against those of the old church of Rome. It is mainly
during the post-Reformation period that foreignness within
Europe appears to have become noticeable. As far as Englishmen were concerned, for example, their Scottish, Welsh
and Irish neighbours were simply regarded as "absurd devia-
tions of the English norm". So were the other better known
Europeans such as the Dutch and the French with whom they
shared the same social status. It would appear, therefore, that
even after emerging linguistically, culturally and politically as
distinct entities, the European nations were not yet distinct
enough from each other in their world outlook to consider
one another as foreigners. They might have regarded each
other as strangers but not as foreign to one another.

For a full-fledged contrast, according to Hunter, the Elizabethan author had to seek his characters outside Christianity
and Europe altogether and "draw on oppositions that were
older than ethnographic differences, on the conflict between
God and the devil, between Christian and anti-Christian"
(Hunter, 1964:48). The first strangers or outsiders whom the

Elizabethan creative writers found useful in this regard were the Jews, whose non-Christianity, like that of pagans, infidels, Moors and Turks, gave depth of meaning to foreignness. Thus the old religious framework of assumptions was used effectively in literature to create myths and stereotypes about the Jews which the European public internalized over time.

It is obvious also that the same framework of theological assumptions was used for the treatment of Africans or "Moors" in Elizabethan literature. In fact, it appears that very little distinction was made between the Jews and Moors in some cases as the pamphlet written by S. Wing in 1648, entitled *The Blessed Jew of Morocco, or a Blackmoor Turned White*, clearly indicates. It seems that the failure to distinguish the various groups of foreigners from one another was partly due to lack of personal contact between them and the English people, and partly due to religious bias and lack of concern. Africans, for example, were often confused with Arabs and other non-European peoples in the literature of the day and terms such as "Blacks" and "Moors" were often used interchangeably. "To most Elizabethans", as Charles H. Lyons has rightly pointed out, "a black person meant just about any non-white individual. Hence, they did not feel discomfort when sixteenth-century poets...described all kinds of people as "blacks" or "Moors" or "Negroes"" (Lyons, 1975: 3, Hunter, 1964: 51). Other terms used by Englishmen and by other Europeans for describing dark-skinned peoples in Africa and elsewhere since the Middle Ages were "Blackmoors", "Aethiopians" and "tawny Moors". Shakespeare's *Othello*, for example, was referred to as a "Moor" even though he was not an Arab. He was a "coal-black Negro" just as Eleazer in *Lust's Dominion*, Aaron in *Titus Andronicus* and Muly Hamet in *The Battle of Alcazar* were (Hunter, 1964: 51). This is abundantly clear in the context in which the term is used.

There were other cases, of course, in which the word Moors meant Arabs, half-Arabs, Berbers or other peoples altogether as has already been mentioned. This means that the word "Moor" was very vague ethnographically and seems to have generally meant little more than a dark-skinned outsider. But as Hunter has stressed, "it was not vague in the antithetical relationship to the European norm of the civilized white Christian" because Moors, whatever their actual identity was, were all "in that outer circuit of non-Christian lands where, in the *mappae mundi*, they appear with the other aberrations" or undesirables such as savage men, apes, skiapods, cannibals and "men whose heads/Do grow beneath their shoulders" (Hunter, 1964: 51). This close association with strange creatures and animals throughout the Elizabethan period makes Hunter wonder whether indeed the 'Moor' was a human being or a monster. But I think that this problem of lumping together all creatures which were considered by Christian Europeans to be despicable or undesirable, be they human or animal, was partly due to religious ethnocentrism as Hunter himself has correctly suggested elsewhere in his article, and partly due to lack of precise knowledge about the peoples and animals concerned.

From the imprecise knowledge of Africa and Africans which medieval and renaissance Englishmen obtained from poetry, drama and religious bias, they came to associate them with evil and the devil presumably because to them black colour or blackness stood for evil. If a "prominent nose" or a large "bottle nose" was often used for portraying a Jew in English plays and portraits, it was the black colour of the Moor's skin which was regarded by renaissance Englishmen and other Europeans as "an emblem of Hell, of damnation, as the natural livery of the devil". Even "the devil himself", as Hunter has emphasized, "appeared to many in the body of a black Moor" (Hunter, 1964: 52). Many references in this regard are numerous in the literature of the Renaissance and later periods. Examples are Thomas Heywood, who said in one of his writings that 'a Moor/of all that bears man's shape, likest a divell'; Reginald Scott, who said in his *Discovery of Witchcraft* in 1584 that 'A damned soule may and dooth take the shape of a blacke Moore'; and Samuel Butler, who wrote that 'Some with the devil himself in league grow/By's representative, a Negro" (Hunter, 1964: 52). Thus the hypothetical African or black man was identified, in medieval and renaissance European minds, with evil personified in the form of the devil.

It was not until the second half of the sixteenth century that Englishmen and other northern Europeans began to travel overseas and establish direct contact with Africans and other non-European peoples in Africa, Asia, the Pacific and the Americas through commerce and explorations. In so doing, they began to differentiate these non-European peoples and to refer to the inhabitants of sub-Saharan Africa as 'Negroes', a name whose origin Martin Bernal has now undertaken to trace in an article at the beginning of the present volume. However, these contacts and the information which became available as a result of them, do not seem to have led to a better understanding of these peoples or to the production of objective knowledge about them in later centuries. In the case of Africa, for instance, the published accounts of voyages and land travels, which started appearing towards the end of the sixteenth century, did not change very much the fabulous ideas and fancies which people in England and other parts of Europe had before they became available. On the contrary, they seem to have confirmed most of the old notions and fancies because very often they were written in such a way as to reinforce old images and stereotypes of individual Africans and their communities or to create new ones.

This problem arose because instead of confining themselves to reporting, as accurately as possible, what they saw, experienced or heard about in the regions which they visited, the European travellers, traders and sailors often included in their reports the legendary stories of monsters and strange beings which they extracted from classical and medieval sources. The earliest publication of this kind and the most fanciful of them all was John Mandeville's *Voyages and Travels* which appeared in the fifteenth century. It was the book which introduced Englishmen to the legend of Prester John as the Christian emperor of the fabulously rich oriental empire which included Ethiopia, describing its splendours, wonders, and numerous other phenomena on Africa (Letts, 1953). Other accounts, less fanciful, but nevertheless providing a similar blend of fact and fiction were those describing Thomas Windham's visit to the Guinea coast and the kingdom of Benin in 1553 and John Lok's visit to the same region in 1554-55 (Hakluyt, 1962: 38-57).

It is obvious enough that, given the way it was presented, the new information on Africans made available by European travellers, merchants and sailors in the fifteenth, sixteenth and seventeenth centuries could have done anything other than to reinforce the classical-medieval European image of them. I tend to agree with Hunter that the establishment of contacts between peoples and the availability of information about them alone cannot change old attitudes and existing knowledge in a given society as long as the "framework of assumptions" remains unchanged (Hunter, 1964: 37). In the case of Europe during the Renaissance, the framework of assumptions concerning non-European peoples remained basically the same as it had been in the Middle Ages. Africans and other non-European peoples were still seen as being religiously, ethnographically and culturally different from Christian Europeans and therefore foreign and strange.

Eighteenth-Century European Racism and Africans

In view of the kind of attitudes and distortions which Europeans received about Africa and Africans from their clasical-medieval based literary and travel accounts of the fifteenth, sixteenth and seventeenth centuries, it is perhaps understandable why their image of them became uglier in the eighteenth and nineteenth centuries than before. This is evident in the views expressed by members of what became known in artistic and literary circles in the eighteenth century as the Romantic Movement and in the treatises of contemporary racist pseudo-scientists and philosophers of the Enlightenment. It has been suggested, for instance, that as the Romantic Movement gathered momentum and became preoccupied with the so-called savage peoples of the world and promoted some of them to some kind of "nobility", it was the native American who became the ideal type "noble savage" (Curtin, 1964: 49-51, Cohen, 1977: 70-73). Africans failed to qualify for inclusion in this category apparently for two reasons. First, it was because they were still being used as slaves in the Americas, the Indian Ocean region and in the Muslim states of the Mediterranean region and the Persian Gulf area at a time when members of other racial groups had already been relieved of the burden of slavery; and second, it was due to their black skin colour, which by then was regarded in the European dominated world as a mark of inferiority (Lyons, 1975: 8). For human groups whose complexion was relatively closer to that of the Europeans such as the native Americans and the peoples of Southeast Asia, it was only their "savagery" and their being non-Christian which marked them low in the human social scale as envisaged by Europeans, while for the Africans there was the additional factor of black skin colour.

The colour question was not only used for placing Africans at the bottom of the human social scale but also for justifying their use as slaves in the Americas. Apparently in order to justify the use of African slave labour in the Americas in the Renaissance, slave owners and their intellectual supporters started claiming that the Africans were black and inferior because they were the descendants of the cursed Ham as the *Genesis* part of the *Bible* says, while Europeans were white and superior because they were the descendants of one of the blessed sons of Noah called Japhet (*Genesis*, 9: 22-23). For this reason, the Europeans felt that they were not violating any law against humanity by enslaving Africans.

However, neither *Genesis* nor any other part of the *Bible* suggests in any way that the so-called descendants of Ham are black and that those of Shem and Japhet are white. It seems that the *Genesis* story was picked up and popularized because it appeared to be a reasonable explanation for the peopling of the world by different human races. In order to give more credibility to their interpretation, the European supporters of the enslavement of Africans borrowed variants of the story of Ham from a collection of Jewish legends known as the *Babylonian Talmud*. One of these variants speaks of Ham having received the punishment of becoming black for copulating with a dog in the Ark. Another explains the curse in some detail, suggesting specifically that Ham's descendants were black and were preordained for slavery (Sanders, 1969: 522). Being more explicit than the *Genesis* story these *Talmud* variants of the story of Ham offered a more attractive explanation of the black complexion and degradation of the Africans for those Europeans who sought to legitimize their social and economic exploitation of them in the seventeenth and eighteenth centuries.

All these attempts to justify the superiority of Europeans over Africans indicate clearly that modern racism dates back to the Renaissance when Christian Europe started expanding overseas and exploiting non-European peoples in all sorts of ways. Nevertheless, before the eighteenth century, racist notions and theories did not go beyond Christian rationalization and justification of what was happening at that time by explaining why Africans and native Americans were inferior human beings who deserved the treatment which they were getting from the "civilized" Europeans.

As some of the leading scholars of the eighteenth century lost their faith in Christianity and started using scientific methods in the production of knowledge, they rejected the Biblical explanation that all human racial groups had a common origin in God's creation. This rejection of the religious explanation of the origin of human groups divided the leading scholars of the period into two main groups. One group consisted of those who continued to uphold the common origin of all human racial groups in God's creation or monogenism, while the other was made up of all those who rejected the common origin theory and instead advocated a multi-origin theory or polygenism.

Among the prominent supporters of monogenism were John Locke, Baron Charles de Secondat Montesque, Count Georges de Buffon, J. Friedrich Blumenbach, Oliver Goldsmith and James Prichard. They maintained that all human beings were created equal and endowed with the natural rights of life, liberty and property and that Africans and some other non-European peoples had lost their equality with Europeans due to adverse climatic and environmental factors and degeneration (Laslett, 1966: 302, Buffon, 1785: 207, Jordan, 1968: 222-23). Moreover, they suggested that Africans were the most degenerate human group because they had lost not only their "orginal" white colour but also beauty, intelligence and civilization. For them, Europeans were not only superior over non-whites in terms of material culture and religion but even in terms of physical features.

Although they accepted the hierarchical arrangement of human racial groups of the monogenists, which placed Europeans at the top of the hierarchy and Africans at the bottom of it, the polygenists such as Voltaire, David Hume, Edward Long and Charles White rejected the single origin for humankind idea and offered their own different explanations. Voltaire, for example, is reported to have said that "the negro race is a species of men as different from us as the breed of spaniels is from greyhounds" (Lyons, 1975: 39). Similarly, David Hume maintained that there was no single linear development of humankind but a multiple series of development involving transformation from a lower or barbarous stage to a higher or civilized stage. It was particularly in his essay on human differences that he revealed his preference for polygenism and his contempt for Africans and other non-whites

(Popkin, 1980: 93). Because of his reputation and standing as an empirical social scientist, his historical writings had a tremendous influence on other racist scholars such as Edward Long and Charles White. Long, for instance, explained the emergence of human beings in evolutionary terms as Hume had done. That is, he explained the evolution of humankind from simple organisms to perfect human beings in their different racial groups. By perfect human beings he meant, of course, the Europeans whom he placed at the top of the hierarchy, while he placed Africans at the bottom of it and suggested that they belonged to a subhuman species which was closer to the ape than any other human group (Jordan, 1968: 491-93).

Surprisingly enough, Long's attempt to dehumanize Africans by associating them with apes received strong support from contemporary studies in human anatomy and physiology in Europe and the United States of America. These anatomical investigations included the work of comparing human and animal skeletons and skulls by Pieter Camper in Holland, S.T. von Sommering in Germany, and Dr. John Augustine in the United States. Among these anatomy investigators, it was Charles White who came out with the most racist conclusions and pronouncements on the subject made in the name of science. Like Long, White established a hierarchy of humankind in which Europeans were at the top, followed by Asians and native Americans in a descending order, and Africans at the bottom next to the apes. He asserted also that African mental ability was inferior to that of the European because the size of his brain was smaller than that of the European (White, 1799: 42-59 and 94-95). He supported these contentions partly with his own findings and partly with evidence from studies of fellow natural scientists and social scientists such as Thomas Jefferson and Edward Long (Curtin, 1964: 46, Jordan, 1968: 499-502, Lyons, 1975: 340).

In conclusion, White declared flatly that humankind belonged to several species which had sprang up differently. According to him, Africans and Europeans, for instance, were not members of the same human species and could not have emerged from a common origin given their physical, mental and cultural differences, and the resemblance of the former to apes. Thus in the name of science, Africans were dehumaniz and made permanently inferior to all other human beings by the racist theories of the eighteenth century.

Conclusion

From what has been discussed in the different sections of this paper, it is evident that the nineteenth-century European image of Africa was mainly based on earlier European attitudes and prejudices which are traceable from antiquity to the eighteenth century. By the nineteenth century Africa was regarded by Europeans and North Americans as "the dark continent" and Africans as "fallen men" who were incapable of development on their own and were inferior to white people in every respect. That is probably why Europeans in the late nineteenth century gave themselves the self-appointed duty or burden of helping their unfortunate African brethren by colonizing them in order to put them back on the road to "progress" and "civilization".

Notes

[1] Henry Morton Stanley was the first nineteenth-century traveller to popularize this image of Africa as "the dark continent" in his writings. He did so especially in two of his books: *Through the Dark Continent*, London: Sampson Low, Marston, Searle and Revington, 1878, and *In Darkest Africa*, London: Sampson Low, 1890.

[2] Sudan is the short form of the Arabic term 'bilad al-Sudan', meaning 'the land of the blacks'. It is sometimes referred to as the 'Sudanic Zone'. In its wider sense, it is the grassland region lying between the edge of the Sahara desert and the forest zone and stretching from the Nille Valley in the east to the Atlantic coast in the West. See its description by H.J. Fisher, "The Eastern Maghrib and the Central Sudan", in R. Oliver (ed.), *The Cambridge History of Africa*, Cambridge: Cambridge University Press, 1977, vol. 3, pp. 238-39.

[3] The Arabs call North Africa west of Egypt 'al-Maghrib', meaning the western part of the Arab World. This region is then sub-divided into the so-
ern and western Maghrib. See, for example, Fisher, "The Eastern
the Central Sudan", in Oliver, *Cambiridge History of Africa*,
5-36; and A. Laroui (trans. by R. Manheim), *History of the*
nceton: Princeton University Press, 1977.

Works Cited

Buffon, Comte de(translated by W. Smellie) *Natural History, General and Particular*, London, 1785, Vol. 3, Section 9.

Cohen, W.B., *The French Encounter with Africans*, Bloomington: Indiana University Press, 1979.

Cooley, W.D., *Claudius Ptolemy and the Nile*, London: J.W. Parker and Son, 1954.

Curtin, P.D., *The Image of Africa: British Thought and Action, 1780-1850*, Madison: University of Wisconsin Press, 1964.

Debrunner, H.W., *Presence and Prestige: Africans in Europe*, Basel: Basler Afrika Bibliographien, 1979.

Devisse, J., "Africa in International Relations", in D.T. Niane (ed.) *General History of Africa*, London: Unesco-Heinemann, 1984, Vol. IV.

Fisher, H.J., "The Eastern Maghrib and the Central Sudan", in R. Oliver (ed.) *The Cambridge History of Africa*, Cambridge University Press, 1987, Vol. 3.

Freeman-Grenville, G.S.P., *The East African Coast: Select Documents*, Oxford: The Clarendon Press, 1962.

George, K., "The Civilized West Looks at Primitive Africa: 1400-1800", *Isis*, Vol. 49.

Ghent, H.C. (translator) *The History of Diodorus Siculus*, London: Giles Culvert, 1653, Book IV, chap. 1.

Hakluyt, R., *Voyages* (Originally published as *Principal Navigations*) London: Everyman's Library, 1962, Vol. IV.

Hunter, G.K., "The Elizabethans and Foreigners", in A. Nicoll (ed.) *Shakespeare in His Own Age: Shakespeare Survey*, volume 17, Cambridge University Press, 1964.

Hrbek, I., "Africa in the context of World History", in M. El Fasii (ed.) *General Historical of Africa*, London: Unesco-Hernemann, 1988, vol. III.

Laroui, A (translated by R. Manheim) *History of the Maghrib*, Princeton University Press, 1977.

Laslett, P. (ed.) *Locke's Two Treatises of Government*, Cambridge University Press, 1966, Second Treatise, Section 23.

Law, R.C.C., "North Africa in the Period of Phoenician and Greek Colonization, c.800 to 325 B.C.", in J.D. Fage (ed.)

The Cambiridge History of Africa, Cambridge University Press, 1978, vol. 2.

Letts, M. (ed.) *Mandeville's Travels*, London: The Hakluyt Society, 1953, vol. 1.

Levtzion, N., "The Western Maghrib and the Sudan", in R. Oliver (ed.) *The Cambridge History of Africa*, vol. 3.

Lyons, C.H., *To Wash an Aethiop White*, New York: Teachers College Press, Columbia Universty, 1975.

McCrindle, J.W., *The Commercial Navigation of the Erythraean Sea*, London: Trubner and Co., 1879.

_____, *The Christian Topography of Cosmas, an Egyptian Monk*, London: Hakulyt Society, 1897.

Pliny (translated by H. Rackham) *Natural History*, London: W. Heinemann Ltd., 1947, vol. II, Book V.

Popkin, R.H., "The Philosophical Bases of Modern Racism", in R.A. Watson and J.E. Force (eds.) *The High Road to Pyrrhonism*, San Diego, California: Austin Hill Press, Inc., 1980.

Preiswerk, R. and D. Perrot, *Ethnocentrism and History: Africa, Asia and Indian America in Western Textsbooks*, New York: Nok Publishers International, 1978.

Rawlinson, G. (ed.) *History of Herodotus*, London: John Murray, 1862, vol. III, Book IV, chap. 191.

Rennel, J., The Geographical System of Herodotus, Examined and Explained, London: Bulmer and Co., 1800.

Riad, H., "Egypt in the Hellenistic Era", in G. Mokhtar (ed.) *General History of Africa*, London: Unesco-Heinemann, 1981, vol. II.

Salama, P., "The Sahara in Classical Antiquity", in G. Mokthar (ed.) *General History of Africa*, vol. II.

Sanders, E.R. "The Hamitic Myth: its Origin and Functions in Time Perspective", *Journal of African History*, X, 4 (1969).

Snowden Jr., F.M., *Blacks in Antiquity*, Cambridge, Mass: Harvard University Press, 1970.

Stanley, H.M., *Through the Dark Continent*, London: Sampson Low, Marston, Searle and Revington, 1878.

_____, *In Darkest Africa*, London: Sampson Low, 1890, 2 volumes.

Stevens, E.L. (ed.) *Geography of Claudius Ptolemy*, New York: The Public Library, 1933.

Tamrat, T., "Ethiopia, the Red Sea and the Horn of Africa", in R. Oliver (ed.) *The Cambridge History of Africa*, vol. 3.

White, C.W., *An Account of the Regular Gradations of Man*, London: C. Dilly, 1799.

PART II
Western Imperial Ideology in Theory and Practice

Strategic Amnesia: Versions of Vasco da Gama on The Kenyan Coast[1]

Janet S. McIntosh
University of Michigan

On the edge of the Indian Ocean in Malindi, Kenya, a tall plaster model of a sailboat faces seaward, its stunning white sails emblazoned with a red cross. The monument was inaugurated by Portuguese sponsors in 1960 to honor Prince Henry the Navigator,[2] and its design evokes the vessels commanded by Vasco da Gama that arrived in East Africa in 1498 on their way to India. In April 1998 a committee planning a fete to mark the 500th anniversary of da Gama's arrival in Malindi decided to repaint the icon and add an informational plaque. But as the result of a printing error, the plaque announces not the "Vasco da Gama Commemoration" but the "Vasco da Gama Commemotion"--a remarkable neologism, for by the time the fete was over it had been by turns both commemoration and commotion. Those on the side of commemoration portrayed da Gama as a kind of latter-day tourist, folding the time line so that his arrival corresponded symbolically with that of today's travelers seeking benign cultural contact. Those on the side of commotion--or, to do justice to their intentions, political protest--folded their version of history as well, aligning da Gama's mercenary zeal and Christian orientation with contemporary threats to Islam and a self-determined Africa. In the confrontation, the narration of Africa's past was caught between two forces: the exigencies of an economy increasingly dependent on the pleasure-seeking international traveler; and the self-definition of a complex ethnic group, the Arab-African Swahili, whose shifting ethnic orientation will critically shape its socioeconomic future.

The Vasco da Gama controversy in Malindi illuminates some of the crosscutting forces that influence representations of Africa today. In the pre-colonial and colonial eras, Western discourse widely degraded and dehumanized Africans while obliterating Africa's claim to a history of its own. But in the post-colonial era, of course, political imperialism is no longer the central Western orientation towards Africa; instead, Westerners tend to regard Africa as a victim of political mishandling and "ethnic strife," and as a potential resource for new forms of economic exploitation. And, most crucially for this paper, the stance of the Western explorer to Africa has undergone a radical shift. Just as in orientalist literature the transition from travelogues to tourist guides marked what Bedhad terms "a passage in orientalist vision from perceiving the Orient as the object of cultural domination to seeing it as an object of desire" (Bedhad 1996: 48), so too has the Western view of Africa shifted to focus on the exotic pleasures the continent can provide the tourist. As will be seen, the representational peculiarities of the tourism industry make my discussion more delicate, for the industry's distortions do not emerge from malicious intent, and in fact boost the tourism sector on which many African economies (one third of Kenya's, for example) depend. In so doing, they provide many Africans with a powerful incentive to collude in the new Western images of their own continent.

Yet even as Western fantasy tells one tale of Africa, more and more Africans are engaged in the construction and dissemination of different narratives about themselves and their histories. Although constrained by economic, political, and infrastructural limitations, formally educated Africans since independence have enjoyed greater control over informational media, and have cultivated a heightened sense of how the rest of the world both represents and ignores them. Higher literacy rates and involvement in academia and journalism also place a growing minority of citizens in a position to tell stories about themselves that counter those generated by the West. But to assume that any historically oppressed people, given "voice," will sing only clear and true is to overlook the sociopolitical dynamics that give self-representation (by anyone) strategic overtones.[3] In Malindi, as will be seen, the protests to the da Gama fete were orchestrated by a group of Swahili Muslims with a complicated dual agenda that involved aligning themselves against Christians and with the Arab world, while simultaneously establishing their right "as Africans" to be the mouthpiece of the town.

In the da Gama controversy of 1997, then, malevolence was not the origin of Western distortions of African history, nor was the Western myth the only one generated. In this paper I examine the motivations of both Western and African players in the dispute, and suggest that the event cannot be reduced to a simple case of "oppressive" versus "resistant" images of Africa. Nor does the concept of the Other aptly characterize any of the distortions involved, for both Westerners and Africans were just as concerned with imagining the Self, through the reconstruction of their own historical actions and, it follows, their current relations to others. To understand these dynamics I have found it useful to draw on David Cohen's exhortation that, in approaching the production of history, we explore the appropriating and organizing involved in "remembering," and the "remembering [found] in... 'forgetting'" (Cohen 1994: 22). Hence, I examine here not only the historical claims made but also the historical silences and omissions by both parties; the strategic acts of forgetting that provide eloquent signposts to the priorities of those telling the story.

A brief history of the Portuguese encounter with Malindi, and Malindi's subsequent history, sets the stage for my discussion. Vasco da Gama's arrival in East Africa was not a neutral, exploratory maneuver; rather, it emerged from Portugal's realization in the fifteenth century that supplies of its key trading commodity, gold, were growing scarce. The Portuguese crown set its sights on the lucrative Indian Ocean trading routes and commissioned da Gama, a nobleman with extensive experience as a navigator and captain, to explore the possibility that Portuguese ships might one day monopolize commerce in the area. After rounding the Cape of Good Hope in November 1497, da Gama's fleet touched down at Mossel Bay and Mozambique, arriving in Mombasa (in what is now Kenya) with high hopes but moving swiftly northwards after relations soured and several rounds of fire were exchanged. Arriving in Malindi in April 1498, the Portuguese found that a preexisting feud between the rulers of Mombasa and Malindi worked in their favor. The King of Malindi welcomed them in grand style with several days of splendid festivities, and loaded their ships with spices, succulent foods, and one Arab pilot, Ahmad ibn Majid, who steered the fleet expertly to Goa. The fleet returned to Lisbon to find that their spices were worth 60 times what it had cost to equip the voyage (Strandes 1961), a triumph that ensured there would be more voyages to come.

On their arrival in East Africa, da Gama and the Portuguese who followed him were surprised by the relative wealth and cultural sophistication of coastal culture. The elegantly built towns on the shoreline were dominated by Arab traders and settlers claiming Persian ancestry, and a unique Muslim Arab-African culture, "Swahili", that emerged from centuries of settlement and intermarriage. The economy thrived on the agricultural labor of African slaves, and through a lively trade in gold, ivory, tortoiseshell, and other goods that circulated through the African coast, Arabia, and India (Strandes 1961: 92). The hospitality of the Malindi rulers toward the Portuguese endured for a time, and a modicum of cultural exchange took place there and at other coastal locations. In 1998, fete organizers would take advantage of this dynamic, playing up the Portuguese expressions of admiration and popularizing anecdotes about cultural exchange—the Swahili, for example, were said to have taught Portuguese to use rectangular wooden water containers at sea, rather than the round pottery jars that broke so easily, while the Portuguese in turn introduced maize, cassava, and new agricultural and maritime techniques.

Fete organizers did not, however, draw attention to the general consensus among historians that the new era of international relations begun by da Gama's fleet was heavily tilted in Portugal's favor. Eventually, the Portuguese were able to monopolize most Indian Ocean trade, mining the riches of the East without losing profits to Arab middlemen. They exacted tribute from Kings in the African coastal towns of Kilwa, Mombasa, Dondo, Siyu, and Pate; deposed and replaced other rulers; imposed numerous customs stations; and razed Mombasa twice (in 1505 and 1528) with great loss of life for the inhabitants. Encouraged by two fifteenth century Papal bulls that mandated "the redemption of ignorant peoples from the curses of Islam and paganism" (Strandes 1961: 10), Portuguese mercenaries obstructed pilgrimages to Mecca and interfered with Muslim legal arrangements (Pouwels 1987: 39). In Malindi itself, Portuguese behavior was less than noble from the start; a dispatch from the Viceroy Francesco de Almeida to the King of Portugal in 1508 reads:

> Your Majesty, as you know, owes much to the King of Malindi...His reward, however, is that the captains of your Majesty's ships requite his good deeds by disrupting the peace of the country and behaving so badly that the King would already have left the country had I not managed to keep him there by writing him letters full of empty promises which are never fulfilled..." (Strandes 1961: 98).

The town withered under Portuguese influence, its Arab population living in poverty by 1606 (Martin 1973: 41; Salim 1973).

After the Portuguese chapter came to a close in the late eighteenth century, Malindi's fortunes lay dormant until its late nineteenth century rebirth as an agrarian center. Numerous Arab and Swahili families migrated to the town from Arabia and other areas of the coast, rebuilding and vastly extending the agricultural industry dependent on African slave labor. Town culture once again centered on a thriving Swahili way of life, fed by multiple influences including Hadrami, Omani, and Bantu. Coexisting with the Swahili and Arabs, but living slightly inland or on the periphery of town, were members of nine closely related coastal groups known today as the Mijikenda. Mijikenda were for centuries mutually dependent on the Swahili through patron-client and trade relationships, and while a small number were among the Africans enslaved by Swahilis and Arabs, they usually entered slavery not by violence but through arrangements such as the exchange of a family member for food in times of famine (Willis 1993). Slavery was eventually abolished by colonial law, but the basic hierarchies of the pre-colonial and colonial era remain today: most land is Arab, Swahili, or European owned, while thousands of Mijikenda take odd jobs for wages and squat in improvised villages on the periphery of town.

After slavery ended Malindi's profits as a granary dwindled, but the economy picked up again in the late twentieth century as the town became a popular colonial resort and tourist destination. Malindi's current reputation as a "sex safari" hot spot has brought prostitution and drug use to the town while attracting managerial staff for its hotels from upcountry tribes, whose economic privileges are resented by locals. Many Arabs and Swahili have managed to attain a degree of autonomy from the tourism industry, by owning businesses while receiving capital from friends and relatives in the Arab world. But most Malindi residents are directly or indirectly dependent on foreign visitors—these include European hotel owners; Mijikenda, and upcountry hotel workers and tour guides; and a prominent handful of Maasai transplanted from the Amboseli area to cash in on their exotic looks as the tourists snap their pictures and pay for their beers.

With so much of its land and labor dedicated to tourism, Malindi's fortunes rise and fall on the whim of the international traveler. But in late 1997 and early 1998, the Kenya coast was rocked by the traumatic effects of the El Niño weather phenomenon, epidemics of malaria and cholera, and politically orchestrated "ethnic" violence that pitted coastal interest groups against each other. Not surprisingly, the tourists fled and the town sank into a miasma of economic depression. The Vasco da Gama organizing committee was born, then, in hopes that a boost of publicity might attract visitors, refresh the town's sense of unity, and "put Malindi back on the map" (Robertson 1998a)—the "map" being that carried by the Western history buff and traveler. Although a handful of Indian and African business owners joined the committee, the most influential planners, and those targeted by protesters, were British expatriates with prominent civic roles in the administration of the Malindi Museum Society, Green Society, and Tourism Board. These organizers took pride in their efficiency and vision, and adopted a proprietary attitude towards Malindi's fate as they planned the great tourist attraction.

There are, of course, imperialist overtones in the act of tourism itself, given that at the tourist's destination "others must serve while the tourist plays, rests, cures, or mentally enriches himself" (Nash 1989: 45). And because the tourist has arrived precisely to escape worry and guilt, and to fantasize about a more exotic lifestyle while maintaining enough comforts of home to avoid feeling disoriented, a tourist destination must accommodate these demands as it represents itself. Accordingly, the Kenyan tourism industry never digs into the fraught history of colonial conflict, invoking instead glamorized colonial figures such as Baroness Blixen and Lord Delamere. The postcards, curios, and clothing sold in hotel gift shops urge the tourist to identify with colonials rather than critique them, cultivating an aura of nostalgia for the colonial's supposed blithe mastery of power and danger. The asymmetries cloaked by this nostalgia become still more insidious in the visitor's interaction with "the natives," for the colonial image of Africa as a dark continent of degenerate savagery has become the undercurrent of exoticism that flavors the tourist's fantasies of leisure and discovery. In Malindi, the frisson of cross-cultural contact is heightened by the titillating "native dances" around the hotel swimming pools, and by the male and female prostitutes who solicit tourists, sometimes (by their own admission) using their "traditional dress" as a kind of lure.

For the da Gama committee, the concern for the tourist's comfort remained, but there was a crucial difference that would set the fete apart from Malindi's typical promotional efforts. The hope, said committee members, was to make the festival an educational experience that would edify locals and visitors alike about the centuries of contact between Europe and Africa, and that would promote Malindi as a "quality tourist destination" capable of attracting visitors more interested in history than in hedonism. This didactic strain was evident during the fete week in the lectures at a local museum, in the instructive brochures distributed by the organizing committee (cf. Robertson 1998b), and in the essay competitions that challenged local schoolchildren to write about their history. This mental workout was to be supplemented during the fete week by vigorous athletic competition—boat races, bicycle races, and the like—all in the mode of the British preparatory school. Indeed, the fete seemed calculated to reshape the dissolute tourist, who typically arrives in Malindi planning to melt his brain and abuse his body. But the message was equally aimed at locals, who, some organizers felt, are not responsible proprietors of their own culture or history.

As they nurtured both foreign and local intellects, fete organizers also hoped to spread a sense of peace and unity through the town. Some expatriates in Malindi regarded the violent political-ethnic clashes of 1997 as embarrassing, unnecessary, and naive, preferring that locals adhere to less destructive, more decorous forms of political confrontation. The hope, then, was that the fete would foster some kind of "multicultural cheer", and that the fete's unruffled surface could function as a performative that might enact and hence effect an enduring harmony. Accordingly, Swahili and Portuguese dignitaries dined together at a cheerful public party, and at the parade depicting Malindi's cultural diversity, "da Gama" himself appeared in costume, waving benignly at the crowd. The festival brochure took pains to emphasize "friendly relations" between Portuguese and Swahili, while enumerating the unique forms of knowledge--of agriculture, of navigation, of water containers--that each side had to offer the other (Robertson 1998b). The essay and art competitions, meanwhile, encouraged local children to portray both Portuguese and indigenous cultures, but explicitly discouraged them from focusing on the arrival of Christians in a Muslim town. The total portrait of da Gama and his contemporaries, as portrayed in public lectures, brochures, and even the Vasco da Gama commemorative stamps, froze them in a moment of innocuous contact with a friendly port, obliterating the tensions and iniquities that marked African experiences of the encounter.[4]

There is little doubt in this observer's mind that the organizers wanted the town as a whole to profit from the fete week, but at the same time, their tactics contained a subtext about their own role in Malindi town. By constructing a festival that transcended both the sybaritic tendencies of the tourist and the perceived agitation of the locals, fete organizers positioned themselves as a wholesome force for the good, or latter-day champions of the "civilizing mission." It is as if the post-colonial context has provoked a need on the part of Europeans to justify their presence in Africa in new terms, and the fete provided a unique opportunity for Europeans to assert their entitlement. The displays of efficiency, conflict mediation, and intellectual self-improvement by fete organizers all constructed a message (aimed, perhaps, at themselves as much as at Africans) that the European presence and power in Malindi are mandated, if not necessary, for the well being of the town.

Meanwhile, how did Malindi's African residents respond to the sanguine historical vision purveyed by the fete organizers? For many, including some Muslims, the notion of exposing the moral messiness of coastal history seemed an idealistic fancy compared to their urgent material needs. "We were really crying," said one Mijikenda townsman of the Kenya coast's recent disasters. "Maybe the Portuguese did some bad things, but we really needed the tourists." But other Africans took a trenchant interest in the history of Portuguese-African interaction, generating a struggle over historical narrative that explicitly pit Muslims against Westerners but more subtly reflected internal African dynamics. Under the banner of SUPKEM (Supreme Council of Kenya Muslims) and local organizations, Swahili and Arab Muslims in Malindi decried da Gama's arrival, deeming it the first dark maneuver in the social, economic, and religious destruction of what had been a prosperous trading culture. Rather than celebrate da Gama, they argued, Malindi should commit to a day of mourning, and the Portuguese should offer compensation to the descendants of African victims for their oppressions, including slavery. Several letters appeared in the national newspapers invoking the spirit of Pan-Africanism, excoriating the fete arrangements as "neocolonialist" in tone and content, and rebuking the fete organizers for side-stepping the destructive elements of the Portuguese presence (Akumu 1998; Patel 1998).

Public letters and interviews indicate that most protesters saw the fete organizers as not only callous but conspiratorial. The rhetoric of protest foregrounded the British origins of some of the fete planners, speculating on a sinister alliance with the Portuguese government today, and assuming their political sympathy with all of the European mercenary, colonial, and missionary damage in the centuries that followed da Gama's arrival. In keeping with such suspicions, one circular argued that enhancing tourism could not be the central motive behind the fete, because Portuguese tourists are unheard of in Malindi. "The reason [for the festival] is to heighten tourism? God forbid! These are pretenses-- the truth of the matter has been hidden, and [the fete organizers] know how to cheat us" ("Kusheherekea" 1998). The intent of the fete, Muslims felt, was to glorify the advent of European domination, from the political to the religious domains. The attempt to involve Muslim school children in the fete competitions, for example, was considered evidence of an impulse to gloat while infusing the Muslim community with ideological messages of Christian victory. And while fete organizers regarded Malindi's ancient Portuguese stone pillar as a benign logo for the fete, Muslims read the stone cross atop it as a symbol that continues to speak of Christian aspiration for religious dominance. Meanwhile, a rumor claimed that the Portuguese government was pumping millions of shillings into the fete (Robertson 1998b), money supposedly used to pay off Muslims who appeared to support the fete.[5]

Protesters knew their complaints would not successfully block the fete, but this did not deter them, for they perceived the *representation* of their point of view, now and in the future, as a kind of end in itself. They wanted their narrative to penetrate the town's festive mood, rectifying the fete's benign historical account while "[Putting] into history...that the locals, the indigenous [people], the Muslims of Malindi were against these celebrations and what happened 500 years ago" (Interview, "Wazee na vijana..." 1998). And they knew that rhetoric was critical to their efforts. While fete organizers had hoped to de-couple historical fact and value, rejecting, for example, the phrase "Vasco da Gama celebration" in favor of "Vasco da Gama commemoration," protesters repeatedly subverted the notion that this historical moment could be marked without judgement, describing the fete plans with the English word "celebration" and the Swahili terms *"kusheherekea"* (to display, rejoice, or celebrate) and "*uadhimisha*" (glorification). In their contest for historical validation, they placed the Portuguese-East African relationship on the same footing as other widely decried historical events: "Are the Jews ready to commemorate the 2nd World War and remember Adolf Hitler as a Hero?" ("R. E. Demonstration," 1998). They organized a protest march through town, culminating at the District Commissioner's office, and ensured that the press were there to report it. And they chose a mode of attack subversive in both content and form: graffiti. Anonymous, enduring, and disruptive, the graffiti monopolized public space and put an elbow in the eye of Malindi's blithe Western tourists, disturbing their breezy jaunts through town with epithets ("Vasco da Gama the Butcher"; "Vasco da Gama the Pirate"). Significantly, the graffiti was written in English--a self-conscious tactic to convey their message to the international media, and to reach European conference organizers, whom the protesters termed "ignorant" for their lack of fluency in Kiswahili.[6] All these strategies indexed the protesters' conviction that representations themselves, particularly representations that are printed, preserved, and fated to "go down in history," constitute a kind of redress.

But an exclusive focus on their drive for historical justice obscures a crucial undercurrent of the protesters' actions, for as they castigated the fete organizers, they were also engaged in a two-tiered announcement of their identity. Swahili have long been in complex and shifting orientation to their Muslim and Arab ties on the one hand and their African ties on the other, with one or the other element strategically foregrounded depending on the exigencies of the political moment (Eastman 1971; Salim 1973; Pouwels 1987). The da Gama controversy seemed to fall at a time of complex alignment, when both elements of Swahili identity could serve as useful political and economic tools.

On the one hand, close connections to the Muslim-Arab world are generations old and have served coastal Swahili well in recent years. A significant number of Swahili youth travel to Middle Eastern countries in search of employment and higher education, and many of these send capital and school fees back to their relatives in Kenya. Several Muslim NGOs, partially funded by Arab nations, support needy Kenyan

Muslims and help to pay for their Quranic school (*madarasa*) education, while other Arab agencies help finance the construction of mosques. Such assistance is undoubtedly contingent on Kenyan Muslims' ability to present themselves as a religious community with promise and a globally conscious, activist spirit. There are, furthermore, local reasons for coastal Arabs and Swahili to assert their unity and strength by rallying around a protest. Christianity has long been pitted against Islam in Kenya in a contest for converts and resources (O'Brien 1995). The former political hegemony of Muslims on the coast was quashed by colonial rule and the failure of a movement for coastal autonomy (*Mwambao*) at independence. Coastal Muslims feel persecuted by the Christian-dominated government, a sense heightened by the government's refusal to register the Islamic Party of Kenya in the early 1990s. The current speculation about a new federalism (*Majimbo*), then, has some Muslims hoping to restore a new era of Arab-Swahili glory. The da Gama protests thus took on special import as a means to assert the vigilance and self-determination of Muslim community (*umma*) at both global and local levels.

Despite their alliance with the global Muslim community, Swahili protesters explicitly stated that they objected to the fete in their capacity as both Muslims and "indigenous people", or "Africans". To establish the latter element of their identity, protesters not only framed the da Gama fete in "neocolonialist" terms; they also erased a critical element of their own history: slavery. Arab-Swahili enslavement of East Africans--both within Africa and for overseas sale--has origins at least a thousand years old (Beachey 1976: ix). In 1873, at a high mark of its plantation life, Cooper estimates there were about 4-5,000 slaves in Malindi, with imports "arriving at the rate of 600-1000 per year" (Cooper 1972: 5). Yet the descendants of these former slave owners now broadcast slavery as a major Portuguese offence against East Africans.

Coastal slavery was already contested in the months leading up to the da Gama controversy. Mijikenda memories of slavery, while often vague, are nonetheless easily tapped in conversation, and are acutely charged with resentment against Arabs and Swahili that is compounded by their current low status as squatters and petty wage-laborers. During the Kenyan election campaigns of 1997, President Moi and Mijikenda politicians both urged voters to reject certain Muslim parliamentary candidates with the argument that, from the Mijikenda point of view, "Their people enslaved ours." In response, some Muslims leapt to the defense of their ancestors. One Swahili man in Mombasa, descended from a former coastal governor, sent a letter to national newspapers during the run-up to the elections in which he contends that the number of slaves on the entire East African coast totaled only 2000 at the time of abolition, and that "the real importation and exportation of slaves in the East African Coast was greatly influenced by the Portuguese" (Mohamed 1997). Early coast dwellers, he went on, could not have enslaved Africans on a large scale because as good Muslims they surely followed the Quranic dictate that only prisoners of war can be enslaved, and that if any of the conditions on slavery set by Islamic law (*sheria*) are not fulfilled, the slave would be freed automatically. In conversation, he added that only a tiny handful of "greedy people" and "bad Muslims" were slaveowners--and those, out of self-defense in an insecure urban environment.[7]

Along similar lines, then, some da Gama protesters argued that Arab-Swahili slavery is a myth rather than an historical fact (Interview, "Wazee na vijana..." 1998); a fabrication promulgated first as anti-Muslim propaganda by European missionaries, and more recently by politicians hoping to marginalize Muslim candidates. "How could we have enslaved Africans?" asked one protester. "They are just like us!" One man assured me no Mijikenda would agree they or their parents had been enslaved by Muslims ("I'll give you two thousand shillings if you can find just one"). This tactical amnesia about Arab-Swahili slavery was accompanied by an overstatement of the Portuguese role in East African slaving.[8] When fete organizers--and the author of this paper--noted that few history books supported a portrait of the Portuguese as major players in the East African slave trade, and that Swahili and Arabs themselves had owned slaves, protesters pointed out that many such history books are authored by Europeans and, as such, subject to the distortions of wishful thinking.

This discourse about slavery is not merely about blame, reputation, and an election campaign, but about the question in the back of fete organizers' minds as well; namely, who "belongs" in Africa in the first place. Why did coastal Muslims use the da Gama fete as the moment to declare the coast "theirs" by contrasting themselves with colonial invaders and aligning themselves with other Africans through an erasure of the divisive history of Arab-Swahili slavery? At least part of the answer lies in the enduring coastal conflicts over land ownership and entitlement that have taken on fresh significance in recent years. In the Malindi area Arabs and Swahili are in a dominant position with respect to land ownership, some holding title deeds that date back to the coastal sultanates, while others are accused of buying land out from under destitute Mijikenda squatters who have already built their homes and farms on it. Most Mijikenda have insufficient funds to purchase the land they live on, and resentment over the issue is at high pitch. Last fall, during the politically orchestrated "ethnic" clashes that began as conflict between "coastal" and "upcountry" people, Mijikenda antagonisms toward large land-owners were forced to the surface, and in Malindi some Arabs and Swahili had leaflets pushed under their doors telling them to "go back to Arabia." Some Mijikenda frankly express their vision of Majimboism as one in which upcountry people will be sent back to "their lands," and Arabs too will be chased out of Kenya. [9] In such a context, and particularly within a culture of complexly mixed bloodlines (who, after all, can draw a clean line between "Swahili" and "Arab"?), issues of belongingness come to the fore. Interestingly, in conversations about the conflict it seems that some Mijikenda and Swahili are trying to push back the time of their arrival on the coast; the locution "we have been here since time immemorial" is not uncommon, and seems to have displaced, for some, the earlier origin stories that locate Mijikenda and Swahili roots in Shungwaya, a territory in or near southern Somalia (cf. Spear 1978; Willis 1993). Hence, there were tactical reasons for protesters to object not simply in their capacity as Muslims, but "as indigenous people," "as Africans."

I have explored a controversy that was steered by multiple agendas: the hope—shared by Europeans and some Africans--

of economic renewal through the erasure of a history unpalatable to the Western visitor; the British assertion of their own moral and practical competence and, by implication, their right to control municipal events in Malindi; the Swahili construction of an activist religious identity in order to align with the Arab-Muslim world; the Swahilis' strategic amnesia about their past domination in their current struggle for territorial entitlement. The lesson that the past is up for grabs is by now a truism, but representational struggles like this one are sure to arise with ever-new dimensions of complexity in the future. As tourism and global markets expand, for example, they will set increasingly important boundaries on what kinds of self-representations will profit Africa and what kinds will not. And this economic survivalism will continue to rub up against internal political dynamics, an unwillingness to be represented in the terms set by outsiders, and increasing access by Africans to the media that determine how and to whom widespread narratives will be told. Africa's past will no doubt be continually re-represented in acts of remembering, distorting, and forgetting that emerge not from simple oppositions of oppression and resistance but from all the messy, cross-cutting motives of economic, religious, and political survival.

Notes

[1] I would like to thank Athman Lali Omar and Fred Cooper for their helpful comments. Special thanks also go to Attas Sherif Ali, Abdalla Ali Alaussy, Maxwell Phares Kombe, Ann Robertson, and Kainga Kalume Tinga for their generous help. The support of the Malindi Museum Society and the Institute for African Studies at the University of Nairobi was invaluable to this project. Finally, my deepest gratitude goes to the many residents of Malindi and Mombasa who assisted me during my fieldwork. This research was funded by a Fulbright-Hays Fellowship.

[2] Prince Henry (1394-1460) was a famed navigator who organized and funded voyages of discovery that eventually led to the rounding of Africa and the establishment of sea routes to India. A devout Christian and administrator of the Order of Christ, Prince Henry's motives in exploration were religious as well as mercenary.

[3] For an example of how such dynamics have emerged in another site, see Gyan Prakash's detailed analysis of the indigenous politics of Indian historiography (Prakash 1992).

[4] As the protests began and fete organizers were taken aback by the reaction to their plans, they wondered why da Gama should cause such a stir when five years earlier in Mombasa, the 400th centennial of the erection of Fort Jesus by the Portuguese was celebrated without a hitch. Beyond the dynamics I describe in this paper, there may have been specific reasons why that fete transpired peacefully and the da Gama one did not. Fort Jesus had changed hands nine times over the centuries, passing back and forth between Omani, British, and other powers--a varied history that culminated in full Kenyan ownership and the Fort's conversion to a National Museum for the general public. But da Gama, as an individual with his own designs, was portrayed by protesters as the guardian of the most malevolent Portuguese efforts, even those that took place after his death. It was as if a mute, inanimate artifact could be re-appropriated by one interest group after another, and as such was morally neutralized. Da Gama's human agency, on the other hand, rooted him too deeply--too *intentionally*--in Portuguese mercantilism for him or his representatives to back out of the connection.

[5] The suggestion of anti-Muslim conspiracy is a common theme in Malindi's Muslim community. Some Swahili, for example, have circulated what appears to be a forged 1993 memo from John Major to the Foreign and Commonwealth office (addressed to "Douglas Hogg" rather than Douglas Hurd), in which Major articulates his concern that Muslim triumph in Bosnia-Hercegovina could give Islam a dangerous political wedge into the E.C, and announces that a stable Europe in the future "must remain based on a 'Christian-Civilization' and ethic" (Letter, "Prime Minister John Major" 1998). More recently, at a March 1998 symposium, Sheikh Ahmed Khalif of the Supreme Council of Kenya Muslims accused Western scholars of "[aiming] to denigrate and vilify Islam" by perpetuating distortions such as the notion that the religion itself encourages terrorism (Oyuga 1998). Accordingly, some Malindi Muslims believe the August 1998 bombings in Nairobi and Dar-es-Salaam were orchestrated by the FBI and/or CIA, merely to provide an excuse for open season on Muslims--a theory that President Clinton's hasty retaliatory bombings of Sudan and Afghanistan compounded.

[6] The accusation of "ignorance" was not an isolated barb; it emerged in response to fete supporters' recurrent complaint that the protests emerged from "lack of education." Yet protesters had amassed a considerable body of information--culled from history books, newspaper articles, and the Internet--to support their arguments against the fete. Why such an accusation, then? There were the disputes over who the slaveowners were, as described below. But setting aside this contest over the facts, the concept of "being educated" has an additional subtext, illuminated by one fete supporters' words: "If [the protesters] were educated they would see it's for

Malindi's own good." Arguably, then, the notion of "education" in Kenya is currently aligned with a secular, capitalist stance that sets priorities according to the economic exigencies of the moment. Self-advertisement is crucial to the economy, and the educated person recognizes that antagonistic representations of the past are economically reckless or irresponsible.

[7] To an extent, the Swahili-Arab objection to their reputation as slavers is justified, inasmuch as the Western notion of "slave" conjures up a condition of total debasement that does not map neatly onto the range of social roles played by slaves in coastal society. Most slaves arrived in Swahili society without kin and with a concomitant dependence on their masters, yet many located their relationship in a patron-client framework, and some became assimilated as extended kin. The multiple, shifting distinctions between types of slaves is reflected in the array of terms relating to slavery: *utumwa* (slavery or service, depending on context); *mtwana* (male slave); *mjakazi* (female slave); *suria* (concubine); *suriama* (half-caste); *mshenzi* (raw slave); *mzalia* (home-born slave); and *kibarua* (day laborer), among others (cf. Eastman 1994; Glassman 1991). Treatment of slaves varied considerably depending on whether the slave worked in fields or at home, with domestic slaves having "more comfortable living quarters and better food than field hands, as well as more intimate personal relations with the master" (Cooper 1977: 183). Suria concubines were often married, and immediately freed upon marriage and accepted as viable members of Swahili society. In some areas such as northern mainland coastal Tanzania, slaves themselves strove to assimilate to their masters' customs, avoiding the stigma of a separate "slave culture" (Glassman 1991) and abetting a situation in which the opposition between free and slave was not a fundamental one for many. Most slaves converted to Islam under duress or by choice, and while many retained elements of their traditional ethnic beliefs (Curtin, 1983: 117), they "[could not] always be distinguished from their masters" (Beachey 1976: 31). For those masters who followed Quranic dictates closely, Islam does mitigate the condition of slavery, urging kindness, charity, and manumission of the worthy who request it (cf. Beachey 1976: 33; Gordon 1987). However, slaves did sometimes live under conditions of abject exploitation, and the suggestion that no large-scale system of compulsory labor ever occurred is contradicted by much documented coastal history.

[8] Most Portuguese slaves were drawn from West, not East Africa. According to Beachey:

> the slave trade on the East African coast declined in importance under Portuguese rule...even after 1645, when their export from East Africa to Brazil was permitted...the traffic [in slaves by Portuguese mariners] never amounted to much (Beachey 1976: x-xi)

Beachey contends that Portuguese slaving activity on the East African coast was "of comparatively short duration", centered at the end of the eighteenth and first half of the nineteenth centuries (4).

[9] The politically orchestrated clashes on the coast in late 1997 were facilitated by some Mijikenda leaders who administered an oath of allegiance to clash participants. One such oath explicitly linked God-given ethnic identity and language to a God-given territory on earth. Arabs, then, were given Arabic by God, and according to this argument divinely entitled to Arab, not African lands.

Works Cited

Akumu, J.D. Letter. "We Can't Celebrate Slavery." *Daily Nation*, 4 Apr. 1998: 21.

Beachey, R. W. *The Slave Trade of Eastern Africa: A Collection of Documents*. London: Rex Collings, 1976.

Bedhad, Ali. *Belated Travelers: Orientalism in the Age of Colonial Dissolution*. Durham, NC: Duke University Press, 1994.

Cohen, David William. *The Combing of History*. Chicago: University of Chicago Press, 1994.

Cooper, Frederick. "The Treatment of Slaves on the Kenya Coast in the Nineteenth Century." Unpublished staff seminar paper. University of Nairobi, Department of History, 1972.

---. *Plantation Slavery on the East Coast of Africa*. New Haven and London: Yale University Press, 1977.

Curtin, Patricia Romero. "Laboratory for the Oral History of Slavery: The Island of Lamu on the Kenya Coast. " *The American Historical Review* 88.4 (1983): 858-882.

Eastman, Carol M. "Who are the Waswahili?" *Africa* 41 (1971): 228-236.

---. "Service, Slavery ('Utumwa') and Swahili Social Reality." *Africanistoshe Arbeitspapiere* 37 (1994): 87-107.

Glassman, Jonathan. "The Bondsman's New Clothes: The Contradictory Consciousness of Slave Resistance on the Swahili Coast." *Journal of African History* 32 (1991): 277-312.

Gordon, Murray. *Slavery in the Arab World*. Paris: Editions Robert Laffont, S. A., 1987.

Martin, Esmond Bradley. *The History of Malindi: A Geographical Analysis of an East African Coastal Town from the Portuguese Period to the Present.* Nairobi: East African Literature Bureau, 1973.

Mohamed, Abdulkarim Ali. Letter. "The Real Meaning of 'Slave' in Islam." Sent to national Kenyan newspapers in hopes of publication. Nov. 1997.

Nash, Dennison. "Tourism as a Form of Imperialism." *Hosts and Guests.* Ed. Valene Smith. Philadelphia: University of Pennsylvania Press, 1989. 37-52.

O'Brien, Donal B. Cruise. "Coping with the Christians: The Muslim Predicament in Kenya." *Religion and Politics in East Africa.* Eds. Holger Bernt Hansen and Michael Twaddle. London: James Currey. 200-219.

Oyuga, Chris. "Islam Does Not Back Violence." *Kenya Times,* 26 Mar. 1998.

Patel, Zarina. Letter. "Neo-colonialism at Fort Jesus." *East African Standard,* 22 May, 1998.

Pouwels, Randall L. *Horn and Crescent: Cultural Change and Traditional Islam on the East African Coast, 800-1900.* Cambridge: Cambridge University Press, 1987.

Prakash, Gyan. "Writing Post-Orientalist Histories of the Third World: Indian Historiography is Good to Think." *Colonialism and Culture.* Ed. Nicholas B. Dirks. Ann Arbor: University of Michigan Press, 1992. 353-388.

Robertson, S. A. "Putting Malindi Back on the Map: The Report of the Vasco da Gama Commemoration Week, 9th to 15th April, 1998, Malindi, Kenya." Unpublished Report, 1998a.

---. "Malindi and Vasco da Gama." Pamphlet printed for the Vasco da Gama Commemoration Week 9th to 15th April 1998 for the Malindi Museum Society, 1998b.

Salim, A. I. *The Swahili-speaking Peoples of Kenya's Coast.* Nairobi: East African Publishing House, 1973.

Spear, Thomas T. *The Kaya Complex: A History of the Mijikenda Peoples of the Kenya Coast to 1900.* Nairobi: Kenya Literature Bureau, 1978.

Strandes, Justus. *The Portuguese Period in East Africa.* Trans. J. F Wallwork. 1899. Nairobi: East African Literature Bureau, 1961.

Willis, Justin. *Mombasa, the Swahili, and the Making of the Mijikenda.* Oxford: Clarendon Press, 1993.

Anonymous Circulars and Letters

"Kusheherekea Vasco da Gama ni Haramu [To Celebrate Vasco da Gama is Forbidden by Muslim Law]." Circular written by objectors to the Vasco da Gama fete, Malindi. Apr. 1998.

Letter, apparently forged, from "Prime Minister John Major" to "Douglas Hogg of the Foreign and Commonwealth Office." May 2, 1993. Copies in circulation in Malindi, Kenya, 1998.

"R.E. Demonstration". Letter written by objectors to the Vasco da Gama fete to the District Commissioner of Malindi, Kenya. Apr. 10, 1998.

Interviews

Mohamed, Abdulkarim Ali. Personal interview. 11 Dec. 1998.

Wazee na vijana wa Malindi [Elders and youth of Malindi, a Swahili group who objected to the Vasco da Gama fete.] Personal interview. 11 Sept. 1998.

The "Literature of Empire" and the African Environment

Mahamadou DIALLO
University of Ouagadougou, Burkina Faso

*I must say when I saw the Congo again--when its vast and gaunt waters
broke on my view, and the blaze of its intemperate sun made me close my
eyes in sheer physical pain, I felt like turning tail at the mouth of the river.*
Roger Casement, *Letter to Sir Martin Gosselin*[1]

*Dick and John were quite heroes among their companions, who looked
with envy at the boys who were going to live in a land where lions and
elephants and all sorts of wild beasts abounded, to say nothing of warlike
natives.*
George A. Henty, *The Young Colonists*[2]

1- Introduction

The purpose of this study is to investigate the intellectual relationship between, on the one hand, a sample of British literary figures, and, on the other hand, the African environment. The period under consideration is the late 19th-early 20th century-- a period which corresponds to the height of European imperialism in Africa. European fiction writers who, in this period, wrote about Africa and other conquered lands have been put under the generic term of "Novelists of Empire," and their works under that of "Novels of Empire."[3] Our sample includes authors like George A. Henty, H. Rider Haggard, Gerald Hanley, Nicholas Monsarrat, Joseph Conrad, Graham Greene, Talbot Mundy, Van der Post, Evelyn Waugh and Joyce Cary. In a nutshell, the aim of the study is to see how these novelists intellectually perceived the African environment, and how they dealt with it in their literary works.

Let us say right away that on the whole, their attitudes will be shown to be largely negative. And this is where the important question arises: it has often been argued that our thoughts, words and deeds alike are necessarily influenced by our cultural molds. We shall see how far this applies to our sample of writers. We shall also examine the question whether they were not compelled by other forces. For this purpose, we shall place them and their works in the broader context of the imperial period. In so doing, we hope to be able to bring out what their real motives were.

It goes without saying that "Man" is an integral part of the environment in general. However, in the present context, the African as a human being will be deliberately left out so as to concentrate the study exclusively on the environment in its closest meaning to what is commonly called "nature;" this in spite of the fact that there certainly remains a lot to be said about, say, the warring, "spear throwing" African tribes of our writers--tribes on whom much, perhaps a little too much, has already been said.

2. The African Environment and British "Novels of Empire"

2-1. The African Soil

The supposed evil character of the soil and its primitivism are the two main features out of which the novelists of Empire have made their pet subjects in their writings; it is not, however, the positive type of primitivism that would simply refer to something of the earliest times and would thus, for example, go along with the recognition of the continent as the cradle of the *homo sapiens sapiens* that we are; it is rather the type of primitivism that could be equated to retardation and backwardness.

The continent is seen as a living example of the early stages of creation, but where all things have been standing still almost in the forms in which God first created them. The reader of the novels is constantly reminded that if s/he wants to get an idea of what the world was in the beginning of time, all s/he has to do is take a look at Africa in the present times.

For example, the vegetation in the African forest is often referred to as "primeval," and some types of trees compared to "skeletons"--another way of presenting as vestiges of the past. That is the image that formed in the heads of Frank and Goodenough, the protagonists of Henty's *By Sheer Pluck,* as they traveled in the forest along the Bight of Benin.

> Passing through Assaibo they entered the thick brush. The giant cottontrees had now shed their light feathery foliage, resembling that of an acacia, and the straight, round, even trunks looked like the skeletons of some giant or primeval vegetation rising above the sea of foliage below[4].

The endeavor to present the African land as an evil land appears to be a strikingly coherent feature common to most, if not all, the works of our authors. For example, they seem to be color blind when looking at it: eyes are thus closed on the ochre of the well known laterite crust that covers many areas; this in order to present the soil as black--the color of evil from the Eurocentrist perspective.

On page 7 of his *Drinkers of Darkness* (1955), Gerald Hanley describes the setting for his Eastern African settlement as "that blackish soil...and that impending evil which the sensitive felt at Mambango."

Even the degree of humidity in the soil is often viewed in terms of extremes: either it is too dry and appears as a hellish desert, or it is too wet, in which case it is presented as a marshland covered with impenetrable forests and seething swamps. The reader is thus put in the presence of decaying vegetation, and marshes that exhale poisonous, lethal gases--the notorious *miasma* which, at the height of Empire, was still blamed for most infectious diseases.[5] Before the discovery of the anti-malarial properties of quinine around 1820, it was the *bête noire* of Europeans who visited the continent. Henty refers to it as "the malarious exhalation...arising from the swamps."[6]

This description clearly reflects the attitudes of some characters in the novels: thus, we see Frank and Goodenough in Henty's *By Sheer Pluck* take all necessary precautions to protect themselves during their trekking across the Gabon; when, for example, they came to that village where they decided to stay for a few days, the type of house they started hunting for was not just any type of house, but, to use Henty's own words, "one consisting of three rooms, built on piles;" and the author goes on to add that this is "an important point in a country in which disease rises from the soil."[7] Where that kind of facility was not available, where they did not have the privilege of being perched a few feet above the ground on piles, the type of tent they slept in was conceived to ward off the dangerous emanations.

> It was a double-poled tent, some ten feet square, and there was a waterproof sheet large enough to cover the whole of the interior, thus preventing the miasma from arising from the ground within it.[8]

It goes without saying that such an evil soil can only bear what is evil. The plants, the animals and the birds are not just different from what the characters in the novels are used to in their homeland. This difference is abused and exploited to the same end--bringing out the negative aspects of those elements in order to establish the supposedly evil nature of the African environment.

2-2. The African Fauna and Flora

2-2-1. The Fauna:

Again, Henty is one of the novelists of Empire who did most in painting Africa 'blacker" than it actually is through, among other things, the description of its animals, big and small. The comparisons he makes between African animals and their European counterparts is quite edifying: he speaks of "the monotonous too-too of the doves--not a slow dreamy cooing like that of the English variety, but a sharp quick note repeated in endless succession...."[9] For him, African pigs are inordinately bellicose. "They quarrelled energetically in side lanes and courtyards, and when worsted in their disputes galloped away grunting, careless whom they might upset."[10] As for African dogs, they simply are not normal creatures. Witness this short exchange between the fellow explorers in his *By Sheer Pluck;* the younger one visibly finds it a wonder of Mo-

ther Nature that an African dog should be endowed with the
anatomic ability to bark at all.

> - Frank: "Surely, Mr. Goodenough, I can hear some dogs
> barking! I did not know that the native dogs barked ."
> - Mr. Goodenough: "Nor do they. They yelp and howl, but
> they never bark like the European dogs"[11].

The treatment reserved to the African bovine species is
not any better. Still in Henty, the cattle of the Gulf of Guinea
is presented in almost contradictory terms, this in order to
bring out the extremes in them, and therefore their abnormal
character: one moment they are described as energetic and
susceptible of utter ferocity, and the next moment they are
shown without the slightest energy, as totally lifeless creatures. He writes that "The very bullocks which drew the gliding
wagons seemed to move more slowly than bullocks in other
places." And he goes on to add that

> If English cattle possessed the strength and obstinate fury
> of these little animals, Copenhagen Fields would have to
> be removed further from London, or the entrance swept
> by machine gun, for a charge of the cattle would clear the
> streets of London.[12]

Even the tiny ants are given much more attention than
they perhaps deserve. It is true that as a rule, there is no
common measure between the destructive powers of ants on
the one hand, and their size on the other; but in the fiction of
Empire, African ants are made more destructive than ants can
be anywhere else in the world. Many of our writers have dealt
with those pests, but among them all, Nicholas Monsarrat
stands out as an author almost obsessed with the problem of
ants and rats. The island of Pharamaul which allegorically
stands for Africa in his *The Tribe That Lost Its Head* is swar-
ming with them. David Bracken, the British "Secretary designate" for this scheduled territory, wakes up on his first morning there, observing at one time "a million ants crawling and
hurrying on their pathway of destruction," and at another

time "armies of ants intent on destroying everything wrought by the hand of man."[13]

Under the pen of such authors as Evelyn Waugh, African ants are simply a wonder in the negative sense: for although these insects can undeniably damage just about anything that stands in their way, they are not known to systematically attack certain materials such as rubber and the like; yet in Waugh's *Black Mischief,* we see a motor car that had been put out of use because "white ants had devoured the tyres."[14] Obviously, what is quite explicitly stressed here is the supposedly uncommon voracity of African ants. On the same page, for that matter, we also see the Legation syce "moodily flick[ing] his whip at a train of ants"--a gesture that may seem ludicrous at first sight, but gives an idea of the constant war that is being waged against these mortal enemies.

This is to say nothing of the predator lions and crocodiles in Haggard's *Elissa* (1900), the "cannibal crabs" and the "hopeless jackals" in Talbot Mundy's *The Ivory Trail* (1919), the "mosquito and tse-tse fly and other minute parasites" in Van der Post's *The Dark Eye in Africa* (1955).

2-2-2. The Flora

Where there is vegetation in the novels of Empire, it is almost always in the form of thick, impenetrable forests teaming with dangerous beasts, and run through by fabulous rivers no less filled with monstrous animals. In the usual attempt to always bring out the negative side of the African environment, the plants in the forests are transformed into almost living creatures among which the law of the jungle prevails.

Henty and Stuart Cloete are unbeatable in this respect. The former depicts the African forest as "a perfect wilderness of climbers clustered round the trees, twisting in a thousand fantastic windings, and finally running down to the ground, where they took fresh root and formed props to the dead trees their embrace had killed.[15] The latter, in *Congo Song,* writes of a "wall of solid jungle" with "lianas choking the trees with thick brown arms, garroting them; where orchids in scentless, decadent surrealism clung to dying trees."[16] This kind of description is so common that it would be space consuming to even attempt an overview of it. However, we also have Monsarrat's novel above mentioned and Joyce Cary's *Essays,* to add only these two works in passing.

These forests form an eerie world where what Haggard calls "boiling" or "deep sullen pools" lie dormant, breeding "large quantities of a hideous black water-snake, of which the bite is dangerous." But it should be noted that Haggard has gone further than any novelist of Empire in the common goal of "demonizing" things African in general, and the African environment in particular: the comparison he makes of the Tana river in Kenya with the mythological Styx[17] is a case in point; for instance, in the second phase of the adventure in *Allan Quatermain* (1949), we see this Kenyan river, which we can find on any physical map of the country, turn suddenly into a Stygian waterway, and rush the adventurers into the African underworld of his own creation.

Even the atmosphere is shown to be particularly unhealthy; above "the gloom and quiet of the great forest" in Henty (1884: 324) hangs "the dampness and heaviness of the air, and the malarious exhalation and smell of decaying vegetation arising from the swamps."

As for deserts, although they are given far less attention in our corpus, it is nonetheless true that where there is no vegetation to constitute a green hell, the setting is usually a desert far more hostile than deserts normally are. The hunger and thirst that prevail there are ruthless, and are often seen taking their toll among imprudent European travelers who venture into such areas. That is what exactly happened, in Henty's *Young Colonists,* to the Scot merchant MacGregor, who was stupid enough to lead his caravan through a waterless stretch of the Kalahari[18].

3. A "Prospero Complex"

In literary circles, Shakespeare's *The Tempest,* through the works of authors like Mannoni and Memmi, has inspired the conceptualization of the notion of "Caliban Complex."[19]

Similarly, if we look at Prospero as a character, we see a man subject to a most wonderful contradiction: he is all powerful--so powerful that he can control Sycorax's god; yet, at times, he appears to be such a weak and helpless master in the face of Caliban that he ends up behaving accordingly, using physical constraint and threats, swears and curses. The master is obviously suffering from a kind of reverse fear and suspicion vis-à-vis the slave; he has developed an interrelational counterpart to the Caliban Complex, and which we can call the *Prospero Complex.*

One thing, however, should be kept in mind: what constitutes a real problem for Prospero is not the plot staged by Caliban in itself; it is rather the very possibility for such a plot to take place at all. So much so that Prospero feels he is failing in his role as an absolute master-reformer. And this is due to no other thing than the Evil that is personified in Caliban, and which results in a situation where Caliban the conquered somehow remains unconquered, Caliban the tamed remains untamed.

Intent upon bringing out the evil of the African land, this is exactly the kind of psychological relationship that our authors have established between their characters and the continent.

3-1. Africa the Unassailable, the Untamable

History amply proves that Africa has been brutally assailed and lastingly tamed by Europe. Yet our authors present the continent as naturally protected from any external intrusion--a condition which makes it both unassailable and untamable. In this respect, Haggard deserves special attention. Quite peculiar is the *Romanesque* setting of his works, this for a simple reason: he intended them to be adventure novels for boys, and to this effect he operated on two different levels--the real and the fantastic, with a special stress laid upon occultism. Almost invariably, his stories revolve around the theme of the quest; they begin in the real world and end in the unreal, where the object of the quest stays hidden: this object can be a lost treasure as in *King Solomon's Mines,* a goddess as in *She* (1951) or a lost tribe as in *Allan Quatermain* and *The Ivory Child.* The two worlds are usually separated by an impassable obstacle, so that the explorers who venture from the one into the other, are always faced with a boundless tract of marshes, or a bottomless gulf, or a wall-like forest. In *Allan Quatermain* for instance, we see the companions run into a "thorn forest, so thick that even the elephants could not get through it, much less men."[20] The only link between the two worlds is, according to each case, a narrow plank thrown over the precipice, or a unique and only knowledgeable guide through the marshland, or a fabulous waterway.

But before the explorer reaches the unreal world, he naturally has to face the real one. And obstacles are not lacking there either. We have already mentioned the evil-spitting soil with its disease generating miasma, its dangerous animals and destructive insects. More interestingly, however, what our authors seem to suggest here and there is that the African land has been made naturally impenetrable by mother Nature herself. Again, in Haggard, both the physical layout and the aspect of the real world are presented as repelling, therefore protective in themselves: on page 23 of his *Black Heart and White Heart* (1898), he speaks of an "amphitheater of the most gloomy forest, ringed round in the distance by sheer-sided hills," and on page 88 of his *She,* the valley of Kôr is described as a expanse of "miles and miles of quagmire, varied only by bright green strips of comparatively solid ground, and by deep and sullen pools fringed with tall rushes."

However, the ways in which the continent makes itself physically unassailable appear most striking when seen in authors as "different" as Conrad and Van der Post. Thus, the former, hinting at the protective role of the African seas, speaks of "the formless coast bordered by dangerous surf, as if Nature herself had tried to ward off intruders."[21] The latter, for his part, gives credit to the tse-tse fly and the anopheles and their likes, for keeping watch over the continent: "as if to make quite sure that her defences completely sealed Africa off from the outer world," he writes,

> nature developed the most redoubtable champions in the mosquito and tse-tse fly and other minute parasites, all able to strike down any invader with a wonderful selection of deadly diseases, from sleeping sickness, malaria, dysentery, and typhoid to leprosy and bubonic plague.[22]

3-2. The Impact, or Africa the Beater[23]

Most of our fiction writers of Empire are also convinced of one thing--that, in spite of all the protective arsenal that Africa keeps stored in its environment, if the intruder still manages to penetrate the land, then so much the worse for him/her. He is sure to be severely dealt with and ultimately beaten; and this at all levels--physical, psychological, and spiritual. Again, there is no half way with Africa: either the invader is destroyed, or, if he is tough enough to be among the rare survivors, then he cannot but emerge a super man. This is the idea that Gerald Hanley puts in the head of one of his characters as the latter speaks to his colleagues in their Eastern African settlement.

> It's the country, Browning told them. It's something in the air. It brings out the worst in us, and the best too, if you take the other view. Ultra violet rays acting on the spine or something.[24]

An interesting point, however, is that the best in Europeans is hardly ever shown to be actually brought out by Africa. It is astonishing how our fiction writers have managed to ignore those Europeans who were very successful, from the European point of view, on the African soil: even a man like Rhodes who landed in the Cape an ill and insignificant person, but who ultimately rose to the pinnacle both economically and politically, is mentioned only incidentally by a deeply chauvinistic author like Henty. Military leaders, particularly George Gordon, are but an exception that confirms the rule.

This is no matter for surprise, though, since the obvious aim is to expose the evil side of Africa. To this end most of the authors have indeed devoted a lot of space in their works. The heat of the continent, as already mentioned, is most often taken to task and the reader is constantly "shown" how the intruders are both stunned and numbed by it. For example, in Greene's *The Heart of the Matter,* the author is observing his central character, Scobie, who is in such a condition, and whose behavior reflects the presumption that Africa knows no measure in anything, only extremes.

Scobie walked rapidly back into the lounge. He went full tilt into an armchair and came to a halt. His vision moved jerkily back into focus, but sweat dripped into his right eye. The finger that wiped it free shook like a drunkard's. He told himself: Be careful. This isn't a climate for emotion. It's a climate for meanness, malice, snobbery, but anything like hate or love drives a man off his head.[25]

On the surface level, some of the novelists have tried to touch upon the push factors that impelled Europeans to go out to Africa. Gerald Hanley did so in his *Drinkers of Darkness* (1955), where the characters went out mostly to make something of their failed lives. Rider Haggard's characters were pushed out mainly by their unquenchable thirst for adventure. Greene's Querry in *A Burnt Out Case* (1961) *is* a burnt out case, an architect who has reached the limits of his creativity, and who needs to experience something else. Henty uses the same procedure in virtually all his works, but just as a writing strategy: most of his protagonists are forced to leave home by financial stress and other misfortunes, predominantly accidental. But again, we hardly see Africa do them any good: rather, what Africa does to them is either destroy them, or fashion their characters for good, often leaving them with deep, indelible scars.

On the whole, stress is laid upon the supposedly inescapable, devastating effects of Africa--Africa the destroyer. Heavy drinking is commonly resorted to, as is often the case in situations of despair. The comments made by Mr. Goodenough in Henty are quite eloquent. "Unfortunately," he says,

the European in Africa speedily loses his vigor and enterprise. When he first lands he exclaims, 'I certainly shall have a bungalow built upon those hills; ' but in a short time his energy leaves him. He falls into the ways of the place, drinks a great deal more spirits than is good for him, stops down near the water, and at the end of a year or so, if he lives so long, is obliged to go back to Europe to recruit.[26]

Europeans in Africa are also frequently assailed by psychological problems, with such symptoms as irritability, nightmares, and all sorts of irrational patterns of behavior, sometimes even verging on madness. For instance, in Henty's *Gilligan's Last Elephant,* Miller, one of the big game hunters, nearly perishes in the bush when he gets lost tracking a herd of elephants. After he is rescued, he turns to the wilderness and starts talking to it: "Well, you didn't get me after all." Then he turns to his fellow hunter Jama, saying: "Go on, laugh..." But it gets you, this country. You lose your goddam head in it.[27]

In other instances, stress is placed upon the utter boredom and the meaningless side of the men's lives. In *The Consul at Sunset,* another novel of Hanley's, the only thing the Europeans who are lost in this East African territory can do to fill up their dull evenings is to

> sit for hours at night with a forgotten book on your knee, a glass of brandy in your hand, watching the ants swarm on to a piece of biscuit and laboriously convey it to their nest.[28]

Still worse are the conditions of Harris and Wilson in Greene's *The Heart of the Matter,* where the two Europeans are shown engaging in their evening pastime--a competition which consists in killing the most cockroaches before bedtime.[29]

What tops it all, though, is that Africa affects not only the physique and the mind of Europeans, but also their souls. Even their religious faiths seem to literally disintegrate on the continent, where the perpetual struggle between Good and Evil, between God and the Devil, is believed to be largely in favor of the latter. What could make more sense for a place supposedly without religion? In *The Heart of the Matter,* Scobie, who is afraid he is losing his faith, says to Father Rank: "I'm not sure that I even believe." To which Rank replies: "It's easy... to worry too much about that. Especially *here* (my italics) The penance I would give to a lot of people if I could is six months' leave. The climate gets you down. It's easy to mistake tiredness for--well, disbelief."

The Father is here obviously trying to downplay the situation in order to comfort his disciple. But it is possible that deep down in himself, he is convinced that the African climate can actually break a man's faith; so he feels it his duty to stop Scobie from being definitively lost out of the Christian creed. But whether that is the case or not, what is really important here is the very idea that the African environment can instill religious doubt into the spirits of intruders. It can even affect the faiths of the religious leaders: Father Rank himself, as his name indicates, is steeped in sin. Wilson calls him "the biggest gossip in town."[30]

However, nowhere else have all these views about Africa as inviolable, untamable, and a beater been more masterly condensed than in the death of the big game hunter in Hanley's *Gilligan's Last Elephant*. Lying in his death bed after his unfortunate encounter with a vicious pachyderm, Gilligan, in his delirium, is heard uttering a Kurtzian type of last word: "'They're all right, elephants,' he says. 'No harm in them. No, it's not luck. It's just stupid, that's all.' He shouted it, despite the pain it brought on. 'Stupid!'."[31]

So in their attempt to draw the darkest possible picture of Africa, our authors have clearly put more than enough to make any one, just like Roger Casement[32] at the mouth of the Congo river, feel like "turning tail."

But the fact also is that this picture did not stand in the void; it was contained in a supporting canvas--a wider cultural context with its intellectual and philosophical concepts and trends.

4. The Context: Eurocentrism and the Issue of Cultural Relativism

To say that it is difficult to express one's ideas independently from one's own cultural background sounds like a truism. Our culture is necessarily central--we are culturally centered. Hence the numerous terms that have been coined to designate that notion: we have "ethnocentrism," "cultural egocentrism," "cultural relativism," and so on. In the particular case of the European culture, we have "Eurocentrism," to which Martin Bernal and Edward Said prefer the heavy-sounding term of "Europocentrism."[33]

How far were our authors influenced by this phenomenon of cultural relativism in general, and more particularly by that of Eurocentrism, with the numerous ideas, concepts and philosophies that prevailed at the time?

4-1. The Darwinian Evolutionism

The informed reader cannot have missed the fact that the notion of evolution is rampant in most of the above references and quotations. When, for example, Africa is presented as a "primitive" place and its environment as "primeval," this unequivocally means that the continent has, like everything on earth, gone through the first stages of evolution, but that it has, somehow, remained blocked there so far; that if, as already said above, one wants to see how much distance one has covered on the path of progress and evolution, all one needs to do is look at Africa. Africa is taken almost as a yardstick for evolution. A great part of our authors' ideas and perceptions are based on the evolutionary laws and principles.

Among the animals and between the animals and the people, there prevails a merciless competition in which the stronger eats the weaker in order to keep alive in this lawless jungle that is the African environment. One of Talbot Mundy's settings is a place "where cannibal crabs devour all helpless things;" and "where lean, hopeless jackals crack today men's dry bones left fifty years ago by the slave caravans..."[34]

The humans are not spared either, for they can be dined on by the ever present predators. That, in Haggard's *Elissa,* was the fate of the caravan escorting the European treasure hunters, on their way to the Mythical Golden Ophir in the ancient city of Zimboe. Not only had they "died...by the scores" of "the pestilential fever of the low lands," but

> Twice also they had suffered heavily through hunger and thirst, to say nothing of their losses by the fangs of lions, crocodiles, and other wild beasts with which the country swarmed.[35]

But obviously, the vegetable world, as it is seen by our authors, is where the workings of evolution are most manifest. Plants are turned almost into living things and shown to conduct savage interactions between themselves; for instance, through some of the above quotations, we see the lianas and other creepers "choking" and "killing" their closest neighbors by "embracing" or "garroting" them. The Darwinian "struggle for survival" prevails in this world where "natural selection" is the unique and only law. The reference to creepers, not known to be particularly big in the vegetable world, is no matter for surprise: in spite of their apparently weak constitution, they are among the fittest, because in the process of evolution, they have developed ways to fight and kill their neighbors.

4-2. Environmentalism[36]

German-born U.S. scientist Franz Boas--who early in this century brain fathered the theory of environmentalism--was, as an anthropologist, certainly preoccupied primarily with the human species. Our authors, however, did not hesitate to transpose the theory to the African setting, just as they did with evolutionism. When going through the above sections about the soil and the climate, the flora and the fauna, the reader has certainly not missed this point. The general idea that shows through the different descriptions is that the African environment is naturally evil; and that everything it breeds is necessarily bad, since everything it breeds is influenced by it, better, molded by it.

4-3. A Eurocentric Discourse[37]

In the European *episteme* , there exists a striking similitude between the notion of the Orient and that of Africa. Witness the fact that the two are often lumped together in such institutions as, say, the School of African and Oriental Studies in London. So the same type of discourse that has been developed for the Orient has also been applied to Africa. There actually exists what I have called a "European Africanist discourse,"[38] in other words a replica of Said's Orientalist discourse as applied to the African context.

And the European texts on Africa are replete with a language and a style that are characteristic of that discourse. To stay just in the realm of vocabulary, let us say that anyone familiar with the literature of Empire must also be familiar with words and concepts that I shall only mention here in passing: "nigger," "nig-nog," "wog," "blackie," "fuzzy wuzzy," "boola boola," "Sambo," "Tambo," and so on and so forth.

In our corpus, the striking fact is the similitude in both the ideas of the authors and the language they use to express them. We can clearly perceive here a form of discourse. The similitude of the ideas is what we have been dealing with in the foregoing. As for the language, let us just consider a few examples, by comparing Haggard and Henty. We can find it quite normal to read akin words and phrases in two different authors writing about the same thing. So we can find it normal, for example, to read in Henty "smell of decaying vegetation" (*Pluck,* 324), and then "smell of rotting vegetation" in Haggard (*She,* 88-9); or "the malarious exhalation" in Henty (*Pluck,* 324), and then "the pestilential fever" in Haggard (*Elissa,* 2), or again, about the natural defenses of Africa, "ward off" in Conrad (*H of D,* 69), and then "seal off" in Van der Post (*Dark Eye,* 44-5). But when we find fragments of sentences or entire sentences that are almost the same, then there is obviously something fishy around. Examples: "the gloom and quiet of the great forest" in Henty (*Pluck,* 324), and "the amphitheater of the most gloomy forest" in Haggard (*Black Heart,* 23-4); "as if Nature herself had tried to ward off intruders" in Conrad, and "as if to make sure that her defenses completely sealed Africa off from the outer world" in Van der Post; "the malarious exhalation and smell of decaying vegetation arising from the swamp" in Henty, and in Haggard, "the worst feature of the swamp was the awful smell of rotting vegetation...and the malarious exhalations that accompanied it."

Of course, we can assume that one of the authors read the other and then simply did some lifting. But that's another story.

Even then, though, it appears incontrovertible that there is something common between them: they were working with the same frame of mind in the same context--that is their cultural background, more precisely the imperialist culture of the time: and they were using the same, pre-established tool--that is the same discourse, the European Africanist discourse. They were the "victims" of their Eurocentric culture, just as everyone necessarily is *vis-à-vis* one's own culture. But is that a sufficient reason for such a negative attitude toward Africa and its environment? There seems to be a lot more to it, and a short look at their non-literary lives could shed some more light on the issue.

4-4. How Innocent Were Our Authors?

As already mentioned above, some of our novelists were not at all unacquainted with the imperialist movement. They can even be counted among the Empire builders, for the simple reason that they served, in various capacities, in the British rule of the colonies; a few were directly involved in the administration: Haggard, from 1875 to 1881, served under Sir Henry Bulwer in Natal and then under Sir Theophilus Shepstone in Transvaal;[39] Cary, in the second decade of this century, served as District Officer for Borgu, Western Nigeria'[40] others did close business with the colonial armies: among them Haggard, who got involved with both the Boer war and the battle against the "Matabele,"[41] and Cary who served as an Army Lieutenant in the Cameroons campaign during WWI;[42] still others were, on the African soil, engaged in various activities such as land reform, intelligence, or the media; for instance, during WWII in Sierra Leone, Greene worked on confidential wartime missions for the British government;[43] after the war, Monsarrat, for his part, took up the position of Director of the U.K. Information Office in South Africa;[44] even Conrad, in 1890, found himself serving with the Belgian Congo Company as a steamboat captain.[45]

So it clearly appears that the way in which our authors treated Africa in their works is far from innocent. It could, of course, be argued that we can serve a system that we disapprove, but that also is another story. What is sure is that a sizable group were unquestionably writing to justify the colonial enterprise, in some cases even to defend their class interests, which were hardly different from those of the Empire builders.

5. Conclusion

In the present study, we have seen how British fiction writers of the colonial period--generally known as "novelists of Empire," have dealt with the African environment in their works. We have seen that, on the whole, they have painted quite a negative picture of that environment. We have placed this literary attitude in the wider context of the imperial enterprise, and classed its aggressiveness with the wholesale aggression of Europe toward Africa in general.

Why exactly these novelists wrote about Africa the way they did was a more difficult question to answer. We have, however, tried to show that they were--as every writer necessarily is--compelled, if not influenced by their cultural background, the Eurocentric culture.

A good evidence of this is the use they made of the ideas and theories of the time on the one hand, and on the other hand, of an established discourse that we have called "European Africanist discourse."

But we have also come to the conclusion that cultural influence is not a sufficient reason, and that a number of the authors were not just blindly following a trend; they were also defending their class interests. For, as a matter of fact, the imperial enterprise was largely the concern of the upper and middle class citizens--at least intellectually. But through and beyond these classes, many saw the larger entities that were their nation, and its civilization. Usually happy and proud to belong in a powerful, conquering nation, they used their talents as writers to, among other things, depict a negative picture of the conquered lands, this for two main goals: firstly to justify the domination itself (a bad environment in a savage land needs to be transformed for the better by the providential hand of civilization); secondly, they were hoping to bring out "their" positive image against the negative one that they were making of Africa.

Western media are decried today for doing the same thing, but few people are aware that it is an old practice which assumes different forms as time passes: British information highways today are doing what British novels of Empire did yesterday.

Notes

1 Roger Casement, *Letter to Sir Martin Gosselin* in Paul Hyland, *The Black Heart: A Voyage into Central Africa.* London: Victor Gollancz, 1988, p. 19.

[2] G. A. Henty, *The Young Colonists,* Boston: Charles E. Brown & Co. (1st published 1888), p. 27.

[3] See Susanne Howe, *Novels of Empire:* New York, Columbia Univ. Press, 1949.

[4] George A. Henty, *By Sheer Pluck:* New York, A.L. Burt, 1890, p. 322. [1] Queen Victoria was crowned Empress of India in 1857, but it was not until 1864-65 that the relationship of cause and effect between germs and infectious diseases was clearly established by French biologist Louis Pasteur.

[5] Queen Victoria was crowned Empress of India in 1857, but it was not until 1864-65 that the relationship of cause and effect between germs and infectious diseases was clearly established by French biologist Louis Pasteur.

[6] George A. Henty, op. cit., p. 324.

[7] Ibid, p. 126.

[8] Ibid., p. 132.

[9] Ibid., p. 324.

[10] Ibid., p. 309.

[11] Ibid, pp. 314, 309, 143.

[12] Ibid., pp. 114; 315.

[13] Nicholas Monsarrat: *The Tribe that Lost its Head:* New York, William Sloane Associates, 1956, pp. 99 and 133.

[14] Evelyn Waugh, *Black Mischief:* Harmondsworth, Penguin, 1938, p. 152.

[15] George A. Henty, op. cit., p. 232.

[16] Stuart Cloete, *Congo Song:* Boston, Houghton Mifflin, 1943, p. 111.

[17] According to Webster's Dictionary, the Styx is, in Greek mythology, "the chief river of the lower world, which it encircles seven times."

[18] George. A. Henty, *The Young Colonists:* New York, F. M. Lupon, 1888, p. 258.

[19] Within the general framework of the colonizer/colonized or master/slave relationship, the notion describes the situation of the slave who, being well aware of his subjugation, tries to put up some kind of resistance, constantly fighting back using weapons from the master's very arsenal--language in particular.

[20] H. Rider Haggard, *Allan Quatermain:* London, Macdonald, 1949, p. 116.

[21] Joseph Conrad, *Heart of Darkness:* New York, Signet, 1961 (1st publ. 1899), p.69.

[22] Van der Post, *The Dark Eye in Africa,* New York, William Morrow & Co., 1955, p. 44.

23 I prefer here the word "beater" to, say, the word "winner," because to me, "beater" sounds more of a verb of action, and therefore adds more strength to the idea of what, in the eyes of our authors, Africa can do to invaders.

24 Gerald Hanley, *The Year of the Lion:* New York, Macmillan, 1954, p. 64.

25 Graham Greene, *The Heart of the Matter:* London, William Heinemann and The Bodley Head, 1948, p. 26.

26 G. A. Henty, *By Sheer Pluck:* op. cit., p. 115-16.

27 Hanley, *Gilligan's Last Elephant:* Cleveland, World, 1962, p. 256.

28 Hanley, *The Consul at Sunset:* New York, Macmillan, 1951, p. 9.

29 Greene, *The Heart of the Matter:* op. cit., p. 77 ff.

30 Idem., pp. 176 & 83.

31 Hanley, *Gilligan's Last Elephant:* op. cit., p. 239.

32 Sir Roger Casement (1864-1916; knighted 1911) was a noted British diplomat and humanitarian. In 1915, he resigned his position as a British Consul in order to devote his life to the Irish national cause; as a humanitarian, he got closely involved in the fight against the inhuman system that was established in the Congo by King Leopold II of Belgium. He was one of the brain fathers of the Congo Reform Association (established 1903), and in the early 1900s, he visited the region where he met Conrad. See P. Brantlinger, *Rule of Darkness:* Ithaca, Cornell University Press, 1988.

33 For details about this, see Mahamadou Diallo, *Aspects of British-African History as Reflected in Contemporary British Literature: Colonial and Postcolonial Periods:* unpublished Ph D Dissertation, The University of Iowa, 1993, introductory chapter.

34 Talbot Mundy, *The Ivory Trail:* Indianapolis, Bobbs, Merrill & Co., 1919, p. 66.

35 H. Rider Haggard, *Elissa, the Doom of Zimbabwe:* New York, Longman, Green & Co., 1900, p. 2.

36 According to most encyclopedias, the theory holds that "environment rather than heredity is the primary influence upon intellectual growth and cultural development."

37 The term discourse will here be given the same content as the one it has in Edward Said's *Orientalism.* It will therefore be taken to broadly mean a cultural and intellectual system for dealing with the Orient in particular, and with non-European civilizations in general.

38 See Diallo, op. cit., pp. 156-7.

39 Norman Etherington, *Rider Haggard:* Boston, Twayne Publishers, 1984, p. v.

40 See Forward to *Cock Jarvis:* 1974, and Jeffrey Meyers, *Fiction and the Colonial Experience:* Totoa, New Jersey, Rowman and Littlefield, 1973.

41 Etherington, op. cit.

42 Meyers, op. cit.

43 Ibid., p. 97.

44 Nicholas Monsarrat, "Note about the author" in his *Richer Than All His Tribe:* New York, William Sloane Associates, 1969.
45 Joseph Conrad,*Heart of Darkness:* New York, Signet Classics, 1960, p. 12.

Works Cited

1. Fiction

Cary, Joyce. *Cock Jarvis.* London: Michael Joseph, 1974.

Cloete, Stuart. *Congo Song.* New York: Monarch, 1958.

Conrad, Joseph. *Heart of Darkness.* New York: Signet, 1961.

Greene, Graham. *The Heart of the Matter.* London: Heine-mann, 1971.

-------. *A Burnt Out Case.* London: Heinemann, 1961.

Haggard, H. Rider. *Allan Quatermain.* New York: Dover, 1951.

-------. *She.* New York: Dover, 1951.

-------. *Elissa.* London: Longmans, Green and Co., 1900.

-------. *Black Heart and White Heart.* London: Longmans, Green and Co., 1900.

Hanley, Gerald. *Gilligan's Last Elephant.* Cleveland: World, 1962.

-------. *The Year of the Lion.* New York: Macmillan, 1954.

-------. *The Consul at Sunset.* New York: Macmillan, 1951.

Henty, George A.. *The Young Colonists.* New York: F. M. Lu-pon Co., (1st publ. 1888).

------. *By Sheer Pluck.* New York: Hurst and Co., 1884.

Monsarrat, Nicholas. *The Tribe That Lost Its Head.* New York: William Sloane Associates, 1956.

------. *Richer Than All His Tribe.* New York: William Sloane Associates, 1969.

Mundy, Talbot. *The Ivory Trail.* Indianapolis: Bobbs, Merrill and Co., 1919.

Post, Van der. *The Dark Eye in Africa.* New York: William Morrow and Co., 1955.

Waugh, Evelyn. *Black Mischief.* Harmondsworth: Penguin, 1938.

2. Non-fiction

American Heritage Dictionary(The). Boston: Houghton Mifflin, 1982.

Brantlinger, Patrick. *Rule of Darkness*. Ithaca, Cornell University Press, 1988.

Diallo, Mahamadou. *Aspects of British African History as Reflected in Contemporary British Literature: Colonial and Post colonial Periods*. unpublished Ph D Dissertation, The University of Iowa, 1973.

Etherington, Norman. *Rider Haggard*. Boston: Twayne Publishers, 1984.

Howe, Susanne. *Novels of Empire*. New York: Columbia University Press, 1949.

Hyland, Paul. *The Black Heart: A Voyage into Central Africa*. London: Victor Gollancz, 1988.

Mannoni, Dominique O. *Prospero and Caliban: The Psychology of Colonization*. Transl. Pamela Powesland. London: Methuen & Co., 1950.

Memmi, Albert. *Portrait du Colonisé, précédé de Portrait du Colonisateur*. Paris: Gallimard, 1985.

Meyers, Jeffrey. *Fiction and the Colonial Experience*. Totowa, New Jersey: Rowman and Littlefield, 1973.

Said, Edward W. *Orientalism*. New York: Pantheon Books, 1978.

Shakespeare, William. *The Tempest*. Harmondsworth: Penguin Books, 1968.

From Crusades to Colonies: Africa in French Literature

Kristof Haavik
University of Botswana

The evolving image of Africa in French literature shows progressive stages in European attitudes toward the continent and its inhabitants. A study of selected texts from the Middle Ages, Enlightenment, and colonial period reveals how the geographical and sociological knowledge or misconceptions of European writers developed over time and ultimately led to beliefs that are still current today.

Medieval texts such as the *Chanson de Roland* or *Song of Roland* show extremely limited knowledge of Africa. Composed between 1100 and 1150 and generally considered the foundation epic of French literature, the poem depicts a massive battle between Charlemagne's Christian forces and the combined might of the Muslim world. Although conclusions are difficult to draw since many of the place names used have not been positively, or even tentatively, identified, those that can be recognized are limited to the areas known to classical antiquity: the Mediterranean coast, Egypt, Ethiopia. Similarly, Joinville's *Vie de saint Louis* or *Life of Saint Louis*, an eyewitness account of the Seventh and Eighth Crusades written in the early 1300's, limits its references to African geography to the fringes of the Mediterranean. In both texts, there is no coherent idea of something called Africa, only a collection of regions lying near each other.

As at so many times throughout history, the Nile is the corridor to the African interior for medieval French writers,

and the only mention of any area beyond the Mediterranean
littoral is of the upper Nile. The legend of Ethiopia as the
Christian kingdom of Prester John, though widespread at the
time, finds no echo in the *Chanson de Roland*, for the
country is listed as belonging to one of the Muslim chiefs, and
called "a cursed land" ["une terre maudite"] (161 [CXLIII])[1].
Joinville, who had been to Egypt and Tunisia on crusade with
Louis IX, takes the opposite point of view, stating that the
Nile flows through "earthly paradise" ["Paradis terrestre"]
(121 [187]) before entering Egypt. He describes this
mysterious place as a land full of strange plants and animals
that stare at explorers sent by the Sultan of Cairo, a kind of
positive exoticism that would find many echoes in Western
attitudes, and his account may be the first example of this
trend in European literature. Joinville mentions Prester John
in other passages, placing him in an ill-defined Asia where he
fights against Persians and Mongols, but mentions no
connection between the fabled Christian monarch and
Ethiopia. Indeed, Joinville's description of the upper Nile
contains no mention of any human inhabitants, leaving
readers with the impression that only wild animals live there;
if Africa is perfect, it is so without Africans.

   This ambivalence about the African interior--is it blessed
or cursed?--is reflected in the depiction of Africans in the
Chanson de Roland. Geography is less important than
ideology, and Africans are condemned not as members of a
different race but as adherents of a rival religion and therefore
enemies of Christ. The Muslim world is shown as a negative
double of Christian Europe, in which kings lead their feudal
lords into battle to defend the faith and win glory;
Charlemagne's Twelve Peers, an obvious imitation of the
apostles, fight against twelve Islamic noblemen. In this
aristocratic atmosphere even the enemy must have certain
positive traits in order to be a formidable foe worth defeating:
Corsalis of Barbary, the one clearly African member of these
twelve Muslims, "knows the evil arts" ["sait les arts
maléfiques"] (177 [LXXI]) but still "speaks as a true baron:
for all God's gold he would not want to commit an act of
cowardice" ["parle en vrai baron: pour tout l'or de Dieu il ne
voudrait faire une couardise"] (177 [LXXI]). The portrait of
another champion of Islam, presumably African though it is
never stated, edges closer to judgment based on race: named

Abisme, or Abyss, he is "full of vices and great crimes... as black as melted shoe polish" ["plein de vices et de grands crimes... aussi noir que poix fondue"] (125 [CXIII]). Black skin, it seems, is starting to be associated with evil.

Joinville shows slightly more objectivity and interest in learning about other cultures. He acknowledges the good even in particular Arabs who held the French army prisoners, and takes time out from his narrative to describe the life of Bedouins, whom he recognizes as a distinct ethnic group, separate from the other Arabs. But he shows little understanding of his African enemies: the term Turks ["Turs"] is used interchangeably with Saracens ["Sarrazins"] as though the two were the same (114, 118, 120-21, 123-24, 127, 128, 164-65 [155, 173-76, 185-86, 197-99, 217, 220, 391-94]). To him, and to Western Europeans of his time, they are: both mean Muslim and consequently enemy. The enduring image of Africa presented by Medieval French writers is that of hostile Islam.

Writers of the French Enlightenment show a different kind of ambivalence toward Africa, and lay the foundations of attitudes later to play a vital role in Europe's relationship with the continent. Fénelon's *Télémaque* or *Telemachus*, written in the 1690's to instruct the heir to the French throne in proper statecraft, is remarkably similar to texts written two or three hundred years later, and may lie at their ideological origin. It is difficult to draw solid conclusions about the places depicted in the novel, for it is a *roman à clef* that uses a facade of classical antiquity to represent Europe at the time of Louis XIV, but it is still interesting to note that, while Egypt is presented as a model of a well-governed state, a nameless African interior is chosen as the wild and uncouth land in need of civilization. Other regions in Spain and Greece are shown as simple and rustic, but in a positive way; only Africa outside Egypt is barbaric. Clearly, the modern tendency to consider Egypt a Mediterranean state like Greece or Rome, divorced from Africa, had already begun. The inhabitants of this wasteland are "shepherds as savage as the country itself" ["des bergers aussi sauvages que le pays même"] (87-88), and the tigers and bears with which they share the land show how little the author knew or cared about what Africa was really like. Furthermore, all that is necessary to uplift these poor benighted souls is the beneficent presence of an educated

European, Ulysses's son Telemachus: two centuries before Kipling, the White Man's Burden is already here.

Later Enlightenment philosophers show the increase in geographical knowledge brought about by the commerce of the eighteenth century but retain similar attitudes toward Africans. Montesquieu's epistolary novel *Lettres persanes* or *Persian Letters*, written in the 1720's, makes reference to French navigators on the Guinea coast; thirty years later, Rousseau describes inhabitants of the Congo and the Cape in his *Discours sur l'origine de l'inégalité* or *Discourse on the Origin of Inequality*. Furthermore, European scholars were becoming more aware of the limits to their knowledge at this time, and Montesquieu repeatedly states that little can be said about the interior of Africa because it is unknown. What information was available, however, was almost invariably drawn from one source: the slave trade. For writers of the period, Africa was essentially a source of slaves, and little else about it mattered. Enlightenment philosophers are nearly unanimous in condemning this commerce. Chapter 19 of Voltaire's *Candide* shows a miserable, mutilated victim of the trade as an example of man's cruelty, and in the *Lettres persanes* Montesquieu displays graphically the abuse suffered by slaves in Asia. In his later work of political science, *L'Esprit des lois* or *The Spirit of the Laws*, a famous passage dripping with sarcasm offers a series of frail arguments in favor of slavery:

> Sugar would be too expensive, if we didn't have the plant that produces it worked by slaves.
>
> Those of whom we are speaking are black from the soles of their feet to their heads; and they have such flat noses it is almost impossible to pity them.
>
> One cannot accept the idea that God, who is a very wise being, put a soul, and above all a good soul, in a completely black body.
>
> It is impossible for us to suppose that those people are men; because, if we supposed they were men, one would start to believe that we ourselves are not Christians.
>
> *[Le sucre serait trop cher, si l'on ne faisait travailler la plante qui le produit par des esclaves.*

Ceux dont il s'agit sont noirs depuis les pieds jusqu'à la tête; et ils ont le nez si écrasé qu'il est presque impossible de les plaindre.

On ne peut se mettre dans l'idée que Dieu, qui est un être très sage, ait mis une âme, et surtout une âme bonne, dans un corps tout noir.

Il est impossible que nous supposions que ces gens-là soient des hommes; parce que, si nous les supposions des hommes, on commencerait à croire que nous ne sommes pas nous-mêmes chrétiens.] (vol. 2, 59-60 [XV, 5])

Yet at the same time as they condemn the slave trade, French Enlightenment writers consider Africans themselves primitive and barbaric. Continuing in Fénelon's wake, Montesquieu describes the absurd vanity of a king on the Guinea coast seated "on his throne, that is to say on a piece of wood, as proud as if he had been on that of the Great Mogul" ["sur son trône, c'est-à-dire sur un morceau de bois, aussi fier que s'il eût été sur celui du Grand Mogol"] (80 [XLIV]). Nor can this be construed positively as justifiable pride: Montesquieu scornfully goes on: "all his ornaments and those of the queen, his wife, consisted of their black skin and some rings" ["tous ses ornements et ceux de la reine, sa femme, consistaient en leur peau noire et quelques bagues"] (80 [XLIV]). Voltaire carries the degradation further and explicitly links it to race. A servant girl in *Candide* insists that Africans are naturally given to violence and sexual excess: "Northern peoples don't have hot enough blood. They don't have the mania for women to the extent that it is common in Africa. It seems that your Europeans have milk in their veins; it's acid, it's fire that flows in those of the inhabitants of Mount Atlas and the neighboring countries" ["Les peuples septentrionaux n'ont pas le sang assez ardent. Ils n'ont pas la rage des femmes au point où elle est commune en Afrique. Il semble que vos Européens aient du lait dans les veines; c'est du vitriol, c'est du feu qui coule dans celles des habitants de mont Atlas et des pays voisins"] (163). Another of Voltaire's philosophical stories, *La Princesse de Babylone* or *The Princess of Babylon*, shows a king of Ethiopia who violently ravages Egypt and is killed when found in bed with a rival's girl; in his *Dictionnaire philosophique* or *Philosophical Dictionary*, Voltaire asserts that the Siberians and Hottentots of his time, though superior to early primitive man, are nevertheless "animals that live six months of the year in caves, where they eat ravenously the vermin by which they are eaten" ["des animaux qui vivent six mois de l'année dans des cavernes, où ils mangent à pleines mains la vermine dont ils sont mangés"] (Lagarde and Michard 180). Rousseau takes most of his examples of admirable primitive man from classical antiquity or America, but cites some Africans as savages; though intended positively, the label continues the depiction of Africa as a wild, uncivilized place. The most alarming characteristic of this trend is the philosophers' attempts to find a scientific basis for judgments of racial inequality. Despite his opposition to the cruelty of the slave trade, Montesquieu suggests that the influence of climate on people's willingness to work may justify slavery in some countries; specifically, it is in tropical climates that forced labor could be justified, while in Europe it is clearly unacceptable. Montesquieu hesitates to accept the conclusion of his own argument, but others go further. Voltaire, another outspoken critic of slavery's barbaric treatment of its victims, still organizes humanity into separate races, not descended from a common ancestor but created distinct from each other, among whom the black race occupies the bottom rank. "Negroes are beings almost as savage, as ugly as monkeys" ["les Nègres sont des êtres presque aussi sauvages, aussi laids que les singes"] (Duchet 28), which explains, even if it cannot justify, their relegation to slavery by higher races. Even Rousseau, the admirer of primitive peoples, discusses reported Congo animals half way between men and monkeys, thus opening the door to evolutionary theories that declare Africans to be subhuman, or less human than the rest of humanity.

The philosophers of the French Enlightenment thus have a complex view of Africa. If the slave trade is an abomination that should be abolished, its victims are no less primitive for their sufferings; Africa may not deserve its fate, but all the worst things said about it are true, and can be explained through science. The irony is that these contradictory attitudes toward the continent and its inhabitants would both give fuel to the scramble for Africa: colonial ventures would be justified by the endlessly repeated mantra of ending the slave trade and spreading civilization. In this way those who were at least in one sense Africa's first defenders against European depredation would provide the excuse for full-scale invasion and conquest a century later.

Writers of the colonial era have more first-hand information about Africa but echo some of the attitudes of their predecessors. Their geographical knowledge is greater than that of earlier authors; Daudet's comic novella *Tartarin de Tarascon*, written in the 1870's, gives extensive descriptions of French-controlled Algeria, which had been thoroughly explored by Europeans. But the role of this Europeanized colony in the mind of the story's French characters shows how little was still known of the rest of Africa. To Tartarin and his friends in southern France, the Algerian coast is indistinguishable from the heart of the Sahara, the Congo rain forest, or even other exotic places on different continents; six hundred years after the *Life of Saint Louis*, these Frenchmen still lump all Africans together under the inaccurate name of "Turks." The very fact that Daudet mocks their ignorance, however, ridiculing the would-be lion killer's disillusionment in a heavily Europeanized colony that refuses to live up to his romantic preconceptions, suggests that at least educated Europeans were starting to know something of African realities. Sixty years later, Bardamu, the narrator of Céline's *Voyage au bout de la nuit* or *Journey to the Depths of Night*, discovers a colonial Africa in which European administrators have mapped all of Africa for purposes of control but have little interest in knowing what lies beyond their town or village. To those in the rain forest belt, the interior is simply unbroken wilderness, all the same and not worth exploring.

This lack of interest or energy seems to flow inevitably from the conception of Africa among Europeans at the time. If a single central trait common to French texts of this period can be found, it is the view of Africa as a land of moral decay, corrupt and corrupting. Both Daudet and Céline present most Africans as degenerate in every possible way: the Arabs who entertain Tartarin never fail to charge him for their hospitality; a religious leader courts Tartarin's mistress under cover of delivering the Muslim call to prayer. Bardamu's young African guide not only offers his own sexual services but is quite willing to bring his sister; the forest tribe around his trading station sell him to slave dealers; they, like

Tartarin's black porters, steal everything they can. But this constant depravity is not limited to Africans: European expatriates are just as corrupt. Most of them are, in one way or another, the dregs of Europe, and have come to Africa to make their fortune in ways that would land them in jail at home. Tartarin is fooled and cheated by a pretended Montenegrin prince, in reality a convicted swindler just out of prison in France, who exploits his naivete and ultimately runs off with his wallet. Bardamu goes to Africa to start over after his release from a mental institution, and among his colleagues in the colonial company he finds an endless array of get-rich-quick schemes based on fraud and embezzlement. Bardamu himself ends up burning his trading post and fleeing into the forest with the money his predecessor left behind at the station. Any ideas of personal integrity seem to melt in the African heat.

In this context, the colonial ideology of the white man's civilizing mission can only be a joke. Daudet characterizes the native inhabitants of French Algeria as "a savage and rotten people whom we are civilizing by giving them our vices" ["Un peuple sauvage et pourri que nous civilisons, en lui donnant nos vices"] (161). Céline shows the colonial administration reducing the Africans to slavery to build roads that lead nowhere and are quickly engulfed by the jungle, an apt symbol for the entire colonial venture. He puts in the mouth of the trading company director a eulogy of colonial exploitation almost as comically acerbic as Montesquieu's defense of slavery: "Peanuts and rubber!... To pay the tax! The tax to make more rubber and peanuts come to us! That's life, Bardamu! Peanuts! Peanuts and rubber!" ["Des cacahuètes et du cahoutchouc!... Pour payer l'impôt! L'impôt pour faire venir à nous du caoutchouc et des cacahuètes encore! C'est la vie Bardamu! Cacahuètes! Cacahuètes et caoutchouc!"] (185). The comparison to Montesquieu is revealing in several ways, for, like Montesquieu and his contemporaries, Céline heaps scorn on both African savagery and European exploitation; moreover, following Montesquieu in particular, even if unconsciously, he attributes all this vice to the tropical climate, which brings out the worst in everyone. If white people are already vicious and cruel in Europe, they get worse in Africa, where "their rot invades the surface as soon as the vulgar fever of the tropics stirs them" ["leur pourriture envahit la surface dès que les émoustille la fièvre ignoble des tropiques"] (149). Clearly nothing good can live long here.

Both Céline and Daudet build on the most negative attitudes of previous writers in their depiction of Africa. Rejecting the positive, valorizing exoticism of the Romantic period and of some colonial authors, they present such a negative conception of Africa, devoid of beauty and adventure, full of disease and degeneracy, that it leads inevitably to one persistent question: what are the French doing in Africa? What can possibly justify, or even logically motivate, their presence there? To this penetrating query neither Daudet nor Céline can give a satisfying answer.

These three periods of French literature reveal three moments in Europe's relationship with Africa. Moving from the Middle Ages to the Enlightenment to the colonial period, one sees an evolution of ideas from Africa the infidel to Africa the abused but savage victim to Africa the land of corruption. Clearly many of the attitudes toward the continent that can still be heard today have deep roots: fear of Islam; imaginings of an exotic earthly paradise that has every form of life, except human inhabitants; contempt for perceived backwardness and savagery; assertions of racial inferiority; belief that corruption is inherent and inevitable on African soil. While some of these attitudes may have played a constructive role in abolishing the slave trade and advancing African independence, their continuation today can only be harmful to African development. Those who make it their task to oppose these time-honored prejudices need to know how and why they arose among European intellectuals. To face them today, one might quote again from Voltaire, hardly an Afrophile, who nevertheless provided a forceful reply to the power of entrenched injustice in his philosophical story *Zadig.* Discussing an imminent human sacrifice, one character asks, "Is there anything more respectable than an ancient abuse?" ["Y a-t-il rien de plus respectable qu'un ancien abus?"], to which Zadig responds: "Reason is more ancient" ["La raison est plus ancienne"] (55).

Notes

[1] Page numbers refer to the edition named in the list of works cited. For some sources further information is given in brackets: stanza number in the *Chanson de Roland*, paragraph number in the *Vie de saint Louis*, letter number in *Lettres persanes*, book and chapter number in *L 'Esprit des lois*.

Works Cited

----, *La Chanson de Roland*. Paris: Union générale d'éditions, 1982.

Céline, Louis-Ferdinand. *Voyage au bout de la nuit*. Paris: Folio, Editions Gallimard, 1952.

Daudet, Alphonse. *Tartarin de Tarascon*. Paris: Garnier-Flammarion, 1968.

Duchet, Michèle. "Le temps des philosophes." *Notre Librairie* 90 (Oct.-Dec. 1987): 25-33.

Fénélon, François de Salignac de La Mothe. *Les Aventures de Télémaque*. Paris: Garnier-Flammarion, 1968.

Joinville, Jean de. *Vie de saint Louis*. Sherbrooke: Editions Naaman, 1977.

Lagarde, André, and Laurent Michard. *XVIIIe Siècle*. Paris: Bordas, 1970.

Montesquieu, Charles-Louis de. *De l'esprit des lois*. Paris: Nouveaux Classiques Larousse, 1971.

----. *Lettres persanes*. Paris: Garnier-Flammarion, 1964.

Rousseau, Jean-Jacques. *Discours sur l'origine et les fondements de l'inégalité parmi les hommes*. Paris: Garnier-Flammarion, 1971.

Voltaire. *Romans et contes*. Paris: Folio, Editions Gallimard, 1972.

PART III
Africa, Orientalism and the West

The North African *Motif* in Early American Fiction

Mongi Bahloul,
University of Sfax, Tunisia

Introduction

This paper will be an attempt to disclose a long-continued life of the North African *motif* in early American fiction. First, some data will be supplied to show that the American reading public in the late eighteenth century was interested in "things" Moor (North African). Then, fictional material about North Africa and accounts of Moorish life and histories will be identified through a survey of American magazine publications between 1788 and 1799. As a way of further investigating this issue, a few samples of that fiction will be scrutinised. The aim is to isolate "recurrent patterns" which seem to characterise most of these tales and reports. It will be argued that the African tale has its own specificity and anomalies which may challenge existing models of structural analysis, or at least call for some adjustment. Finally, the conclusions that might be reached and the reflections that will be made are not intended to be definitive.

I. Fascination with "things" North African

Data about post-colonial America show unmistakable signs of American interest in things North African. The readers of the period (1790's) developed a taste for subjects and events related to the part of Africa known as the Greater Maghreb. It includes Egypt, Libya, Tunisia, Algeria, Morocco and Mauritania. This "Afrophilia" can be evidenced through a survey of what was said or written about the region and its people in early American fiction, and most importantly what was currently published in American magazines during the 1780's and 1790's.

A. Background Information

The fascination with the Orient and North Africa was part of a greater tradition which had started in Europe with the advent of the Crusades. It found its artistic expression in Elizabethan and Jacobean drama. One example would be *Lust's Dominion* (1590), a tragedy by Thomas Dekker. The structure of the play is built upon the Moorish figure of Eleazar who through eight soliloquies and ten asides informs the audience of the progress of his ambitious designs. His purpose is to gain vengeance for his father's loss of life and kingdom and his own capture by the "Spanish Tyrant;" he openly voices his intention to "drown Spain with her own proud blood" then make "an ark of carcasses" and "sail in blood to hell"[1]. The Moor is helped in his plans by the Queen Mother whose husband, King Philippo of Spain, is dying. The king chooses his eldest son, Fernando, to succeed him but Prince Philip contests this succession and accuses his mother of making a plot to remove the king with the help of her lover Eleazar. All the blame is then put on the Moor who is called villain and an African demon. Eleazar and the Queen organize the murder of the Prince and the Cardinal, then they both flee away to Portugal to savour their burning passion for each other. Eventually Eleazar mounts the throne of Spain but towards the end, Philip and Hortenzo enter disguised as Moors after having killed Baltazar and Zarack, Eleazar's guards, and Philip stabs the Moor.

The best illustration of the Moorish image would undoubtedly be Shakespeare's *Othello* in 1604. Othello the Moor, a soldier and traveller, has succeeded in winning the love of Desdemona, the daughter of a Venetian Senator and has married her. Jealousy, intrigue and lust for power have led the Moorish general into a series of murders and ultimately a self-inflicted death. As Eldred Jones (1965) points out, the Moor, as an African, is given an exceptional treatment in this play even in comparison with an earlier representation by Shakespeare himself in *Titus Andronicus* (1604). According to Jones, the originality of this treatment lies in Shakespeare's maturity as a dramatist. In *Othello*, he is a creator rather than a follower of popular taste.

B. The North African Image in Early American Fiction:

In America, it was through Royall Tyler's major fictional piece *The Algerine Captive* that the Moorish image came into artistic shape adding thus more fuel to the already existing interest in Africa. Tyler himself testified to that growing interest when he noted that the reading taste of Americans had changed in a very short time, that works of sensation and amusement (probably referring to his own African novel) had replaced those of instruction, and he added that such tales were sending masses of people into such agreeable state of terror that they felt afraid to go to bed on their own.

With regard to Tyler's *The Algerine Captive*, subtitled *The Life and Adventures of Doctor Updike Underhill, Six years a Prisoner among the Algerines*, the principal character, Dr. Underhill, announced himself as the author of his own adventures. In his Preface to the book, he has his friend comment on the topic:

> Your captivity among the Algerines, with some notices to the manners of that ferocious race, so dreaded by commercial powers, and so little known in our own country, would at least be interesting.[2]

The exotic aspects of the novel had wide appeal, as is shown in a favourable review of the book which appeared in the *Portfolio* for 1802:

> The *Algerine Captive*, written by R.Tyler (is) a work of much merit and for which we are happy to see a late and increasing demand... A

second edition of his book ... is greatly
wanted. [3]

Ultimately, this novel must be judged in conjunction with
the whole body of magazine literature about North Africa
produced during the post-colonial period. Indeed, prior to the
publication of *The Algerine Captive*, there had been a plethora of
African tales, travel accounts and anecdotes, as we shall see in
the following section.

C. American Magazine Literature on North Africa (1788-1799):

The corpus which has been collected for the purpose of this
study covers all early American magazine publications on North
Africa from 1788 to 1799. The material has been restricted
within the narrow limits of what is presently known as the
Maghreb (the United Maghreb), that is, Tunisia, Algeria and
Morocco. The abundance of literature written on Egypt makes its
inclusion rather difficult as the scope of this paper is fairly
limited. In an attempt to have a representative sample, no less
than twenty five magazines have been consulted and all their
issues over the 12-year period have been scrutinised for tales,
accounts, anecdotes, apologues or news about the above-cited
North African countries. What follows is a brief presentation of
the identified material. [4]

(i) A Presentation of North African Material

"Facts respecting Africa" was the title of a 2-page article
published in *The American Magazine* for November 1788. The
report gives a detailed description of African climate, land and
habits in the Northern part of the continent. The accuracy of the
data that have been provided remains debatable.

In March 1789, *The Massachusetts Magazine* reproduced a
lengthy study about Algeria; the article is entitled "Concise
History of the Algerines." The same subject was further
investigated in two subsequent issues. Scenes of African distress
were highlighted in a series of poems that were published in *The
American Museum; or, Universal Magazine* for October 1789.

Misery, poverty and ill-health in Africa were described and discussed in a poetic language.

Starting November 1789, *The Columbian Magazine* issued a series of accounts on the History of Morocco. The serialized excerpts contained Moorish anecdotes and vivid descriptions focusing mainly on Muley Ishmael's reign and leadership over the western part of North Africa. In a similar way, Tunis and Algiers were depicted at some length in an article entitled "The Jealousy shown by the Mohamedans to European travellers." These reflections appeared in the December 1790 issue of *the New York Magazine.* The account presented the Tunisian and Algerian Moors under a negative light.

Turkish baths or "saunas" have always been popular and well-frequented by North Africans. *The Universal Asylum and Columbian Magazine* for February 1791 addressed the question in an article entitled "Turkish Baths." The setting is "Barbary" land (a reference to North Africa), and the main actor is a Moor who gives a European traveller full massage culminating in an orgasm. In an earlier issue, the same magazine published an extract from M. de Brison's *Account of the Shipwreck and Captivity.* The passage describes the life and behaviour of Arab females at home and in the fields. The images which have been drawn of Moorish women are tainted with a sense of contempt.

A similar topic was touched upon in the *Massachusetts Magazine* for August 1792. The author shed light on how Moorish women dressed. Throughout the description, there was an attempt to present things as they historically occurred. Still in 1792, *The American Apollo* published a report on the Dey of Algiers in which he was depicted as one of "the petty tyrants of Africa," blood-thirsty when holding those "piratical posts of Barbarity."

The New York Magazine for February 1793 issued "Selico: An African Tale." At about the same time "Ishmael: A Moorish Tale" appeared in another issue of the same magazine. The nine-page account describes the life of the Moors and their land in a way that caters to the public taste for exotic sentiments. Love, violence, intrigue and wild passion are the main ingredients of major incidents in the plot. "The justice of the Sultan Sandjar" is the title of yet another African tale which appeared in *The Massachusetts Magazine* for 1793 with Algiers as a setting and the Moors as brutal and villainous characters. That brutality was further discussed in the June 1793 issue under "The Quarrels of the Moors." The issue also contained "The Vindictive Moor: an African Tale" reflecting a plot which was much in line with "The Wretched Taillah," another African tale published at about the same date in *The New Hampshire Magazine*. "The Wretched Taillah" gives a horrendous account of how slaves were caught and sold to American traders on North African shores. A love affair was also inserted as a flavour to the narrative structure.

Throughout 1794, American magazines published very little about North Africa. The interest seems to have shifted further East with masses of material on Turkey, Irak, Persia and Egypt. Similarly, Gothic stories increased considerably during that year. The reasons for this shift are beyond the scope of this paper.

A regain of interest in things African would be witnessed in 1795 with more Moorish material making the headlines of most American magazines. *The literary Miscellany*, for example, published "Obidah; or, the Journey of a Day." The story is set in the North African wilderness and it involves Moorish and European characters. In another issue printed the same year, "The Story of Abbas" was presented. Again, the setting is the Atlas region and the content abounds in unexpected happenings and dramatic incidents where "love" is a recipe for disaster.

In September and December of 1795, *The Massachusetts Magazine* allocated some space to North Africa. First, it reproduced an article from Chenier's account of Morocco. The personality traits and reign of a Moroccan Emperor were described and commented upon. Then, the December issue run an African tale entitled "The Sultan and his Vizir; or, the Sultan who received a blow." A 3-page report on Moorish women was also included. Both tale and report provide a detailed and vivid description of life styles and customs in North Africa.

The series of North African tales continued in 1796. For instance, "The History of Selim, from the Armenian letters" appeared in *The Rural Magazine*; or, *Vermont Repository* and "Phedima and Abensar" was published in *The Massachusetts Magazine*. Once more, "love," piracy, slavery, and physical violence make up the usual recipe for such Moorish anecdotes.

The North African flame gained more momentum throughout 1797 with more material published in American magazines and newspapers. *The South Carolina Weekly Museum* contained "The Twin-brothers of Mezzorania." The events of the story occur "amidst the extensive wilds of Africa; the main characters are black Moors, tawny Moors and negroes. About the same period, *the New York Weekly Magazine* published the story of "The Great Almanza, King of Cordova in Spain." The tale was supplemented with the King's book of maxims and other accounts testifying to his courage. In another issue, the magazine printed a number of Arabian maxims originating in North Africa. In its April issue, *The Methodist Magazine* carried "a remarkable instance of honour," a narrative in which a Moor offered protection to a Spaniard wanted for killing a Moorish boy. The victim happened to be the protector's son. Faithful to his word of honour, the bereaved Moor helped the assassin to escape. In its spring issue of 1797, *the New York Weekly Magazine* devoted the front page to an article entitled "The African's Complaint." The report denounces the ill-treatment of slaves captured on North African Soil.

More reports on North African urban life appeared in *the Literary Museum* and *the American Universal Magazine* between June and November 1797. These are a few examples:

* "An account of the city of Morocco" is a translation from the French of Mr. Chenier. It is a 6-page description of the people of Morocco and their way of life. The Moroccan Royal family is put under scrutiny; whole sections describe the Emperor's hedonistic habits and his sexual indulgence.

* "The advantages of cleanliness in preventing infectious diseases" gives a grim picture of Algiers when a prey to the great pestilence. Cleanliness and its merits in preventing the spread of the virus have been discussed in connection with the Mohamedan faith.

The reviewed magazines for the year 1798 revealed more material about North Africa and an increasing interest in the exotic lands of the Mediterranean sea. For instance, the *Key,* the *Weekly Magazine,* and the *Rural Magazine* for the period running between February and December 1798 carried further tales and reports about North Africa. Most scenes are set either in Algiers or in major Moroccan seaports. The writers showed little interest in any moral judgement of the Moors; they did however express serious concern about a burning issue in their days: The question of the African world as a way of life and a value system different from anything American at that time. Examples of the tales reviewed are "Schah Abbas the Great," "Abu-Cacem's Slippers" and "Selico: an African tale," among others.

(ii) Reflections on the Presented Material

In the foregoing pages we have traced the African fiction through American magazines from 1788 to 1799. It now remains to present a few reflections on this subject:

- Identical stories or reports were published in several magazines in different parts of the country and at different times. For example, "Selico: An African Tale" first appeared in the *New York Magazine* for February 1793, then it was re-printed as a serial publication in the *Philadelphia Minerva* from February to March 1798. Similarly, the account entitled "Contrast between the African and Christian Soldier" was initially written in *The New York Magazine* for April 1796, and in August 1798, the same material re-appeared in the *Rural Casket*.

- It was not unusual for a story to appear in a different magazine without any reference to its source or to its former appearance and very often under a different title. For instance, the *Dessert to the True American* for Monday 22, 1799 carried the story entitled "Algerine Justice." The same story had already been published in the *Rural Magazine* for Saturday, November 3, 1798 under the caption of "The Difficulty of Concealing Guilt: the Story of an Algerine."

- With regard to workmanship, most reviewed material is less than satisfactory, especially the longer pieces (usually tales run in several issues of a magazine). The phraseology is awkward; the idioms are obscure; the sentences are often involved and frequently unintelligible. The compositions are wrought with no respect for plot, for coherence, or for proportion. Events and occurrences are piled one on the other so rapidly that even to the most gullible they are hardly plausible today. The embedded structure characterises many tales. There are layers beneath layers within a single narrative. Perhaps spiral ways of thinking and circular forms of telling are an African legacy. Embedding has been noted in "Schah Abbas the Great," "Anecdotes of the Moors," and "Selico: An African tale." There seems to be no sense of direction in the tales and this explains why it is hard to pin them down to any definitive structure of the type suggested in the works of contemporary narratologists such as Tomashevski, Propp and Labov.[5] Their models, it has been argued, have mainly focused on the Western tradition of story-telling and can hardly accommodate the peculiarities of Oriental and African stories.[6] Identification of recurrent motifs may therefore help us to define a tentative structure of an African narrative, as we shall see in the final section of this essay.

II. Characteristic Motifs of North African Tales and Accounts

The interest in story-telling is not a new phenomenon; it goes back as far as the time of Aristotle and other philosophers of Ancient Greece. In fact, the Aristotelian definition of "narrative" as "a work with a narrator" is still of great significance to modern critics and narratologists.[7] Although narrow in scope, this definition applies to such literary genres as the novel, the short story, or the tale . The term "tale" is defined for this matter as a story involving adventure or supernatural phenomena; it may also refer to a written account of things that might have happened, especially one that is very interesting and exciting. Here we shall be concerned mainly with the narrative as a semiotic representation of a series of events.[8] The level of analysis will be restricted to "story" as opposed to "plot," in E.M Forster's terms, or *fabula* as distinct from *suitzhet*.[9] I will therefore try to point out in some of the African, Moorish tales identified earlier a number of "recurrent patterns," and see how these may constitute the architectural layout of the African narrative and its structural complexity.

I am aware that I have, with due credit to Labov and Waletzky[10] for the suggestion, employed a similar technique to theirs. In my study, however, the aim is simply to arrive at a tabulation of the recurrent motifs in which the thirty tales are based, and at the same time assess their conformity to or departure from the established norms of narration. The result of my investigation follows.

1. Luxury

All thirty tales that have been surveyed contain elements and descriptions of the splendor of the Mediterranean. They offer vivid accounts of the luxury and beauty of the women of Tunis, Algiers, Oran and cities of Morocco. In "The History of Selim," Zaida, the Moorish lady, is described to have an exceptional beauty and an irresistible charm. When she "threw back her veil" for the first time, Selim was so taken up by her beautiful looks that he "could not take [his] eyes from the window." Similarly, Moorish women in "Dress of the Moorish women" are portrayed as the most beautiful virgins of Africa. Their beauty, the narrator adds, is without equal and their "cheeks were as fresh as the roses of the morning," with glittering solid gold rings and necklaces hanging from various parts of their body: "At the upper part of each ear hangs a gold ring which has at one end a cluster of precious stones."

Other aspects of opulence appear through the detailed descriptions of the fabulous dinners of Kings and Sultans. The ruler of Algiers in "Anecdote of Schah Abbas" was "more luxurious than became so great a prince." His empire is measured by the great "variety of dishes at his table; some were sent to him from the Euphrates, others from Mauritania and the Caspian Sea." There are frequent references to the evening entertainment in the richly decorated harem of the lady of the grand vizier or Kahya, and the marvellous, fantastic landscape of palaces and mansions, as described in "Character of the Emperor of Morocco."

Nearly all tales depict the wonders and exotic sides of Barbary land. You read of wealth and grandeur in places like Algiers, Carthage, Tunis, so much so that such descriptions become ingrained in the mind, and will thus be associated with any tale of this kind. There is no linear pattern to the narration as these descriptive elements appear at many stages of the narration process. In terms of the Labovian framework, the scenic details in the African tales and the motif of luxury may approximate the category called "ORIENTATION"[11] as their effect conveys a picture of time, place, and behavioural situations. In a way, they set the tone and atmosphere of the story, and pave the path for a host of events that will lead to the gradual unfolding of the plot.

2. Royalty

The "Royalty" Motif applies to characters such as Sultans, Viziers, Caliphs, Deys, Cadis, Sheikhs, tribe dignitaries. Most reviewed tales have room for one, two or more of these character types. The power notion has been employed with varying skill and importance depending on the nature and length of the story. One thing is certain, though; these people who hold the reins of power have also the key for the complicating action in Labovian terms. They order the killing of subjects, they capture and torture foes, and they administer justice in special courts. If they are not directly involved in the making of events, they are certainly behind them. For example, the Turkish Agha in "The History of Selim" and the Emperor of Morocco in "Anecdotes of the Moor" have no active role in the course of the narration but their names are repeatedly mentioned with the effect that their presence is strongly felt in the course of the narrative. They also act as catalysts in the power game and its related intrigues within and without the royal palace, inside or outside the kingdom.

In addition to their significant roles at the "COMPLICATION"[12] stage, kings, sultans, and bashas have a say in terms of assessing the events and their developments. The same is true for viziers, and other ruling agents in the stories.

3. Slavery

Another recurrent motif of the African fables deals with the harem. Let it be understood that in the broad context of Oriental fiction, this refers to changing seraglios, eunuchs, palanquins, astrologers, hermits, young boys (ghulems), caged maidens, dervishes, or persons who have been sold or bought as slaves. This last category is most predominant in the North African context.

The tales abound in details describing this last faction of people. For example, in "The story of an Algerine," slaves are "permitted either by shop-keeping or otherwise and on paying their master a certain sum, to earn a little money for themselves." The plot describes the hardships endured by a slave who lost all his savings to a "respectable" thief. The Dey of Algiers assesses the situation and administers justice as the victim lies "prostrated on the carpet at the foot of the throne." Similarly, "The History of Selim" gives a lengthy account of how slaves are treated during their captivity in North Africa; this is conveyed by a long string of events leading to a very complicated situation. Selim thus relates his history: "I was with five others, sold to a young Moor, and conveyed with my companions to a spacious house" near Oran, and then "confined to severe labour." On the whole, African fables exemplify incidents in which persons are bought or sold as slaves with special focus on the inhuman aspect of this trade.

4. Piracy

Like "slavery," "piracy" is a dominant feature of most African tales. The Corsairs of the Barbary Coast were, in plain language, pirates. The Mediterranean had always been plagued by piracy. Algiers was often described as Barbarossa's fiefdom and a base for corsairs who were capable of defeating the fleets of Europe. Commerce in the Mediterranean became a competition to seize and hold hostages for ransom. In Tunis, as stated in one account, the hostages were held in the bagnio at la Goulette. That place still stands and is open to visitors.

The reviewed material tends to portray that period as a contest between high-minded Christians and odious, throat-slitting Muslims. For instance, when European pirates, known as the hard men of the Atlantic, were hired by the beys, they had to "take the turban," i.e. declaring themselves Muslim. In one account, they were driven around Tunis in a cart with a portrait of Christ held upside down. Another requirement for a piracy contract with the Beys was circumcision. This part of the initiation rites could come as a shock. So keen was the Bey of Tunis to secure the services of the English baronet Sir Henry Mainwaring (B.A. Oxon), who was described as "the most accomplished pirate of his time" [13] (he had his own fleet), that the Bey offered to waive the circumcision clause. Sir Henry nevertheless declined the offer.

Sir Henry was an exception. In another tale, Captain Ward readily accepted the deal and confronted the circumcision test with courage and fortitude. He was described as about 55, nearly bald, and with a fringe of white hair around a swarthy face. "Speaks little, always swearing. Drunk from morn till night. Most prodigal and plucky. Sleeps a great deal. A fool, an idiot out of his trade."

The ordinary men were even worse. "They carry their swords at their sides," a disapproving Frenchman noted in one of the travel account. "they run drunk through the town; they sleep with the wives of Moor; in brief every kind of debauchery and unchecked licence is permitted to them." In another report about these pirates, it was stated that:

> The great profit that the English bring to the country, their profuse liberality and the excessive debauches in which they spend their money before leaving the town and returning to war (thus they call their *brigandage* at sea) has made them cherished by the janissaries above all other nations.

The expulsion of the Moors from Spain was vividly described in a number of tales and the displaced people, mostly Tunisian Berbers, returned to the land of their ancestors and to grim economic prospects. The ports of Tunisia and the rest of the Barbary Coast were depicted as "clogged by idle men with sea-faring skills running deep into their veins." This population often turned into piracy as a profession and like the Europeans they would be hired by the beys to man the many pirate fleets operating along the Barbary Coast.

5. Mystery

In their discussion of the section on "EVALUATION," Labov and Waletzky state that "there is an appeal to the element of mystery in most of the narratives."[14] This is certainly true in the tales under examination. The African fiction produces no end of mysterious effects, and supernatural manifestations. Very illustrative examples of these are found in most tales which have been "visited." The atmosphere of mystery is often conveyed by natural phenomena such as forked lightning, roar of thunder, "sulphurous" clouds, driving storm of hail and rain, horrid darkness, "hoarse" roaring of the sea, rocking of earth, walls falling with great force, and so on. The magic motif is predominantly present in the tales,

The element of mystery often acts as a problem-solving agent. The RESOLUTION phase in the Labovian formula[15] may find an answer in the mystery motif. Most crises in the stories are resolved via supernatural forces or agents supposed to govern them. Again, the African fable derails here from the Labovian way. As Robert L. Mack pointed out, moonlit seraglios, poweful sultans, mysterious veiled women, and threatening ginii, make of the tale "a colourfully diverse ... form of writing." He added that it is "a place to be free of the restrictions of the mundane realism tied to the demands of the market place and the goings on of "real" society."[16] The special effects of the tale's "enchanting" conventions -- of its genies and its demons and its magic spells -- convey the freedom of fictional explorations that transcends the limitations and constraints of well-defined analytical models.

6. Morality

Finally, a typical feature of the material surveyed is the presence of a didactic trend which runs throughout the narrative. It seems that the narrator has a debt to pay: **a moral**. Some tales have more than one; they are usually inserted in many parts of the story. Examples of these are numerous, and therefore I will restrict my review to what is striking in terms of originality, subtlety, and wit.

The ending of "The History of Selim" shows suspense and wonder as demonstrated by Selim's exclamation: "Good Heaven, how soon was changed the gladsome prospect of happiness, to the darkest view of misery."[17] In "The Difficulty of Concealing Guilt," the last paragraph of the tale is devoted to the morality of the story: "It requires less ability to procure honour and independence than is necessary to the concealment of guilt." Similarly, "The Wretched Taillah" concludes in the form of a plea to God: "O God why slept thy thunders and crushed not the execrated heads of such monsters of ingratitude and inhumanity."[18]

Usually the moral lesson takes the form of a story within a story. The embedded structure characterises many Oriental and African tales. There are layers beneath layers of meaning within a single narrative. Perhaps, as suggested earlier in this essay, spiral ways of thinking and circular shapes of telling are an African/Oriental legacy, and the Labovian model can do very little to accommodate such a peculiarity. Embedding has been noted in "Anecdote of Schah Abbas the Great," "Anecdotes of the Moors" and "Selico: an African Tale." On a lighter tone, however, "Abu-Cacem's Slippers" and "Ishmael: A Moorish Tale" have no explicit morals but the reader perceives the didactic dimension which lies behind the amusing aspect of the narration. Didacticism is therefore achieved through "showing" rather than "telling"[19].

In terms of the Labovian framework, the "Morality" motif may fit into the section called *Coda*. "The *Coda*" says Labov, "is a functional device for returning the verbal perspective to the present moment."[20] This seems to be roughly what a moral does in an African tale as it brings to the reality of the speaker and listener the lesson to be remembered from an eventful experience. However, in the Labovian model, the status of a *Coda* is optional, just an additional element whereas in the African tale, it becomes the backbone of the story and the entry visa to the African maze.

In the foregoing pages I have tried to explain and flesh out the **Six ----y's motifs** which I see as the **"Six Ways"** that make up the **"infrastructure"** of the North African fictional **world**. With the **Six Road Signs** in mind, I have laboured to map out a scenic "typology" of the Moorish tale. I may add that the identified patterns and characteristics are not only distinctive of short stories, they are equally relevant and valid when applied to a longer narrative. There is no room in this essay for a detailed discussion of Tyler's *The Algerine Captive*, but I can argue that a presentation of the material will reveal that the work fits nicely into the six-motif framework discussed earlier.

Conclusion

In the first part of this essay, I have tried to establish the American fascination with things North African during the early years of the Republic. Then, I scrutinised the periodical publications of that era for African material as evidence. Being from the Maghreb, I have made an attempt to give a scenic view of the African narrative from the inside, hoping thus to sensitise my reader to some typical features of African fiction--such characteristics and *motifs* are not meant to be comprehensive as the material examined has been fairly limited.

Finally, it seems unthinkable to tackle a problem which *smells* "Oriental" without lending an ear to Edward Said who, for that matter, is considered as the most severe and articulate critic of Western complacency regarding the image of the Orient. He thus asserts that Orientalism is "a kind of Western projection onto and will to govern the Orient... [a] collective notion identifying *us* Europeans as against all *those* non-Europeans."[21] Although I endorse what Said has written about the structures of Orientalism, the tales I reviewed in this essay would seem to argue for an analysis which makes more allowances for the specific nature of the Oriental/African tale tradition and involves less sweeping generalisations of the type made by Roland Barthes in the late nineteen sixties.[22] Such views may probably fuel a further investigation of this subject.

Notes

[1] Thomas Dekker, "Lust's Dominion "in *The Dramatic Works*, Fredson Bowers (ed) (Cambridge: Cambridge University Press, 1968), pp. 190-91.

[2] Royal Tyler, Preface in *The Algerine Captive; or, the life and Adventures of Updike Underhill* (Gaisville, Fla: a facsimile Reproduction of the London edition of 1802, 1967), p.2.

3 In *Portfolio* for 1802: 28.

[4] All magazines that have been consulted for North African material will be listed with all necessary data under "REFERENCES" below.

[5] These three narratologists conducted seminal studies on the structure of the tale; for more details, see: :

(i) Boris Tomashevski, *Russian Formalist Criticism: Four Essays*, Lemon & Reis, eds. (Lincoln: University of Nebraska Press, 1965), pp.61-68.

(ii) Vladimir Propp, *Morphology of the Folktale*. Trans. Lawrence Scott and ed. Louis E. Wagner (Austin: University of Texas Press, 1968).

(iii) William Labov and Joshua Waletzky "Narrative Analysis: Oral Versions of Personal Experience," *Essays on the Verbal and Visual Arts*. Ed. Jane Helm (Seattle: University of Washington Press, 1967), pp.12-45.

[6] Mongi Bahloul, "The Oriental Tale: Difficult to Define, Impossible to Resist!," a paper presented at an international conference on "The Arabs and Britain: Changes and Exchanges," Cairo, Egypt: 23-25 March 1998.

[7] Aristotle, *The Poetics*, trans. W. Hamilton Fyfe in *Aristotle: The Poetics* (.Cambridge, Ma.: Harvard University Press, 1927).

[8] Mieke Bal, *Narratologie: Essais sur la signification narrative dans quatre romans modernes.*(Paris: Klincksick, 1977).

[9] E.M. Forster, *Aspects of the Novel* (London: Hodder & Stoughton, 1927), pp.17-29.

[10] In "Narrative Analysis: Oral Versions of Personal Experience," William Labov and Joshua Waletzky suggest to look at a number of narratives which have been produced by "unsophisticated speakers." Their aim is to "isolate elements of narrative" that may lead to the construction of a general narrative framework. Labov and Waletzky propose to examine fourteen examples of data which have been collected from 600 interviews; these oral extracts are essentially meant to be answers to a common question: "Were you ever in a situation where you thought you were in a serious danger of being killed?" Labov and Waletzky have identified five steps in the overall structure of the narrative: orientation, complication, evaluation, resolution and *coda*. In Labov & Waletzky, pp.12-45.

[11] This secrtion serves to "orient the listener to *person, time, place* and *behavioural situations*." In Labov & Waletzky, p.34.

[12] It is defined as a series of events that build up a complicated situation. At that stage, a result is expected or sought. In Labov & Waletzky, p.34.

[13] All quotations in this section on "Piracy" have been gathered from "Anecdotes of the Moors," *The Columbian Magazine* and the supplement of the third volume (November 1789): 669-673 and 769-775 and "Contrast Between the African and the Christian Soldier," *The Rural Casket* (August 14, 1798 No.2,Vol.1: 170-181.

[14] In Labov & Waletzky, 1967, p.34.

[15] It follows the "EVALUATION" section and provides a solution to the crises, in other words, it diffuses the tension which has built up at the "COMPLICATION" phase. Labov & Waletzky, p.41.

[16] Robert L. Mack, ed. (1992), "Introduction," in *Oriental Tales* (Oxford: Oxford University Press, 1992), p.xvii.

[17] In *The Rural Magazine; or, Vermont Repository* (December 1796, vol.2, No.12: 589.

[18] In the *Newhampshire Magazine* (June 1793) : 54.

[19] Percy Lubbock, *The Craft of Fiction* (London: Cape, 1921), p.38.

[20] According to Labov and Waletzky, this section may be optional as many narratives end at the resolution phase. However, *Coda* has an important function since it returns "the verbal perspective to the present moment," and therefore completes the circle of a narrative. In Labov & Waletzky,pp.39-41.

[21] Edward Said, *Orientalism* (New York: NY University Press, 1979), pp.31-110.

[22] In his "Introduction to the Structural Analysis of Narratives," Barthes maintains that his proposed narrative framework can explain any conceivable type of narrative structure. See Roland Barthes, "Introduction to the Structural Analysis of Narratives." *Image, Music, Text.* Ed. and trans. Stephen Heath (New York: Hill & Wang, 1977) pp.79-117.

Works Cited

"Abu-Casem's Slippers, an Arabian Tale," *The Dessert to the True American* (Saturday 8 December 1798) vol.1,No.22: 12-17

"Account of the City of Morocco," *The Literary Museum; or, Monthly Magazine* (June 1797): 394-397.

"Account of the Female Arabs," *The Universal Asylum and Columbian Magazine*(January 1791) vol.4: 33-35.

"Account of the TURKISH BATHS," by the Abbe Poiret, *The Universal Asylum*, (Feb. 1791) vol.4: 80.

"Algerine Justice," *The Dessert to the True American* (22 July 1799) vol.2 No4.

"Almanzor, the Arabian," *The New York Weekly Magazine* (February 1797): 1.

"Anecdotes of the Moors," *The Columbian Magazine* (November 1798) vol.3: 669-673 and 769-775.

"Anecdote of Schah Abbas the Great," *The Weekly Magazine* (August 1798) col.3, No.28.

"A Remarkable Instance of Honour," *The Methodist Magazine* (April 1797): 368.

"Arabian Maxims," *The New York Weekly Magazine* (1796): 148.

"Character of the Present Emperor of Morocco," *Massachusetts Magazine* (September 1795) vol.7, No.6: 331-332.

"Concise History of the Algerines," *The Massachusetts Magazine* (January-April 1789) vol.1, No 1,2,3,.4: 43-198.

"Contrast Between the African and the Christian Soldier," *The Rural Casket* (14 Auguat 1798) vol.1, No.2: 170-81.

"Description of the Moorish Women," *The Massachusetts Magazine* (October 1795): 419-421.

"Dress of Moorish Women," *The Massachusetts Magazine* (August 1792) vol.4,No.9: 490-91.

"Facts respecting Africa," *The American Magazine* (November 1788): 821-822.

"Ishmael: An African Tale," *The New York Magazine* (November 1793) vol.4, No.2: 687-695.

Jones, Eldred, *Othello's Countrymen: The African in English Renaissance Drama* (London: Oxford University Press, 1965), pp. 34-41.

"Moorish Gratitude," *The New York Weekly Magazine* (July 1796), vol.2.: 44

"Obidah; or, the Journey of a Day," *Literary Miscellany* (1795): 13-18.

"On the Jealousy shown by Mohamedans to European Travellers," *The New York Magazine* (December 1790), vol.1, No.12: 702-703

"Phedima and Abensar: An African Tale," *The Massachusetts Magazine* (September 1796),vol.8, No.9: 495-99.

"Pictures of African Distress," *The American Museum; or, Universal Magazine"* (November 1789),vol.4: 228-229.

"Quarrels of the Arabians from Heron's Voyages," *The Massachusetts Magazine* (June 1793), vol.5,No.6: 348-349.

"Selico: An African Tale," *The Philadelphia Minerva* (February, March 1798), vol.4,No.160: 114-119

"The Advantages of Cleanliness in preventing Infectious Diseases," *The AmericanUniversal Magazine* (November 1797) vol.3,No.7: 3-4

"The African Complaint," *The New York Weekly Magazine* (May 1797), vol.2,No.97: 1.

"The Dey of Algiers," *The American Apollo* (1792), vol 1,No 15, part : 165.

"The History of Selim," *The Rural Magazine; or, Vermont Repository* (December 1796) vol. 2, No.12: 584-590.

"The Justice of the Sultan Sandjar," *The Massachusetts Magazine*(March 1793), vol. 5, No.3: 142-143.

"The Story of Abbas by Dr. Langhorne," *The Literary Miscellany* (1795), No. 5: 1-12.

"The Sultan and his Vizier; or, the Sultan who received a Blow," *The Massachusetts Magazine* (December 1795), vol.7, No.9: 558-559.

"The Vindictive Moor," *The Massachusetts Magazine* (June 1793), vol.5, No.6: 343-346.

"The Wretched Taillah: An African Story," *Newhampshire Magazine* (June 1793): 53-56.

"Twin-Brothers of Mezzorania," *South Carolina Weekly Museum* (February 1797), vol.1: 141-143 and 175-178.

"The Difficulty of Concealing Guilt, the Story of an Algerine," *Rural Magazine* (November, 1798) vol.1, No.38: 2-3.

Mediterranean Waterways, Extended Borders and Colonial Mappings: French Images of North Africa

Jonathan Gosnell
Smith College

In the nineteenth century, European writers, artists and a host of others traveled across the Mediterranean Sea to North Africa in search of the exotic, the Orient. Contact with all that they saw, heard, smelled, sensed and perhaps most importantly, imagined there, helped to inspire the works of art and literature that are now well-known to us, by the likes of Eugène Delacroix and Gustave Flaubert to name just two "Orientalists." French colonialism in North Africa, begun in Algeria in 1830, facilitated contact between Europeans and the Orient. The flow of persons, ideas and goods across the Mediterranean Sea grew steady once trade and travel routes were established. French fascination with Algeria in particular was encouraged by its central position within the colonial Empire. Algeria's legal status as a territorial part of France, its North African topography and climate, its indigenous and emigrant populations, and varied cultural traditions contributed to diverse imaginings.

Some of these recorded imaginings provide the substance of this essay. Colonial works of literature from the late nineteenth and early twentieth centuries contain interesting accounts of migration to North Africa and varied perceptions of the land that settlers claimed. This literature conveys the struggles and reported successes of settler activity, the fabled fruits of French colonialism. Colonial texts are particularly revealing, I suggest, in that they helped to create a myth, an image, a "colonial idea," as it was often called, of an extended French territory. Written primarily for a French reading public, they sought to encourage both a metaphoric and a literal fusion of colony and Metropole. This literature claimed that culturally distinct identities resulted from this fusion. In the following analysis, I explore the causes, content and meanings of the colonial consciousness that produced a remapping of the modern French world.

I ask the reader to first picture in his or her mind a steamship transporting people, merchandise, languages, customs, religious beliefs and values from the port cities of Marseilles, Valencia and Naples to the North African hub, Algiers. Spanish and Italian as well as metropolitan French settlers crossed the Mediterranean Sea and made their homes in French colonial Algeria. Sociologist Paul Gilroy uses a ship, a slaveship precisely, as a metaphor for the human diaspora and cultural exchange market of the Black Atlantic (4). Many of the European writers whose works are cited here describe similar kinds of displacement, in this case voluntary migratory activity, across the Mediterranean. They believed the transmediterranean exchange between European and North African populations and cultures to be highly desirable. Well before Gilroy circulated his very interesting notion of the Black Atlantic, these authors imagined the *French Mediterranean*.

In the view of French colonialists, an ensemble of administrators, politicians, intellectuals and assorted supporters of imperialism, France and North Africa were halves of a greater French whole. French colonial activity in Algeria, they declared, progressively collapsed northern and southern shores of the Mediterranean Sea, fostering a reconceptualized sense of national territory.[1] French thought, ethos and development had so permeated Africa in their estimation that fusion had indeed come to pass. French colonialism in North Africa had eradicated borders. Theoretically, there was no longer any distinction between Metropole and colony, between Orient and Occident. Algeria and France were one, part and parcel of "la plus grande France" or "Greater France." They were joined by a sea, the Mediterranean Sea, which did not separate autonomous countries as seas generally do. In this literature, the Mediterranean Sea appears much more like a canal facilitating traffic and joining points on an enlarged national grid. Ferdinand de Lesseps, who oversaw the construction of the Suez Canal in 1869, had such ideas of connecting waterways. Lesseps's canal was built, in the words of Edward Said, "to liberate the Orient and the Occident from their geographical bonds," to symbolically bridge the gap between their shores (219). Said adds, "De Lesseps and his canal finally destroyed the Orient's distance, its cloistered intimacy *away* from the West, its perdurable exoticism" (92). During the late nineteenth and early twentieth centuries, colonialists viewed the Mediterranean Sea as facilitating a similar process.

The French essayist Ferdinand Duchêne wanted readers to think of the Mediterranean Sea as a "French lake," whose waters encouraged travel not from Europe to North Africa, but from one side of France to the other. Duchêne claimed that such "internal" French travel enabled Algerian populations to visit "la plus belle moitié de la France" ("the most beautiful half of France").[2] This was their duty, he claimed, as recently-admitted members of an extended French community:

> C'est un devoir pour eux, devoir d'utilité, de piété, d'aller de temps en temps se tremper les mains, se laver le front, et boire aussi, à la source de grandeur simple, de beauté claire, d'énergie précise, de force mésurée qu'est l'esprit français, plus pur encore dans son cadre, celui que les fées lui ont donné pour berceau: la France (228).
>
> *[It is a duty for them, a useful, pious one, from time to time to wet their hands, rinse their faces and drink of the beautifully clear, replenishing well of simple grandeur, precise energy and tempered strength that is the French spirit, purer still in the natural setting that the gods gave it at birth: France.]*

The value of such travel was not unidirectional. The metropolitan French themselves could allegedly profit from passage across this internal lake and perhaps more fully comprehend the "reality" of France and French society reproduced beyond the Alps and the Pyrénées. Inspired travelers might decide to emigrate to North Africa and help to populate French settler communities. French as well as local colonial officials in Algeria encouraged this throughout much of the nineteenth and early twentieth centuries.[3] They offered French citizenship as an enticement to European settlers from Spain and Italy. Settlers did not leave France or Europe in gaining Algerian shores, according to colonialist views; they simply helped to explore and settle its lesser-known areas. By naturalizing and subsequently reproducing, they revitalized a metropolitan French population depleted by low birth rates.[4]

French colonialist discourse frequently proclaimed the benefits of transmediterranean travel and exchange, perhaps never so profusely as during the Centennial celebration of French presence in Algeria in 1930. Local administrators organized festivities to commemorate one hundred years of Franco-Algerian collaboration. This exchange had supposedly culminated in the dissemination of French culture and thought into the furthest reaches of North Africa.[5] Celebratory events scheduled throughout the spring and summer of 1930--parades, art exhibits, sporting events, scholarly conferences, official proclamations, the unveiling of commemorative monuments--paid tribute to the French landing at Sidi-Ferruch in June 1830 and to the colonial activity that followed. The high point of the Centennial celebration was a weeklong visit by French president Gaston Doumergue to several Algerian cities. This official visit by a French head of state signaled the legitimate place of Algeria within French imperial space. If Paris was the center of metropolitan France, Algiers was the flourishing capital of the French colonial Empire.

Organizers of the 1930 Centennial intended that it reflect:

La glorification des méthodes colonisatrices de la Mère-Patrie, de son action tutélaire et juste. [...] Faire aimer davantage ce grand pays et surtout le faire mieux connaître. Voilà [...] un des buts principaux du Centenaire (Mercier 3-5).

[The glorification of the colonizing methods of the Mother-Country, of its just and protective action ... To inspire love of this great country and especially to know it

in more detail. That is ... one of the primary goals of the Centennial.]

Local leaders in Algeria and colonialists in Paris agreed that the general public on both sides of the Mediterranean Sea knew too little about French life beyond the borders of France. The Centennial provided an occasion to help fill that gap. The official program of the event stated:

La grande affaire, c'est de montrer qu'il existe, à côté de la France millénaire, à vingt heures de Marseille [...] une autre France, âgée de cent ans à peine, déjà forte, pleine de vie et d'avenir, unissant dans sa formule heureuse les races latines et les races indigènes, pour en faire des races également françaises (Mercier 10).

[The main objective is to demonstrate the existence, alongside age-old France and a mere twenty hours from Marseille ... of another France, just one hundred years old, already strong, full of life and vigor, combining in its harmonious mix latin and indigenous races, in order to create an equally French race.]

Through coordinated efforts to disseminate information about Empire, the existence of an enlarged or Greater France would presumably take on concrete meaning for the metropolitan and colonial French populace, and not simply for the colonial enthusiasts whose words are cited here.[6] The 1930 Centennial of French presence in North Africa served this purpose, as did the Colonial Exposition held in Paris the following year.[7] Perhaps most importantly, schools, newspapers, radio, film, travel and military service all helped, supporters claimed, to extend the conceptual boundaries of France for individuals.[8] By way of instruction, exposure, and the heightened imaginations of individuals that resulted, the French nation would expand out from its metropolitan center to the colonial periphery. In the words of Benedict Anderson, colonialism enabled administrators, educators, journalists and novelists alike to stretch "the short, tight skin of the nation over the gigantic body of the Empire" (86).

Notions of Frenchness could thus be extended symbolically to populations far removed from the Metropole.

Advocates of colonialism such as Léon Archimbaud alluded to the charting of a new definition of Frenchness inclusive of colonial lands, populations and cultures. In 1928, Archimbaud suggested replacing the conventional sense of French identity with what he called "l'âme impériale" or "imperial spirit" (8). Contemporary French historian Raoul Girardet refers to such a consciousness as the "colonial idea" (287). An imperial or colonial consciousness would progressively broaden sentiment too closely linked to metropolitan France and allow for the perception of all French territories as a unified French consortium, what Archimbaud called *La plus grande France*.

As a result of coordinated efforts and colonial acquisitions, a "Hexagon" no longer accurately described French national space. Metaphorically, France had outgrown its metropolitan frame. Terms such as "another France," "second France" and "integral France" referred to the larger imperial body, and were commonly used during the 1930s and 1940s.[9] The supporters of French colonial activity believed this body to be stronger and more vital, due to its greater mass, and better able to defend itself in case of attack. A look at the titles of studies written during the first half of the twentieth century, during the apex of French colonialism, reveals curious interpretations of imperial space. Several works allude to an intimate, parental relationship between France and Algeria: *North African France* (1920), *Algeria, Center of French Africa* (1938), *White French Africa* (1949), *In Algeria with France* (1927) *Algeria, Daughter of France* (1935), *Our Child Algeria* (1949), *Algerian France* (1938), *Algeria, French Territory* (1931), *In the French Homeland, the Algerian Homeland* (1952).[10] These titles represent a sampling of writings from a much larger body of work. French colonial Algeria clearly inspired the imaginative fires of a good many observers.[11]

All of these notions fused the peripheral colonial territories, and North Africa in particular, to the metropolitan center, aided by the designation of the Mediterranean Sea as a source of continuity of Frenchness and not a barrier to it. Algeria was officially made up of three French "départements" since 1848 and thus constituted a region not unlike Brittany or Provence. In 1931, the Berber political activist and critic Ferhat Abbas expressed his hopes of witnessing the establishment of identical law in these overseas French territories (135). In 1935, French author Gabriel Audisio echoed the theme of French continuity and geographic extension beyond the former Hexagon. He disregarded the metaphor of a French lake for that of a "liquid continent" linking Europe and Africa. Audisio remarked:

> Il ne fait pas de doute [...] que la Méditerranée soit un continent, non pas un lac intérieur, mais une espèce de continent liquide aux contours solidifiés (*Jeunesse* 16).

> *[There is no doubt ... that the Mediterranean is a continent, not an interior lake but a kind of liquid continent with solidified contours.]*

His fusion of Metropole and colony through the solidification of the Mediterranean Sea, creating a single continent, was supposedly advantageous for France and North Africa. An imperial commonwealth was greater than the sum of its individual parts.

At the height of the colonial period, interested French writers considered Algeria to be emphatically French, not particularly North African, and certainly not African in a sub-Saharan sense. Gabriel Audisio claimed that the Sahara Desert was much more of an actual boundary than the Mediterranean Sea, separating Algeria from the rest of Africa. "Non, le Maghreb n'est pas encore l'Afrique," he wrote. "L'Afrique commence au Sahara" (18) ("No, the Maghreb is not yet Africa. Africa begins at the Sahara.") Italian-born writer and emigrant to North Africa Jean Mélia concurred. He also described the Sahara as a veritable barrier, but in terms that are strikingly sea-like (46). One finds in this particular discourse a metaphorical desertification of the Mediterranean Sea, facilitating exchange between North Africa and Europe, and a liquidizing of the Sahara Desert, cutting the African continent into separate northern and southern halves. While the idea of a French Mediterranean had captured the imaginations of European writers, a French Sahara had not. Such mappings of the French colonial world were clearly inspired by specific concerns. The view that the Maghreb was more European than African served to justify Algerian ties to France.

If European authors, captivated by the reported successes of French colonialism, admitted that Algeria was a part of

Africa, it was specifically a Latin Africa. The very notion of Latin Africa posited authority squarely in European hands and drew attention away from internal, indigenous forces. Turn of the century French novelist Louis Bertrand was one of the leading proponents of African "latinité." Bertrand located the source of African 'Latinness" within the Roman Empire and the early Christian epoch.[12] The Romans had established a culture, religion and language in North Africa that had dispersed over the centuries, but not without leaving lasting traces. In support of lingering "Latinness," Bertrand populated his novels, all set in North Africa, almost solely with Europeans. He rejected what he considered to be romantic portrayals of African life in literature that focused on indigenous peoples and traditions, and relegated Europeans to the margins of narratives.[13] Bertrand defiantly asserted the predominance of European presence in North Africa. In his estimation, French settlers in Algeria were the modern inheritors of the Latin heritage and tradition.[14]

While Louis Bertrand is the author most often associated with the notion of Latin Africa, he was not alone in imagining a European-influenced continent. Others conceived of slightly different configurations that also took into account European designs on North Africa. Early twentieth century novelist Robert Randau imagined the colonial coupling of North Africa and France as *AfroFrance*. He renamed its inhabitants "les franco-berbères" (*Cassard* préface). Colonial advocate Maurice Ricord insisted on a similar change in terminology and consciousness in 1946, through pedagogic reform. He sought to replace the term "colonies" in French school textbooks with *Provinces d'outre-mer* or overseas provinces (179). Essayist Jean Paillard, writing in 1939, hoped to witness the creation of a *Province française d'empire* (French imperial province) in Algeria (109). Ten years later, author Jean Pomier suggested that a more appropriate name, justly honoring France's influential role in Algeria, would be *Francitanie* (4). These views reflect a particularly French, assimilationist manner of envisioning the colonial world.

Still more configurations were imagined, particularly after the Second World War. In 1951, a group of colonial supporters began to circulate the notion of *Eurafrique* or Eurafrica. They founded a journal under the same name in order to promulgate "Eurafrican" ideas. Supporters claimed that the amalgamation of African and European territories and peoples was not a fantasy but rather an attainable goal. An opening editorial stated:

La coupure de la Méditerranée entre Europe et Afrique sera aussi négligeable que la fosse du lac Léman entre Evian et Lausanne (avril 1951).

[The Mediterranean gulf between Europe and Africa will be as insignificant as the distance separating Evian from Lausanne on Lake Léman.]

According to this same editorial, not only countries but also populations would fuse:

Rien n'est plus naturel que d'envisager l'unité de l'Eurafrique, c'est-à-dire la réunion de peuples dont l'intérêt vital est de s'établir en un seul et même peuple.

[Nothing is more natural than to envisage the unity of Eurafrica, that is to say the necessary fusion of peoples whose vital interests lead them to combine into a single, unified people.]

Growing hostility in North Africa at this time between nationalists and European settlers lent an air of urgency to such thought. In what became a motto for the journal, editors insisted that "l'Eurafrique est la dernière chance de l'Europe et la première chance de l'Afrique" ("Eurafrica is the last chance for Europe and the first chance for Africa.")

By the midpoint of the twentieth century, French colonial discourse had begun to change in tone. The views expressed by essayist R.C. Llamo in 1956 provide an example. Llamo claimed that the only possible future for European presence in North Africa required complete separation from indigenous populations. Llamo described his hope of witnessing the establishment of a territory called *Euralgérie* (Euralgeria) that would be reserved solely for French settlers (28). He gave no clarification as to the parameters of this protected space, but he suggested that it was imperative to the survival of Europeans in North Africa.

R.C. Llamo's *Euralgeria* clearly differed from *Eurafrica*. It represented a shift away from the inclusive, fusionist idea of Greater France which by the mid to late 1950s had lost much of its sustaining force. Llamo spoke perhaps only for himself and a small group of followers, but his words conveyed growing concerns about the future of the French colonial empire. In the post-World War II period, when emerging nationalisms began to agitate the French colonial world, boundaries were once again drawn, separating "threatened" European communities from "hostile" indigenous populations.

French colonialism in North Africa had clearly transformed national geographies in the imagination of French writers. Empire had indeed influenced European literary traditions.[15] The contact between different peoples and cultures had perhaps even altered settler society, in narrative form at least if not in reality. In colonial novels, European settlers are depicted as pioneers who faced formidable and life-changing conditions on the Algerian frontier. Their experiences helped to shape a new colonial identity. Some authors contended that emigrants had become Africans by virtue of their extended stay on the continent. This assertion is curious since the Maghreb had been defined as being more European than African. "Soyons des Africains!" ("Let's be Africans!") proclaimed a fictionalized settler in Robert Randau's *Les Colons* (27). European settlers had been physically transformed, their skin blackened by the hot North African sun. Romanticized notions of the emigrant experience in Algeria contributed to such beliefs. The achievements of Roman forefathers centuries earlier, to borrow again from Louis Bertrand, lent a measure of legitimacy to the European idea of "going native."

Several chroniclers of the colonial experience had spent their entire lives in North Africa. They wrote about an area that they knew intimately and created fictionalized accounts of their own families. A theory of "routes and roots" is useful here (Gilroy 190). Long routes across lands and ultimately across the Mediterranean Sea led to a quest for roots among settlers to Algeria. A sense of rootedness replaced that of exile for settlers the longer they remained in North Africa.[16] Rootedness led to appropriations of African land and identity. Some settlers claimed to have become more North African than French with the passage of time.[17] Such assertions of

"Africanness" by European settlers conflicted with legal definitions of identity as determined by citizenship. There was no officially recognized African identity under colonial rule in Algeria. Since 1889, European emigrants had been collectively naturalized and granted automatic French citizenship.

Individual identity was thus not always translated by formalized categories in the colonial world. Colonial Algerian society was richly varied and identities often confused and slippery. Several authors allude to hybridity when articulating the complexities of Algerian identity. They believed peoples of various ethnic, religious and cultural backgrounds to have fused in Algeria, resulting in the "métissage" often associated with North American society. North African-born author Albert Camus referred, favorably, to the Algerian population as bastardized. He called it:

> Une race bâtarde, faite de mélanges imprévus. Espagnols et Alsaciens, Italiens, Maltais, Juifs, Grecs enfin s'y sont rencontrés. Ces croisements brutaux ont donné, comme en Amérique, d'heureux résultats (127-8).

> *[A bastardized race, made up of surprising mixes: Spaniards and Alsacians, Italians, Maltese, Jews and Greeks. Such intermingling has had, as in America, positive results.]*

America is indeed a frequent trope in colonial Algerian ruminations. Writers perceived Algeria as "l'Amérique à la française" or French America, a mineral-rich North African California or Texas. The same pioneering spirit could allegedly be found in the Wild West of North America and North Africa.[18]

Gabriel Audisio agreed that colliding cultures in colonial Algeria resulted in a hybrid Mediterranean identity. In a 1938 essay, Audisio designated the Mediterranean Sea as a veritable "patrie" or fatherland that had sired "L'Homme méditerranéen." A Mediterranean Man was a composite consisting of:

> La narine sémitique, l'oeil andalou, le muscle berbère, le sein provençal, la cheville sicilienne, un doigt des baléares, un cheveu de la Corse (*Amour* 20).

[A Semitic nose, Andalousian eyes, Berber muscle, Provençal breasts, a Sicilian ankle, a finger from the Balarean Islands, a strand of hair from Corsica.]

A racially mixed being, who pledged allegiance to no one nation, a Mediterranean Man worshipped only the sea, sun, and wind, primary elements of the region.[19] A prominent social scientist by the name of E. F. Gautier argued in 1930 that cultural homogenization in colonial Algeria was a myth. Colonial Algerian society was no melting pot but rather a salad bowl made up of autonomous sub-groups (97). Arab, Berber, Jewish and European settler populations often lived in seclusion from others.

"Algerianness" in North Africa was not inclusive of all populations. The epithet *Algerian*, as defined in colonial society, was restricted to persons of European descent born in Algeria. The quintessential Algerian is the fictive settler Cagayous, a loud, uncouth and anti-Semitic representative of the European lower-middle classes, created by the French author Musette at the end of the nineteenth century.[20] To distinguish himself from Jews, Berbers and Arabs, Cagayous defiantly proclaims that he and other emigrants are uniquely Algerian. Contemporary Algerian novelist Mohammed Dib commented that one might be inclined to believe that settlers were natives and the natives settlers from such assertions (45-6). Similar narratives were produced by a group of writers known as *les Algérianistes* who were primarily interested in extolling the virtues and successes of European settlement of Algeria.[21] Louis Bertrand was one of its leading figures.

Colonial Algerian literature evokes as much about metropolitan French thought as about North Africa, if not more. It conveys a great deal about French sentiment concerning Empire through the first half of the twentieth century. Novels and essays echo the concerns of modern European society, of nationalist expansion and capitalism. Many of the authors cited bought into and helped to propagate the notion of a rubbery, expandable France extending itself magnanimously across the ocean. The stated justification for French colonial activity was mutual benefit for France and Africa. Algeria represented a frontier for French vitality and growth, particularly after the loss of

Alsace-Lorraine in the 1870-1871 Franco-Prussian war. Some observers believed that Algeria and the rest of colonial Africa represented France's very future.

What is interesting in the case of Algeria is that French colonialism attempted to wash clean a distinct land, people and cultures of "otherness." While Orientalist depiction often set North African or Islamic societies apart as different and inherently inferior, French colonialists placed Algeria on equal ground with the West. They claimed that Algeria had been transformed, that it was French, a part of France or Greater France. They claimed that settlers themselves had been transformed and sought to make this known to a wider audience. Belief in French universalism, a far-reaching centralized state and a civilizing mission provided the basis for this discourse. "Formally the Orientalist sees himself as accomplishing the union of Orient and Occident," writes Edward Said, "but mainly by reasserting the technological, political and cultural supremacy of the West" (246).

While colonial representations of an extended French nation and population flourished, little was corroborated by legal jurisdiction. Only the French Union of 1946 and the constitution of the Fourth Republic described in real terms a colonial commonwealth resembling Greater France. Only this Union granted French citizenship to all persons living in either metropolitan or imperial France. By this time however, indigenous elites had grown increasingly suspicious of assimilationist declarations. Colonial Algeria had long remained a country in which nine-tenths of the population, Algerian Arabs and Berbers, held no claims to French citizenship rights and privileges. Only a sliver of the North African coast was administered similarly to departments in France. Yet supporters of Greater France continued to laud the fusion of lands and peoples. This colonial idea was never fully realized in the French-speaking world, but it still proved captivating and resistant to change.

Fusionist statements by French colonial advocates continued even as the Empire unraveled in the 1950s and 1960s, during nationalist struggles for autonomy throughout Africa. Today, close to forty years after its demise, French Algeria is still invoked and celebrated. To former inhabitants, it seems a lost paradise in comparison to the one-party rule of the FLN (National Liberation Front) following independence and the current civil war.[22] For European settlers, a new exile far from their North African birthplaces began after 1962. The voyage by steamship back across the Mediterranean Sea, often to unknown lands and "mother-countries," gave rise to a literature of loss, anguish and nostalgia which is still being written.

Notes

[1] See Charles-Robert Ageron, *Histoire de l'Algérie contemporaine*, Paris: PUF, 1964, and more recently, Benjamin Stora's *Histoire de l'Algérie coloniale, 1830-1954*, Paris: La Découverte, 1991.

[2] All translations from French to English are my own.

[3] Ageron, op. cit.

[4] In 1889, non-French European settlers born in Algeria were collectively naturalized. Algerian Jews received French citizenship in 1870.

[5] See *Le Livre d'or du Centenaire de l'Algérie française* (ouvrage honoré d'une souscription du commissariat général du centenaire de l'Algérie), Alger: Fontana, 1931.

[6] See William H. Schneider, *An Empire for the Masses: The French Popular Image of Africa, 1870-1900*, Westport, CT: Greenwood Press, 1982, and Thomas G. August, *The Selling of Empire: British and French Propaganda, 1890-1940*, Westport, CT: Greenwood Press, 1985.

[7] The Universal Colonial Exposition of 1931 brought the colonies to France. See Charles-Robert Ageron, "L'Exposition colonial de 1931" in Pierre Nora's *Les Lieux de mémoire I. la République*, Paris: Gallimard, 1984.

[8] Centralized French institutions had already (arguably) produced a sense of national sentiment by the beginning of the twentieth century. See Eugen Weber, *Peasants into Frenchmen: The Modernization of Rural France, 1870-1914*, Stanford: Stanford UP, 1977.

[9] Léon Archimbaud, *La Plus Grande France*, Paris: Hachette, 1928; Virginie Hériot, *La Seconde France* (Impressions sur les fêtes du centenaire), Paris: L'Imprimerie artistique de l'ouest, 1931. Maurice Ricord refers to "la France intégrale" in *Au service de l'Empire, 1939-1945*, Paris: Editions coloniales et métropolitaines, 1946.

[10] The original titles and authors, respectively, are *La France Nord-Africaine* (Lucien Deslinières), *L'Algérie foyer de l'Afrique française* (Maurice Ricord), *L'Afrique blanche française* (Jean Despois), *En Algérie avec la France* (Edmond Gojon), *L'Algérie fille de France* (André Foucault), *Notre Enfant l'Algérie* (Jean Vignaud), *France algérienne* (Jules Correard),

L'Algérie terres françaises (Armand Megglé), *Dans La Patrie française, la patrie algérienne* (Jean Mélia).

[11] The symbiotic relationship between imperialist expansion and Western cultural production is explored by Edward Said in *Imperialism and Culture*, New York: Knopf, 1993. See also Herman Lebovics, *True France: The Wars over Cultural Identity, 1900-1945*, Ithaca: Cornell UP, 1992.

[12] Louis Bertrand's concept of "latinité" is developed in several works. See for instance *Les Villes d'or. Algérie et Tunisie romaines*, Paris: Fayard, 1921.

[13] Jean Dejeux, "De l'éternel Méditerranéen à l'éternel Jugurtha," *Revue algérienne des sciences juridiques, économiques et politiques* XIV, 4 (décembre 1977): 658-728.

[14] Contemporary novelists, following Bertrand's lead, claimed that European settlers spoke "le latin d'Afrique." For examples, see Ferdane, *Joyeux pêcheurs de la côte oranaise*, Oran: Fouque, 1948.

[15] Edward Said, *Imperialism and Culture*, op. cit.

[16] See Jean Mélia, *Dans la Patrie française, la patrie algérienne*, Alger: La Maison des livres, 1952.

[17] Ferdinand Duchêne examined the distinct sensibilities of first, second and third generation emigrants to Algeria in *Mouna, cachir et couscouss*, Paris: Albin Michel, 1930.

[18] Curiously, while North Africa is generally considered eastern in its attributes, the "Maghreb" refers literally to the west of the Islamic world.

[19] For an authoritative source on the Mediterranean region see Fernand Braudel, *La Méditerranée. Les hommes et l'héritage* (II), Paris: Arts et métiers graphiques, 1978. More recently, see Claude Liauzu, *L'Europe et l'Afrique méditerranéenne. De Suez (1869) à nos jours*, Paris: Editions Complexe, 1994.

[20] Gabriel Audisio, *Cagayous ses meilleures histoires*, Paris: Gallimard, 1931.

[21] For a review of this literature see, Jean Dejeux, op. cit., and Hubert Gourdon, Jean-Robert Henry, Françoise Henry-Lorcerie, "Roman colonial et idéologie coloniale en Algérie," *Revue algérienne des sciences juridiques, économiques, politiques* XI, 1 (mars 1974): 75-85.

[22] See novels and essays written by Marie Cardinal including *Les Pieds-Noirs*, Paris: Belfond, 1988.

Works Cited

Abbas, Ferhat. *De La Colonie vers la Province. Le jeune Algérien.* Paris: Editions de la jeune parque, 1931.

Anderson, Benedict. *Imagined Communities: Reflections on the Origin and Spread of Nationalism.* New York: Verso, 1983.

Archimbaud, Léon. *La Plus Grande France.* Paris: Hachette, 1928.

Audisio, Gabriel. *Amour d'Alger.* Alger: Charlot, 1938.

---, *Jeunesse de la Méditerranée.* Paris: Gallimard, 1935.

Camus, Albert. *Noces* suivi de *L'été.* Paris: Gallimard, 1954.

Dib, Mohammed. *L'Incendie.* Paris: Editions du Seuil, 1954.

Duchêne, Ferdinand. "France-Algérie. La petite patrie et la grande." *Bulletin de la société de géographie d'Alger et de l'Afrique du Nord* 103, 3 (1925): 219-236.

Eurafrique 1 (avril 1951).

Gautier, E.F. *Un Siècle de colonisation.* Paris: Librairie Félix Alcan, 1930.

Gilroy, Paul. *The Black Atlantic: Modernity and Double Consciousness.* Cambridge: Harvard UP, 1993.

Girardet, Raoul. *L'Idée coloniale en France de 1871 à 1962.* Paris: La Table ronde, 1972.

Llamo, R.C. *Essai sur le peuplement européen de l'Algérie. Euralgérie ou de la naissance d'un peuple original.* Alger: Imprimerie moderne, 1956.

Mercier, Gustave. *Le Centenaire de l'Algérie française.* Numéro spécial de la "Presse nord-africaine." 10 décembre 1929.

Paillard, Jean. *Faut-il faire de l'Algérie un dominion?* Paris: Fernand Sorlot, 1939.

Pomier, Jean. "'Algérien?' ... Un mot qui cherche son sens." *Afrique* 242 (octobre-novembre 1951): 3-19.

Randau, Robert. *Cassard-le-Berbère.* Alger: J. Carbonel, 1926.

---, *Les Colons.* Paris: Albin Michel, 1907.

Ricord, Maurice. *Au Service de l'Empire, 1939-1945.* Paris: Editions coloniales et métropolitaines, 1946.

Said, Edward. *Orientalism.* New York: Random House, 1978.

Transposing the Political and the Aesthetic: Eugène Fromentin's Contributions to Oriental Stereotypes of North Africa

Valérie Orlando
Illinois Wesleyan University

The orientalist stereotype[1] was a favorite of 19th century French authors and painters such as Théophile Gautier, Pierre Loti, Gérard de Nerval and Eugène Fromentin who traveled to North Africa.[2] Their works depicted a repertoire of literature and art that exploited the exotic erotica of Eastern lands to its fullest. Manet's *Olympia* 1863, Lecomte de Nouy's *The White Slave* 1888, and Tissier's *The Algerian* 1860 are but a few examples of the fantastic *tableaux* which were on display in 19th century France. In the 20th century, postcards of highly sexualized *oriental* dancing girls have been hawked on Algerian and Turkish street corners to European tourists. Orientalist sets and themes have always drawn wide appeal on the stage and in Hollywood films. Vaslav Nijinsky's 1911 theater performance of *Sherazade*, the 1937 film *Ali Baba Goes to Town* and the infamous James Bond in *The Spy Who Loves Me*, 1977, offer audiences sex appeal and seductive danger in the harem. These are but a few samples of orientalized artistry. Orientalism and its congruent themes can even be seen in the local supermarket on alimentary products such as couscous. To my amusement, I once purchased such a box of couscous with a delicious pair of dark feminine eyes peering out from a veiled face, offering exotic-erotic "memories of Marrakech."[3] I wondered what I was really buying; couscous or the comfort of an age-old stereotype?

In 19th century France, the production of artistic and literary fantasy based on suppositions about the Orient was tightly interlaced with the political policy of the day. One cannot deny the fact that the artistic/literary aesthetic experience was linked to political actions, campaigns and imperial policy. From 18th century novels such as Montesquieu's *Lettres Persanes* (1721), Volney's *Voyage en Egypt et en Syrie* (1787), to 19th century narratives and poetry such as Hugo's *Orientales* (1829), Balzac's *La Roubailleuse* (1841), and Flaubert's *Salambô* (1862), otherness and exotic desire provided a lucrative backdrop for the narratives of the time while also appealing to political policy makers eager for colonial expansion. Paintings such as Ingres's *Grande Odalisque* (1814), Trouillbert's *The Harem Slave* (1874), Gerome's *The Bath* (1880) and *The Slave Market* (1885), and Dinet's *Moonlight at Langhouat* (1897), all exemplify art as a product of the new military conquests of North Africa in the 19th century. These great masters fueled the fire of oriental fantasy for the public and were used to gain approval of the conquest of countries such as Algeria.[4]

Glorious accounts of the military campaigns led by Field Marshal Thomas Bugeaud[5] in the 1830s and 40s as well as the writings of Théophile Gautier honed Eugène Fromentin's interest in North Africa. Although, Fromentin had significant competition in the literary/artistic milieus of his era, I have chosen him as the "poster boy" for the Orientalists because I feel his work is so uniquely linked to both worlds of art and literature. As artist, author, and politician, Fromentin set a standard for the exotic and paved the way for future stereotypes of otherness which have endured in our century. His work, spanning the years 1848 to1857, depicts Arab hunting forays, pastoral scenes, harems, and women in exoticized settings.

Eugène Fromentin contributes to the development of stereotypes associated with the entire region of North Africa during the 19th century by juxtaposing political and artistic arenas that assure a codified Western vision of the Other. Particularly in his two travel novels, *Une Année dans le Sahara* and *Un Eté dans le Sahel*, Fromentin nurtures his own oriental desire, as well as that of the public's. First, the reader remarks that the author creates an overly dramatized exotic world by further exploiting existing Western stereotypes of previous authors and artists associated with the East. Secondly, he specifically collectivizes French oriental desire through explanation to his reading public of what he views as the mysteriously captivating space of oriental lands. Lastly, by writing down what he saw (often these were later embellished versions), the author transmits the idea that travel in these new colonized lands will lead the French individual to self-knowledge and self-expansion.

Eugène Fromentin made his first trip to Algeria in 1846. His second journey, spanning eight months from Autumn 1847 to Spring 1848, would provide the background for his first book *Un Été dans le Sahara*, published in 1857. The author was particularly ecstatic over this second trip because he was the first European painter to venture to the far southern regions of Algeria. A map of Fromentin's 1848 journey shows a route winding from the village of Laghouat, where most of the first novel *Un Été dans le Sahara* takes place, to his final destination, the region of Biskra, where he eventually set his second novel, *Une Année dans le Sahel*. Following the 1848 trip, the artist's pact between brush and pen was sealed, giving credence to and amplifying the importance of a technique known as *transpositions d'art* begun earlier by Théophile Gautier. The world of transpositions was built on universals, upholding the idea that art is eternal and that painted depiction could meld to the written word as well as to music, sculpture, and poetry. Fromentin believed that shifting from paint to ink was a manner through which to extend real depiction one step further forcing, as he thought, "exactitude pushed to the last scruple" (*Un Été* 10). His efforts to link the paintbrush to pen aided the cause of *la littérature pittoresque*, which he felt would take the art of painting and writing further than their normal realms.

Throughout his travel novels the author sought to test his new theory in order to discern if the art of writing could achieve the expression of reality offered by painting. Acting within an interstitial space between these two media, Fromentin calls to task the depiction of reality in earlier artistic works of great masters such as Eugène Delacroix. Did Delacroix's representations of the Orient ring true? Did this famous painter uphold Fromentin's quest for consistency in real life depiction? In an effort to mull over these questions, the author often juxtaposes painted reality with that of the written word in *Une Année dans le Sahel*. Upon deciding to use the secret chambers of an Algerian woman, Hawa, (whom he has recently met) as an example, Fromentin tells his fellow traveler and companion, Vandell, "I am going to see if Hawa's apartment really resembles the admirable painting *Les Femmes d'Alger* by Delacroix" (*Une Année* 149).[6] The painting was brought back to France in 1834 (Brahimi 13).

Eugène Delacroix's rendition of harem women in their chambers colludes with Fromentin's expectations when he does finally gain access to this *lieu interdit*, but only as a point of departure. Unlike the painting, which Fromentin finds "fixed" and definitive, "truer than the true" he seeks in his narrative to draw out not only the painted qualities of a harem scene, but also the real life women within it (Brahimi 13). His odalisque, Hawa, becomes not just a flat representation, but a living, breathing real subject with a past. We are told she is a divorced woman of questionable integrity who is currently living with her second husband in a loveless marriage. The idea of the totality--the three dimensionality--of her existence is clearly represented as Fromentin describes her persona down to perfume, sounds and fabrics; in aesthetic narrative terms, her essence is drawn out to its full potential. She allows Fromentin to enter her chambers, fulfilling his desire to see as well as to depict the Odalisques as in real life.

Up to this point, he has only been able to speculate on their cloistered activities. Delacroix's tableau is transposed onto Fromentin's narrative as he describes the inner sanctum of Hawa's apartment. Elated, Fromentin exclaims: "As she entered the room, she throws off her veil, kicking off her black leather sandals at the edge of the carpet, she arranges herself on the divan, magnificently, like an idol" (*Une Année* 175-176). Hawa, unlike Delacroix's fixed painted woman, moves in unison with the other subjects in her entourage. The reader sees the denouement of the action as Fromentin does, complete with the arrival of the characters and the gestures that they perform. "Arriving at the entrance of the room of her mistress," he states, "the black servant turns her head halfway towards me, making a gesture in order to push back the flowered Muslin curtains, exactly as you can see it in Delacroix's painting" (*Une Année* 150). Paint strokes meld with text, becoming a palimpsest comprised of painted and real gestures as Delacroix's work is transformed into a vehicle through which Fromentin's written word passes and takes us to another realm. This written-painted space displays a living tableau incorporating past and present time, while making the Oriental harem come alive. As Fromentin sends his detailed stories back to journals and serials such as *Revue de Paris*, *L'Artiste*[7] and *La Revue des Deux Mondes*, the public gains privileged access to the complete inner circle of a world still considered mysterious and incomprehensible.

Yet how real is the real Fromentin is relating to his public? I feel that we must question the link between realistic depiction and the author's insatiable public popularity. Like his paintings, which were often painted years after the images were sketched in a notebook, Fromentin re-wrote much of his travel journals from notes more than a year after his return from Algeria in 1853. It was only after numerous revisions, embellishments and input from friends that the finished product was achieved. One might speculate, therefore, on the degree of Algerian reality Fromentin is really exposing to the reader. His, as well as other orientalists' objectification, or what I call "commodification" of the Orient, insidiously assured France's continued love affair with ready made stereotypes--Arabs as representations of the exotic, the despotic, and the barbaric--that conveniently were associated with everything North African. The Orient would now and forever represent a place where one could lose one's self, enraptured by and intoxicated with an idealized otherness. The Orient became the comforting *lieu d'extase* equal to a drugged euphoria. As Fromentin admits in *Une Année dans le Sahel* the Orient is "a place to repose... where one sleeps, where one believes he is thinking... it is a convenient mode in which to finish life in voluptuous suicide" (*Une Année* 85). This zeal for commodities from the Arab world amplified the representation of the Orient as a site of exotic bliss where the European man could achieve all his fantasies. It also fueled the desire for a new era of international prowess for France.

France's fascination with the Orient was directly linked to the notion of great empire, satiating a newly kindled desire for the exploration of difference. Both *Un Été dans le Sahara* and *Une Année dans le Sahel* attest to Fromentin's probing of Algeria by means of the widely accepted political premise that the Arab world equals the barbaric and the debase and, therefore, is readily in need of interpretation by the European. A second important point to note is that in each narrative Fromentin exerts a sense of self-appointed duty to document this new unknown space for those who cannot travel there. He feels compelled to enlighten the public back home so that they may gain true knowledge of this *other* world. *Un Été dans le Sahara* and *Une Année dans le Sahel* are based on ideals of alterity which play essential roles in cultivating enthusiasm from the public for Fromentin's literary projects. This enthusiasm colludes with the European male's sense of adventure. The new wide-open conquered space is seen as a means of bettering one's self through fulfillment gained by manly adventures against hostile elements of opposition, whether they be human or of nature. Gautier, Fromentin, Loti and Nerval, among other orientalists, all expressed the desire to know this opposite as a way of delving into the inner recesses of what they thought was synonymous for their own unknown dark side.[8]

The universal appeal of the total aesthetic experience found in North Africa owes much of its success not only to art and politics, but also to the world of science. Scientific study was linked to colonialism when the first French vessels set sail for foreign lands. African men, women and children found themselves under a microscope as specimens to be scrutinized by the white explorer.[9] Fromentin's descriptive accounts in both travel novels clearly demonstrate his contribution to these early scientific interests. He is caught up in the biological classification of animals, species and humans, which was very much in vogue at the time.[10] *Une Année dans le Sahel* attests to the author's adherence to the parameters of scientific classification, certainly in terms of ethnic groups. On the subject of women and ethnicity, he writes; "much more tolerant than the Arabs, the Jews and the Negroes permit their women to go out unveiled. The Jewish women are lovely, but unlike Arab women, we see them everywhere" (*Une Année* 32). Although Jewish and black women openly offer themselves as subjects for Fromentin's scrutiny, unlike his favored Mauresques (Arab women), they do not possess the Arab beauty, which he finds so seductive. Throughout his travel novels, Fromentin refers to the echelons of race, commenting on the low station of blacks in particular and the fact that they are slaves of both Jews and Arabs. The subordination of blacks, he feels, is due to nature, which has destined them to be "nannies and beasts of burden." They are appreciated for their "robust opulence," yet never considered beautiful or alluring (*Une Année* 32).

Scientific categorization of the Maghreb provided an easy manner by which to divide up the country in terms of race and allowed colonial institutions and bureaucracies to manage the natives militarily and politically. Gender also became a tool, manipulated to oppress. The Arab man was repeatedly feminized, thus making him more easily dominated. Homosexuality was thought to be widespread throughout North Africa and became a popular topic of conversation among European travelers. The homosexual stereotypes that the Arab man was forced to bear, was a favorite topic of Fromentin's. The author does not hide the fact that he feels that there is a certain "Arab vice" that seems to plague the men of Algeria. He blames this on the confinement and the paltry availability of women (Hartman 52). "Effeminate, voilà, I think that's the most appropriate word to define their character," the author notes with disdain (*Une Année* 90). Ironically, it is the very sequestration of women Fromentin believes that has caused homosexuality in men. Women wield their vengeance on men for their diminished place in Arab society, as he states in *Une Année dans le Sahel*:

> Isn't it usual in feminine countries to produce a sort of confusion within the sexes and to weaken one to the extent the other is diminished? Such a bizarre thing, and at the same time that they disappear from public life, women also come out in the temperament of the race; the less they are recognized as having importance outside... [men] must replace them... he substitutes for her in duties, which diminish his status. This is how women gain revenge, in bringing down the species...all the society is punished (*Une Année*, 90).

It is thus through this deformation and the confusion of roles that Fromentin is sure "results in what we see: a people that is quasi-feminine, boys who are almost girls, youths who are mistaken for young women" (*Une Année* 90). Other traits, directly linked to this feminization, are infantile behavior and lack of ambition. Fromentin, aligning his views with the popular imperial French sentiment of the time, suggests that the masculine weakness and childlike behavior of the Arabs automatically authorize a *carte blanche* for Europeans' tutelage. It is his duty to take it upon himself to show "these Arab despots" the way to civilization. As the author declares, "it's our industry, from which they will profit, our commerce, which will offer them means of exchange... force has never been displeasing to them, and, like children, they will accept obedience" (*Une Année* 22). The feminization and categorization of races into convenient stereotypes, particularly in Algeria, undoubtedly aided the colonial mission's full penetration of Algeria by 1872.

The allure of the mysterious and the thrilling exploration of the unknown are common motifs in the orientalist novel. What is automatically implicated in *littérature pittoresque*, and most certainly in travel literature, is that this other world is always synonymous for the far off and the foreign. The author finds himself as both narrator of events and interpreter of those same events for which his readers have no preexisting knowledge. What is at stake is the representation of alterity (which offers the prime appeal) and the sense and comprehension of it that the author can provide for his public. Yet, because the integral essence of his novel--alterity--must be kept in place in order to continue its allure, the picturesque author finds himself not wanting to give too much away.

Fromentin grounds the equilibrium between alterity and its explanation (present in both his travel novels) in order to guarantee continued appeal back home. As an artist of words, he is both he who sees and he who presents what we see--he is a director of representation with the power to play in or cancel the script. He strives to explain the most minute of details concerning the native, while simultaneously embellishing and amplifying the exotic qualities of the inexplicable. Many of his observations are noted down secretly, unbeknown to the observed, thus adding more intrigue to what he is able to uncover, yet cannot explain. Often these intrigues implicate Arab women who, as previously mentioned, are virtually impossible for the Westerner to approach. The Mauresques, the veiled, exotic Arab women of Algeria, are the equivalent of phantasmagoric objects placed in sublime settings as part of the Algerian landscape which like sunsets, flowers, birds, and trees, Fromentin admires from a distance. For the author, the Arab woman is the privileged site of otherness--an other doubly othered--that constantly exasperates him. The veiled feminine figure continually surfaces in both novels. He is fascinated by the large, heavy *haïks* (typical Algerian long robes), which he describes as "this tight envelop" that seals the feminine body behind a locked door of fabric (*Un Été* 188). In *Une Année dans le Sahel*, the painter often wonders what lies at the heart of this feminine space which he views as a sequestered "private life" that is "protected behind impenetrable walls" (*Une Année* 28-29).[11] Fromentin's sense of adventure and love of mystery spur him on to pursue the Algerian woman incessantly. On the rare occasion when the Mauresques venture from their locked domiciles, he is there --waiting: "I often witness," he writes, "[their] carrying on from afar, hidden in a convenient shadowed place of observation. I see all" (*Une Année* 74-75). Such antics are scrupulously depicted for the reader. In *Une Année dans le Sahel*, the author hides behind a tree to observe a group of women visiting tombs in a cemetery. He is elated when they unexpectedly throw off their veils. He and the reader, at last, obtain a glimpse of this unknown feminine presence that has for so long mystified the author.

In addition to the feminine mystery that provides substance for commentary, there is also a more obscure oriental dark side of Fromentin's wanderings that he often exposes. This dark unknown reminds both author and reader that the mystery associated with the new colonies is doubly constructed upon violent domination and a foreignness that escapes explanation. Images of the foreign culture are often upsetting for the orientalist author who finds them unnerving. One such haunting scene in *Un Été dans le Sahara*, entails Fromentin's description of a woman's desiccated corpse and one shriveled severed hand which he picks up to observe. The hand offers a haunting metaphor for this Other that, more often than not, eludes description because it is impossible to fathom or to really *know*:

> I take [the hand] and tie it to the tree of my saddle; it's a funeral relic to take to the sad ossuary of El Aghouat... the hand swayed next to mine; it was a small hand lying, straight, with white nails, which were not without grace, which perhaps, were young; there was something still *encore vivant* in the frightening gesture of the rigid fingers; I ended up by getting scared, and I put it down when I passed the Arab cemetery (*Un Été* 280-281).

The hand is at once a site of fear and curiosity for Fromentin. It equally represents a space where other and self meet head on in symbolic confrontation. This confrontation, in turn, generates a narrative that simultaneously authorizes the communication and the separation of two worlds. This separation is present with respect to women throughout Fromentin's travel novels. Not only is this particular feminine hand detached from its body, it is also haunting because it still is somewhat *vivant*, even though it is not whole (lacking union with a body). The hand is reified as a symbol for an otherness, which is not quite living, nor dead, but held in mysterious limbo between these two spaces. Fromentin is also amazed at its almost life-like qualities when he places his hand next to it, remarking on how it "swung next to" his in perfect unison (*Un Été* 280-81). However, the author falls prey to his own fear perhaps due to the closeness and likeness in the hand he sees to his own and the sudden realization that he will never know this decimated blackened burned woman. She, like the veiled woman, will remain a mysterious feminine other sequestered from view. His fear draws a line of disjunction and disassociation between himself (as French intruder) and the dead colonized Algerian woman. This impenetrable border of otherness brings to the surface an alterity that compels Fromentin to simultaneously see and feel a conjunction and a disjunction, or both a presence and a separation, between the Other and the Self (Racault 37).

The constant schism between the author's feeling of being able to exist as a native and his awareness of the Arab's incomprehensible otherness are noted in many different forms throughout both novels and are, indeed, characteristics of the travel literature of many orientalists of the time. Fromentin and his contemporaries were aware that this dual relationship existed and had to be maintained, not only because it promoted the wide appeal for all that was oriental, but because it continued fueling the dialectic between the dominated and the dominator. This duality was responsible for an entire profitable economy--literary, artistic, economic, and political--which would endure well into the 20th century.

European imperialist policy, in general, not only provided new aesthetic matter for the orientalist painter and author, it also granted the opportunity for expansion of the self; a man's chance to augment his economic ambitions as well as exert his drive for adventure. The fruits of the oriental lands offered the white European male a playground of unfettered possibilities. Through the experience of colonizing the native, the traveling orientalist sought out himself. Colonialism aided the Frenchman to strike out on his own and discover his true masculine hidden identity. Fromentin's travel companion and intrepid *aventurier*, Louis Vandell, in *Une Année dans le Sahel* best exemplifies the "self-made man through masculine actions" image that characterized the protagonists of many orientalist works. Fromentin tells us that Vandell is "solitary," roaming the four corners of Algeria, a man devoted to adventure (*Une Année* 121). He has gone completely native, sporting Arab dress and mannerisms. We are told that he has taken the Arab name, Bou-Djâba, meaning "man with a shotgun." "This country is mine, it has adopted me," the wayfarer remarks (*Une Année* 118). He has renounced any thoughts of ever going back to France, preferring to wander forever in the deserts of Algeria. Fromentin writes, "Vandell has been everywhere where one can go as an intrepid and inoffensive traveler, he has seen everything that merits being seen" (*Une Année* 124-125). The colonizing of Algeria has offered Vandell a platform on which to build another persona. As a "new" man, Vandell enjoys the freedom of exploration and a new identity. The adventurer revels in his escape from French capitalist society which, at this time, is in full expansion mode, leaving less and less space for dreamers, artists, and writers.[12] The aesthetically pleasing stereotypes associated with Algeria and other parts of North Africa promoted in orientalist literature and art opened a window of opportunity, permitting the noble French gentleman relief from the suffocating bourgeois and provincial lifestyles of France. The lives of adventurers, chronicled in detail in works such as Eugène Sue's *Mystères de Paris*, and *La Nouvelle algérienne* (which was a soap opera novella written in 1833 about the sordid affaire of an Algerian woman, Zorah, and a French lieutenant) collectivized an entire nation's will to fantasize and speculate on otherness. The Arab was now the incarnate of an oppositional way of being. Stories promoting redemption by the French sword inspired by the military campaigns of Bugeaud,[13] and by the popular view that the Arab culture was despotic, succeeded in convincing the French public that what their military was doing in the colonies was right and just.

Part of the pleasure of the adventurer's exploits in the colonies was enjoying the Arab woman. According to him, she needed saving from the licentious Arab world. In addition to being portrayed as erotic harem divas in orientalist novels, Algerian women were also considered as pitiful subjects of abjection by religious pundits and missionaries. It was widely thought that the Arab woman was in dire need of rescue from the drudgery of excessively rigid Arab machismo. Feminine abjection became one of a long list of viable excuses for the colonial French Christian mission in Algeria.[14] The French public's compassion for what one French politician of the era stated as "these women who are the most unlucky of creatures and who merit our interest" also weaves its way into Fromentin's texts (Meyer et al. 393). No character better exemplifies the orientalist breadth of Arab feminine representation than does Hawa in *Une Année dans le Sahel.* As previously mentioned, she first appears as an exemplary figure of pure erotica wetting the reader's appetite for a more in depth glimpse of the uncharted space of the harem. Nevertheless, by the end of the novel, Fromentin has brought her full circle, ending her days as a dejected wasted figure. In the closing pages of the novel, she becomes a pathetic woman, following on the heels of Fromentin, Vandell, and her husband as part of a hunting party. In *Une Année dans le Sahel,* Fromentin and Vandell both are surprised at her coming and insist that because of her audacity-- exposing herself in such a public space--she has fallen from her pedestal, condemned by them for her crass and lewd manner of behavior. She and her friend, Aïchouna, have even given to showing themselves "in broad daylight to the curiosity of a troop of soldiers and the insolent gaze of young men who dishonor them" thus breaking the Arab rule, which Fromentin and Vandell seem to have adopted, that women should always be covered (*Une Année* 275). "It is a question of discipline," remarks Vandell. "The entire difference is in the covering: covered up, women are honest, uncovered, they aren't" (*Une Année* 275). As if to save her from further immorality, Fromentin kills her off in the last few pages. Her husband, Amar, murders her for adultery. Bitterly, Hawa is twice condemned, once by her husband and a second time by Fromentin who at no time seems too concerned with her death. In fact, the author surveys the bloody scene with little emotion and expresses no real interest in inquiring as to whether the criminal should be hunted down and justice sought. Nonetheless, if we consider Hawa's death in the context of the imperial mission in Algeria, then her demise may be viewed as a metaphor for the entire conquest of the region. With her tragic end, there is a certain closure of the orientalist's plane of desire, which has been so scrupulously developed by Fromentin in *Une Année dans le*

Sahel. As with Hawa's death, although he expresses some grief at the outcome, he does not demonstrate any tragic emotion over the conquered beauty of Algeria. Both woman and territory are dismissed as unfortunate, but necessary victims, in the scheme of colonial expansion. Though he expresses some regret over the changes occurring in his adopted country because of colonialism, he still is content knowing that "half of French Africa lies before us" (*Une Année* 297). It is regrettable he feels that some of the charms of Algeria have been altered, yet he is pleased to now know that France, by incorporating this majestic country, has regained some of its lost prestige.

Fromentin impresses upon the nineteenth century reader that the opening up of the world through colonization places the western traveler in an optimally exciting position in which to explore. On the heels of the military generals and with the words of the orientalists' travel literature imprinted on their minds, the settlers came to Algeria. Fromentin's dreamy literature of otherness created a new venue for poetic artistic expression while assuring the everlasting melding of art, literature and politics in the interstitial space between seduction and conquest.

Notes

[1] Edward Saïd, as well as many other contemporary critics, has remarked that the first orientalist depictions were responsible for adhering labels to the Arab world. These labels included decadence, sexual licentiousness, corruption, nepotism, effeminate behavior, weakness and childishness and were most notably cultivated by Western authors and painters who traveled in North Africa. See Saïd's famous work, *Orientalism*, (NY: Vintage Press, 1979).

[2] At this point it is necessary to clarify the terms "Maghreb" and "North Africa." The Maghreb refers to the countries of Algeria, Morocco and Tunisia while North Africa encompasses these countries as well as Egypt and Libya. Confusion might arise for English speakers reading 19th century orientalist texts due to the French term "Afrique du nord" which was primarily used to refer to the Maghreb.

[3] On this particular box of couscous the words, "Memories of Marrakech" are written on the box.

[4] Military campaigns in Algeria were fiercely condemned in the beginning as being purely politically motivated by French government officials who wanted to conserve the precarious throne of Louis-Philippe.

[5] Thomas Bugeaud, organizer of the first large military conquest of Algeria in

the late 1830s, was later nominated Marechal de France and governor of Algeria from 1840-1847.

[6] All translations of both Fromentin's texts are my own.

[7] A periodical founded by the painter Théophile Gautier. He first published a portion of Fromentin's *Une Année dans le Sahel* under the title, *Alger, fragment d'un journal de voyage* (See Emanuel Mickel, *Eugène Fromentin*, Boston: Twayne Publishers, 1981: 45).

[8] This space of alterity as a place of confrontation manifested in various literary and picturesque forms throughout the 19th century. Dark against light, East opposite West, and the feminine juxtaposed to the masculine were oppositionalities that provided the fodder for what Joseph Conrad would later call the "heart of darkness"--a synonym for the colonized world. Fromentin's expansion of his own Self through colonial exploration had a cathartic affect on readers and politicians back home in France. Therefore, the fine line between literature and political rhetoric concerning the colonized demonstrates the influence authors like Fromentin had on the political arena. These authors gave confidence to the public and assured them that this unknown world would not only lead to material wealth but also recreate the French man; fortifying the individual and, in turn, the nation.

[9] Frantz Fanon wrote, "Le language du colon, quand il s'agit du colonisé, est un language zoologique" [The language of the colonizer when referring to the colonized is a zoological language]. The link between science and colonialism took on its most heinous attributes towards the end of the 19th century when "human zoos" became the rage in Paris. After the successful "dog exhibition" in 1874, human exhibitions boasting African specimens became widely popular. Humans behind bars and put on display became a common occurrence across Europe. In Berlin in 1879 six Zulu warriors were displayed and from 1877 to 1893 several "tribes" were exhibited in the Jardin d'Acclimatation in Paris. Such fascination, however, does not end with the 19th century. As recent as 1994, a zoo near Nantes, France wanted to create a "village ivorien" [Ivory Coast Village], but were discouraged by a wave of antiracist organizations (*"Zoo humains,"Le Monde*, Jan. 17, 2000).

[10] "The first Order of Nature" and scientific study "were a colonial affair" as Donna Haraway attests. African men, women and children found themselves under a "system of unequal exchange...[an] extractive colonialism" (Donna Haraway, *Primate Visions*, NY: Routledge, 1989: 119). The scientific leaps and bounds made on the heels of military advancement in North Africa generated growing government interest in further study of the exotic flora and fauna of the newly founded colonies. The enthusiasm of Napoléon III for the scientific ventures of the colonial missions accumulated eventually into the founding of the *Société Zoologique d'Acclimation* in the Spring of 1855. Fromentin's descriptive accounts in both travel novels clearly demonstrates his contribution to these early scientific interests.

[11] Frantz Fanon remarks a century later in his work *A Dying Colonialism* that it is precisely these veiled women who entice the "European's persistence in

his irrational conviction that the Algerian woman is the queen of all women."
Therefore, she must be conquered because "unveiling the woman is revealing
her beauty; it is bearing her secret, breaking her resistance, making her
available for adventure" (*A Dying Colonialism*, NY: Grove Press, 1965: 43).
Fanon refers here to the popular French colonial ideal that gaining access to
the Algerian woman would subdue any further resistance from Algerian men.
It was thought that once Algerian men saw that their women had been
conquered, they would put down their arms. The French of course were
mistaken and were taken aback by the incredible roles Algerian women played
during the Algerian revolution. The war would not have been won without
women's participation.

[12] Fromentin's choice to become an artist caused him much personal anxiety
throughout his career (his father wanted him to become a lawyer). Where
Vandell and Fromentin differ is in their perception of the colony and the
escapism it provides. Vandell views it as an expanse in which to become lost,
"to become part of the desert" he states. In contrast, Fromentin never gives up
on being French and following his aesthetic drive to understand the oriental
experience as an appendage to his own life. This experience, he hopes, will
lead him to understand himself in terms of his own spiritual essence explored
because of Algeria. Nevertheless, although arriving at self-knowledge in
different manners, both the author and his protagonist share the view that the
great realm of the colonial space offers a means of transcendence to greater
self-understanding. Fromentin also implies in his texts that self-
understanding through colonial actions allows the individual to find pride
in his own country. He admits that in the wake of France's loss of Alsace-
Lorraine in 1871 (duly signed over in the Treaty of Frankfurt), he was deeply
embittered by the defeat and the humiliation. He blamed France's diminished
international importance on the ailing monarchy, which he held directly
responsible for corruption of the political system (Mickle 22). Fromentin
turned to the world of the colonies, hoping to demonstrate that it was there,
in Algeria particularly, where France would regain her national pride and
international prestige.

[13] Most notably his various military campaigns of the late 1830s.

[14] Some critics assert that the period of colonial expansion in Algeria really
marked a new era of the Crusades. It was thought that this Christian view of
world politics should be *de rigeur* if France was ever going to reassert itself
as a major imperial power. The new fight of the *Croix* against the *Croissant*
was under way. Christianity was readily applied as the third integral part of
the imperialist triptych--adding its dimension to colonial military and
economic zeal. The hard line Christian rhetoric (brought with the influx of
missionaries following the military campaigns of Algeria in the early 1840s),
often used the treatment of women by Algerian men as one of the examples of
the many ills of Islam. Much of the military/Christian political dogma, which
was hinted at in the colonial orientalist novel, was due to the general
conception held by French colonialists that Algerian women were subject to
a pitiful existence and that it was up to white Christian men to save them.

Works Cited

Brahimi, Denise. *"Enjeux et risques du roman exotique français."* *L'Exotisme.* Paris: Cahiers CRLH-CIRAOI, no. 5, 1988: 11-18.

Chenet, Françoise. *"L'Art sarcophage ou la place de l'autre dans la relation de voyage: trois artistes sur le Nil: Flaubert, Maxime du Camp et Fromentin."* *L'Exotisme.* Paris: Diffusion Didier-Erudition, 1988: 149-159.

Cooke, James. *New French Imperialism 1880-1910.* Hamden, CT: Archon, 1973.

Croutier, Alev. *Harem: The World Behind the Veil.* NY: Abbeville, 1989.

Fanon, Frantz. *A Dying Colonialism.* NY: Grove Press, 1965.

Fromentin, Eugène. *Une Année dans le Sahel.* Paris: Plon, 1884.

_____. *Un Été dans le Sahara.* Paris: Georges Crès, 1924.

Haraway, Donna. *Primate Visions.* New York: Routledge, 1989.

Hartman, Elwood. *Three Nineteenth Century French Writer/Artists and the Maghreb: The Literary and Artistic Depictions of North Africa by Théophile Gautier, Eugène Fromentin, and Pierre Loti.* Tubingen, Germany: Gunter Narr Verlag, 1994.

Lafouge, Jean-Pierre. *Étude sur l'orientalisme d'Eugène Fromentin dans ses "récits algériennes."* NY: Peter Lang, 1988.

Marcos, Fouad. *Fromentin et l'Afrique.* Québec: Editions Cosmos, 1973.

Meyer, Jean, Jean Tarrade, Annie Rey-Goldzeiguer, Jacques Thobie. *Histoire de la France Coloniale: Des origines à 1914.* Paris: Armand Colin, 1991.

Mickel, Emanuel. *Eugène Fromentin.* Boston: Twayne Publishers, 1981.

Moussa, Sarga. *"Dire l'Orient."* *L'Exotisme.* Paris: Diffusion Didier-Erudition, 1988: 179-188.

Osborne, Michael A. *Nature, the Exotic, and the Science of French Colonialism.* Bloomington: Indiana UP, 1994.

Queffelec, Lise. *"La Construction de l'espace exotique dans le roman d'aventures au XIXe siècle."* *L'Exotisme.* Paris:

Diffusion Didier-Erudition, 1988: 353-364.

Racault, Jean-Michel. *"Instances médiatrices et production de l'altérité dans le récit exotique aux 17e et 18e siècles."* *L'Exotisme*. Paris: Diffusion Didier-Erudition, 1988.

Saïd, Edward. *Orientalism*. NY: Vintage Press, 1979.

Shohat, Ella and Robert Stam. *Unthinking Eurocentrism: Multiculturalism and the Media*. NY: Routledge, 1993.

PART IV

Africa in the Americas

"In Brightest Africa": Naturalistic Constructions of Africa in the American Museum of Natural History, 1910-1936

Jeannette Eileen Jones
State University of New York at Buffalo

On May 19, 1936, a group of people gathered at the base of the Roosevelt Memorial Statue on the steps of the American Museum of Natural History (hereafter AMNH) in New York City. They awaited the dedication of the Akeley Memorial Hall of African Mammals, an event the Museum had promised since the death of naturalist Carl Akeley in 1926. A rumor that Africa was "coming" to America had circulated the city for weeks. Many spectators awaited confirmation of their knowledge of the so-called "Dark Continent," gleaned from the pages of H. Rider Haggard's *King Solomon's Mines* and Edgar Rice Burroughs' Tarzan series, and viewed through the lenses of Cherry Kearton's wildlife films.[1] Previously unknown and unseen animals waited to be viewed on the other side of the Roosevelt Rotunda.

Beyond the rotunda, a museum staff member opened the doors and escorted some 2,000 guests to the African Hall. They entered a "vast room of black and grey marble, dimly illuminated from overhead by a light like dusk in the jungle" (*Time Magazine*, June 1, 1936: 52). Looming in the shadows of the room was a herd of elephants; seven females facing the entrance, and a bull facing the opposite direction in a stance of protection. Fifteen dioramas depicting various scenes of animal life surrounded the herd, illuminated by light, bright like sunshine (*New York Times* 1936; *New Yorker* 1936).

Against the backdrop of beating "tom-toms," African paintings, and sculptures of African people, wildlife posed in its "natural" environment. "In the damp uplands of the Belgian Congo a glowering male gorilla beats his breast, while the female leans placidly against a tree, watching her baby eat wild celery" (*Time* 1936: 52). Nearby "[o]n the plains of the Tanganyika a group of mottled, sinister wild dogs" watches a herd of zebras and poses for attack (*Time* 1936: 52). "A superb black-maned male" lion rests on the plains as well. "A pair of Bongo antelopes" push through a bamboo jungle and a forest hog "heaves up from its bed among ferns and orchids" (*Time* 1936: 52). *The New York Times* hailed the dioramas for "their artistic beauty, dramatic realism, and scientific accuracy" (1936: 5), and because they had accomplished the impossible. They had brought Africa to Central Park.

Visitors claimed to have been transported to Africa as they viewed the carefully crafted dioramas of African wildlife. Combined with music, lighting, sculptures, and paintings, the habitat groups seemed to work magic on their viewers. "One [could] almost hear the drip of water from recent rains" (*New York Times*, 1936: 5), smell the smoke from the volcanoes of Kivu, and feel the winds sweeping across the Serengeti Plains. African Hall was an illusion *almost* strong enough to make one forget the tales of a Dark Continent with impenetrable jungles, wild beasts, and "savage" men.

The opening of the Akeley African Hall symbolized the triumph of a vision of Africa almost twenty-five years in its conception. Led by Carl Akeley, naturalists at the AMNH dreamed of "Brightest Africa" (C. Akeley 1924), epitomized in an exhibit that would capture the true essence of the continent and dispel myths of steaming jungles, ferocious beasts, and primitive savages. For them, the Hall was the culmination of years of expedition, research, and discovery in the "Dark Continent," supported by scholarly publication, radio broadcast, and cinematic production. African Hall was scientific proof that "Deepest Darkest Africa" was nothing more than the figment of two imaginations fused; those of Henry Morgan Stanley, a reporter in search of an elusive governor, and Joseph Conrad, a former soldier reminiscing about the realities of colonialism.

Wild Beasts, Savage Men, and Impenetrable Jungles

Fifteen years before the opening of the African Hall, Carl Akeley wrote a letter to his wife, Mary, in which he lamented "that horrible darkest Africa the public has accepted" (C. Akeley, 3 February 1921). The tone of the missive is one of annoyance, if not outright disgust. This was neither the first time, nor the last, that Akeley would express his disenchantment with what he saw as the public's willing acceptance of false images of Africa. In his book *In Brightest Africa*, Akeley commented that he hoped African Hall would "tell that story" of "jungle peace...so convincingly that the traditions of jungle horrors and impenetrable forests may be obliterated" (1924: 254).

In the letter to his wife, Akeley challenged one of the most influential texts on the image of Africa: Henry Morgan Stanley's *In Darkest Africa* (1890), which had introduced the Western world to an Africa filled with strange tribes and exotic landscapes. Contributing to the existing plethora of travel narratives on Africa, Stanley's book enjoyed acclaim in the Victorian Era (Murray 1993: 140). Of particular fascination for Stanley was the "primeval forest," specifically the forests of Central Africa (1890: 67).

It is in Stanley's description of the Central African forest where many of the tropes associated with "Darkest Africa" emerge. Stanley draws his audience into a world of "venom, fury, voracity, and activity" (1890: 70). The forest is the site of a Darwinian struggle between man and nature, where "death from wounds, sickness, decay, hereditary disease and old age, and various accidents [thin] the forest, removing the unfit, the weakly, the unadaptable, as among humanity" (1890: 71). Stanley wrote that in all forests, except the primeval forest, "wild men" render nature "prostrate." Yet it is the forest where "there are few places penetrable...without infinite labour" (1890: 72) that Stanley romanticizes as a place of resplendent horror.

Stanley narrates the darkness of the "ruthless forest" where trees do battle with the elements in a "Berseker rage":

The lightning darts here and there with splendour of light and scathing flame, the thunder explodes with deafening crashes, reverberating with terrible sounds among the army of woods, the black clouds roll over and darken the prospect; and as a cloud becomes involved within cloud, in the shifting of pale light, we have a last view of the wild war, we are stunned by the fury of the tempest, and the royal rage of the forest, when down comes the deluge of tropical rain—which in a short time extinguishes the white heat wrath of the elements, and soothes to stillness the noble anger of the woods (Stanley, 1890: 76).

Stanley's description of the African jungle, however romantic in its language, nevertheless depicted a place whose barely suppressed danger emanated from its darkness and impenetrability. Akeley found this portrait of a ruthless forest filled with venomous flora and insects, savage men, and dangerous animals, incredible. To counter this mythic Africa, he designed the African Hall.

The Akeleys reinforced their commitment to challenging the myth of "darkest Africa" by deliberately selecting titles for their African travel books that suggested an opposite vision of the continent. Mary Jobe Akeley titled her book on the Congo expedition *Congo Eden* ([1950] 1961), in much the same way that Akeley called his account of the East African expedition *In Brightest Africa* (1920). Clearly, the Akeleys saw Africa as neither "hellish" nor "dark."

The Akeleys, as well as other AMNH naturalists, reserved their most scathing critiques for the American film industry, whose portrayals of Africa were sensationalistic and ahistorical. Together with filmmakers Osa and Martin Johnson, the Akeleys launched a campaign against the famous "Snow Films" of the 1920s. The AMNH contracted the Johnsons to film wildlife in East Africa as part of its African Hall project (Imperato and Imperato, 1992: 91), to make "scientifically true motion picture records of the primitive tribes of Africa and its rapidly disappearing wildlife" (AMNH 1923).

H. A. Snow and his son Sydney produced *Hunting Big Game in Africa with Gun and Camera* (1922), and other films under the auspices of the African Expedition Corporation (Munden 1971). These films depicted African wildlife, featuring original footage and horrifying hunting scenes. In his endorsement of the Martin Johnson African Expedition (1921-23), Carl Akeley claimed that "[t]he Snow films were largely faked and in addition were entirely misleading from the standpoint of truth and fearfully brutal from the standpoint of the sportsman" (C. Akeley, 22 January 1924). His criticism was well received, particularly since rumor had it that Snow's hunting scenes were staged on Hollywood lots.

Echoing Akeley's critique of the Snow films, Martin Johnson denounced other films besides Snow's. In a report of the National Better Business Bureau, "Film Americaine 'Ubangi'" [sic], he called the film *Ubangi* a "mockery." Supposedly a cinematic portrayal of a Belgian expedition into the jungles of the Congo, *Ubangi* contained scenes of African wildlife and natives outside of "their real geographic situation" ("Film Americaine 'Ubangi'"). Many of the animals photographed were not native to the Congo. Moreover, the featured Meru people were depicted as living in the western region, when in reality the group was eastern in origin. These types of historical inaccuracies disturbed naturalists like Johnson.

The naturalists' critique of cinematic representations of Africa was symptomatic of a larger body of criticism of popular and public images of the continent. The AMNH's naturalists argued that not just film, but literature, radio and museum exhibits as well, had seduced the public with the myth of "Darkest Africa." More importantly, they appropriated those same media to present and disseminate their own vision of the continent.

AMNH naturalists understood that the success of the African Hall depended on more than its ability to challenge old myths. It required the captivation of the public imagination and an arousal of the public mind, without sacrificing the scientific validity of the exhibits. Thus, the Hall's creators had to engage in a curious dialectic. They had to employ both popular and scientific discourses on Africa by taking on the popular roles of storyteller, hunter, and explorer, while maintaining their scientific reputations as naturalists and conservationists.

As storytellers, the Hall's creators recounted experiences in the wilds of Africa. These scenes were recreated in numerous articles, radio talks, and films produced by the AMNH, as well as memoirs published by the naturalists themselves. Perhaps the most sensational safari episode was Carl Akeley's almost fatal encounter with an elephant on

Mount Kenya. Although this mission was on behalf of the Field Museum in Chicago, the story became part of the lore of safari and expedition associated with Akeley wherever he traveled, and it became a favorite among Akeley's New York colleagues (C. and M. Akeley 1930: 8-13, 15).

As explorers and hunters, Akeley and his fellow naturalists brought back trophies from Africa to create dioramas as symbols of their conquest over nature. (Akeley's bulls were part of "The Charge," the centerpiece of the African Hall, and "The Fighting Bulls" at the Field Museum.) However, at the same time that AMNH naturalists shot game with gun and camera, they warned the world of the inevitable depletion of game in Africa. This conservationist role was manifest in the cooperation of Akeley and the AMNH with the Belgian government to create Parc National Albert (Department of the Interior 1924).

The multidimensional persona of the naturalist—explorer, hunter, scientist, and conservationist—emerging from the written word, film, and radio alone could not create a "bright Africa" for the American public. If all that was required to achieve this feat were crafty narratives and moving and still pictures, how would the AMNH's naturalists differ from the Snows and Haggards of the world? How could their work eclipse those fictitious images of Africa? The practices of natural history, which included taxidermy, diorama, and museum display, offered a vehicle for distinguishing "darkest" from "brightest" Africa.

Carl Akeley and the Aesthetics of Natural History

Carl Akeley's approach to creating his hall was a product of late nineteenth and early twentieth century practice in the discipline of natural history. Natural history during this period was overwhelmingly concerned with display and the dissemination of natural historical knowledge to a wider public—a public beyond the traditional elite consumers of museum culture. Developments in lithography and photography, advancements in taxidermy, and the evolution of habitat diorama techniques helped to make natural history aesthetically pleasing to public consumers, primarily through museum exhibits (Jenkins 1978: 73; 85; Wonders 1993: 23-140; Dance 1978: 87; 191-196).

The evolution of the habitat diorama technique and its adoption by museums enhanced the illusionistic presentation of natural history. By giving scientific legitimacy to the new "artistic" display of zoological specimens, through the vehicles of taxidermy and landscape painting, naturalists hoped to challenge the dominant exhibition philosophy of the period. Coined by Louis Daguerre—inventor of the daguerreotype—and taken from the Greek words, *dia* and *horama*, diorama literally meant "through what is seen" or "through sight." Dioramas were designed to capture "through sight" the natural environment of specimens, as well as to suggest "movement without motion" (Wonders 1993: 12; 24).

Taxidermy was the most important element in the success of a habitat group/diorama. Although the ultimate goal of the diorama was to place the specimen in its "natural environment," what drew the public's attention was the realism (or lack thereof) of the stuffed animals. Thus, poses were key to the diorama. Capturing the perfect pose of the subject necessitated a trip to the field—a first-hand experience with the natural world. As a result, museum curators insisted on field collection. Field naturalists argued that isolated specimens of flora and fauna mounted by men unfamiliar with the landscape could never make nature "real" for the public (Browne 1884: 312-316; 1896: 381; 397; Ward 1913: 32-33; 40; 70). Akeley argued that this was especially the case for portraying Africa in a "bright" light.

Akeley advocated the mixing of techniques to create the most faithful portrait of wildlife in its natural habitat. He was a proponent of sketching, photographing, and filming animals before "bagging" them. He also suggested that field naturalists make photographs, paintings, or sketches of the various landscapes where the specimens were found, as well as collect rocks, leaves, tree bark, and other portable pieces of the landscape (Osborn 1924: 12-15; Akeley 1924: 1-19). Akeley's diorama technique dated back to his days with the Field Museum, but became most associated with his work for the AMNH. President Osborn wrote in his Annual Report of 1924 that Akeley "invented an entirely new method of mounting... nobly exemplified in his African Elephant Group, far more artistic and lifelike than his previous method" (1924: 12-13). He goes on to say that Akeley's gorilla group afforded "the finest example of Mr. Akeley's new art in mounting and modeling, especially in the facial expression of these great primates" (*Ibid.*).

Osborn was among the many people who praised Akeley's technique of display for transforming the image of the "Dark Continent." However, Akeley's presentation of "Brightest Africa"—a zoological wonderland authentically preserved in habitat dioramas—did not go uncontested. Could the exhibit include natives and remain "bright"? Would the presentation of African peoples and cultures somehow diminish the brightness of Africa in a natural history exhibit?

Displaying Africa and the Cultures of Natural History

Akeley's position on the displaying of Africans in the hall must be reconciled with two specific trends in viewing natural history in the early twentieth century. The turn of the twentieth century saw an increasing separation of zoology and anthropology within the discipline of natural history. Zoology (the scientific study of animals) became associated with "traditional" natural history. Anthropology (the study of humans with an emphasis on measurement and classification) was viewed as an extension of ethnography/ethnology ("the physical and civil history of foreign and particularly non-Christian peoples") (Bravo, in Jardine, Secord, and Spary, 1996: 338-339). The separation of the two fields into distinct disciplines played a key role in the way in which the AMNH would display Africa.

Tensions between zoologists and incipient anthropologists can be seen in the Congo Expedition (1909-1915) for the African Hall. While the expedition was designed to be principally zoological, naturalist Herbert Lang showed more interest in the Africans he encountered. In his recounting of the expedition for the museum's journal *Natural History Magazine*, Lang wrote extensively about the peoples of the Ituri forest, whom he called "Pygmies" (1919a: 696-713). He took extensive photographs of the Ituri peoples and made plaster casts of their faces, which became the bases for his "Pygmy Group" (1919a: 701-702). In another article, he wrote about the Mangbetu and neighboring peoples (1919b: 527-552).

Lang's departure from the zoological mission of the expedition is significant because it represented the movement away from a more "traditional" naturalistic picture of Africa that focused on flora and fauna. Although not impervious to the presence of Africans, Akeley made little use for them in his image of Africa. In fact, the hall's opening in 1936 did not feature Lang's group. The hall did, however, include various bronzes of Africans that Akeley had sculpted.

The exclusion of Lang was not the first incidence of zoology eclipsing anthropology in the AMNH's naturalistic representation of Africa. According to a 1911 history of the museum, the Department of Anthropology housed an African collection that dated back to 1902. African acquisitions from 1902 to 1908 included specimens of basketry, weaving, pottery, musical instruments, masks, idols, "fetishes," and woodcarvings (Osborn 1911: 103-104). These items appeared to have disappeared after the hiring of Akeley in 1909. In reality, the emphasis on Africa shifted in the museum from anthropology to zoology. Many of those early ethnographic specimens would not resurface again until the after 1950 when Colin Turnbull visited the Congo in 1951. Turnbull's visit renewed the museum's interest in African ethnography and led to the creation of a permanent exhibit dedicated to the peoples and cultures of Africa (Rexer and Klein 1995).

The inclusion of African objects and cultural profiles of Africans may have broadened the scope of the museum's images of Africa. However, ethnography did not remedy the limited image of Africa that Akeley embraced.

Towards a "Brightest Africa"

The AMNH's image of Africa, while often hailed as new, revolutionary, or progressive (cf. Beauregard 1995; Houston 1986; Imperato 1992; Bodry-Sanders 1991) was in fact an old image reconfigured. Akeley's image of Africa was of an "ageless continent" (M. Akeley 1940: 368). Like most Americans, Akeley chose to see Africa as a timeless, unchanged land—a place where modernity and civilization had not yet triumphed. Africa held within its borders mysterious beasts, exotic flora, and "primitive men"—all the symbols of a past long gone—or so the story went. Thus, to understand the problematic—how an exhibit designed to dispel myths about a "Dark Continent" reinforced those myths—we must look not only at the content of the hall, but at the institutional context in which the hall was constructed.

"Primitive men" were so much a part of the static image of Africa. Yet Akeley chose not to include images of Africans in any substantial way in his exhibit. Understandably, Akeley was primarily a zoologist. However, his personal identification as a naturalist does not explain why the museum did not propose an adjoining hall that would emphasize African anthropology. The lack of commitment to including Africans in any exhibit seems puzzling—especially in light of the approach the museum took to the North American wing.

In the North American wing of the museum, both a zoological and an anthropological hall were constructed. Franz Boas' hall of Native American peoples and cultures was not at odds with the zoology hall. Both views—of peoples and cultures, and of flora and fauna—were acceptable in presenting the natural history of North America. Why was this not applicable to Africa? First, North America was not understood as an ageless continent, despite the presence of people who had been "naturalized" in the American imagination. The presence of whites in America seems to have rescued the continent from the designation "primitive," by bringing it into a narrative of modernity and civilization—into history. The presence of Europeans in Africa appears not to have had the same effect. Second, the racial ascription placed on Africans, while at times similar to that projected on Native Americans, was unique due to the circumstances under which Westerners encountered Africans.

Europeans' presence in Africa was initially in the context of trade in commodities and humans. By the late nineteenth and early twentieth centuries, Europeans were in Africa, primarily to extract natural resources back to the mother country, employing African labor. With the exception of the southern African colonies, Europeans generally did not envision colonizing Africa on a permanent basis, unlike British colonization of America. Thus, Africa could never be truly a "white man's country"--"modern" and "civilized" (Pieterse 30-51).

In the case of North America, displaying images of Native American peoples and cultures (i.e., the natural historical past of the continent) bolstered the image of a continent transformed by the presence of Europeans. North America had a clear historical narrative, which began and ended with the Americans of European descent. The North American Hall served to highlight this contrasting of these "two Americas." The Native Americans depicted were the "noble savages," symbols of the valiant struggle for and conquest of America. Africans, on the other hand, were not seen to be as noble in their struggle for the continent. After all, they had been subject to intercontinental slavery and colonialism, yet somehow they survived. They could not be martyred as a bygone race in an age of modernity. They were still "savage" and resistant to "civilization."

The decision to view Africa through the lens of natural history predetermined the extent to which Akeley's new image of Africa would challenge the old. The discipline of natural history was caught in a moment when Africa could not escape naturalization—because it was applied to the study of non-Western lands and peoples. In a climate of scientific and popular racism, any naturalistic approach to Africa was fraught with images that echoed that of those associated with "Darkest Africa" and colonialism, which emphasized the "naturalness" of Africa and the "White Man's Burden" to bring order to nature. Describing Africa as "natural" was synonymous with characterizing it as "primitive" or "uncivilized," for in Western thought the mark of civilization is the ability to subdue and conquer nature.

The extent to which Akeley achieved his goal of recasting the public's image of Africa is debatable. What is clear is that in his effort to obliterate the myth of the "Darkest Africa," Akeley created a new image of Africa plagued by many of the same fictions that underlined Stanley's portrait of the continent. Africa remained the home of mysterious flora and fauna, and of "natural" men.

Notes

[1] The novels of H. Rider Haggard were popular in both America and Great Britain. Haggard presented the public with characters who ranged from great white hunters and imperial white men, to "savage" natives. Among his more celebrated novels are *She* and *King Solomon's Mines*. Edgar Rice Burroughs became famous in the early twentieth century for his serial novels, which featured the character "Tarzan." His novel *Tarzan, the Ape*

Man was brought to the big screen as a feature movie, and was one of the top twenty grossing films in 1933. Cherry Kearton was best known for his wildlife films, particularly his documentary of Theodore Roosevelt's hunting trip to Africa.

Works Cited

"Africa Comes to New York." *New York Times.* 17 May 1936: 17+.

"Africa Transplanted." *Time* 1 June 1936.

Akeley, Carl. *In Brightest Africa.* Garden City, New York: Doubleday, Page & Company, 1924.

_____. Letter to Mary Jobe Akeley and Herbert Lang. 3 Feb. 1921. Papers of Mary Jobe Akeley. AMNH Special Collections, New York.

_____. Letter to Mr. -----. 22 Jan. 1924. Papers of Mary Jobe Akeley. ANMH Special Collections, New York.

Akeley, Carl and Mary L. Jobe. *Adventures in the African Jungle.* New York: Dodd, Mead, and Company, 1930.

Akeley, Mary L. Jobe. *Congo Eden: A Comprehensive Portrayal of the Historical Background and Scientific Aspects of the Great Game Sanctuaries of the Belgian Congo with the Story of Six Months Pilgrimage Throughout that Most Primitive Region in the Heart of the African Continent.* New York: Dodd, Mead & Company, 1950; reprint, 1961.

_____. *The Wilderness Lives Again: Carl Akeley and the Great Adventure.* New York: Dodd, Mead, & Company, 1940.

"Akeley Memorial." *New Yorker* 2 May 1936.

"Akeley Memorial Dedicated by 2,000." *New York Times* 20 May 1936: 3+.

American Museum of Natural History. *The Martin Johnson African Expedition Under the Supervision of the American Museum of Natural History.* New York: American Museum of Natural History, 1923.

Beauregard, Erving E. "Explorers: The Two Mrs. Carl Akeleys." *Journal of Unconventional History* 6 (1995): 28-59.

Belgium. Ministère des Affaires Étrangères du Commerce Extérieur et de la Coopération au Développement. Archives Africaines. "Film Americaine 'Ubangi'." *Informations relatives aux puissance d'Amérique*—E.U.A., 1275-1393. Etats-Unis d'Amérique. Ministère des Colonies, AE/II no. 1388 (3240) 8516.

Bodry-Sanders, Penelope. *Carl Akeley: Africa's Collector, Africa's Savior*. New York: Paragon House, 1991.

Bravo, Michael T. "Ethnological Encounters." *Cultures of Natural History*. Eds. Jardine, N., J. A. Secord, and E. C. Spary. Cambridge: Cambridge University Press, 1996. 338-357.

Browne, Montagu. *Artistic and Scientific Taxidermy and Modelling: A Manual of Instruction in the Methods of Pre-Serving and Reproducing the Correct Form of all Natural Objects Including a Chapter on the Modelling of Foliage*. London: Adam and Charles Black, 1896.

_____. *Practical Taxidermy: A Manual of Instruction to the Amateur in Collecting, Preserving, and Setting Up Natural History Specimens of All Kinds. To Which is Added a Chapter Upon the Pictorial Arrangement of Museums*. London: L. Upcott Gill, 1884.

Dance, S. Peter. *The Art of Natural History: Animal Illustrators and their Work*. Woodstock, New York: The Overlook Press, 1978.

Department of the Interior. Memorandum for the Press. 10 Mar. 1924.

Houston, Dick. "The Boy and Girl Next Door Made Movies Far Away." *Smithsonian* 17 (1986): 144-49, 150, 153-155.

Imperato, Pascal James and Eleanor M. *They Married Adventure: The Wandering Lives of Martin and Osa Johnson*. New Brunswick, New Jersey: Rutgers University Press, 1992.

Jenkins, Alan C. *The Naturalists: Pioneers of Natural History*. New York: Mayflower Books, Inc., 1978.

Lang, Herbert. "Famous Ivory Treasures of a Negro King." *The American Museum Journal* (1919): 527-552.

_____. "Nomad Dwarfs and Civilization." *Natural History* XIX No. 6 (1919): 696-713.

Munden, Kenneth W., ed. *The American Film Institute Catalog of Motion Picture Produced in the United States: Feature Films, 1921-1930.* New York and London: R. R. Bowker Company, 1971.

Murray, John A. *Wild Africa: Three Centuries of Nature Writing from Africa.* New York and Oxford: Oxford University Press, 1993.

Osborn, Henry Fairfield. *The American Museum of Natural History: Its Origins, Its History, the Growth of Its Departments to December 31, 1909.* With the Cooperation of Members of the Administrative and Scientific Staffs. New York: Irving Press, 1911.

_____. *President's Annual Report.* New York: American Museum of Natural History, 1924.

Pieterse, Jan Nederveen. *White on Black: Images of Africa and Blacks in Western Popular Culture.* New Haven and London: Yale University Press, 1992.

Rexer, Lyle and Rachel Klein. *American Museum of Natural History: 125 Years of Expedition and Discovery.* New York: H. N. Abrams in association with the American Museum of Natural History, 1995.

Stanley, Henry M. *In Darkest Africa or the Quest, Rescue, and Retreat of Emin, Governor of Equatoria.* New York: Charles Scribner's Sons, 1890.

Ward, Rowland. *A Naturalist's Life Study in the Art of Taxidermy.* London: Rowland Ward, Ltd., "The Jungle," 1913.

Wonders, Karen Elizabeth. "Habitat Dioramas: Illusions of Wilderness in Museums of Natural History (Sweden, United States)." Diss. Uppsala Universitet, Sweden, 1993.

From Race to Class: The African American Literary Response to the Italo-Ethiopian War

John Gruesser
Kean University

The two excerpts below from Hughes' "Ballad of Ethiopia" and Tolson's "The Bard of Addis Ababa" reveal the intensity of the African American reaction to Italy's invasion of Ethiopia in 1935:

All you colored peoples   The Black Shirts slump on the camels,
No matter where you be   Haggard and granite-eyed;
Take for your slogan   No longer the gypsying Caesars
AFRICA BE FREE!   Who burnt-faced breeds deride:
Be a man at last   In the river Takkaze their vanity
Say to Mussolini   Lies with the Caesars who died.
No! You shall not pass.   (Melvin Tolson)
(Langston Hughes)

These excerpts also typify the special place that Ethiopia, with its history of resistance to foreign intrusions, has held in the African American psyche. Fascist Italy's October 1935 invasion and May 1936 annexation of Ethiopia figure not only in several poems by Langston Hughes but also in a lengthy prose fragment and poetry by Melvin B. Tolson. Early in the war, Hughes adopted a racial approach to the besieged nation; late in the conflict and after the Italian takeover, he looked at the Ethiopian situation from a Communist point of view. Set in East Africa just before and during the war, Tolson's unfinished novel "The Lion and the Jackal" (1935?)[1] and a companion piece,

"The Bard of Addis Ababa," included in his first published book of poems *Rendezvous with America* (1944), take a decidedly pro-Ethiopian stance and evince an impressive familiarity with Ethiopian history, culture, and geography. Like Hughes, in the wake of the Italian victory, Tolson's position toward the Ethiopian conflict shifted from a racial to an economic approach, as revealed in the "Caviar and Cabbage" columns Tolson wrote for the *Washington Tribune* in the late 1930s and early 1940s.

In two recent books devoted to the African American response to the Italo-Ethiopian War, Joseph E. Harris (1994) and William R. Scott (1993) emphasize the intensity and the massive scale of black American identification with and moral support for Ethiopia. According to Scott, "The pro-Ethiopian crusade of African-Americans represents an extraordinary episode in modern U.S. black history. A mass impulse, its scope was broad and its force intense, exceeding in size and vigor all other contemporary black freedom protests" (1994: 210). The black press covered the conflict at length, roundly condemning Italy's aggression. No African American publication devoted more attention to the war than the *Pittsburgh Courier*, which in 1935 had the largest circulation of any black newspaper. The *Courier* presented Italy's invasion and the major powers' tepid response as a conspiracy designed to bolster white imperialism and keep black people in submission. The paper dispatched J.A. Rogers to the front, the only correspondent from a black paper to report on the battles firsthand. Rogers achieved a journalist coup when the *Courier* on 7 March 1936 published his exclusive interview with Haile Selassie, the first granted to a foreign reporter (Buni 1974: 245-47, Weisbord 1972: 237-38). Scott (1993) suggests that as a result of all the news coverage, African Americans in 1936 knew more about Ethiopia's history and culture than that of any other African country. Several organizations were formed to raise money for Ethiopia, although the amount of money collected was quite small and very little of this actually found its way to Addis Ababa. During the war and immediately following Italy's victory, tensions between African Americans and Italian Americans escalated, resulting in riots in Brooklyn, Harlem, and Jersey City.

A major obstacle to concrete, long-lasting cooperation between black Americans and Ethiopians was the perception, apparently not without some basis in fact, that members of the

Ethiopian ruling class did not regard themselves as black people and were reluctant to associate with African Americans. Two major supporters of the Ethiopian war effort later condemned Haile Selassie and the ruling elite's racial attitudes. When the exiled Emperor refused to meet with him, Marcus Garvey, long a champion of the Ethiopian cause, attacked the ruler, warning that "The Negro Abyssinian must not be ashamed to be a member of the Negro race. If he does, he will be left alone by all the Negroes of the world" (qtd. in Isaacs 1963: 153).[2] Likewise, Willis N. Huggins, who had headed the International Council of Friends of Ethiopia, subsequently criticized the Ethiopian regime. Despite efforts at damage control by Rogers and others as well as by Ethiopian representatives themselves, the combination of the rumors of Ethiopians' disavowal of racial kinship and the swift defeat of the country dampened African American enthusiasm for Haile Selassie's cause considerably.

Harris and Scott differ markedly on the long-term significance of the African American response to war in Ethiopia. Regarding the black American reaction as "a watershed in the history of African peoples," Harris sees a clear link between it and the freedom movements in the United States, the Caribbean, and Africa following World War II (1994: xi, 159). Scott, in contrast, noting that despite extensive coverage in the black press the restoration of Haile Selassie to power in 1941 generated little interest among the African American masses, does not see the connection: "...during the era of the civil rights revolution in America and the rising tide of black power all over colonized Africa, a generation of black Americans who had not been nurtured on the gospel of Ethiopianism or the veneration of the Ethiopian state tended to look beyond racially ambivalent Ethiopia toward other openly avowed black African nations for inspiration in their own liberation struggle against white oppression" (1993: 219-20).[3] The truth appears to lie somewhere between Harris' and Scott's widely divergent positions. Although key figures in the effort to aid Ethiopia during the war later proved instrumental in founding the Pan-African Federation, which organized the Fifth Pan-African Congress held in Manchester in 1945, these men, who included George Padmore and Jomo Kenyatta, were West Indian and African rather than African American, and their base of operation was London rather than New York (Hill 1994: 37).

A gradual move from a racial to an economic reading of the

Italo-EthiopianWar can be seen in the six poems that Langston Hughes published between September 1935 and September 1938 that either directly address or in some way allude to the conflict. In his biography of Hughes, Arnold Rampersad observes that Hughes responded to the Ethiopian crisis in two different ways: "Hughes seemed sometimes to endorse the communist view, sometimes the more racial perspective" (1986: 322). The dates of the poems are significant, however, because they reveal a progression, rather than an inconsistency or alternation as Rampersad seems to assert, in Hughes' thinking. In the two poems published before the Italian invasion, Hughes clearly adopted the racial perspective, but once the fate of Ethiopia was sealed he espoused the Communist view.

In "Call of Ethiopia," a nineteen-line lyric published in *Opportunity* in September 1935, Hughes' calls on "all Africa" to "arise" and "answer ... the call of Sheba's race" (11, 13), concluding with the lines, "Be like me, / All of Africa, / Arise and be free! / All you black peoples, / Be free! Be free!" (15-19). This Pan-Africanist recruiting pitch recurs in "Ballad of Ethiopia," a fourteen-stanza poem published the same month in the Baltimore *Afro-American* that contains more topical references and employs a more belligerent tone. The speaker, personifying the black race throughout history, calls upon his reader to "Take as your slogan: / AFRICA BE FREE" (23-24) and then, echoing the sorrow song, issues a warning, "O nobody knows / The trouble I've seen-- / But when I rise I'm / Gonna rise mean" (29-32). After recalling Joe Louis' defeat of the Italian fighter Primo Carnera, the speaker boasts, "Mussolini's men / They may swing their capes-- / But when Harlem starts / She's a cage of apes!" (37-40), calls for black unity, and ends with the admonition, "Listen, Mussolini, / Don't you mess with me!" (55-56). Significantly, these two poems resemble racially inflected poems inspired by the war published elsewhere in the world. For example, "A Poem on Ethiopia," appearing in Accra's *Vox Populi* on 21 September 1935, concludes, "From East and West, South and North / To Ethiopia we'll come, a fighting band / To drive imposters out of the Black Man's land; / If we win not, we will die trying / To keep our land, and freedom flag flying / Greedy man, let your war madness cease / The Ethiopian wants his land, and peace" (qtd. in Asante 1977: 217).

Beginning with the 132-line "Air Raid over Harlem," published in *New Theatre* in February 1936, Hughes looks at the

Ethiopian conflict and its significance for African Americans in more than just racial terms. Subtitled "Scenario for a Little Black Movie," this poem implicitly and explicitly connects conditions in doomed Ethiopia with those in Depression-era Harlem. Two-thirds of the way through, the speaker not only continues to link Italian oppression of blacks in Africa with white oppression in America, particularly that of the police in Harlem, but pinpoints capitalist greed as the source of both instances of oppression:

> BLACK WORLD
> Never wake up
> Lest you knock over the cup
> Of gold that the men who
> Keep order guard so well
> And then--well, then
> There'd be hell
> To pay
> And bombs over Harlem. (91-99)

This stanza suggests that if African Americans were to become aware of how capitalism exploits them and try to do something about it, then they would be just as likely to be the victims of the white world's firepower as the Ethiopians. Nevertheless, the speaker proceeds to imagine Harlem "waking," "see[ing] *red*," and "shak[ing] the whole world with a new dream"--a Marxist dream of "Black and white workers united as one / In a city where / There'll never be / Air raids over Harlem / FOR THE WORKERS ARE FREE" (103, 108, 110, 122-26, emphasis added).

The three relatively brief poems concerning Ethiopia Hughes published in the wake of the Italian victory likewise consider the takeover of Ethiopia from a Marxist viewpoint. "Broadcast on Ethiopia," which appeared in the July/August 1936 issue of the *American Spectator*, concerns May 4, 1936, the day Haile Selassie fled his country, but also the day Communists gained seventy-five seats in the French Parliament. The poem refers to the defeated nation as a "Tragi-song for the newsreels" (6); reveals the African American disillusionment with the racial aloofness of the Ethiopian ruling class discussed by Scott, and asserts that the Ethiopians did not stand a chance, "Haile/ With his slaves, his dusky wiles, / His second-hand planes like a child's, / But he has no gas--so he cannot last" (7-10); and laments that "Civilization's gone to hell!" (35). Yet because "Italy's cheated / When *any* Minister anywhere's / Defeated by Communists" (27-29, emphasis in original), there is cause for hope in the French election results. "White Man," published in *New Masses* in December 1936, begins by emphasizing the racial perspective but suddenly shifts to the Marxist view. The speaker, identifying himself as "a Negro," directly addresses the "White Man": "You take all the best jobs / And leave us the garbage cans to empty" (4-5); "You enjoy Rome-- / And *take* Ethiopia" (12-13, emphasis in original); " Let Louis Armstrong play it-- / And you copyright it / And make the money" (14-16). The last third of the poem, however, suggests that the real source of exploitation lies in class rather than race differences. Stating "I hear your name ain't really White / Man" (21-22), the speaker asks, "Is your name in a book? Called the *Communist Manifesto*? / Is your name spelled / C-A-P-I-T-A-L-I-S-T / Are you always a White Man?" (28-32). Finally, in "Song for Ourselves," published in the *New York Post* 19 September 1938, the speaker links "Czechoslovakia! Ethiopia! [and] Spain!" as victims of "the long snake of greed" (7, 10).

Melvin's Tolson's fiction, poetry, and political commentary about Ethiopia in the late 1930s and early 1940s follow a similar path from racial identification to global economic analysis. The fifteen chapters of Tolson's incomplete "The Lion and the Jackal" are divided into two books. The title refers to Haile Selassie and Benito Mussolini respectively, although neither actually appears in the manuscript. The action begins in Djibouti, Ethiopia's French colonial neighbor, on 1 October 1935, two days before the Italian invasion. The major figure in Book I is Abba Micah Soudani, a renowned poet and patriot, who is a close friend of the Emperor. In Book II the scene shifts to Ethiopia itself as a motley group of passengers travels by train from Djibouti to Addis Ababa on the day the war begins. The novel then jumps ahead to late December 1935 after the Italians, despite the setback of the Ethiopian counteroffensive in the vicinity of the Tekkaze River, have pushed deeply into the country, and Soudani's son, Lionel, a lieutenant in the Ethiopian army, emerges as a key figure in the story. At the end of the manuscript, the outcome of the conflict remains very much in doubt as Lieutenant Soudani speculates that guerrilla tactics may be the most effective means of defeating the

Italians.

Although there are no African American characters in the manuscript, Haile Selassie has an American advisor and two white Americans ride the French train to the Ethiopian capital. One is a journalist who has come to report on the conflict. The second, a missionary who identifies himself as a descendent of John Brown, offers to take up arms against the invaders. Here implicitly and elsewhere in the novel much more openly Tolson equates fascism and slavery. The manuscript does allude to the "Black Condor," John C. Robinson, the African American pilot who served as the leader of Ethiopia's small air force in the war, as well as to the flamboyant Hubert Fauntleroy Julian, also known as the Black Eagle of Harlem (but referred to by one of Tolson's characters as "the big-mouth, Colonel Peacock" [89]). West Indian by birth and a Garveyite during the 1920s, Julian first came to Ethiopia in 1930 to organize Haile Selassie's air force, but left the country soon after crashing the emperor's best plane. He returned shortly before the war and once more served as aviation chief, only to anger the ruler yet again and lose his position to Robinson.[4] Most intriguing of all are references in "The Lion and the Jackal" to rumors among the Ethiopians that a group of five thousand African Americans, "freed and led by the great Dedjazmatch [General] Abraham Lincoln, were on their way to Addis Ababa, with tanks and bombers" (19).

Not enough of "The Lion and the Jackal" exists to determine for certain where Tolson intended to go with the story; however, it does not contain his only thoughts on the Italo-Ethiopian War. Allusions to the conflict are scattered throughout *Rendezvous with America* and "The Bard of Addis Ababa" is completely devoted to the early months of the Italian invasion.[5] Like Tolson's unfinished novel, this 112-line poem adopts the racial approach. Each of the three sections of "The Bard" provides evidence that the poem derives from and/or was written in conjunction with "The Lion and the Jackal." The description of the accoutrements of the Bard in section one identify him as Abba Micah Soudani. In the second section, the Bard's exhortation to the Ethiopian soldiers to "Rise up, ye warriors, do or die" (55 and 73), linking their cause to a wide variety of freedom movements mentioned in *Rendezvous* (especially that of the American soldiers at Valley Forge), and his prediction of defeat for Italy--part of which serves as an epigraph for this paper--appear exactly as they do in "The Lion and the Jackal." Finally, the celebration of Ethiopia's Christmas offensive in the third section closely resembles that of the second half of Book II of the novel.

After the Italian conquest, Tolson abandoned the racial approach to the war. Writing about the then-concluded conflict in a "Caviar and Cabbage" column in the *Washington Tribune* entitled "Drama: 'The Tragedy of Ethiopia,' May 28, 1938," Tolson offers a coldly economic analysis that differs markedly from the passionate partisanship of "The Lion and the Jackal" and the "The Bard of Addis Ababa." Like Hughes, Tolson blames capitalism for Ethiopia's defeat and for the undermining of international law, yet he is less cynical about the exiled Emperor than Hughes in "Broadcast on Ethiopia," describing Haile Selassie begging for assistance at the League of Nations as a tragic figure worthy of Shakespeare. Whereas at the end of the novel and "The Bard" Ethiopia's fate has not yet been determined, Tolson claims in the column to have predicted a swift Italian victory on the day the conflict began because "spears and old-fashioned guns are no match for mechanized modern warfare" ("Drama" 105). Tolson makes no distinction between Italy's occupation of Ethiopia and Britain and France's colonial rule in Africa and elsewhere; rather, referring to these countries as "The Unholy Three," he states, "England and France and Italy now exploit 500,000,000 colored people. For what? For dollars. For profits in gold and oil and rubber and agricultural products" (106). However, Tolson suggests that the capitalists have been sowing the seeds of their own destruction, "But at home the masses of the population in these countries tear out their lives against economic injustices. That's the cancer that will eat away these dishonorable governments" (106), and he concludes the column with the assertion that "The white man--I mean the big white man--has messed up the world. He's had two thousand years to make good. He's had the best soil of the earth at his command. Nature and fortune have smiled upon him. But he started out wrong. Because he started out to exploit" (106). Although he echoes many late nineteenth- and early twentieth-century African American writers in asserting that the West is destined to fall, Tolson differs from them by failing to express any hope that this will result in a better world for people of African descent. Instead, with bitter sarcasm he can only urge his readers to "laugh" at the "worst of all possible worlds" white people have created (107, 106).[6]

As reflected in the texts of Hughes and Tolson written in 1935 and early 1936, the Italian invasion of Ethiopia elicited intense feelings of racial solidarity from African Americans. However, in the wake of the Ethiopian defeat, these authors devoted their energy to analyzing the political and economic causes for the Italian takeover, with Hughes adopting an openly and Tolson an implicitly Marxist reading of the situation.

Notes

We are greatful to the UP of Kentucky for authorizing the inclusion in this article of elements from chapter 4 of John Gruesser's *Black on Black: Twentieth Century African American Writing about Africa* (2000).

[1] Assigning a precise date to "The Lion and the Jackal" presents a serious challenge. Although Joy Flasch (1972) claims that Tolson wrote it in 1935 (27), in her chronology of his life she claims he finished the novel in 1939 (16). The 105 typewritten papers of the manuscript in Tolson's papers, however, do not amount to a complete story. Further complicating matters, the folder containing it in Tolson's papers at the Library of Congress bears the description "Novel: *The Lion and the Jackal,* C. 1945." I suspect that the 1935 date is correct and that the rapidity of the Ethiopian defeat took Tolson by surprise and caused him to abandon the manuscript. I am grateful to Aldon Nielsen for providing me with a copy of this novel.

[2] For information on Garvey's reactions to the Italo-Ethiopian War and his criticism of Haile Selassie, see Lewis 1988: 168-75.

[3] Scott here elaborates an assertion first made by Harold Isaacs: "Nowadays... Ethiopia does not figure prominently in the new shape of Negro interest in Africa" (1963: 153).

[4] For information on Robinson and Julian, see Scott 1993: 69-95 and Weisbord 1972.

[5] For a discussion of the numerous references to the Ethiopian War in *Rendezvous*, see Doreski 1998: 82-83.

[6] Tolson's assertion that capitalism was responsible for the defeat of Ethiopia is repeated in another "Caviar and Cabbage" column entitled "Frankenstein and the Monster," which appeared in 1940.

Works Cited

Asante, S.K.B. *Pan-African Protest: West Africa and the Italo-*

Ethiopian Crisis, 1934-1941. London: Longman, 1977.

Buni, Andrew. *Robert L. Vann of the "Pittsburgh Courier": Politics and Black Journalism*. Pittsburgh: U of Pittsburgh P, 1974.

Doreski, C.K. *Writing America Black: Race Rhetoric in the Public Sphere*. New York: Cambridge UP, 1998.

Flasch, Joy. *Melvin B. Tolson*. New York: Twayne, 1972.

Harris, Joseph. *African-American Reactions to War in Ethiopia, 1936-1941*. Baton Rouge: Louisiana State UP, 1994.

Hill, Robert A. Introduction. *Ethiopian Stories*. By George S. Schuyler. Boston: Northeastern UP, 1994. 1-50.

Hughes, Langston. "Ballad of Ethiopia." *Afro-American* 28 September 1935: 3.

_____. *The Collected Poems of Langston Hughes*. Eds. Arnold Rampersad and David Roessel. New York: Knopf, 1994.

Isaacs, Harold. *The New World of Negro Americans*. New York: Day, 1963.

Lewis, Rupert. *Marcus Garvey: Anti-Colonial Champion*. Trenton: Africa World, 1988.

Rampersad, Arnold. *The Life of Langston Hughes*. Vol. I. New York: Oxford UP, 1986.

Scott, William R. *The Sons of Sheba's Race: African Americans and the Italo-Ethiopian War, 1935-1941*. Bloomington: Indiana UP, 1993.

Tolson, Melvin. "Drama: 'The Tragedy of Ethiopia,' May 28, 1938." *Caviar and Cabbage: Selected Columns by Melvin B. Tolson from the Washington Tribune 1937-1944*. Ed. Robert Farnsworth. Columbia: U of Missouri P, 1982. 104-07.

_____. "Frankenstein and the Monster, May 25, 1940." *Caviar and Cabbage: Selected Columns by Melvin B. Tolson from the Washington Tribune 1937-1944*. Ed Robert Farnsworth. Columbia: U of Missouri P, 1982. 125-27.

_____. "The Lion and the Jackal." Melvin B. Tolson Papers. Library of Congress. Washington, D.C.

_____. *Rendezvous with America*. New York: Dodd, 1944.

Weisbord, Robert G. "Black Americans and the Italo-Ethiopian Crisis: An Episode in Pan-Negroism." *Historian* Feb. 1972: 230-41.

The Herero in the Harz: Pynchon's Re-Presentation of Race Relations in *Gravity's Rainbow*

Victoria Ramirez
Weber State University

In an article that offers a historical re-reading of Thomas Pynchon's *V.* , Robert Holton notes: "There is an almost Pynchonesque irony in the way in which many critics have maintained a blind spot in their readings of Pynchon's texts, a blind spot that occludes the explicitly social and political dimensions of the work." Critics may have identified Pynchon's unrelenting attack on what Michael Bérubé calls the "totalizing unities" that underlie Western discursive strategies of control and oppression, but they have failed to connect this attack to Pynchon's simultaneous interrogation of race relations. Yet protagonist Slothrop's drug-induced racist fantasy alludes to the American civil rights and black power movements of the 60s, while the novel includes an entire "sub-plot" that historically re-interprets the German imperialist enterprise in South West Africa.

This paper asserts that Pynchon's politically radical rereading of that German colonization, and his dramatization of the "Schwartzkommando"--the fictitious African rocket troops that assemble Hitler's V-2 rockets--help clarify for readers America's deepest, yet most unacknowledged, problem: racism. I will argue that Pynchon's re-presenting of race relations at the heart of both European imperialism and America's greatest social problems provides its radically revised historical record through a narrative that at the time of the novel's publication helps re-create a hitherto underrepresented history of the oppressed that directly questions the authority of pervasive Enlightenment "dichotomizing" discourses. Pynchon effects this re-presenting of race relations, which reveals white America's own racial attitudes, through manipulating readers into adopting textual positions complicitous with a number of racist beliefs and behaviors.

Pynchon's use of the Herero has been taken by many of Pynchon's critics to be important as a "sub-plot" that furthers the "main" plot surrounding the making and firing of the V-2 rockets. Thus, while commentators seldom fail to discuss the fictional African rocket troops, they rarely offer an interpretation connecting these troops, comprised of survivors of the Herero's 1904 genocide by the Germans, to larger issues of Euro-American imperialism and neo-colonialism, or in America to white supremacist attitudes and practices. A few symptomatic examples will demonstrate what I consider an avoidance of the "explicitly social and political dimensions" of *Gravity's Rainbow*. John Dugdale locates Pynchon's politicism in his "unofficial version" of historical events, but does not clarify what precisely constitutes this illegitimate version. Dugdale notes that although Pynchon appears to create a novel sympathetic to the so-called "Third World," he stops short of writing the type of novel produced by "oppressed minorities and dissident elements within developed nations" (188). But Dugdale's focus on what he calls Pynchon's "allusive parables of power" does not offer specific insights into the novel's connection between power's numerous control systems and how these oppress socially and politically marginalized groups. Another example is Khachig Tololyan's otherwise informative article, "War as Background in *Gravity's Rainbow*," which claims that Pynchon deploys the African rocket troops to remind us that "we live in a dangerous age where our deepest fears and nightmares, threaten at any moment to become real" (59). Tololyan's reading of the Herero as the literal embodiment of Freud's dictum concerning history as the return of the repressed goes no further than to repeat a representation of the African as a terrifying Other to the Western mind, a depiction of Otherness that Pynchon critiques. Finally, even Molly Hite's estimable *Ideas of Order in the Novels of Thomas Pynchon* does not link the Herero and their decision to choose the Rocket as their "death totem" to broad issues of racial oppression and Western hegemony. Thus, with the exception of a few critics such as Robert Holton, Thomas Schaub, and Michael Bérebé[1], research on *Gravity's Rainbow* has been notably deficient in acknowledging the novel's radical re-historicism, which necessarily involves issues of gender, class, and race.

Turning for the moment to Pynchon's pre-*Gravity's Rainbow* article treating the race riots in Watts during those hot summers of the mid-60s, we find even more clear-cut evasion by critics of Pynchon's re-presentations of race relations. Pynchon's *New York Times Magazine* article, "A Journey into the Mind of Watts," has elicited an astounding array of avoidance strategies concerning the critical engagement of the article's core thematization of white supremacy and its socio-political effect on the inhabitants of Watts. In *The Grim Phoenix* William Plater depicts the article as "clarifying the recurring theme of colonialism" in Pynchon's fiction, but goes on to add, "colonialism consists of the forcible displacement of land by landscape, the conscious imposition of a synthetic reality onto an already existing reality" (109). Nowhere does Plater speak about the *people* of Watts, whereas Pynchon uses literal geography as a metaphor for psychic geography throughout the piece, offering the brutalized landscape as a metaphor for a people systematically--and systemically--brutalized through the overt and covert operation of white supremacy. Even more amazing is Charles Hollander's "Pynchon's Politics: The Presence of an Absence," which deems the Watt's piece "overtly political," only to conclude that "Pynchon sees L.A., white culture, as refined away from its human, primal, violent origins. Watts, black culture, is closer to the primordial, the pagan, the magical" (56). While Pynchon could be accused of lapsing at certain points into an essentialist discourse in his treatment of Herero women,[2] his Watts article is clearly designed to counter widely held assumptions by white Americans about what they believe to be the "nature" of blacks; to that end, Pynchon explains violence as a function of legal and economic terrorism on the part of the white bureaucracy and its white taxpayers.

The cataloguing of errors and omissions by commentators regarding Pynchon's depiction of race relations does more than simply justify yet another article on *Gravity's Rainbow* in the context of an already enormous body of criticism. By foregrounding what I consider chronic under or mis-reading of Pynchon's thematization of race relations, I am also providing a profile of the psychic geography of Pynchon's target audience: white, middle-class males. This audience, not coincidentally, also comprises the "Elect" in the discourse of preterition that functions as one of the novel's underlying thematic and structuring principles. In keeping with this essay's assertion that *Gravity's Rainbow* is a prolonged meditation on, among other things, contemporary American attitudes towards racial matters via its foregrounding of Herero history, let us turn to Pynchon's depiction of the Herero and explore its thematic possibilities.

As readers of *Gravity's Rainbow* know, Pynchon dramatizes a fictional scenario that inversely parallels German penetration into the African Sudwest by placing formerly colonized Hereros within the heart of Hitler's war industry. Thus, Herero tribal groups have been commissioned to work secretly at Nordhausen, the site of Hitler's "Mittelwerke" inside the Harz mountains where the deadly rockets are created and assembled. Unknown to almost everyone (including the reader for much of the novel) is their private agenda of salvaging enough rocket parts for both Herero factions--the Empty Ones and their philosophical adversaries, the Schwartzkommando--to build their own rockets for tribal purposes. Since so much has been written not only about this plot-within-a-plot, but also about Pynchon's detailed description of the Herero culture upon contact with the Germans, I refer readers to any of the existing studies that focus on explaining Pynchon's use of Herero language, customs, and beliefs. [3]My primary interest here is in exploring the thematic function of the Herero beyond their immediate role in furthering the "plot" of this radically re-historicized war saga, Pynchon's "fractured fairy-tale" of our most cherished and usually unambiguous war.[4] As we will see, the thematization of Herero history acts as a crucial signifier for a type of thinking, codified within Western "grand narratives," that legitimizes drearily monotonous types of socio-political oppression based on race, class, and gender, and that echoes forms of oppression constituting various human relations in the main story of *Gravity's Rainbow*.

Pynchon foregrounds the saga of the Herero to set in motion a powerful reversal of the traditional historical record, creating a version of Africa's colonization by Europe indigestible to widely disseminated, and highly motivated, Eurocentric history. Two interrelated facets of the official historical version arising out of Western "power/knowledge" discourses as early as the 18th-century are important to my argument: first, what Victor Mudimbe calls the Eurocentric "identity of the Same" (12), a cultural assumption that one group of people constitutes a norm with everyone outside this default group labeled as defective and pathological. Mudimbe notes, "human civilization was Western in the eyes of the colonizers and Africans weren't human" (68). This tendency in European thinking, which Wilson Harris calls "fortress homogeneity" (xviii), results in the pervasive European belief in the inferiority of races other than the Caucasian, spawning various tropes designed not only to label the non-white's supposed difference, but to culturally perpetuate belief in non-white racial inferiority. Albert Memmi notes that "racism"-- and I would add, "white supremacy"--"is not incidental to, but consubstantial with, colonialism" (87). The African, within a monologic and seemingly omnipotent Western discourse that constitutes such hegemonic areas of knowledge as Anthropology and History, "is the negation of all human experience" (Mudimbe 71). As such, Africans offer to the Eurocentric gaze a blank space on the map that recalls Marlow's boyhood fantasy in *Heart of Darkness*. The white supremacist assumption that all non-white societies lack culture, civilization, and history is not, of course, limited to literature--or to the 19th-century. Mudimbe observes that the late Carl Sagan, when asked to assess the scientific validity of the Dogon cosmological model, displayed a type of cultural reasoning about "primitives" that reveals the deeply regressive nature of contemporary ethnocentrism (17).

Pynchon's strategy to counteract this first facet of official History is to adopt what Edward Said terms a "contrapuntal perspective" (32) in relation to Western assumptions about the African's alleged absence of history and culture. If, as Said insists, European imperialist discourse is predicated on the silence of the African within politically motivated Africanist discourse, then Pynchon's portrayal of the Herero as having possessed a vibrant, complex, and deeply spiritual culture prior to German colonization constitutes an example of what Said calls a "voyage in" (244). I take Said to mean by this term, which he calls "an interesting type of hybrid cultural work" (244), the reversal of the fixed system of values underlying Western Us/Them thinking, a system of values that must necessarily de-value anything that does not originate from the metropolitan center. Pynchon textually punctures the certainty of traditional history by making available to readers his own imagined version of the Herero's rich and deeply philosophical pre-conquest life, remnants of which Pynchon weaves into the narration as he unfolds the on-going tribulations of a tribe almost entirely decimated by the Germans. The reader soon realizes, for example, that the Zone Herero are motivated by such strong tribal and communal affiliations that, despite the existence of competing factions, members in each group work cooperatively together. Also, ancient Herero moral and ethical systems still guide the tribal members in exile and prove to be a match for those of Western culture. But Pynchon's revision of the historical record also includes a portrait of the Herero as rocket scientists in Hitler's Reich, a re-presentation of Africans that belies such Eurocentric tropes as "primitive," "lazy," "child-like," and "mentally defective. "Enzian, the Schwartzkommando's leader, develops into one of the novel's main characters.

When we first meet him as we journey with Tyrone Slothrop in search of the V2 rockets, Enzian and Slothrop happen to be atop a moving train. Threatened by one of the novel's most evil characters, Major Marvy, Enzian fights him and manages to throw him off the train. This scene automatically places the African in the role of a heroic man of action--a role readers can readily identify with, but one usually reserved for the white male. At this point, however, the American "WASP" Slothrop is a mere onlooker, his position forecasting the novel's end in which he is ousted from narrative prominence as he psychically disintegrates, while Enzian develops great courage and vision. Slothrop's mental "scattering" will become correlative with emotional as well as historical amnesia, in stark contrast to Enzian's growing awareness that "[w]e can't believe Them any more.

Not if we are still the same, and love the truth" (728), which frees him from the bonds of concocted History into his own, authentic history.

The second facet of traditional history that Pynchon problematizes is the characterization of imperialism as a positive boon to "primitives" in need of a Christian God, Progress, Education, and a step up into World History, which of course means history from the viewpoint of the metropolitan center. Early anti-imperialist critics such as Aimé Césaire and Franz Fanon underscore this negative aspect of colonialism, causing Césaire to insist in his polemical *Discourse on Colonialism* that colonialism be identified not by its alleged positive features, but rather by its negative ones of economic exploitation and social disruption, mordantly concluding that it is a "sick civilization that justifies force against people" (21). Fanon's plea to all colonized to throw off the psychic and emotional chains of Eurocentrism-- "Leave this Europe where they are never done talking of Man, yet murder men everywhere they find them" (311)-- segues into Pynchon's often cited parodic characterization of German colonizers in *Gravity's Rainbow*:

> What's a colony without its dusky natives? Where's the fun if they're all going to die off?... --wait, wait a minute there, yes it's Karl Marx, that sly old racist skipping away with his teeth together and his eyebrows up trying to make believe it's nothing but Cheap Labor and Overseas Markets. ... Oh, no. Colonies are much, much more. Colonies are the outhouses of the European soul, where a fellow can let his pants down and relax, enjoy the smell of his own shit. Where he can fall on his slender prey roaring as loud as he wants, and guzzle her blood with open joy ... Christian Europe was always about death, Karl, death and repression (317)

By invoking Marx's avoidance of the issues surrounding imperialism's *systemic* exploitation and its pernicious impact on the lives of the colonized, Pynchon takes us beyond the type of brutality dramatized above, which could be excused by apologists of "overseas development" as the isolated transgressions of a few excessive individuals.

Which brings us to the last of Pynchon's thematic deployments of the Herero in *Gravity's Rainbow*. The presence of the Herero, a racial Other located at the center of the socio-political upheaval of WWII, affords Pynchon the opportunity to explore a host of white supremacist attitudes towards blacks in the novel, which savvy readers will ultimately connect to the politically motivated genocide of various non-Aryan Others conquered by Hitler. Pynchon lampoons the novel's most flagrant racists, Major Duane Marvy, the American sent out to kill the black rocket troops- -"They're a childlike race. Brains are smaller" (288)--together with "Old Bloody" Clayton Chiclitz, whose dream is to find children he can turn into galley slaves (558). Marvy and Chiclitz are perhaps the most egregious racists, ones that most readers can safely differentiate themselves from. It is harder, however, to distance oneself from more subtle forms of white supremacy within a story whose narrator continually shifts narrative viewpoint from outside, to inside, a character's mind.[5] This form of "indirect free speech" is a style "marked by the use of words denoting mental processes, by use of the features of direct speech, by idiosyncratic idioms and exclamations, and by a sense of heightened subjectivity" (Smetak 94). This type of narration regularly collapses the boundaries between narrator, character, and reader, enabling Pynchon to establish a field of indeterminacy surrounding precisely who is engaged in various thoughts, speech, or actions. Within this field of indeterminate textual play the numerous unattributed and, therefore, ambiguous "yous" add up. By eliminating the certainty surrounding who is speaking and who is being spoken to, the narrator tells a story that covertly interpellates readers who, despite their class, gender, or race, "are faced with their own complicity in both individual and social, collective behavior" (Ramirez, 291).

A particularly clear example of this technique occurs when the Zone Hereros are introduced to us. We are told that they had been converted by early missionaries and sent to the Metropolis, or brought back as servants, or recruited before the war by the Nazis to help rid black Africa of British and French colonies. These Herero ironically adopt the aardvark as their totem, for it is the totem of the poorest group of Herero in South West Africa. The speaker explains this in typically distanced narratorial fashion, directing comments to readers who are by necessity spatially and temporally detached from these events. Speaking of these original "aardvark" Herero, the narrator observes: "Considered outcasts, they lived on the veld, in the open" (315), but almost imperceptibly changes the register of address in the very next sentence with: "You were likely to come across them at night, their fires flaring bravely against the wind, out of rifle range from the iron tracks..." (315). This ominous turn in the narration results in complete slippage between the German colonizers and the reader in the next sentence: "You knew what they feared--not what they wanted, or what moved them. And you had business upcountry, at the mines: so presently, as the sputtering lights slipped behind, so did all further need to think of them" (315). Whether the event is wholesale genocide or drug-induced racist fantasy, readers unwittingly "enter" an alien mind and are then unwittingly trapped into sympathizing with the type of thoughts normally reserved for minds not our own.

This erosion of identity on various levels of narration parallels evidence of rampant white supremacy central to the novel's unfolding and dramatizes racism's awful ubiquity. Marvy is not the only one who has been sent out by bureaucrats to eliminate the African rocket troops: the novel's early protagonist Tyrone Slothrop, intelligence operative out of Harvard and a family with ancestral ties to New England's Puritans, has been sent by British Intelligence's Sir Marcus Scammony to locate and kill the Herero. Speaking of the Americans, Sir Marcus insists: "They'll want to see how we do with *our* lovely black animals ... before they try it on their own, ah, target groups" (616). The Russian Tchitcherine is obsessed with murdering his half-African sibling Enzian, while behavioral scientist Edwin Treacle laments the racism of his colleagues, "their feelings about blackness ... tied to feelings about shit, and feelings about shit to feelings about putrefaction and death" (276). The Dutch female double-agent Katje detests and fears the African rocket troops because of their ... *blackness* (658), while the megalomaniac film-maker, Von Göll, betrays unintentional irony in his obsession that his propaganda film featuring black troops has literally given birth to the actual Schwartzkommando (388).

Not only does Slothrop's genocidal quest to locate the Herero in the Harz intersect with all the novel's numerous plots and characters, but he serves as the crucial link in the novel's rendering problematic American racial attitudes through its re-presenting of widespread racism and white supremacy among many characters connected to the Rocket. It is Slothrop whom we learn most about and follow in his ongoing "quest" for various types of information. It is also Slothrop who is ancestrally and temperamentally connected to the novel's Puritans, those unstinting believers in such self-serving notions as Predestination, salvation of God's Elect, and perdition of everyone else--namely, the Preterite masses. Further conditioned into the "Puritan Mysteries" (267) of elitism at Harvard, Slothrop is full of "bland ignorance" (268) concerning what is really at stake in any socio-political situation. At one point he is in a plane fantasizing about flying away from the war to any place he remembers from the films: "Sure, what about--well, that Spain? No wait, they're Fascists. South Sea Islands! Hmmm. Full of Japs and GIs. Well Africa's the Dark Continent, nothing *there* but natives, elephants, 'n' that Spencer Tracy" (266).

From a long line of economic exploiters and spoilers, Slothrop reflects sentiments that seem silly and even harmless enough, incapable of causing serious problems for anyone. But early on we witness Slothrop, whose body undergoes repeated "colonization" by various institutions such as "Harvard and the U.S. Army" (83), descending into drug-induced narcosis to "help illuminate racial problems in his own country" (75). His interrogator takes Slothrop to Roxbury and the Roseland Ballroom, involuntary fantasy uprooting from his mind's deepest corners memories of fear, danger, and "Red" Malcolm amid a narcotic nightmare in which Slothrop imagines his head is stuck in a toilet and Malcolm X and crew are about to sodomize him. Slothrop hallucinates that he swims down into the toilet, his memories now connecting Negroes, blackness, shit, and death, eventually broadening out to include racist tropes about communists, mulattoes, Japs, and Indians. Although the precise meaning of this narrative segment's surreal imagery continues to baffle readers, an ominous sense of terror prevails and matches the overall mood of the novel's characters, one of the most fearful and paranoid of which is Slothrop. Although his subsequent quest is most often discussed by critics as an attempt to discover secret clues to his identity, it is seldom acknowledged as the death mission to wipe out the Zone Hereros that it actually is, motivated by the irrational and unwarranted fears of a white supremacist power structure.

Slothrop's lack of awareness regarding his deepest attitudes towards non-whites parallels his ignorance regarding the true aim of his mission, but we eventually learn something that Slothrop and They don't: the Zone Hereros are gathering rocket parts to build missiles intended to return them--literally as well as figuratively--to a space/time of mythic wholeness. Thus, within the larger story of the war the Herero are the harmless ones whose very presence terrorizes whites, and sets in motion secret plans for their own elimination if and when they are located by Slothrop. Terror has been cited as fundamental to the thoughts and feelings of the novel's characters, but most often terror is connected either to the real and imagined machinations of pervasive control systems the novel depicts, or it is linked in Cold War America to the dreadful reality of nuclear attack from airborne rockets. In the context of Pynchon's radical rehistoricizing of race relations, however, readers discover through the enormously irrational and terrified white response to the Hereros' presence Pynchon's oblique presentation of white America's own unwarranted fear of African Americans and other non-white people.

Nightly newscasts of Black Panther rallies, rioting in Watts and other cities, clashes between civil rights' demonstrators, white supremacists, and the police added to everyday footage of non-white criminals on America's TVs, serve as incessant and visually alarming reasons why white America at the time of the novel's publication should feel terrified and besieged within its own borders. What has not received equal representation is a view of the situation from a non-white perspective, what Bell Hooks calls a black "ethnographic gaze" (167) leveled at whites. This gaze retrieves from the exclusions of traditional history the notion that "all black people in the U.S., irrespective of their class status or their politics, live with the possibility that they will be terrorized by whiteness" (175). The long history of imperialism responsible for Herero suffering reaches back over hundreds of years and projects itself into the neo-colonial present and future, making clear to readers that events and situations transpiring under the aegis of white supremacy cannot be limited to discreet cultural moments. The Herero hidden deep in the Harz dramatize the reality of contemporary America, where according to Pynchon's re-interpretation of the situation, Watts "lies impacted in the heart of this white fantasy, a bitter pocket of reality" (150).

Pynchon attempts in this essayistic precursor to *Gravity's Rainbow* to clarify for white readers the argument from the other side. As in his earlier novel, *V.*, the Watts article acknowledges two separate worlds comprised of us and everyone who is not us, at the same time making evident who wields the power. The foremost exercise of power, often misunderstood, is the power to decide on a value system and then designate the position of everyone within, or outside, this hierarchy of value. Thus, we read that people in Watts are angry and may turn to violence, but the reasons for rioting, just like the order of values on the good/bad scale controlled by white Los Angelenos, are overturned as Pynchon reveals white injustice to be the actual impetus for black violence: "As for violence, in a pocket of reality such as Watts, violence is never far from you: because you are a man, because you have been put down, because for every action there is an equal and opposite reaction. Somehow, sometime" (156). The Watts journey may be billed as a voyage through the psyche of the black Other, but do not be fooled: it is actually a journey through white consciousness, a mind-set that not only terrorizes its Other, but in doing so, terrorizes itself.

The ending of *Gravity's Rainbow* contains a series of surreal episodes seemingly disconnected from the foregoing story of the V-2 rocket that occupies most of the novel's 760 pages. Set in what appears to be Slothrop's hometown of Mingeborough, Massachusettes, these segments carry us anachronistically to America under Nixon's watch, and under siege. Our town seems to be under occupation and we cannot return, but it appears to be our own army, and not, say, the Herero or Malcolm X, that is preventing us from reaching safety. In a hallucinatory interview staged near the novel's end, the "interviewee," in his role as "SPOKESMAN"--and we are left to speculate who or what he actually represents, confesses, "I am betraying them all ... the worst of it is that I know what your editors want, *exactly* what they want. I am a traitor. I carry it with me. Your virus" (739). And he later adds, "We drank the blood of our enemies. The blood of our friends, we cherished" (739). The "bloody" acts which readers are "betrayed" into result in our own interpellation and collusion as we metaphorically sit in that L.A. movie theater on the novel's final page awaiting annihilation, though not, it seems, at the hands of the Other. Pynchon's re-conceptualization of our shared history, black and white together, is in the words of Wilson Harris, "the ceaseless mediation of energy between all partial structures masquerading as totality" (48). In *Gravity's Rainbow*, this mediation and its explicit critique of Enlightenment discourses enacted through the Herero's story leads into an implicit questioning of the status, and consequences, of "Whiteness" in contemporary American culture.

Notes

[1] See Holton's article and Bérubé's book in Works Cited. For Schaub, see *Pynchon: The Voice of Ambiguity.*

[2] Although Pynchon takes pains to incorporate a detailed portrait of Herero life and mores into his novel, his main Herero characters--Enzian, Josef Ombindi, and Christian--are male. And, at those textual junctures where Herero women do appear, it is limited to the context of their childbearing capacity. Thus, we learn about Enzian's Russian father, but nothing of his Herero mother. Later we learn that Christian's sister, Maria, has had an abortion, but she does not even make an entrance into the novel.

[3] For a listing of Pynchon's sources for his information on the Herero, see Steven Weisenburger's "Pynchon's Hereros: A Textual and Bibliographic Note. " *Pynchon Notes* 16 (1985): 37-45.

[4] In Michael Bérubé's *Marginal Forces, Cultural Centers*, the author discusses the reluctance of many Pynchon commentators to engage his "heretical rendering of History." Bérubé queries why critics have not questioned "what it might mean that Pynchon's "version" [of *Why Are We In Vietnam*] is not about Vietnam at all but about the one war within living memory which, for most Americans ... was 'the good war,' unambiguous in purpose and outcome" (273).

[5] The nature of *Gravity's Rainbow*'s narration is a much contested issue in Pynchon criticism. While Molly Hite (*Ideas of Order in the Novels of Thomas Pynchon*) calls the narrative voice "protean," Thomas Schaub (*Pynchon: the Voice of Ambiguity*) insists it is "omnipresent," while

Charles Hohmann (*Thomas Pynchon's "Gravity's Rainbow": A Study of Its Conceptual Structure and Rilke's Influence*) believes there may be multiple narrators. The assumption in this study closely matches the narrative theory of Jacqueline Smetak (see Works Cited).

Works Cited

Bérubé, Michael. *Marginal Forces, Cultural Centers: Tolson, Pynchon, and the Politics of the Canon.* Ithaca: Cornell UP, 1992.

Césaire, Aimé. *Discourse on Colonialism.* New York: MR, 1972.

Dugdale, John. *Thomas Pynchon: Allusive Parables of Power.* New York: St. Martins, 1990.

Fanon, Franz. *The Wretched of the Earth.* New York: Grove, 1963.

Harris, Wilson. *The Womb of Space: The Cross-Cultural Imagination.* Westport, Conn: Greenwood, 1983.

Hollander, Charles. "Pynchon's Politics: The Presence of an Absence. " *Pynchon Notes* 26-27 (1990): 5-59.

Holton, Robert. "In the Rathouse of History with Thomas Pynchon: Rereading *V. " Textual Practice* 2 (1988): 324-44.

Hooks, Bell. *Outlaw Culture: Resisting Representations.* New York: Routlege, 1994.

Mudimbe, Victor. *The Invention of Africa: Gnosis, Philosophy, and the Order of Knowledge.* Bloomington: Indiana UP, 1988.

Plater, William. *The Grim Phoenix: Reconstructing Thomas Pynchon.* Bloomington: Indiana UP, 1978.

Pynchon, Thomas. *Gravity's Rainbow.* New York: Penguin, 1987.

---. "Journey Into the Mind of Watts. " *New York Times Magazine* 12 June, 1966. Rpt. In *Man Against Poverty: World War III.* Ed. Arthur Blaustein and Roger Woock. New York: Random, 1968. 146-58.

Ramirez, Victoria. "'Writing Is But Another Name for Conversation': Dialogism, Narrator, and Narratee in Sterne's *Tristram Shandy,* Aidoo's *Our Sister Killjoy,* and

Pynchon's *Gravity's Rainbow.* " Diss. State U of New York, Binghamton , 1997. DAI 58: 5, 1702.

Said, Edward. *Culture and Imperialism.* New York: Knopf, 1993.

Smetak, Jacqueline. "Who's Talking Here: Finding the Voice in *Gravity's Rainbow.* " *Pynchon Notes* 20 (1987), 93-103.

Tololyan, Khachig. "War as Background in *Gravity's Rainbow.* " *Approaches to Gravity's Rainbow.* Ed. Charles Clerc. Columbus: Ohio State UP, 1983.

PART V
Media-ting Africa

In the Heart of Sickness: A *Life* Portrait of Dr. Albert Schweitzer

Jessica Levin
Harvard University

On November 15th, 1954, approximately 5,613,000 readers of *Life* Magazine made the acquaintance of Dr. Albert Schweitzer.[1] To be sure, many had been previously introduced to the man through his scholarship on Johann Sebastian Bach. Some were familiar with his philosophical investigations of Goethe and Kant. Still others knew of his various contributions to theology. But, as the doctor himself explained, "No one knows me who has not known me in Africa" (*Life* 161). One week after Dr. Schweitzer accepted the Nobel Peace Prize, *Life* Magazine published his iconic portrait, formally presenting "A Man of Mercy" to the American public.

To shoot the photographic essay, *Life* photographer W. Eugene Smith worked on location in Africa, shadowing Dr. Schweitzer at his hospital in Lambaréné for seventy days. At the end of his stay in French Equatorial Africa, in the territory now known as Gabon, Smith selected 25 photographs to represent the doctor in his African surrounds. As the table of contents attests, both Smith and Schweitzer understood well the communicative power of each image. The copy reads, "When Smith tried to photograph [the doctor] at work, he balked, saying, 'People will think Schweitzer has picked up a shovel to show the world he works!' Smith placated him by replying, 'If the story looks like that then we've both failed'"(*Life* 27). The folio was indeed a success, depicting the doctor as a saintly figure wanting to cure the ills of Africa.

Outside of missionary materials, few visual images of disease in Africa circulated in America prior to Schweitzer's *Life* portrait. There were, however, numerous news articles, travelogues, and medical fiction novels promoting the idea of Africa as a land of affliction.[2] While there certainly was disease in Africa (as elsewhere in the world), sickness was selected as a defining trait of the continent and its people. As V.Y. Mudimbe (1988: 49) explains, there was a tendency in the West to see in Africa only those features which necessitated help. To diagnose Africa as sick was to establish the need for medical care and to offer a rationale for colonial intervention.[3] The photographs of Dr. Albert Schweitzer and his patients in Lambaréné gave visual expression to the idea of an ailing Africa in desperate need of medical attention.

By force of personality, Dr. Schweitzer won his "jungle hospital" worldwide recognition. For Americans, W. Eugene Smith's camera lens brought Schweitzer's star quality into sharp focus. On the opening page (figure 1), the doctor is seen in black and white, watching over hospital construction. The shadow of a handsaw is cast over his white-collar shirt, which matches his white full mustache and white safari hat. Behind him is an African man, with shredded clothes and large muscles providing evidence of hard work. Neither the doctor nor the builder looks at the camera. Instead, they look to their left, presumably at other workers busy with the task at hand. With furled brow, Schweitzer appears as if about to correct their method. The text explains that "amid primitive conditions, Europe's saint is forced to become a remote, driving man who rules his hospital with patriarchal authority" (*Life* 161). The scale of the project here is difficult to determine since both Dr. Schweitzer's lower body and the building's beams extend beyond the picture frame. Readers are left to imagine the expansive construction site and its forest environs.

The following two pages showcase scenes from a typical day at the hospital. In one photograph, men carry a new mother in a wooden stretcher from the delivery room to the maternity ward.

Fourrès, Schweitzer and a carpenter, watch hospital building

A Man of Mercy

a's misery turns saintly Albert Schweitzer into a driving taskmaster

"No one knows me," Albert Schweitzer has said, "who has not known me in Africa." In Norway last week, where he had come to acknowledge a Nobel Peace Prize, crowds jammed streets to cheer a great figure of our time. As they cheered they were convinced that they knew him well; he is the humanitarian, warm and saintlike. In full manhood he had turned away from brilliant success as a preacher, writer and musician to bury himself as a missionary doctor in Africa.

All this was truth—but admirers who have followed Dr. Schweitzer to French Equatorial Africa know a different man. There, amid primitive conditions, Europe's saint is forced to become a remote, driving man who rules his hospital with patriarchal authority. For those seeking the gentle philosopher of the legend, he has a brief answer: "We are too busy fighting pain." Then he turns back to the suffering and the work that make up the African world of Albert Schweitzer.

Photographed for LIFE by W. EUGENE SMITH   161

Figure 1: "A Man of Mercy"
Photo by W. Eugene Smith/LIFE Magazine©Time Inc.

Here they cross the compound's main street, which is simply an earthen floor. In another photograph, a baby is being fed on the floorboards of the nursery. There is no cradle or crib to keep the child clean and safe. Rather, an outstretched arm empties food into the child's mouth while he grabs his caregivers' toes. Schweitzer is pictured checking his post-operative patients upstairs, while three more patients wait downstairs. The doctor's busy open-air office and waiting room speak to the demand that his service fulfills. In the final image, a woman wearing a print wrap and headscarf walks barefoot as she smokes a pipe and balances a bowl of kitchen utensils on her head. The caption explains that she has just finished cooking her husband's meal on an open fire. In the style of many African hospitals today, the patients' families bring food to and even live with their loved ones during treatment and recovery.

American readers expecting pristine conditions may have found the hospital grounds quite unsettling. After visiting the site himself, biographer Norman Cousins (1960: 91) commented, "The idea of a hospital creates instant images in the mind of immaculate corridors, white sheets, total sanitation. These images were badly jolted when one saw the Hospital at Lambaréné for the first time." Dr. Schweitzer did not try to impose Western life on the Africans, but rather allowed them to live as they would. In the years preceding Schweitzer's death, this approach came under attack by writers who accused the doctor of maintaining low standards and unclean conditions at the hospital despite large contributions of money and medical supplies from the West. In *Verdict on Schweitzer: The Man Behind the Legend of Lambaréné*, Gerald McNight explains:

> In surprising discord, the occasional dissenting voices have growled lamentations that Schweitzer's kingdom is unnecessarily primitive; that he refuses to treat with progress, or to move forward on any wings other than his own; that Lambaréné is no more than a shrine of the sentimental and the vicarious do-gooder; in reality, a jungle sore suppurating into the fresh body of emergent Africa (1964: 13-14).

Dr. Schweitzer felt strongly that he should treat the patients on their own terms, in their own environment. To this end, he recreated the village within the hospital grounds, allowing for communal bathrooms and freely roaming animals. The doctor followed this village model, convinced that the Africans would be too shocked by modern equipment and too alienated by sterile hospital conditions to come for his care.

Turning the page, readers encounter scenes of hard physical labor. As an African man pushes the weight of his whole body against a crowbar, men around him try to move the large rock beneath. Here the black body is pictured toiling, close to the earth. The caption reads "Although there are quicker ways to move rocks, this one was muscled out in arduous tradition of African hand labor" (*Life* 164). In two other photographs, Africans and Europeans work together setting down a portable railroad for transporting materials to the new leper hospital. The heavy moving and lifting is a sign of the strenuous work that is done at Lambaréné. Dr. Schweitzer's personal involvement is symbolized here by the central photographs of his umbrella stuck in the sand and of his 30-year-old shoes. The viewer can imagine him supervising construction, firmly planting his umbrella when he too must go to work. The old, worn shoes prove that Dr. Schweitzer knows best, since no other man has walked in those shoes. They also recall his years of being in the mud--in Lambaréné, he is truly in the thick of things.

It was from this perspective that Dr. Schweitzer viewed colonialism. The doctor spoke of the colonial project not as a foreign official, but rather as one who could make informed judgments based on his experience living with the people of French Equatorial Africa. In the introduction to his essay on colonialism, he writes

I wish to discuss Colonialization, and the relations of the White and Coloured Races which it involves, as a peasant talks of his cabbages, and not as an artist or a poet would depict the same cabbages. It is the point of view of the man who is in the work, who has to dig and sow, manure, and tend the plants (Schweitzer 1928: 5).

The doctor's direct involvement in Africa granted his voice a degree of authenticity and authority in political debates. For him, promoting health was one of colonialism's most beneficial aspects, as it helped Africans to attain a state of well-being. The famous hospital at Lambaréné stood as an exemplar of the restorative aspects of colonial rule and served as a claim to its legitimacy.

The next pages (figure 2) reveal the most striking image of the *Life* portrait. Here Smith has photographed the faces of two lepers as they wait in line for pills and the water to wash them down. After taking the medicine, a patient "is given a vitamin tablet against possible bad reactions and a glass of milk because Dr. Schweitzer thinks it is good for him whether he likes it or not" (*Life* 167). While they are certainly treated like young children, the lepers' ages are not clearly distinguishable. What is clear is that they wait, open-mouthed, for the kind hand of the good doctor. A seemingly heavenly light comes from above, gracing the face and medicine cup of the first patient. Smith focuses on this face at close range while blurring the immediate background. Caught in shadows, the second patient's form is difficult to discern. The viewer must struggle to make out the shape of her leprous body.

Beyond its visual impact, the photograph of "despairing lepers" derives meaning from religious symbolism. While in diagnostic language leprosy is an illness marked by patches of discoloration, by thickening of the skin, and by loss of sensation, in Christian scripture it is an illness characterized by a physically and ritually unclean body. In the Bible, it was used by God as a punishment for Miriam, and so was thought of as a punishment for sin. That the leper was regarded as ceremonially unclean was a reflection of the laws of hygiene in Leviticus, laws designed to prevent the spread of infections for which there was no effective treatment. Upon being pronounced leprous by a priest, the affected person was quarantined. "All the days wherein the plague shall be in him he shall be defiled; he is unclean: he shall

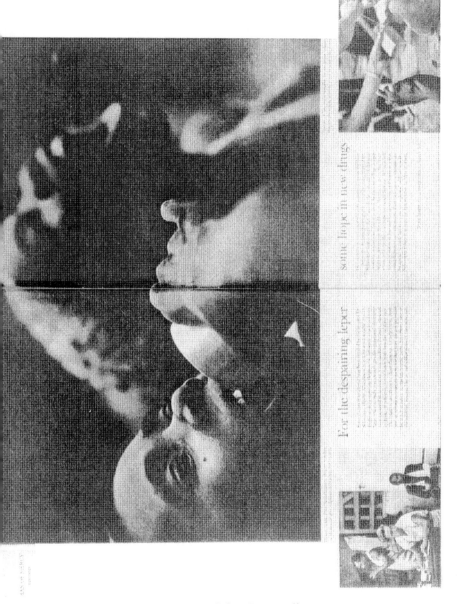

Figure 2: "Despairing Lepers"
Photo by W. Eugene Smith/LIFE Magazine©Time Inc.

dwell alone; without the camp shall his habitation be" (Lev. 13:46). The leper was placed outside the camp not only for fear of contagion, but also to protect the wholeness and well-being of society as well as to demonstrate the excluded status of the afflicted. When healed, the patient had to undergo a cleansing ceremony and bring special offerings to the temple. In the New Testament, Jesus healed people who had leprosy, and on one occasion healed ten lepers, only one of whom returned to be thankful. In the Gospels,[4] it is pointed out that whereas the cure of disease is called healing, the cure of leprosy is called cleansing, because the restoration of skin allowed the leper to be ceremonially clean, and therefore restored to the worship and service of God. In both the Hebrew Bible and the New Testament, the discourse surrounding leprosy is intimately tied to a larger idea of cleanliness, a quality which Dr. Schweitzer did not believe so-called primitive and semi-primitive people possessed.[5]

Treating people with leprosy elevated Schweitzer to the status of saint in the minds of many who believed that only Christian compassion could save the otherwise abandoned souls. Without the doctor and his medical mission staff, a viewer might assume, the lepers would be banished by their community and shunned by the world. On the bottom of figure 2, we meet Danish Nurse Erna Spohrhanssen who is willing even to tend the oozing sores on lepers' mangled feet. By building a leper colony adjacent to the hospital grounds, Dr. Schweitzer rescued the lepers from their exclusion and isolation while heroically risking contagion himself.[6]

As at any hospital, many patients died at Lambaréné. The next two pages chronicle the death and funeral of one of Dr. Schweitzer's patients, Eugenia Mwanyeno. In the last moments of her life, she sits upright on her death bed, eyes closed. In another photograph, Eugenia's daughter and granddaughter are seated at her bedside, sorrowfully leaning their faces against their hands. Smith shoots the funeral procession from behind so as to capture Dr. Schweitzer grasping his hands behind his back in a gesture of sadness and respect. The caption tells us that the doctor rarely attends funerals, but here made an exception since Eugenia had long been a familiar figure at the hospital. Nearby we see a close-up of palm leaves used to cover the coffin along with grave-digging tools. As symbols of victory, the palm leaves acknowledge Death's victory over Schweitzer's best efforts. Lastly there is another shot from behind, this time featuring a white nurse holding flowers at her back, in a stance much like Schweitzer's. This image is particularly resonant, with the flowers set against the nurse's pure white skirt. Even her rolled down bobby socks and penny loafers recall American innocence, somehow hardened by witnessing the loss of life.

Amidst images of sickness and disease, Schweitzer appears strong and healthy throughout the photographic essay. In fact, the doctor gained fame and recognition for remaining in good health and overseeing his hospital until his death at the age of 90.[7] During colonialism and before, Africa came to be known as "the white man's grave" as news emerged that numbers of colonial officials and their wives had died from such diseases as malaria and dysentery. As a result, many feared that to migrate to Africa in the name of colonial governance or entrepreneurial riches was to risk one's life and family. This fear was allayed by Dr. Schweitzer, who lived and worked in what was considered the heart of sickness for 52 years.

The following two pages feature the doctor alone with his studies. After the long day that has passed conceptually over the previous pages, Dr. Schweitzer still makes time for intellectual pursuits of music and philosophy. In solitude, he plays his organ, which is actually a piano with organ petals. Across the top is a series of photographs showing the doctor's frugal methods of reusing old paper and binding paper together so as to protect it from insects and larger animals. In the central image, he labors intently at his desk, carrying on with his intellectual work "long after the hospital is asleep" (*Life* 170). Here the reader learns that this relentless man is determined to study music and write books despite all hardship. Whereas his African patients are always seen as sick, the doctor is seen as hearty despite his old age. While the African assistants perform only manual labor, the white doctor engages in cerebral activities as well.

While in Lambaréné, Dr. Schweitzer wrote his sweeping work entitled *The Philosophy of Civilization*. Based on his theory of "reverence for life," the two volumes address the doctor's concern for life and the future of civilization. Worried about the integrity of the individual within the modern collectivist state, Dr. Schweitzer calls for personal will to guide moral judgments. He writes that only ethical decisions can lead to the progress of civilization; one such ethical decision is to undertake humanitarian efforts on behalf of others. The doctor spoke of this ideal in America in 1949 when he visited Aspen, Colorado to give the main address at the bicentennial celebration of Goethe's birth.

The Goethe conference in Aspen provided the occasion to bring the doctor's ideas to the American public. He was incredibly well received, as his philosophical orientation appealed to American sensibilities. One year after his visit, a readers' poll taken by the *Saturday Review of Literature* (Dec. 1950: 381) named Dr. Schweitzer as the world's greatest living non-political person. At a time of American expansionism in the post-WWII era, he embodied the American model of the frontiersman who boldly ventures into new lands. He also conveyed a Thoreau-like self-reliance, living as he was in the jungle forest with few modern conveniences. Furthermore, Dr. Schweitzer enjoyed the respect and prestige accorded to doctors, and surgeons in particular.[8]

Surprisingly, neither Dr. Schweitzer nor his patients appears on the final page of the portrait. Instead, there is a single photograph of four European goats standing on an aluminum rooftop in Lambaréné. Like their owner, the old goats could make even the farthest reaches of Africa their home. At this point in the essay, this seemingly incongruous image appears less so to *Life* readers who have become accustomed to European adaptability.

The November 15th, 1954 photographic essay, "A Man of Mercy," presents a number of striking oppositions: black and white; body and mind; sanitation and contamination; sickness and health. In the interplay of photograph and caption, these oppositions identify Schweitzer as the hero-doctor and the African as sickly patient. By way of Dr. Albert Schweitzer's *Life* portrait, American readers came to see Africa not only as a locus of disease, but also as a place in need of Western care.

Notes

I wish to thank Suzanne Preston Blier, Daniel Mengara, and respondents at SORAC '98 for their valuable insights and suggestions. Travel to Gabon in July 1999 and February-April 2000 was supported by the Mellon Foundation and the Harvard CE Norton Grant, respectively.

[1] According to *Life* Magazine circulation staffmember. Telephone interview. May 22, 1998.
For an illustrated biography, see Sonja Poteau and Gérard Leser, eds. *Albert Schweitzer: Homme de Günsbach et Citoyen du Monde*. Mulhouse: Editions du Rhin, 1994.

[2] Most notable is the widely circulated writing of missionary explorer and doctor David Livingstone. According to the Comaroffs, Dr. Livingstone "invoked images of disease very similar to those of his medically untrained colleagues: of illness as the product of exposure and contagion, the result of bodies improperly set off from each other and from the natural elements." John and Jean Comaroff, "Medicine, Colonialism and the Black Body" in *Ethnography and The Historical Imagination*. (Boulder: Westwood Press, 1992) 225.

[3] In this context, sickness functions as a sign of a primitive state (Mudimbe 1988: 53). Like orientalism, primitivism is a mode of discourse with a supporting vocabulary and imagery that negatively defines Africa in an effort to secure the superiority of the West. In this way, it serves as a justification for colonial domination. See Edward Said, *Orientalism*. New York: Vintage Books, 1994 and Linda Nochlin, "The Imaginary Orient" *Art in America* vol. LXXI. May, 1983.

[4] In St. Luke's Gospel, the leper is chosen by God for salvation. He was therefore considered to be dead to the world and reborn in God.

[5] For a discussion of hygiene in colonial discourse, see Anne McClintock, *Imperial Leather: Race, Gender and Sexuality in the Colonial Contest*. New York & London: Routledge, 1995.

[6] Megan Vaughan describes models of leprosy colonies in *Curing Their Ills: Colonial Power and African Illness*. (Stanford University Press, 1991) 79.

[7] *Life* Magazine covered "The White Wizard's 90th" birthday celebration in its February 19th, 1965 issue.

[8] He also bore a striking resemblance to Dr. Albert Einstein, complete with messy crown of white hair and crooked bowtie. On Schweitzer's trip to New York, a young woman asked him to sign a picture of Einstein. Schweitzer jovially signed the photo "Albert Einstein, by way of his friend Albert Schweitzer." William Sargeant, "Albert Schweitzer," *Life* (25 July 1949) 75.

Works Cited

Bible, King James Version.

Cousins, Norman. *Dr. Schweitzer of Lambaréné*. New York: Harper & Bros., 1960.

"Leprosy." *A Dictionary of Christ and the Gospels*, vol. II. New York: Charles Scribner's Sons, 1912.

McNight, Gerald. *Verdict on Schweitzer: The Man Behind the Legend of Lambaréné*. New York: The John Day Company, 1964.

Mudimbe, V.Y. *The Invention of Africa: Gnosis, Philosophy, and the Order of Knowledge*. Bloomington and Indianapolis: Indiana University Press, 1988.

Saturday Review of Literature. December 1950.

Schweitzer, Albert. "The Relations of the White and Coloured Races". *The Contemporary Review* vol. CXXXIII. January 1928.

Schweitzer, Albert. *Philosophy of Civilization*, trans. C.T. Campion. 1st American edition. New York: Macmillan Co., 1949.

"A Man of Mercy." *Life*, 15 November 1954.

"Scarred for Life?" Representations of Africa and Female Genital Cutting on American Television News Magazines

Martha S. Grise
Eastern Kentucky University

The practice of cutting external female genitalia, euphemistically referred to as female circumcision or pejoratively as female genital mutilation, has existed for over 2,000 years.[1] Few Americans realize that up to about 1950, doctors in this country and in England were removing the clitorises of women to treat lesbianism, masturbation, and other supposed sexual deviancies (Toubia, *Female* 2 1). And as recently as fifteen or twenty years ago few Americans knew that female genital cutting was practiced extensively in certain parts of Africa and the Middle East. Medical personnel in the United States sometimes encountered immigrant women who had undergone genital cutting, and medical literature as well as anthropological studies treated the subject; but the subject reached a large audience only when the popular media began to cover international convocations of women during the International Decade for Women and when representatives of African and Middle Eastern women sought media attention to garner public support for their clients' efforts to remain in the United States to avoid genital cutting of themselves or their daughters.

In the 1990s, the subject of female genital cutting was treated in documentaries and news programs of various types on public television, CNN, and the three major commercial networks. I propose to examine in detail treatments of the subject in the ABC television news magazines, *Day One*, *20/20*, and *Nightline*, and to suggest some of the likely negative consequences of these treatments. First, however, a review of some of the facts about genital cutting may indicate some of the challenges that confront those who attempt to present this complex and sensitive subject to American audiences.

Genital cutting occurs in at least 28 African nations, affecting perhaps as few as 5 percent of girls and women in Uganda and as many as 98 percent in Djibouti and Somalia.[2] It is performed at different stages of female development from infancy to marriage but is performed most often between the ages of four and 12 years as a part of complex rituals intended to prepare girls for their adult roles in society. In rare instances, the cutting may involve little more than a superficial nick that leaves the clitoris fully intact and sexual responsiveness undiminished. More extensive operations fall into three basic categories: clitoridectomy, excision, and infibulation. Clitoridectomy, the cutting away of part or all of the clitoris, and excision, in which both the clitoris and labia minora are removed, account for about 85 percent of genital cutting. Infibulation involves not just the removal of the clitoris and labia minora but the creation of raw surfaces on the labia majora which are joined and allowed to heal, leaving only a small aperture for the passage of urine and menstrual blood.

These procedures cause not only pain and anxiety at the time they are performed but also negative health consequences that range from hemorrhage and infection to painful intercourse, infertility, obstructed labor and birth defects, abscesses, and fistulas. Increasingly, practitioners are medical personnel doctors, midwives, and nurses, who perform the procedures under sanitary conditions; but the majority of practitioners are still the traditional birth attendants, who sometimes operate with relatively crude implements in unhygienic conditions. The practice is an important source of revenue for medical personnel and traditional practitioners alike, and their vested interests contribute significantly to its continuance.

The reasons for the cutting of female genitals are as varied as the cultures that perform the procedures. Often the motive is to enhance male sexual pleasure or to curb female desire, thereby assuring males that their brides will be chaste and their wives faithful. Preventing the female from becoming promiscuous is perceived as being in her own best interest as well, since promiscuity may result not just in the loss of reputation but also in the contraction of venereal disease and consequent infertility. In some cultures, the cutting is believed to enhance fertility in and of itself, or enduring the cutting may be considered essential preparation for the ordeal of giving birth. Other cultures consider the unaltered female genitalia ugly or unclean. Certain West African societies believe that the clitoris is dangerous, causing impotency in the male organ that comes into contact with it and/or death to the newborn whose head touches it. Some mistakenly believe that their religion requires the practice, and there are also areas in which there seems to be no awareness of either practical or religious foundation for genital cutting: it is done in the present because it was done in the past and is perceived as an essential part of the culture. In some cases, Western derogation of African cultural practices during and after the colonial period has resulted in the retention of genital cutting as an act of defiance when it otherwise might have been abandoned.

To the Westerner, none of the reasons underlying the alteration of female genitalia are likely to be seen to justify a practice so injurious to women's health and dignity. Given the prevalence of negative images of Africa in the Western media, the practice is likely to be understood in the West in the context of stereotypes of Africa rather than in the context of worldwide devaluation of girls and women and repression of their sexuality, a context that includes, for example, the killing of infant females in poor societies in which girl children are seen as financial liabilities, the killing in some Middle Eastern cultures of adult females whose premarital or extramarital sexual activity is perceived as having brought dishonor on the family, or the systematic use of rape as a weapon of war. Few Westerners are likely to associate female genital cutting of girls and women in Africa with breast augmentation surgery in the United States or with domestic abuse so prevalent and severe that it leads to the deaths of over a thousand American women a year at the hands of their husbands or boyfriends (Flores A9).

A heavy burden falls on anyone who undertakes the presentation of a complex and highly sensitive subject like female genital cutting to a television audience with very limited understanding, perhaps even serious misunderstandings, of the cultural contexts in which the practice occurs. In my judgment, a responsible treatment of the subject must make clear at least the following:

1) that there are a wide variety of types of ritual female genital cutting and that they range from symbolic superficial incisions to infibulation;
2) that these practices are not limited to Africa and that they are not practiced in almost half of the 54 countries on the African continent;
3) that the practices are found among adherents to Islam and Christianity as well as among adherents to traditional religions;
4) that these practices, especially in their most extreme forms, have serious immediate and long-term negative consequences on the physical health of girls and women and on their babies and that they almost surely have serious negative psychological consequences as well, though these are not well documented;
5) that these practices are carried out because they are sincerely believed to be in the interest of the girls or women themselves and/or the community and that they are done for widely varying reasons, including religious, aesthetic, hygienic and medical, and sociological reasons;
6) that because of the history of colonialism and continuing unequal power relations between Westerners and Africans, the influence that Westerner--and even Africans who are perceived as Westernized--can have on these practices is severely limited and that such influence as may be exerted is negated by the use of inflammatory language and the demonization of the girls' families and of the practitioners, mostly women, who do the cutting;
7) that given the urgent needs of many African women for clean water, sufficient food, and adequate medical care, the eradication of ritual genital cutting, even where its dangers are well understood, might not be a preeminent concern;
8) that the incidence of genital cutting is decreasing slightly as a consequence of the educational initiatives undertaken by African women in their communities and to a lesser extent as a consequence of urbanization and improved formal education; and
9) that within the Western world there are also practices that are highly prejudicial to the well-being of women and children, that, although these practices are impossible to justify in rational terms and difficult to make comprehensible to those

outside the cultural context in which they occur, they are nevertheless profoundly resistant to correction and their correction is perceived as a matter to be addressed within the culture.

To set forth such standards is to be struck immediately by the unlikelihood, given the nature of the genre--especially the time constraints for preparation and presentation and the competition for audience share--of even minimally satisfactory presentations of the subject of ritual cutting of female genitalia in television news magazines. One treatment, in fact, met only one of the criteria that I have posited. The *Nightline* program that aired on May 2, 1996 made it clear that female genital cutting posed serious threats to the lives and health of African girls.

In this program, host Ted Koppel interviewed Stephanie Welch, a 22-year-old American photojournalist; 19-year-old Fauziya Kassindja, who had fled Togo to avoid ritual female genital cutting; and David Martin, chief counsel for the United States Immigration and Naturalization Service. The central question that the program explored was whether the granting of political asylum to one young woman, Fauziya Kassindja, would lead to an unmanageable incursion of female African immigrants: "You do understand," Koppel earnestly asked Ms. Kassindja, "that if . . . if you are granted political asylum for that reason it could open the door for many, many thousands, possibly hundreds of thousands, of other young girls to want to do the same thing?"

Such a question is based on a number of very doubtful assumptions: first, that large numbers of African girl children and adolescents are so weakly socialized that they resist the practice and that their resistance would be so strong that they would be willing to separate themselves from their families and communities to avoid it; second, that they would understand the concept of political asylum and would know that political asylum was available in America on the basis of female genital cutting; and third, that these children and adolescents would be able to obtain the resources--money and social support--they would need to make their way from their homes to America.

Before the end of the program it became clear that the theme was a calculated appeal to xenophobia. Koppel revealed that he had prior knowledge that Canada had extended political asylum on the basis of female genital cutting and that only two or three women had made asylum claims on that basis. Had Koppel not already known that there was no real likelihood of "many, many thousands, possibly hundred of thousands" of young African girls seeking political asylum, he would have learned as much from two of his guests. Ms. Kassindja explained that she, though a member of a privileged class, had not known what political asylum was even as she asked for it upon her arrival in America. She was simply acting on the advice of a German friend. And David Martin told Koppel how the INS was putting into place guidelines that would strictly limit eligibility for political asylum on the basis of ritual female genital cutting.

Before the program began to explore the dangers of "opening the floodgates," as it were, it was necessary to make certain that the audience was educated about the nature of female genital cutting. Toward that end, Koppel devoted the first five minutes to an interview of Stephanie Welch, a 22-year-old employee of the *Palm Beach Post* whose pictures of the genital cutting of a Kenyan girl had won her the Pulitzer Prize. Welch, a student at Syracuse University, had gone to Kenya to work as an intern for a Nairobi newspaper. Having read a copy of Alice Walker's *Possessing the Secret of Joy* given her by her sister, Welch wanted to photograph a ritual female genital cutting (Minor 1D). She managed to get an invitation to a village where a sixteen-year-old named Seita, the first girl from her village to go to school, was returning home to undergo cutting. Her teachers had made her aware of the pain and dangers involved, but Seita feared the pain and danger less than she feared being spurned by family and friends.

What the audience saw through Ms. Welch's lens was a young woman experiencing terror and excruciating pain and a father whose exclusive interests in the proceedings were the opportunities to enrich himself by means of the gifts brought to celebrate his daughter's coming-of-age and to spend several days drinking beer with his friends. They saw villagers who came from near and far to eat and drink and sing and dance, and they saw sympathetic peers whose attempts to help their friend took the form of beneficent deception. They saw adult women who quite literally turned their backs on the young girl's fear and suffering. Welch presented herself as a person of superior sensitivity: "Seita," she said, "understood that I was probably the only person that empathized with her."

Welch did not speak the language, had no training in social anthropology, and seemingly had no sense of having abused the hospitality of those who permitted her to share a significant cultural event. These lacks may have been understandable in terms of her youth and inexperience. What is most troubling is the producers' choice of her to present the subject to the American public when persons of much greater knowledge and experience were almost certainly available. In *Do They Hear You When You Cry*, the account of her experiences that Fauziya Kassindja co-wrote with Layli Miller Bashir, Kassindja tells how her attorneys located Merrick Posnansky, Professor Emeritus of Anthropology of the University of California, who had spent 30 years in Ghana and Togo and whose depth of understanding of West Africa in general and of her small ethnic group in particular made him a powerful advocate in her effort to have the denial of her request for political asylum overturned on appeal (423-24). Professor Posnansky, or if he was unable to appear, his research assistants or other experts in West African cultures would surely have presented the subject in a way more suggestive of its sensitivity and complexity.

The use of Welch and her arresting images was probably due to the program's having been aired during what is commonly called "sweeps week," one of the two two-week periods each year when audience share is measured. The amount of advertising revenue that a series can command is based on audience share, and thus sweeps week is the time when standards of responsible journalism and canons of good taste are most likely to be violated.

In a *20/20* segment that aired on June 20, 1997, veteran ABC newswoman Barbara Walters interviewed Somalian supermodel Waris Dirie, who had been infibulated at the age of four or five and who, as an adolescent, had made her way alone across 200 miles of desert between her nomadic family and Mogadishu to escape an arranged marriage to a man she believed to be some 40 or 50 years older than she. Because Ms. Walters lacks expertise in African cultures in general or female genital cutting in particular, she was unable to contextualize the experience of her subject. Thus Ms. Dirie's experience was made to seem representative. Viewers who had no prior knowledge would have thought that female genital cutting was limited to infibulation, which actually accounts for only about 15 percent of such procedures (Toubia, *Female* 11), and that the solitary rationale for infibulation was man's determination to protect his exclusive right to his female sexual property. Considerable emphasis was placed on the initial trauma and the immediate danger to life as well as the enduring psychosexual consequences, but little attention was given to the long-term health consequences, such as painful menstruation, obstructed labor, neuromas, abscesses, and fistulas. The term "female genital mutilation" was used consistently and both Barbara Walters and Waris Dirie used such terms as "torture," "horrible," and "brutal." Both Walters and Dirie left the false impression that no one is working to eradicate infibulation; and incidental comments, such as that by Hugh Downs that Dirie had been able to make her way from Africa to the "modern world" and Barbara Walters' explanation that female genital mutilation was practiced not just in Africa but in "other countries" reinforced the stereotype of Africa as an undifferentiated primitive mass.

The most comprehensive treatment of female genital cutting was the *Day One* segment entitled "Scarred for Life," which aired on March 20, 1993. Host Forrest Sawyer and reporter Sheila MacVicar made it clear that the term female circumcision covered a wide variety of practices, and they used a map to show the occurrence of female genital cutting on the continent. Something of the complexity of the issue was conveyed by MacVicar's interview of a middle-class Atlanta couple, naturalized American citizens born in Somalia, who were agonizing over whether to take their three young daughters to a foreign hospital to have clitoridectomies performed on them. The father remembered how his sisters suffered when they were infibulated and wished to spare his daughters the danger, pain, and disfigurement. The mother, however, worried about betraying her culture and about making her daughters "different" and making them unacceptable marriage choices for Somalian men. She was convinced that her own capacity for sexual response had been unaffected by the procedure.

Much of the *Day One* segment was devoted to discussions with women from The Gambia who, despite scant funding and stiff resistance, are engaged in a campaign to eradicate female genital cutting. Using powerful language, they described the practice, which they attributed to both the unquestioning acceptance of tradition and to male attempts to control female sexuality. They provided a disturbing video of solemn girl children awaiting the procedure, crying out as it was performed, suffering pain and shock afterwards, and being feted in the village after they had healed.[3] Much prominence was given to the awesome figure who performed the cutting, Auntie Adama, celebrated in circumcision songs as the Crocodile.

The program showed clips of African anti-circumcision activists conducting workshops in which adolescent girls were educated about sexuality in general and about the dangers of circumcision. Ms. MacVicar also spoke with the mothers of the girls whose response to the cutting of their daughters was sad acquiescence. She did not interview the village men, who, by all accounts, refuse to marry uncircumcized women, but who distance themselves from the consequences of that refusal: "it is women's business," they say.

The segment ended with a dialogue among Efua Dorkenoo and Dr. Nahid Toubia, who work in England and the United States respectively to combat genital cutting among immigrant populations, and Dr. Mark Belsey of the World Health Organization, James Grant of UNICEF, and Sandra Kotok of the United States State Department. Toubia insisted on the parallel between breast augmentation surgeries performed in the US and genital cutting, in both of which women's bodies are altered to conform to a social definition of what it means to be a woman. UN officials, when pressed by Dorkenoo and Sawyer to explain why so little funding has been allocated for the support of eradication efforts, and Ms Kotok of the State Department, when pressed to explain why the United States has not ratified the United Nations Declaration on the Rights of the Child, resorted to excuses, evasions, and equivocations.

The major shortcomings of "Scarred for Life" were the failure to acknowledge the complex motivations of the women who perform the genital cutting[4] and the failure to recognize the limitations of the moral suasion of the United States and the dangers contingent on U.S. involvement in this sensitive issue. The segment, though flawed, suggested at least the possibility of a responsible treatment of the subject in the popular media. Even if there were an exemplary presentation in the popular media, it would mean the addition of another negative image of Africa to the images of famine, war, and corruption that predominate in the news. There is little in the popular media to countervail such images. Even a late night news program like *Nightline*, which competes for an audience with comedians Jay Leno and David Letterman, attracts hundreds of thousands of viewers. Programs that show positive aspects of African culture, aspects that might well be emulated in the West, are presented in classrooms, recital and lecture halls, and theaters before groups of only dozens or hundreds. A recent issue of the African Literature Association *Bulletin* rejoiced that a thousand persons had heard Africa's best-known novelist Chinua Achebe, when he delivered the keynote speech at a recent ALA meeting (Nichols 12).

Regrettably, sensationalizing treatments of female genital cutting have prevailed in the popular media and will probably continue to prevail. Such treatments have served the interests of the women seeking political asylum. The more outraged the American public became the more likely it was to exert pressure on government agencies to grant asylum. In one regard, sensationalizing treatments also serve the interests of African activists, since an aroused public may also pressure international agencies to provide funding to support the activists' efforts. And sensational treatments certainly serve the needs of the news media as they compete for audience share and advertising dollars.

The consequences of the media's mishandling of the subject of female genital cutting are serious and far-reaching. It reinforces the perception that Africa is primitive and that Africans are irredeemably Other, the sense that there is an unbridgeable chasm between Them and Us. In the general public it exacerbates racism, and in the academic community it exacerbates tensions between Western and African feminists and between African scholars and Africanists. Ironically, the more television news contributes to American shock and indignation the more it increases the isolation of Africans living in the West and thus undermines the efforts of social workers attempting to educate them about the dangers of genital cutting. And the more television news contributes to American shock and indignation the more it encourages clumsy intervention in African affairs and thus exacerbates Africans' sense that their culture is under siege and deepens resistance to change. Well-intentioned Americans thus unwittingly contribute to the persistence of the very practice they hope to eradicate.

A critique of the American popular media's handling of the subject of female genital cutting is not intended to minimize the fear and suffering of girl children or the threat that genital cutting poses to their well-being; it is not intended to imply an endorsement of the idea that girls and women *as they naturally are* are somehow dangerous, or ugly, or unclean; neither is it intended to condone the gender power imbalance that has permitted the practice to persist for over two millennia. It is intended rather to suggest why it is unlikely that Americans who have no expertise in African cultures will move beyond their shock and indignation to an understanding of the sensitivity and complexity of the issue, why it is unlikely that they will embrace the attitudes and adopt the language that will enable them to offer the most effective support to the African women who are working to eradicate female genital cutting.

Notes

[1] The cutting of female genitals is believed to have begun in Egypt during the first millennium BC. Early written references to the practice are found in the works of Herodotus (5th century BC) and the Greek geographer Strabo (25 BC). Doctors in Alexandria and Rome left rather detailed descriptions of the practice in the early Christian era (Coquery-Vidrovitch 207). See also, however, Efua Dorkenoo's discussion of alternative explanations of the origins of infibulation (33-34).

[2] See Nahid Toubia, *Female Genital Mutilation*, pp. 24-25, for a map showing the African countries in which female genital cutting is practiced and a chart indicating the estimated number and types of procedures performed in each country. The discussion of the types of genital cutting which follows is drawn largely from Toubia (10-11). However, see also Dorkenoo (5-8) for a similar classification with some additions and refinements.

[3] In the book which she co-wrote with Alice Walker, Pratibha Parmar casts serious doubts on the veracity of MacVicar's statement that the video was given ABC by anti-circumcision activists. When Parmar and Alice Walker were filming *Warrior Marks*, their documentary on "genital mutilation" in The Gambia in January 1993, they worked with a woman named Bilaela, who had served as local liaison for the film crew from "a major U. S. television network." Bilaela offered to arrange for Parmar and Walker to film an excision if they "were willing to pay for it." She said that she had made similar arrangements for the network film crew. Bilaela did not prove to be absolutely reliable in her dealings with Parmar and Walker, but her description of the scenario filmed by the ABC crews was accurate: "The circumciser had had two rooms, separated by a curtain. The girls were taken in, one by one, which was filmed. They'd recorded the screaming and then had filmed the girls being taken out again" (161-62).

[4] For a discussion of the complex motivations of the circumciser, see Toubia, "Social and Political Implications," pp. 151-52.

Works Cited

Coquery-Vidrovitch, Catherine. *African Women: A Modern History.* Trans. Beth Gillian Raps. Boulder: Westview, 1997.

Dorkenoo, Efua. *Cutting the Rose: Female Genital Mutilation: The Practice and Its Prevention.* London: Minority Rights, 1994.

"Female Genital Mutilation." *Nightline.* Narr. Ted Koppel ABC, 2 May 1996.

Flores, Veronica. "Domestic-Violence Services Seem to Save More Lives of Abusers." *Lexington Herald-Leader.* 9 Apr. 1999: A9.

Kassindja, Fauziya, and Layli Miller Bashir. *Do They Hear You When You Cry?* New York: Delacorte, 1998.

Minor, Emily J. "A Blur, A Scream." *Palm Beach Post.* 21 Apr. 1996: 1D.

Nichols, Lee. Interview with Bernth Lindfors. "1998 ALA (Texas) Conference Wrap-Up and Interviews." *ALA Bulletin* 24.2 (1998): 26-29.

"Scarred for Life?" *Day One.* Narr. Forrest Sawyer and Sheila MacVicar. ABC. 20 March 1993.

Toubia, Nahid. *Female Genital Mutilation: A Call for Global Action.* New York: Rainb, 1993.

---. "The Social and Political Implications of Female Circumcision: The Case of Sudan." *Women and the Family in the Middle East: New Voices of Change.* Ed. Elizabeth Warnock Fernea. Austin: U of Texas P, 1985. 148-59.

"Waris Dirie." *20/20.* Narr. Barbara Walters. ABC, 20 June 1997.

Walker, Alice, and Pratibha Parmar. *Warrior Marks: Female Genital Mutilation and the Sexual Blinding of Women.* New York: Harcourt Brace, 1993.

(U.S.-Centered) Afrocentric Imaginations of Africa: L.H. Clegg's *When Black Men Ruled the World,* and Eddie Murphy's *Coming to America*

Jean Muteba Rahier
Florida International University

Africa has been imagined and re-presented on the white screen since the very beginning of Western cinema's history. Western cinema, and particularly the white Hollywood industry, has usually represented sub-Saharan Africa as a place of safari-like adventures and/or missionaries' enterprises for white heroes revolving among savage people and beasts ("The African Queen," "The Naked Prey," "Tarzan, the Ape Man," "Congo," etc.) (see Cameron 1994). On the other hand, Africa has rarely preoccupied black U.S.-produced and directed cinema. When it refers to Africa at all, the latter seems to prefer the portrayal of Africa as a site of ancient grandeur and fantastic monarchies (that is the case of the two films analyzed here). I argue that in both cases, today's Africa is erased, as well as her strengths, her specificities, and her numerous problems and struggles.

In this paper, my objective is to examine the representations of Africa, Africans, and African history made in two African-American films: a non-fiction or documentary film, "When Black Men Ruled the World: Egypt During the Golden Age," produced independently by Louis Henry Clegg (1991), and a fiction film, "Coming to America," produced by Eddie Murphy and the Hollywood cinema industry (1989). These two African-American films illustrate different popular, "Afrocentric" and geographic orientations: the obsessive focus on Egypt, and the "Sub-Saharan Africa of Kings and Queens."

At this point, some readers could already raise a few questions: Why am I taking Eddie Murphy's comedy seriously? How can I compare Murphy's fiction film to a non-fiction or documentary film such as Clegg's? Shouldn't fiction films and documentaries be treated separately?[1]

Common sense distinctions between fiction and documentary films are less obvious than what they might seem. Today's scholars of film and media studies agree on the fact that the boundaries between fiction and non-fiction films are, at best, fuzzy and variable. Film and media studies specialists distance themselves from previous definitions of the genre of "documentary films" that ascribed an inherent and "objective" reality to their contents (see for example Barsam 1976; Stott 1973; Allen 1985; Grierson 1966). Dirk Eitzen, among others, finds the past definitions unsatisfactory because they are grounded, in different ways, on too simplistic and limited understandings of what documentaries are and do. Relaying Nicholas Wolterstorff's philosophy of art (Wolterstorff 1980a; 1980b), he writes:

> Every representation of reality is no more than a fiction in the sense that it is an artificial construct, a highly contrived and selective view of the world, produced for some purpose and therefore unavoidably reflecting a given subjectivity or point of view. Even our "brute" perceptions of the world are inescapably tainted by our beliefs, assumptions, goals, and desires. So, even if there is a concrete, material reality upon which our existence depends (something very few actually doubt), we can only apprehend it through mental representations that at best resemble reality and that are in large part socially created. Some film theorists have responded to this dilemma by claiming that documentary is actually no more than a kind of fiction that is constituted to cover over or "disavow" its own fictionality (Eitzen 1995: 82).

Representations in so called fiction and non-fiction films are projected with various "stances." While the storyteller will typically take a "fictive stance" for the projection of his/her representations, in contrast the documentary filmmaker will adopt an "assertive stance." This opposition between "fictive" and "assertive" stances is what—according to Plantinga—distinguishes documentaries from fiction films. Just like fiction films, documentaries re-present or imagine a world; unlike fiction films, they make claims about it (Plantinga 1997). The latter statement is subject to intense discussions among film critiques, since claims about reality can also be found in fiction films (see Eitzen 1995; Plantinga 1997).

Both the comedy "Coming to America" and the documentary "When Black Men Ruled the World" disclose imaginings of Africa and the African past made from an identified positionality: a black American perspective very much embedded in Western history. Both are directed to the American public, and both obviously resist the white supremacist and white hegemonic discourses that characterize the history of the United States, and which consist in asserting that African people and their descendants in the Diaspora are inferior people, whose ancestors were savages, cannibals, lazy social predators, and so on, who did not deserve better than to be enslaved and colonized, and who presently continue to suffer from their racial limitations: "lower I.Q.," African famine and internal wars, propagation of the HIV virus, drug addiction, etc. Both films reject Hegel's claim that: "African history did not exist prior to European colonization." One could say that, borrowing Franz Fanon's words, these two films project—in their own distinctive way—a "passionate research...directed by the secret hope of discovering beyond the misery of today, beyond self-contempt, resignation and abjuration, some very beautiful and splendid era whose existence rehabilitates us both in regard to ourselves and in regard to others" (Fanon 1968: 170).

If the representations of Africa and Africans in "Coming to America" and in "When Black Men Ruled the World" can be compared--they point to the two most visible versions of U.S.-centered Afrocentrism--, the two films are nevertheless very different in that the first aims to entertain and provoke laughter while the second's main objective is to educate and divulge what the filmmaker and producer think is a "scientific truth."

The term "Afrocentrism" has meant different things when used by different people in different locations and situations. Sometimes it has only been used in a looser sense to refer to, or emphasize the African origins shared by the black people of the world. It has been used to qualify the work of some scholars whose research has been focused, almost exclusively, on African cultural survivals in the Americas and other locations of the African diaspora, as well as to characterize the work of researchers dedicated to the study of African cultural influences on various cultural formations in western cultures. Some black artists have also called their work "Afrocentric" because of their exclusive orientation to celebrate Africa, African people, history, and cultures.

"Afrocentrism" has also been used with a stronger sense by a diverse group of thinkers self-labeled "Afrocentrists" because of their shared belief (or faith) in a "cohesive, dogmatic and essentially irrational ideology" (Howe 1998: 1). This ideology, by seeing Africa as the source of any and every civilization, does nothing but replace the role that Europe plays in Eurocentric dogmas as the origin of everything. Following Eurocentrism, this kind of Afrocentrism falls in the trap of the analytical simplicity brought by unicentric views (Boyce Davies 1999; Gilroy 1993: 187-223). The British scholar Stephen Howe, who has recently published a book entitled *Afrocentrism: Mythical Pasts and Imagined Homes* (1998), presents a critical history of this "Afrocentric ideology." After underlining the fact that "strong" Afrocentrism resembles the extreme forms of cultural nationalism specific to nineteenth-century Europe as well as to 1930s Germany and 1990s Serbia, he writes at the beginning of the book:

> From all of this follows extreme intellectual and cultural separatism, involving belief in fundamentally distinct and internally homogeneous "African" ways of knowing and feeling about the world, ways which only members of the

group can possibly understand. Even those who are apparently in-group members, by birth, ancestry or pigmentation, can be excluded from it on ideological grounds if they fail to accept the ideology's doctrines; for such failure can be attributed, quite simply, to brainwashing by the dominant Eurocentric culture. Thus the belief system is insulated from the possibility of critique or falsification. (Howe 1998: 1-2)

I call the two films under scrutiny here "Afrocentric" because they both display a dream of a world without whites by presenting two different versions of an allegorical African past (and present), devoted to African ancestry and blood, grounded on traditions of kingship which demonstrate African nobility. They are preoccupied with the celebration of a lost way of life. They are both driven by the desire of getting back African honor and pride (Early 1995: 39).

"Coming to America," faithful to the (white) Hollywood tradition of fairy-tale happy endings, presents the story of a young African prince, Akeem (Eddie Murphy), who travels to America in order to find the right bride and escape from the tradition of his country, the imaginary Zamunda, which would want him to marry a young woman who was chosen at birth by his parents, the king and the queen. The vast majority of the actors are African Americans. The few white characters are at most peripheral and in a subordinate social position.

A bit of the basic story line is appropriately recounted for clarity: the film begins with a long scene, taken from above, of a dense and unpopulated rain forest. There are no cities, no slums, no markets, nothing else than the fairy tale palace with an architecture resembling European castles in which the king, the queen, Akeem, and a multitude of servants live. The story continues with the morning ritual of Akeem, on the very day he is supposed to be introduced to his future bride. Musicians playing instruments (violins and bugles) softly awaken Akeem. African women servants lead him to a small swimming pool, which is in fact his bathtub, where they wash him from head to toe. Blasé, he stays indifferent to the presence of the young and attractive, naked women servants in the bathtub with him. We later learn that just like his father, he sometimes engages in sexual play with them. While his gaze is lost in the horizon, one of the female servants exclaims, surging out of the water: "the royal penis is clean, your Highness." They then help Akeem to gargle and to brush his teeth. Then, the depiction of Africa and African kingship continues in an extravagant display of modern wealth irrespective of the plans of black cultural nationalists, for whom Africa has to be thought of exclusively in terms of very old (nonmodern) traditions. Akeem rejoins his parents in an "aristocratic" dining room, which in fact evokes European grandeur by the size of the table, the chandeliers, the use of intercoms to communicate, etc.

In the dining room, Akeem is told by his father that today, the day of his birthday, he will have to meet his future bride during a solemn ceremony. After the breakfast, Akeem goes to practice some martial arts with Semi, his friend, confidant, and servant: a character played by Arsenio Hall. During the exercises, Akeem shares with Semi his doubts about the woman that he is supposed to marry. He does not like the tradition of having imposed upon him a bride whom he does not even know and whom he does not love. To Semi, who reminds him that this is an old tradition of the kingdom of Zamunda, Akeem responds: "Times must and always do change, my friend!" During these first scenes, inoffensive elephants walk by trumpeting with kind giraffes, Semi makes allusions to hippopotamus excrement, and zebras gently run in the background...

Later that same day, at the ceremony of the presentation of the "future bride," the members of the royal court are present. Men wear tuxedos and women African garb. Dancers perform a supposedly African dance for a little while and then regroup in two lines to allow the future bride to walk in a submissive fashion down the center of the room to meet the prince. Surprising everybody, the prince suddenly takes her to a side room to talk to her in privacy and, supposedly, to get to know her. Once away from the public eye, she tells him: "I've been trained to serve you!"

"Yes, but what do you like?" asks Akeem, who supposedly wants to see her freed from old traditions of servitude. "I want a woman who will arouse my intellect as well as my loins!" continues Akeem. She keeps repeating that she entirely surrenders her physical and mental being to his will. The scene ends with the prince—who wants to test how far she will go to please him—asking the young woman to bark. She obeys and leaves the room barking and hoping on one foot while Akeem's father comes in.

After getting the authorization from his father to travel, Akeem goes to America with his servant/friend to find the bride of his dreams, who must be—unlike African women—independent. He is obsessed with being loved for himself and not for his royal status. For that reason, he will hide his aristocratic origin until the very end of the film, when he marries, in a fairy-tale like conclusion, the pretty, intelligent, independent, U.S. black woman of his dreams.

It seems to me that "Coming..." does not follow what Paul Gilroy argued in the last chapter of *Black Atlantic* (1993). There, Paul Gilroy explained how racial and political discourses in various communities of the African diaspora have both been embedded within and without the West. He suggests that the very particularity of these discourses consists in referring to, recalling and/or re-appropriating in a variety of ways, an African essence with great "African (non-modern) traditions." These traditions are conceived as constituting the pole definitely opposed to white/European modernity, with which no reconciliation is possible. He thinks here at political movements such as Garveyism, Négritude, Asante's kind of Afrocentrism, Rastafarianism, etc.:

> This gesture sets tradition and modernity against each other as simple polar alternatives as starkly differentiated and oppositional as the signs black and white. In these conditions, where obsessions with origin and myth can rule contemporary political concerns and the fine grain of history, the idea of tradition can constitute a refuge. It provides a temporary home in which shelter and consolation from the vicious forces that threaten the racial community (imagined or otherwise) can be found (Gilroy 1993: 188-189).

As I interpret the film, I do not see that "Coming to America" deals with African traditions in a way that opposes Africa to the western world in a definitive fashion. On the contrary, and that is what the conclusion of the film suggests I think, Africa and the modern world can inter-marry. And this is made even easier because the imagined Africa of "Coming..." is not deprived at all of the signs of capitalist modernity. There, there is no place for "obscure rituals, esoteric spirituality, and strange behaviors" (from a western perspective), and demonstrations of wealth and consumerist values abound (Cameron 1994: 154-155): servitude for the master's "refined pleasures" ("the royal penis is clean, your Highness"); Akeem and his family possess a great many "modern objects" and have unlimited financial resources which allow them to buy whatever and whomever they want in Africa and in the West; Akeem and his friend Semi can travel to the United States with an unrealistic amount of luggage; Akeem and Arsenio do not have one of the "typical accents" of African English speakers but speak an English that has a vast vocabulary which surprises black Americans; Arsenio remodels their dirty American studio as soon as he has the opportunity to do so by purchasing modern western furniture; etc.

Indeed, the Africa of "Coming..." is not the Africa of Asante, Karenga, Jeffries and others, although like theirs, it is an Africa that intends to heal the wounds left by slavery, racial discrimination and segregation, white supremacy and white hegemony. The Africa of "Coming..." does not participate in the opposition "tradition *versus* modernity" previously mentioned. It is an Africa which, instead, seems to suggest that there is a place for African modernity. The numerous exaggerations and dream-like depictions point to an Africa that does not exist anywhere. It is an Africa that is in direct contradiction with the Africa of uneducated or poorly educated (lower class and some middle class) African Americans. The latter often imagine an Africa of savage animals living in an unconquered and dangerous natural environment. Laughter in the film's audience is often provoked by the juxtaposition of both imaginations of Africa, Eddie Murphy's Africa of aristocrats, and the Africa of black U.S. masses: "Excuse me if I was being brusque but sometimes we get bubbas without a dollar to their name. But, obviously you gentlemen, you came in another boat," says the landlord of the building where Akeem finally rents a studio. Later on, after showing the floor's filthy and insect infested communal bathroom that Akeem and Semi will have to share with the other tenants, the same landlord adds: "There is a little bit of an insect problem. But, you guys, from Africa, you are used to that." Darryl, the boyfriend of Lisa—Akeem's future wife—asks Akeem at the basketball game: "What kind of games do you play in Africa? Chase the monkey?" I cannot resist mentioning the scene when Akeem goes to the barbershop and the Jewish patron who is always there exclaims: "Hey, it's Kunta Kinte!" which provokes general laughter in the shop. Later, to convince Lisa that he is poor, Akeem lies and manipulates the myth of rural, non-modern and poor Africa by saying that he is a deprived goat herder; and so on.

In "Coming..." women have a subaltern role. The only ones who seem to have somewhat escaped from male authority and have more autonomy than the others are the queen, Lisa, and her sister. All other women, and particularly African women, are fundamentally in a position of submission. They are portrayed as closer to traditions than men, and therefore less independent, less modern than men are. This is expressed, among other things, in the clothes they wear. From the beginning of the film to the end, African women are always dressed in traditional African garments. They never wear Western (i.e. modern) clothes. This is the case, for instance, in the ceremony—which is supposed to be "traditional"—during which the young African woman who has been trained or domesticated to marry Akeem is introduced to the court: all men are dressed in tuxedos while the women are dressed in African clothing. In the same order of things, the only bodies that the viewers see naked or half naked—in a similar fashion as in the pages of the National Geographic Magazine (Lutz 1993)—are the bodies of African women servants in Akeem's bathtub and private apartments in the palace in Zamunda. Neither African men, African-American men, nor African-American women are seen naked or bare breasted.

A comparable male dominated perspective is found in "When Black Men Ruled the World" (1991). As suggested earlier, the stance in "When Black Men..." differs significantly from the tone of "Coming..." Instead of being fictive it is assertive. "When Black Men..." makes a series of claims about the African past and about the importance of Africa in the development of "civilization" (used in the singular in the film's text). It is a didactic film directed to primary school, high school and even university students. It comes with a "Learning/Activity Guide" which has probably been more useful to schoolteachers than to university students and professors. The guide presents short texts about the origin of the Ancient Egyptians, the Ancient Egyptian social structure, the pyramids, the hieroglyphs, the Egyptian medical science, etc. It is followed, in the same booklet, by an activity guide which asks the students to reproduce a definition or a geographic map, as well as to identify a pharaoh, a particular dynasty, and so on.

The didactic tone of the film is made obvious from the very beginning. The first scene reveals Henry L. Clegg in a black tuxedo, which interestingly enough parallels the tuxedos of the African men in "Coming..." He recites Countee Cullen's poem, "What is Africa to Me?":

What is Africa to me?
Copper sun, a scarlet sea,
Jungle star and jungle track,
Strong bronzed men and regal Black
Women from whose loins I sprang
When the birds of Eden sang?[2]

Then, Clegg identifies the project of the film by explaining that when the poem was first written, people knew very little about Africa, which was then called "the Dark Continent." Today, he adds, things have not changed much because when we hear about Africa in the news or read about it in the paper, it is more often than not to be informed about a famine, an ethnic war, or whatever other plague. This is the case even when the news coverage is valuable. Few journalists have taken the time to reveal the great Ancient past of Africa. The reason for this being that they too probably know little about it. After complaining about a similar ignorance in academic circles, Clegg explains that the viewer is about to engage in an unforgettable experience which has been designed by a number of teachers, scholars, ministers, school board members and others who have sought ways to teach "black history and culture" (in the singular). Clegg continues, while he buttons up his tuxedo as if he was about to be himself shaken by the whole experience: "With this film, we are going to take you on an exciting journey into the black past. We will focus on Egypt's Golden Age. This will be a fascinating expedition into Antiquity." These words—which present Ancient African history as a travel log/neo-colonial diary—are followed by the captions introducing the film: "Strong Arm Entertainment proudly presents... the new edition of 'When Black Men Ruled the World'." This introduction is followed by almost four minutes of a globe gyrating in the infinity of space, which probably symbolizes the world that was once ruled by black men...

The voice over decisively states that the film's focus will not be on today's Egypt—now populated by Arabs whose ancestors conquered the country in the 7th century AD—or on today's Sub-Saharan Africa, but on Africa's Golden Age, that is to say the Egypt of the pharaohs. This interest on Egypt's past will allow the viewer—who is thought of as being an African American person, to discover his/her roots. The voice over continues: "So, just as Alex Haley, the distinguished African-American writer who also unearths his roots in Western Africa, ...we too must turn away from the lure of the modern world and then search the Ancient sites, monuments, legends, and documents to discover our Golden Past." The style of the film is dramatic. The "black genius of yesteryear" is celebrated over and over again, and the film's narrative retraces a movement from south to north: "The journey must begin where the human race began, in the very heart of Africa," says Clegg wearing then an African *bubu*. The greatness of Ancient Egyptian civilization is presented as the result of migrations and/or conquest of Lower Egypt by people coming from the kingdom of Nubia (and Kush) and before that from southern regions in Central Africa. The presentation of the argument is made while applying uncritically concepts which have been socially and culturally defined and re-defined throughout U.S. history, and which are still at the center of animated scholarly debates. That is the case of the concept of "race" and of "black" or "blackness," for instance:

> Perhaps, the most convincing argument for a southern or Nubian origin of the ancient Egyptians and their civilization is that the people of these two nations were of the same Black or African racial stock. Once again, the evidence for this is found in the testimony of ancient eyewitnesses as well as in the discoveries of modern science (Clegg 1991: 13).

Then, the film goes on to explain how ancient Egyptians invented everything, from the first medical treatments, the production of iron, mathematics and other sciences, to monumental architecture, philosophy, spirituality and genial social organization. Ancient Egypt, Clegg continues, has influenced all the other civilizations of the Mediterranean: Ancient Greece, Rome, etc. Therefore, and this is the main point of the film, black Africa (via Egypt) has in fact been the primary origin of "Civilization," a civilization which allowed the development of Europe. In that sense, the claims of the film repeat the arguments elaborated by Cheikh Anta Diop, Ivan Van Sertima, Chancellor Williams, and others: Africa is at the source of modernity. My goal here is not to discuss the validity, or absence thereof, of these claims. Such an endeavor does not draw my interest whatsoever.

This brief and—I admit—uncompleted examination[3] of the representations of Africa in "Coming to America" and in "When Black Men Ruled the World" gives me the opportunity to underline a few things.

1) The complete absence of information in these two visual texts about today's Africa, her struggle against neo-colonial economic and political structures, her difficulty—in specific regions—with ethnic tensions and devastating civil wars that lead to the disintegration of the state, her suffering under the yoke of still too

numerous dictatorial tyrants, and so on, is quite edifying in the sense that they illustrate quite well a known tendency of contemporary African-American films. The rare African-American films in which we can find Africa imagined do not depict the continent in a way that some of us Africans who came to live in this country (the U.S.), can directly relate to. We were born there and still maintain on her lands parents to whom we send money every month to allow them to survive. This is not the Africa we can find in the pages written by Wole Soyinka, Ngugi Wa Thiong'o, Ali Mazrui, Nina Emma Mba and so many others who reflect upon Africa's immense challenges and propose concrete solutions. The Africa of "Coming..." and of "When Black Men. . ." is far from the Africa depicted in numerous films by Senegal's Sembene Ousmane, Cameroon's Jean-Marie Téno in "Africa, I will Fleece You," by the Haitian filmmaker Raoul Peck in "Lumumba: Death of a Prophet," by Anne-Laure Folly in "Women with Open Eyes," or by the Guinean David Ashkar in "God's Will"[4]--to name only a few. These filmmakers—unlike Eddie Murphy and Henry Louis Clegg—address the tyranny of African dictators, the role of the African elites in the suffering of so many people, the neo-colonial structures of domination, the struggle for gender equality and the successes of African women against patriarchal societies, etc. In Clegg's and Murphy's imagined Africa, Africans have no say. They are not participating in the elaboration of the visual text, and their voices seem to have no importance. It is an Africa that corresponds to the Africa referred to by Stuart Hall in an article entitled "Cultural Identity and Cinematic Representation":

> But whether [Africa] is, in this sense, an origin of our identities, unchanged by four hundred years of displacement, dismemberment, transportation, to which we could in any final or literal sense, return, is more open to doubt. The original "Africa" is no longer there. It too has been transformed. History is, in that sense, irreversible. We must not collude with the West which, precisely, "normalizes" and appropriates Africa by freezing it into some timeless zone of the "primitive, unchanging past." Africa must at last be reckoned

with…. But it cannot in any simple sense be merely recovered. It belongs irrevocably, for us, to what Edward Said once called an "imaginative geography and history" … Our belongingness to it constitutes what Benedict Anderson calls "an imagined community." To this "Africa," … we can't literally go home again (Hall 1996: 217).

2) "Coming to America" and "When Black Men Ruled the World" are two expressions of the still growing influences of "Afrocentrism" in black U.S. circles of academics and artists. Afrocentric ideology—of the "strong" type defined earlier—exists exclusively as a defensive posture to Eurocentrism and falls into the same traps it wants to criticize in the latter. Afrocentrism, which rightfully combats Eurocentric claims, unfortunately tends to profess intolerance against all white folks, who are simplistically demonized, and who are thought of as being incapable of understanding any aspect whatsoever of black peoples' lives because they do not share the "racial essence." What has been called here "strong" Afrocentrism, most of the time a U.S.-centered ideology, is also eager to silence or erase voices of black people, from Africa or from other locations in the Diaspora, particularly when these voices do not support its dogmas. Two anecdotes illustrate this point. Recently, in Florida's Broward County, located north of Miami-Dade County, Molefi Kete Asante—one of the leading figures of Afrocentrism—made a speech to educators who had invited him to talk and give some advice about how to teach to a culturally, and "racially" diverse student body. They had invited him because they have black students coming from different areas of the United States, but also from Haiti, Jamaica, the Bahamas, Central and South America, etc. and wanted to deal better with this rich variety of cultural backgrounds. Asante responded to their request by proudly repeating his Afrocentric dogmas: "No person left Africa as an African American, a Haitian or Jamaican. There were no Costa Ricans. They left Africa as Yoruba and Ashanti. This is the way the Africans landed here" (Charles 1998: 3-B).

Kwame Anthony Appiah reports another anecdote:

The notion that there is something unitary called African culture that could thus be summarized has been subjected to devastating critique by a generation of African intellectuals. But little sign of these African accounts of African cultures appears in the writings of Afrocentrism. Molefi Asante has written entire books about Akan culture without referring to the major works of such Akan philosophers as J.B. Danquah, William Abrahams, Kwasi Wiredu and Kwame Gyekye. And I am reliably informed that, on one occasion not so long ago, a distinguished Zairian intellectual was told by an African-American interlocutor that "We do not need you educated Africans coming here to tell us about African culture" (Appiah 1997: 731).

In addition to the Middle Passage and the experiences of slavery and colonialism, one of the major reasons why black people all over the world feel connected to one another is because of their relationship—recognized as more or less problematic—to Africa. Black individuals and black communities all over the world have developed through time, from the specificity of their quite different subjectivities, a variety of affective, political, spiritual, economic, cultural, etc. relationships to Africa. Black peoples have been imagining Africa from different positionalities. The examination of black peoples' relationships to Africa is an informative way to approach the plurality of black subjectivities.

Notes

[1] Although I prefer the expression "non-fiction film" to "documentary film," I use them here as synonymous.

[2] This poem, entitled "Heritage," was included in Alain Locke's *The New Negro* (Locke 1975: 250).

[3] Representations of gender roles in these two films could be the object of another paper.

[4] All these films are distributed by California Newsreel.

Works Cited

Allen, Robert C. and Douglas Gomery. *Film History: Theory and Practice*. New York: Alfred Knopf, 1985.

Appiah, Kwame Anthony. "Europe Upside Down: Fallacies of the New Afrocentrism." *Perspectives on Africa: A Reader in Culture, History, and Representation*. Christopher Steiner and Roy Richard Grinker, ed. Pp. 728-731. Cambridge, Massachussetts: Blackwell, 1997.

Barsam, Richard Meran, ed. *Nonfiction film: theory and criticism*. New York: Dutton., 1976.

Boyce Davies, Carole. "Beyond Unicentricity: Transcultural Black Intellectual Presences." *Research in African literatures* 30, 2 (1999): 96-109.

Cameron, Kenneth. 1994. *Africa on Film: Beyond Black and White*. New York: The Continuum Publishing Company.

Charles, Jacqueline. "Educators learn how to teach black history." *The Miami Herald* (September 19, 1998): Pp. 1-B & 3-B.

Clegg, Legrand H. and Karima Y. Ahmed. *When Black Men Ruled the World. Part One: Egypt During the Golden Age (Learning Activity Guide)*. Compton, California: The Clegg Series, 1991.

Early, Gerald.. "Understanding Afrocentrism." *Civilization* (July-August 1995): 31-39.

Eitzen, Dirk. "When is a Documentary?: Documentary as a Mode of Reception." *Cinema Journal* 35, 1 (1995): 81-102.

Fanon, Frantz. *The Wretched of the Earth*. New York: Groove Press, 1968.

Gilroy, Paul. *The Black Atlantic. Modernity and Double Consciousness*. Cambridge, Massachusetts: Harvard University Press, 1993

Grierson, John. "The First Principles of Documentary." *Grierson on Documentary*. F. Hardy, ed. London, England: Faber & Faber, 1966.

Hall, Stuart. "Cultural Identity and Cinematic Representation. "*Black British Cultural Studies: A Reader*. Houston Baker,

Manthia Diawara, and Ruth Lindeborg, ed. Chicago: The University of Chicago Press, 1996: 210-222.

Howe, Stephen. *Afrocentrism: Mythical Pasts and Imagined Homes*. London: Verso, 1998.

Lemelle, Sidney and Robin Kelly. *Imagining Home: Class, Culture and Nationalism in the African Diaspora*. London: Verso, *1994*.

Locke, Alain, ed. *The New Negro*. New York, 1975.

Lutz, Catherine and Jane Collins. *Reading National Geographic*. Chicago: University of Chicago Press, *1993*.

Plantinga, Carl. *Rhetoric and Representation in Nonfiction Film*. New York: Cambridge University Press, 1997.

Stott, William. *Documentary expression and thirties America*. New York: Oxford University Press, 1973.

Wolterstorff, Nicholas. *Art in action : toward a Christian aesthetic*. Grand Rapids: Eerdmans, 1980a.

Wolterstorff, Nicholas. *Works and Worlds of Art*. New York: Oxford University Press, 1980b.

PART VI
Feminism and Women in Africa

Perceptions of African Feminism:
A Socio-Historical Perspective

Daniel M. Mengara,
Montclair State University

Approaching things feminist in North America nowadays, specifically in the United States, has grown to become something of a "risky" business. Similar "risks" are indeed present in any cultural studies approach that tackles issues pertaining to minorities, above all as they relate to Africa and African-Americans. However, whereas racial issues have been dealt with more openly in one way or another in the political arena, feminism seems to be of a much more sensitive nature as it requires of both men and women a much deeper sense of diplomacy and political correctness that would not only ensure that no gender-based sensibilities are hurt, but also guarantee that no outrageous assertions relating to females are made. Thus, whereas the Ku Klux Klan is still able to organize itself into a national movement, and freely go to national television not only to declare its belief in the purity of the white race, but also to re-assert its hatred for minorities and foreigners, no movement for the domination of women has been able to surface in America and practices such as polygamy, that are often viewed as symbols of male domination, have been solidly kept in check by laws protecting the rights of women not only in the workplace of economic capitalism, but also in the more private or semi private realm of society at large. This is indeed an enormous behavioral shift from the western world of only about sixty to seventy years ago when women were still second-class citizens not only in the United States, but also in many other western countries that, paradoxically, have now suddenly vowed to become the champions of women's rights both at home and abroad. As far as the United States is concerned, it is certain that feminism, as a result of women's activism, has been able to evolve somewhat positively therein as women and men alike have striven to define, *for America*, the kind of feminism that is best suited for *its culture and society*. Such has also been the case for other western countries such as France or Great Britain, among others. The problem, however, often poses itself when feminist thinking or policy seeks to export itself just like any other economic commodity because, from a western perspective, its principles are, in essence, deemed universal. This assumed universality of feminist thought is therefore going to be the main object of this paper as we seek to explore the African side of the feminist story.

Several questions do come to mind when one is faced with the issue of feminism worldwide. What is feminism? Will feminism express itself the same way across cultures, irrespective of the particular experiences and conditions of women around the world? Should African feminism,[1] for instance, be the exact twin copy of Western feminism?

These questions are not easily answered. They pose a problem not only because of the inherent sociocultural complexities that underlie the notion of feminism, but also because of the fact that the idea and practice of feminism as we "know" it today was born in the West and later exported to other regions of the world. Thus, as an ideology about women, feminism as the West defines it, seeks to be universal. However, because Western feminism, as we shall see, stems mostly from historically rigid gender considerations, its often asserted universality can be easily dismissed as a sex or gender-based universality, rather than one based on sociocultural motivations.

This paper will therefore attempt to answer the above questions not only through a brief exploration of the notion of feminism in general terms, but also through a study of the particular way "African feminism" has expressed itself throughout known history in the African context.

According to Rosalind Delmar:

> [Feminism is a position that] holds that women suffer discrimination because of their sex, that they have specific needs which remain negated and unsatisfied, and that the satisfaction of these needs would require a radical change (some would say a revolution) in the social, economic and political order (Delmar 1986: 8).

In other words, women are dominated, negated, discriminated against and exploited by men in all spheres of human life, that is, social, economic and political. As a consequence, they wish to emancipate, liberate themselves from the status of second-class citizens in which men have confined them throughout history. They are therefore demanding equality with men in these and other areas.

Indeed, when one talks of liberation or emancipation, the idea that comes to mind is that one is not free. So the natural tendency in any state of "imprisonment", whether physical or psychological, is that one must liberate oneself. Thus, applying the notion of feminism to the African context automatically entails that the African woman is not free. As a result, she must be liberated. The problem however, as Molara Ogundipe-Leslie (1994) puts it, is that, because it originates mostly from a Western definition that derives its essence from the western context, feminist thought of the alleged "universal" kind has, too often, translated itself into a paternalist (or maternalist) discourse from Western feminists who basically tell the African woman that she is not free; that, because she cannot free herself from the domination of her male, the western woman, probably with the help of the western man, is the one who will free her or teach her how to free herself. Because of the problems inherent in this paternal-maternalist approach, cross-cultural practice of feminism has not always produced the expected result. For instance, most of the meetings between Third-World feminists (from Africa, Asia and South America) and feminists from the western world seem to have, more often than not, ended up in irreconcilable deadlocks, differences and misunderstandings that have dealt a terrible blow to the notion of a universal feminism that would not take into account the particular experiences of women in their own socio-historical and sociocultural contexts (Ogundipe-Leslie 1994).

These failures by women of the world to agree on a universal approach to things feminist are, in themselves, very revealing. At the same time, they prompt the alert observer who wants to go beyond the superficiality of stereotypical considerations to look for a response in the cultural ideologies underlying the various idiosyncratic sociocultural practices and expressions of feminism. In this regard, a study of the principles and spirit of Western imperialism holds a number of plausible answers that are worth exploring, above all when they are, later in this study, contrasted with gender relations as practiced in the African world.

A careful observation of western civilization reveals that its assortment of Judeo-Christian traditions tends to define relationships between humans, or between humans and things, mostly as relationships of domination in which the strong and the weak are constantly engaged in a deadly struggle for the domination of one over the other (Sudarkasa 1987: 26-27). In this system of thought--which places great value on the natural laws that condition the competitive survival of the fittest, and which was fueled by biblical religion and later expanded through the Aristotelian models of categorical exclusions--things and beings are always either evil or good, black or white, superior or inferior, dominant or dominated (Linton 1936, Whyte 1978). In this approach, one is either "in" or "out". To belong to a particular entity or category, one has to fulfill all the *necessary* conditions. *Sufficient* conditions are not enough to justify belonging. There is no go-between, no fuzzy lines that may help to justify inclusion.[2] Needless to say, the Bible's Old Testament itself, as the supreme informer of Judeo-Christian morality, has condoned such a view of the world for centuries and, because of the sacred place it holds as a constant definer of Christian morality, still does.[3] This is why no one in the West seems to have rejected the teachings of such "messengers of God" as Deuteronomy (7: 1-3) who, as was mentioned in the introduction to this book, advocates that:

> When the Lord your God brings you into the land which you are entering to occupy and drives out many nations before you (...), when the Lord delivers them into your power and you defeat them, you must put them to death (...). (...) you must not intermarry with them, neither giving your daughters to their sons nor taking their daughters for your sons.

It is therefore such exclusive views that for millennia before and after the Bible, have conditioned the relationships between the Western man and the Western woman. As a result, for most of Western history from antiquity to the first half of the 20th century, gender statuses were defined specifically and assigned exclusive functions that could not suffer any amendment as such functions were often consigned into written, therefore rigid, laws. Thus, since the Bible says a woman must obey and be the servant of her man, so should it be. It is therefore not surprising to read what Aristotle, one of the fathers of Western philosophy, has to say about it:

> For that some should rule and others be ruled is a thing not only necessary, but expedient; from the hour of their birth, some are marked out for subjection, others for rule (...). (...) The rule of the inferior is always hurtful. The same holds good of animals in relation to men; for tame animals have a better nature than wild, and all tame animals are better off when they are ruled by man; for then, they are preserved. Again, the male is by nature superior, and the female inferior; and the one rules, and the other is ruled; this principle, of necessity, extends to all mankind (Aristotle, *The Politics*, I.v.2, Jowett's translation).

Islamic, and middle-eastern civilizations,[4] as Omoyajowo (1991) explains, are based on similar models of gender exclusions:

> The Jews had a strictly masculine concept of God: We read of the God of Abraham, of Isaac, and of Jacob and not of Sarah, Rebecca, Leah, or Rachael. In their

synagogue assemblies, they never counted women to make a quorum. This prejudice was chrystallized in the miracle of feeding performed by Jesus. The figure of five thousand was said not to include women and children. To Paul, it was an anathema for a woman to speak in the church; if there was anything she wanted to know, she should ask her husband at home. In Islam, women could only lead prayers for a congregation of women. In the mosque, women are not to stand in the same row with men but separately behind the rows of men (Omoyajowo 1991: 74).

Because Western man was blessed with the chance of possessing a writing system, he thus took pleasure in creating and codifying cultural behavior into written laws that would confirm the woman and other lesser beings into their roles of second-class citizens in the service of him, the Western man.[5] It is only in the 20th century that such laws, in many places officially consigned into various national constitutions, started to be dismantled, and still are: for instance, the United States gave women the right to vote only in 1920, Britain in 1928 and France in 1944. However, this dismantling of male privileges did not come without its own load of paradoxes. For instance, whereas, in this 20th century of alleged gender equality, supposedly "less democratic", "more sexist" societies such as India or Pakistan have been able to elect women at the highest political position in their countries (Prime Minister), America cannot yet come to terms with the possibility of a woman being elected President of the United States.

As far as African cultures are concerned, questions about the status of women equally need to be addressed. More specifically, can one expect of indigenous[6] African cultures that they function based on the same models of Biblical and Aristotelian exclusions? We may want, before tackling the African side, to note here that the development of Western societies into nuclear families in a context of multinational capitalism may be the main reason for the alienation of western man from western woman. As a result of the gender conflicts that emerged in its own nuclear-family universe, the West has come to look at other cultural systems of male-female interactions mostly from the perspective of the western nuclear family. In other words, the West has basically perceived the African marital and social universe based on gender considerations specific to the particular conflicts, social or interpersonal, that oppose man and woman within the confines of the Western family nucleus. Yet, can an extended family of hundreds constructed on a communal model be understood from the narrower perspective of a nuclear family of only two evolving in a context of multinational capitalism? Can the conflicts between man and woman in a family of two be equated with the complexities to be found in the family as it is practiced in Africa?

Some of the traits that make such an equation problematic are that the western nuclear family functions based on principles of conjugality (see Fig. 1 below) where duties are defined within a unit of two, whereas the African extended family operates based on principles of consanguinity. In the latter model, the duties and functions are family and blood-related, and the couple is seen only as part of a larger and higher system of communality in which roles and functions have a symbolic value in which gender plays only a very minimal, if not peripheral, role.

**Fig. 1: Principles of Western Conjugality:
The Aristotelian/Biblical Model[7]**

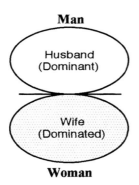

Thus, when looking at the issue of feminism in Africa, the West, in both popular thinking and academic scholarship, seems to have simply superimposed its own models of male domination over the gender structures of African societies. By so doing, it perverted or, rather, misconstrued, the processes that condition gender relations in an African context where the relationships between humans are defined mostly in terms of the role that each individual has to play in society, in *complementarity* with, not exclusion of, others. African mythology more accurately explains this from the perspective of symbiosis. In Africa, nature and humans are not discrete and autonomous boxes. Rather, they are different substances of the same entity and complement each other with reciprocal energy. These traits of reciprocality and complementarity exist not only between nature and humans, or between the living and the dead, but also between man and woman and all the other elements of the universe. Thus, as Sudarkasa (1987) and Whyte (1978) point out, a man in African societies *cannot* claim to be *superior* because, on the one hand, he does not necessarily see his interactions with his wife or any other woman as relations of domination, and on the other hand, relationships of allegiance are much more intricately woven around considerations that go beyond rigid gender bounds. In other words, in the African context, relationships of allegiance are based on permeable, not absolute gender boundaries. In fact, relationships of allegiance between males and females in indigenous African traditions are built on a network of functions that transfer such allegiances back and forth between males and females depending on the context. Such is for instance the power of seniority: in both patrilinear and matrilinear societies, the order of birth usually prevails. Thus, in these systems, senior sisters will always outrank junior brothers, and males will prostrate before their elders even when such elders are women (Sudarkasa 1987).

One of the requirements for understanding the condition of women in Africa is that any type of judgment must not limit itself to the perception of Africa as it stands today. The problem with a perception confined to present-day Africa is that it would tend to obliterate huge chunks of African history that could have helped to sort out the various behaviors therein with a view to determining the ways of doing that are specifically African, and the ways that are alien. The point of the matter is that the Africa that we know today *is not* the Africa that has always been. Because of its double colonization history (Arab and European colonizations), present-day Africa is a syncretic Africa in which features of civilizations that are alien are amalgamated with traits of civilization that are indigenous. Thus, in order to understand the true essence of African cultures, the various layers of foreign influence must first be removed. In fact, if one is to simplify the "modern" African universe based on its major cultural legacies, it appears that this universe is made of at least three sorts of societies of which the various formative layers must be defined as follows (see Fig. 2 below for a visual representation):

Fig. 2: Macro-Structure of Postcolonial[8] African Societies

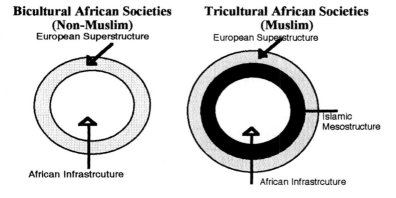

Bicultural African Societies (Non-Muslim)
European Superstructure
African Infrastrcuture

Tricultural African Societies (Muslim)
European Superstructure
Islamic Mesostructure
African Infrastrcuture

Note: Because Islam penetrated Africa well before European colonization, trilateral African societies have three competing civilizations. Source: Original.

1) Monocultural societies: these can be seen as both pre-Arabic and pre-European cultures devoid of foreign cultural influences. Of course, all African societies may be said to have now been touched by these foreign influences; in this sense there are practically no "pure" African societies left, except perhaps some of the forest pygmy tribes of central Africa. As a result, these types of societies can only now be an idealistic construct which, for the sake of our argument, we will call *African infrastructure*, that is, all the values and traits of civilization specific to the African world, prior to the Arabo-Islamic and European invasions.

2) Bicultural societies: these are societies composed of an African infrastructure and a *European superstructure*. The latter is made up of all the values and traits of civilization specific to the European world, and how these values came to affect and mold the African universe during and after the event of colonization. Their "superstructuredness" comes from the fact that they represent a layer that came to superimpose itself *over* the African one. Most sub-Saharan societies below the equator are of this type.

3) Tricultural societies: These are societies made of an African infrastructure, an *Islamic mesostructure*, and a European superstructure. The Arabo-Islamic penetration of sub-Saharan Africa (east, north and west) having occurred prior to the European intrusions, the Arabo-Islamic culture thus became a "meso" culture, that is, a middle culture between the African cultures and the European culture (the latter came last). Most of western and eastern Africa's Islamicized peoples are of this type. Note however that in a postcolonial world embodied by the arbitrary borders established by the colonial empires, all three types of societies could be represented within one African country, and would sometimes view themselves as culturally different from one another on the basis of the foreign cultures and/or religions that now define them. The recent Nigerian religious crises, triggered by the forced introduction of Sharia (Islamic law) in the Northern States of Zamfara, Kaduna and others, are a good example of how foreign cultures and religions can pervert the African universe and generate therein conflicts such as the ones opposing Islamicized creeds to Christianized creeds in Nigeria. Thus, whereas precolonial[9] African cultures, as we shall see, used to be integrative, foreign influences have transformed them into internally and/or externally exclusive societies on the basis of religion, culture, education, social and gender status, among others.

In other words, when the European *superstructure* and the Islamic *mesostructure* have been peeled away to reveal the *infrastructure* of indigenous African cultures, it becomes evident that African societies are characterized by socio-cultural features that set them aside not only in terms of the way power is communally distributed among all members and groups in society, but also in terms of how males and females conduct their affairs.

In this respect, a fact that one must keep in mind is that indigenous African societies are mostly genderless societies (see Fig. 3 below). Not only does the wife in most cases keep her name in marriage, but women's names and males' names are often interchangeable. Thus, for instance, a boy could easily be named after a female ancestor that the family would like to honor, and vice-versa. What is more, the whole structure of family ties and relationships is so complex that gender is not defined exclusively in terms of sex, but rather in terms of the complementary function or role that each individual plays in society at the consanguine level. However, these roles are neither absolute, nor rigid. Rather, they are played and interplayed on a social scene where functions are constantly taken, transferred, exchanged and replayed depending on the context.

Because of this permeable transferability of gender values, roles and functions, words such as "husband", "wife", "son", "brother", etc., are only vaguely and peripherally loaded with gender considerations. Due to the fact that tradition accords a semantic elasticity to apparently genderful terms such as these, a woman in African societies can be considered the "husband" of her brother's wife simply because, as her brother's sister, and according to the principles of African consanguinity, a sister automatically "inherits" the gender status of her brother in that context, and vice-versa. It is therefore expected of a brother's wife that she will show to her sister-in-law the same consideration she owes her own husband. Similarly, a particular man can be the "wife" of another man, just because this other man married his sister. In addition, a man who marries the daughter of a given clan or family automatically becomes the "daughter" or "son" of that family, which means that this man is going to owe to this family the same sort of reverence as would be expected from an actual daughter or son. In fact, it suffices at times that a girl of five be given the name of the deceased mother or father, and the rest of the family would venerate her as the "mother" or "father," and respectfully call her "mama" or "papa".

Fig. 3: Principles of Genderless Consanguinity in Africa: The Network Model[10]

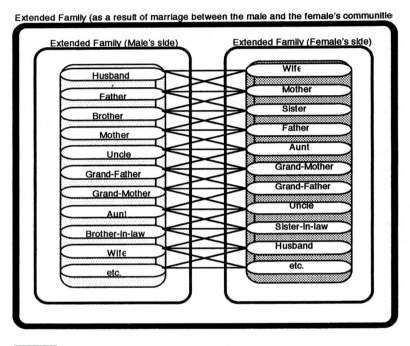

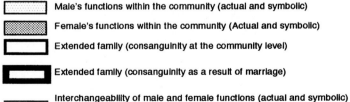

Male's functions within the community (actual and symbolic)

Female's functions within the community (Actual and symbolic)

Extended family (consanguinity at the community level)

Extended family (consanguinity as a result of marriage)

Interchangeability of male and female functions (actual and symbolic)

Thus, when analyzing the power structure within such societies as Africa's, the principles of power distribution that, in another civilization, could have been expected to be genderful are, in this context, rendered rather genderless simply because they are defined within a network of relationships that go beyond rigid and absolute modes of behavior. Interestingly enough, even within the structure of polygamy, the senior wife usually considers herself the "husband" of the younger wives of her spouse. Of course, tradition does often recommend that she take a part in the choice of who her husband should marry. What one may therefore derive from the above comments is that principles of genderful conjugality make no sense in traditional, indigenous African societies, above all if one is to attempt to see therein structures of male domination. Any such attempt probably has to stop at the door of Western conjugality and try to penetrate the African universe with a mindset that could grasp the rationale behind the African practice of gender relations. In other words, one will have to come to terms with the idea that, because an African can be defined socially as both "male" and "female" at the same time, male power is constantly kept in check by social structure that "effeminate" this power by making the male "go woman" wherever and whenever the context lends itself to such metamorphoses. In other words, the male is forced, through the very mechanisms of consanguinity, to feminize himself and take on, symbolically or not, the *various statuses* of the female in contexts that require such social metamorphoses or impersonations.[11]

Fig. 4: Social Parallelism in Traditional African societies

CUSTOM	MALE	FEMALE
Polygamy (polygyny (male) vs. polyandry (female)) In fiction, see Achebe, *Things Fall Apart* (1958), Kourouma, *Soleil des indépendances* (1970), Ousmane, *Les bouts de bois de Dieu* (1960)	Yes* (**)	No, but... (see endnote #12).
Circumcision (male and female) In fiction, see Kourouma, *Soleil des indépendances* (1970) & Laye, *L'enfant noir*(1953)	Yes*	Yes
Positive values (social demands of courage, self-reliance, determination, respect for elders, etc.) In fiction, see Laye, *L'enfant noir*(1953)	Yes	Yes

Reverence (attached to gender functions such as motherhood and fatherhood, including respect for seniority, etc.)	Yes	Yes*
Work (including domestic, daily management of family wealth, trade, child care, etc.). In fiction, see Ousmane, *Les bouts de bois de Dieu* (1960)	Yes	Yes*
Education (Storytelling was a function of traditional education. In this area, women excelled as much as they excelled and were preponderant in the overall education of children, decorative arts and artifacts).	Yes	Yes*
Property (including land possession, etc.)	Yes*	Yes
Intellectual life (arts, orature, history, philosophy, dances, etc.)	Yes	Yes*
Chieftancy (including kingship) In fiction, see Kane, *L'aventure ambiguë* (1961).	Yes*	Yes
Spiritual leadership (religion, priesthood, traditional medecine) In fiction, see Achebe, *Things Fall Apart* (1958)	Yes	Yes*
Forced Marriages (submission to "forced marriages") In fiction, see Dikobe, *The Marabi Dance* (1973)	Yes	Yes
Mythology (Gods, divinities and various deities) In fiction, see Achebe, *Things Fall Apart* (1958) & *Arrow of God* (1964)	Yes	Yes*

Source: Original. Go to this endnote[12] for details on this table.

Judging relationships of allegiance in traditional African societies is therefore a very complex, sometimes perplexing endeavor. However, after careful examination, one will indeed come to the conclusion that principles of equality and lawfulness existed therein that placed no one—chief (if any), man, woman, elder or youth—above the requirements of traditional law. In fact, as scholars such as Niara Sudarkasa (1987) and Ifi Amadiume (1987)[13] have suggested, one can make a case for the absence of gender-based structures in African societies because of the genderless permeability, transferability and distribution of such structures among males and females. In this sense, depending on the context, male powers and female powers are assumed "hermaphrodizely" and interchangeably by both males and females, while preserving a structure of *social parallelism* where males rule males, and females rule females (Sudarkasa, 1987, Amadiume, 1987).[14]

In fact, as can be seen in Fig. 4 above, when the areas of gender power and benefits are compiled and compared, females in indigenous African societies tend to always end up with the larger share of social influence not only because of their various functions and roles, but also because of the inherently inclusive genderless nature of African customs[15]. As we pointed out earlier, the structures of power permeability and transferability can be understood only from the perspective of African consanguine systems where, not so surprisingly, matriarchy has been the dominant criterion, even within the context of so-called patriarchal systems.[16] In fact, the current gender issues that cripple Africa are themselves a result of foreign influences, and of the transposition of western and Islamic values to the African soil. The transformations brought about by such alien cultural infusions are easily spotted when one looks at the role religion has played not only in the imperial tendencies of both western and Islamic cultures, but also in the definition of the status of women as second-class citizens. As Mazrui (1995) points out, in relation to African religions and, therefore, traditions:

> Of the three principal religious legacies of Africa (indigenous, Islamic, and Christian), the most tolerant on record must be the indigenous tradition. One might even argue that Africa did not have religious wars before Christianity and Islam arrived, for indigenous religions [therefore cultures] were neither universalistic (seeking to conquer the whole of the human race) nor competitive (in bitter rivalry against other [universalistic] creeds). Because they are not proselytizing religions, indigenous African creeds have not fought with each other (Mazrui 1995: 77).

Not only did Africans not fight against each other as has often been suggested[17], they also developed religious practices that would be *fully* inclusive of women (Mazrui 1995; Omoyajowo 1991). Thus, the fact that African mythologies and religions appear to have been far less sexist than most other religions is an argument in favor of a stronger democratic spirit in Africa's inclusive systems of sociopolitical organization. In African mythologies and religions, supreme gods as well as lesser gods could be either man or woman, and the overwhelming majority of deities, divinities and priests have always been female (Omoyajowo 1991; Mbiti 1991). In fact, one could even argue that, based on the very "superstitious" nature of Africans, the person who is dominant in the spiritual domains of mythology and religious-medicinal practice—women in this case—in actual fact controls tradition itself, and therefore society in general (see Fig. 4 above). Because of the communal, decentralized nature of African societies, women seem to have enjoyed more social freedoms and political powers therein than in most other civilizations. It is therefore not surprising to see the amazed astonishment of Ibn Battuta, the Arab traveler of the 14th century, when he came across Islamicized African tribes and kingdoms that seemed to practice Islam in ways that would have appeared utterly sinful to Arabs. For instance, Ibn Battuta found it scandalous that Islamicized Africans should let their women go freely and unveiled about the community, and allow them to be alone with male companions that were not their husbands (Hamdun and King, 1994).

The contemporary reality is therefore that the troubles of the African woman in modern times began with both Islamic and European colonizations. In other words, when Europeans and Arabs transferred their *genderful patriarchies* onto Africa's *genderless patriarchies*, when the Europeans transferred their Biblical and Aristotelian models onto African societies, they brought gender-based stratifications that their developing capitalist economies had helped to foster. Thus, one had, with such intrusions, the ingredients for a cultural disaster that was going to cost the status of women dearly in traditional African societies. In the traditional economic systems of Africa, women were never dependent on men. Women worked the land, had a right to land property--at least more than their Western and Islamic counterparts did--, built houses, and fulfilled many other traditional functions that made them central social, economic, and intellectual assets in their communities. In fact, they were the economic pillars of their communities because they mastered the day-to-day management of family economies. They were the ones in charge of trade in the traditional markets; they kept daily account of the belongings of the family and knew up to the minute the state of the family's wealth. In this context, men would usually rely on their women for the management of traditional wealth. This control over economic as well as religious affairs strongly contributed to giving women a relatively egalitarian say in the political, spiritual, social and intellectual life of the community, despite the apparent subordination which tradition seems to have imposed on them by making man the more visible public figure of the two.

But when westerners took over, they brought in their Judaeo-Christian notions of the dominant male vs. the dominated female. When they built their schools, they gave school instruction to men only, and excluded women from all spheres of public, political, spiritual and social life from there on. By so doing, that is, by giving power and education exclusively to the African men within the confines of modern economy, they gave to men overall control over the future of Africa and actually took away from these women the traditional positions and powers that they had had in society. As a result, the colonialists alienated these women from their men, turned them into dependents of their husbands, and suppressed the interdependent complementarity that existed prior to Islamic and European colonizations. The colonizers actually did to African women what they had already done to their own women in Europe or in the Islamic world, that is, they turned African women into housewives instead of wives that went out, built houses, and worked in the fields as much as their men did. As Obbo (1980) suggests, women's loss of power, which is now translated into the male's domination in modern matters, is strongly reflected in the social, political and intellectual spheres of modern, *not* traditional, Africa. This position is shared by Elizabeth Fox-Genovese (1995) when she states that "[in] the Third World, where Westerners have shaped educational [but also sociocultural and political] patterns, it has normally been preferred to educate and train men, not women, for the advanced economic and governmental sectors."[18]

In other words, the Africa that we know today is an Africa in which, after destroying the fabric of Africa's genderless consanguinity, the European (and Islamic) empires had instilled strong principles of conjugal male domination. Thus, the various conquests of Africa by cultures so different in matters of gender relations transformed African societies into cultures of male predominance. Consequently, all the customs that, in precolonial times, used to ensure gender cohesion within the realm of African consanguinity have now become obsolete in the conjugal structure of modern, multinational capitalism. It is therefore in this context that African feminism is expressing itself today.

However, African women's struggles are different from those of their western counterparts in many respects. Western women are fighting structures that, for millennia as can be testified by classical Greece's exclusion of women in matter of socio-democratic politics (Roberts 1994), were *specifically meant* to maintain them in their assigned status of second-class citizens. They are therefore claiming rights that they *never had* and *that were never given* to them in the first place. But, as far as they are concerned, African women are, rather, trying to *regain,* within the problematic context of modern, postcolonial Africa, the central role that they *used to have* in traditional, precolonial Africa. As Ogundipe-Leslie (1994), herself an African feminist, argues, the struggle of African women can be summarized in the following terms: African women want to force their (westernized) African men to give them back their status within the context of a westernized culture. Will this status be exactly the one they had in traditional Africa? Probably not, because what they are actually looking for is the acquisition, in the context of modern Africa, of an egalitarian education, the unbiased opening of socioeconomic opportunities to them, and access to modern types of knowledges that will enable them to adapt to the structures of modern economy.[19] If this is achieved, they would be able to start playing a central role in society again, in complementarity with their men. Their struggle for equality cannot therefore, from this point of view, be conducted, as it is in the West, on the basis of adversarial behavior and/or separatism. This is why African feminists have been looking for a different method of conducting their battles. Because Western feminism tends to bring to mind gender conflicts that may not necessarily pose themselves under the same terms in Africa, African women have defined their own struggle as *womanism*. What is womanism, and how does African womanist feminism distinguish itself from Western feminism? It is, once more, Ogundipe-Leslie herself who gives us the answer:

> (...) most African women and feminists are *womanists* in Alice Walker's sense of being committed to the survival and *wholeness* of *entire peoples, male and females*; being not in any way separatist or adversarial to men. African women in general wish to *retain* certain features of their traditions; those which are positive for women (Ogundipe-Leslie 1994: 12-13; italics mine).

Notes

[1] In this paper, the term "Africa" and all derivatives will signify "sub-Saharan Africa" or "Black Africa", unless otherwise specified. The term "African societies" will be used to refer to indigenous, "black" African societies from the Sahel region down to the Cape. It excludes the North and East African Arabs or the Whites in the settler-colonies of the southern African region..

[2] Note for example that, at times, in the racial segregation history of countries such as the Unites States and South Africa, the process of belonging has often been a very problematic and sensitive one. In fact, in the racial history of apartheid South Africa, the process of inclusion was often pushed to the limits of science. For instance, the white apartheid government had policies that allowed it to filter the population by scientifically measuring in mixed people (coloureds) that could pass for white the proportion of white or black blood in their veins that would classify them socio-economically as whites or blacks. In the US, anyone who looks dark in complexion is automatically considered black, even when his or her parents are African-American and Asian as in the case of golf champion Tiger Woods, or African-American and White as is the case for tenniswoman Alex Stevenson.

[3] During the apartheid era in South Africa, the Boers (Afrikaners) made full use of the Bible's language of exclusion to justify oppression of the black majority.

[4] Despite the fact that the Arabo-Islamic colonization of Africa also had profound impact on the cultural, commercial and even political structures of the continent, we will be mostly insisting on the much deeper influence of the West. Indeed, Arab intrusions, which occurred much earlier (around

the 7th and 8th centuries AD) than Western conquest (15th century), did bring about the first large scale enslavement of Africans and converted many tribes to Islam. But this was nothing compared with the events that followed the arrival of the Europeans in Africa, events which translated into the forceful and general takeover of the continent and its wholesale transformation, exploitation, subversion and alienation from itself in all spheres of political, social, economic and cultural activity. Because of the scope of these transformations and the fact that Western colonization came last, Western influence has--through the media, schools, cultural imperialism, political structures and economic capitalism--remained increasingly dominant even in those areas that had been Islamicized centuries earlier.

[5] Jack Goody, in his *The Logic of Writing and the Organization of Society* (1986), has suggested that a correlation exists between the possession of writing and the way society organizes its laws and social hierarchies. Thus, as we understand it, written civilizations were able to maintain their social structures much more durably because of the inherent durable rigidity that written laws confer on societies that were able to codify social behavior by means of written constitutions and codes of conduct, often with the purpose of maintaining the privileges of the ruling classes. Indeed, when one extends these principles to international relations, one can easily see why, with the help of writing, the domination of oral civilizations by written cultures was possible. This domination was mostly achieved through the skilful use of writing not only as a tool for the preservation of history as defined by the imperialist culture, but also as a tool of domination. In this equation, oral cultures such as Africa's have consistently lost their battle for history, and, by the same token, have been unable to maintain their identities. Because of the ability of writing not only to codify the spoken word, but also to freeze it into an unshakable law capable of surviving centuries, the history of human civilization seems to have frozen around the Mediterranean area. Note that the current debates, which oppose Afrocentrists to advocates of what Bernal (1987) calls the Aryan Model such as Mary Lefkowitz (1996; 1997), revolve precisely around issues of historical precedence: who did it first and who gave it to the others? Thus, in this debate, history is seen as possessed only by those who made efficient use of writing because they can "prove" they were "first" by simply pointing to evidence from written records.

[6] In this paper, the term "indigenous African societies" will be used interchangeably with "precolonial African societies" and "traditional African societies". By such terms, we mean the state of African societies prior to Islamic and European conquests.

[7] In this model, the functions limit themselves to the specific and palpable arena of conjugal interactions. Thus, the only functions immediately available to the male and the female are those of "husband" and "wife" respectively and exclusively. Because there is no guarantee that the couple will ever want to have children, even the functions of mother and father are

not certain. Indeed, when these functions do emerge, they will be gender-bound: a male can only serve male functions (uncle, grand-father, etc.) and a female only female functions (aunt, grand-mother, etc.). In this context, a woman cannot be considered a "husband" to another woman. Also, the conjugal link of marriage in this western context can be broken irremediably, whereas in the case of African consanguinity (to be discussed later), the marital link will remain even after divorce. Source: original

[8] Based on Ashcroft, *et al.* (1989), and Mengara (1996), the term "postcolonial" is hereby defined as all the continuities and discontinuites triggered in the colonized world from the very moment of colonization up to the present. Thus, post-independence to us is not equivalent to postcoloniality; rather, post-independence is itself a result and part of the postcolonial condition, among other aspects. The guiding principle in this interpretation is that the events and changes that were provoked by colonial contacts left an indelible mark on, at least, the colonized societies, and as a result, things could never be the same again for them, either before or after factual independence. In addition, because the effects of colonization are still felt today in the colonized world, independence did not mean a total suppression or disappearance of these effects after the departure of the empires. The very notion of neocolonialism itself explains it all. All of these events and periods are therefore part of the postcolonial condition.

[9] Precolonial African societies in this work means both pre-Islamic and pre-European sub-Saharan African societies.

[10] Man and woman, as well as both types of extended families (within and without marriage) should be viewed as nodes within a consanguinity network of infinite possibilities, where functions will also vary according to this law of infinity. All lines delimiting the communities should be considered fuzzy and subject to further family expansion (Source: original).

[11] Please refer to the article entitled "Playing Africa: The Fictions of Ferdinand Oyono" in this very volume. In this article, Sharmila Sen does a wonderful job in bringing forth the powerful theatricality of African societies where social "roles" are basically played and exchanged in the theatre of life itself. This ability of Africans to "play" life is therefore a strong supporting point in the context of this paper's suggestion that gender, just like any other social function therein, can be transferred back and forth between males and females depending on the context.

[12] Notes: (*) means *preponderance*. Preponderance here means that the practice mentioned was applied more to the indicated group. Indeed, except in the case of circumcision where both male and female genital cutting brought to both groups equal social values (fertility, masculinity and feminity, etc.), the group marked with an (*) derived from a given practice much more social benefits than the other. Keep in mind, however, that the practice of male circumcision is much more widespread in Africa than that

of the genital cutting of females. Note, also, that the practice of kingship and centralized chieftancy did not exist in all tribes. Nevertheless, when such a function was formalized, it did not have, except in very notable rare instances (Chaka, for ex.), the same meaning as in the Western world, that is, the meaning of a supreme commander who unilaterally and individually gave orders and decided policies. The king or queen was more like a spokesperson who represented the views of the community in both internal and external affairs. His/her representativity was usually due to his/her diplomatic and oratorical skills, as well as to his/her integrity in the community. (**) Polygamy is widely practiced in Africa in the form of polygyny (marriage of one man with many women). Although polyandry (marriage with one woman with many husbands) is not known to have existed officially in Africa, mild forms of it can be found in most African societies in the form of *integrated polyandry* (my own term). Integrated polyandry occurs when, for instance, a husband who cannot have children because of sterility would, unofficially, allow his wives to secretly see other men who could make them pregnant. Because the honor of the husband would, ideally, be safe thanks to the secrecy that would surround the matter, he could officially claim such children as his even if, in reality, such children would be those of a village "brother". But polygamy goes beyond this and includes many variants that cannot all be discussed here. One of these variants, for instance, is that a young male can inherit his older brother's wife even if this wife is so old that they both can no longer have a physical relationship. The practice was developed mostly to allow widows to stay in the family of their husband and to continue not only to benefit from the human and material inheritance of their marriages, but also to continue to get the social affection, protection and warmth that comes from belonging to the family in which they had lived for most of their adult lives.

[13] Note, for instance, the title of Amadiume's book, *Male Daughters, Female Husbands: Gender and Sex in an African Society* (1987).

[14] An important addition here is that, as Fig. 4 shows, social parallelism required that the education of both males and females be similar in all respects. Thus, what was required of males was also required of females, and vice-versa. For instance, both males and females of the same age group had to go through similar rites of passage, including the rite of circumcision where practiced on women. Similarly, it is often a biased misconception that forced marriages should be seen only as impositions on women alone. In fact, both males and females are subjected, equally, to the practice of arranged marriages whenever this occurs, simply because tradition requires of *them both* that it be so. Thus, where a woman is forced to marry a given man, one can assume an equal imposition on the man because the man in question may not necessarily have wanted to marry that precise woman. However, because of the requirements of tradition, they both have to please the community by agreeing to such a union. Also, males are not responsible for the education or guidance of women. Because of the

structures of social parallelism in African societies, men are educated by men and taught the social values that go with manhood, whereas females are taken care of by other females and taught the values inherent in femalehood. Consequently, men will perform circumcision and all necessary rites on men and females will perform genital-cutting and all required rites on women in the societies in which female genital cutting is practiced. However, the overall general socio-cultural socialization of both male and female children was primarily the burden of women.

[15] It just seems that, from the African perspective, female functions tend to carry and require more social reverence on the part of society that those attached to the male. Such is the case of the notion of "motherhood" which, in the African world, carries more weight than that of "fatherhood". In the poetic literature from Africa, one will notice that it is the idea of the mother that is most commonly used. Poets of Negritude such as Senghor made abundant use of the mother image not only as the role model, but also as the only bringer of psychological closure, peace, protection and deliverance in the context of adversity that colonization was. These poetic evocations thus confirmed the centrality of matriarchy in African cultures (see Senghor 1992 for poetic examples in African and diasporic literatures).

[16] Even today, this predominance of matriarchy can still be perceived, although already heavily perverted by the patriarchal systems from Europe.

[17] Mengara and Larson (in Malinda Smith's *Globalizing Africa*, forthcoming in 2001), for instance, have argued that indigenous African cultures were not belligerent cultures, and could not have fought against each other.

[18] Elizabeth Fox-Genovese, "Women in Society", published in the 1995 edition of Grolier Multimedia Encyclopaedia.

[19] Realism forces one to acknowledge that a "pure" return to the lost African values is impossible. The only course of action is therefore to adapt to the modern context first, and then later try to mold this context according to the values of civilization that correspond to one's view of the world.

Works Cited

Achebe, Chinua. *Things Fall Apart*. London: Heinemann, 1958.

___. *Arrow of God*. London: Heinemann, 1964.

Amadiume, Ifi. *Male daughters, female husbands: gender and sex in an African society*. London: Zed Books, 1987.

Ashcroft, Bill, *et al. The Empire Writes Back: Theory and Practice in Post-Colonial Literatures.* London: Routledge, 1989.

Bernal, Martin. *Black Athena:The Afroasiatic Roots of Classical Civilization. Vol. I: The Fabrication of Ancient Greece, 1785-1985.* New Brunswick, NJ: Rutgers UP, 1987.

Delmar, Rosalind. "What is Feminism?" *What is Feminism? A Re-Examination.* Ed. Juliet Mitchell & Ann Oakley. New York: Pantheon Books, 1986: 8-33.

Dikobe, Modikwe. *The Marabi Dance.* London: Heinemann, 1973.

Fox-Genovese, Elizabeth. " Women in Society". Published in the 1995 edition of Grolier Multimedia Encyclopaedia. CD-ROM Version 7.0.2 for Macintosh. Search Keyword: "feminism". 1995 by Grolier Electronic Publishing, Inc.

Goody, Jack. *The Logic of Writing and the Organization of Society.* Boston: Cambridge University Press, 1986.

Hamdun, Said, and Noël King. *Ibn Battuta in Black Africa.* 1975. Princeton: Markus Wiener Publishers, 1994.

Kane, Cheick Hamadou. *L'Aventure ambiguë.* Paris: Julliard, 1961.

Kourouma, Ahmadou. *Les Soleils des Independances.* Paris: Seuil, 1970.

Laye, Camara. *L'enfant noir.* Paris: Plon, 1953.

Lefkowitz, Mary R., and Guy MacLean Rogers, eds. *Black Athena Revisited.* Chapel Hill: U of Northern California Press, 1996.

Lefkowitz, Mary R. *Not Out of Africa: How Afrocentrism Became an Excuse to Teach Myth as History.* 1996. New York: Basic Books, 1997.

Linton, Ralph. *The Study of Man.* New York: Appleton-Century, 1936.

Mazrui, Ali A. "Africa and Other Civilizations: Conquest and Counterconquest". In John W. Harbeson, and Donald Rothchild. *Africa in World Politics: Post-Cold War Challenges.* San Francisco: Westview Press, 1995.

Mbiti, John S. "Flowers in the Garden: The Role of Women in African Religion." *African Traditional Religions in*

Contemporary Society. Ed. Jacob K. Olupona. New York: International Religious Foundation, 1991: 59-72.

Mengara, Daniel M. "Postcolonialism, Third-Worldism and the Issue of Exclusive Terminologies in Postcolonial Theory and Criticism." *Commonwealth* 18, 2 (1996): 36-45.

Mengara, Daniel, and Victoria Larson. "Africa and the Invention of Democracy". Forthcoming in *Globalizing Africa*, Edited by Malinda Smith. Trenton, N.J.: Africa World Press, 2001 (tentative date).

Obbo, Christine. *African Women: Their Struggle for Economic Independence.* London: Zed Press, 1980.

Ogundipe-Leslie, Molara. *Re-Creating Ourselves: African Women & Critical Transformations.* Trenton (N.J.): Africa World Press, 1994.

Omoyajowo, Joseph Akinyele. "The Role of Women in African Traditional Religion and Among the Yoruba." *African Traditional Religions in Contemporary Society.* Ed. Jacob K. Olupona. New York: International Religious Foundation, 1991: 73-80.

Ousmane, Sembene. *Les bouts de bois de Dieu.* Paris: Le Livre Contemporain, 1960.

Roberts, Jennifer Tolbert. *Athens on Trial: the Anti-Democratic Tradition in Western Thought.* Princeton: Princeton UP, 1994.

Sen, Sharmilla. "Playing Africa: The Fictions of Ferdinand Oyono". See Chapter VII of this volume.

Senghor, Léopold Sédar, Ed. *Anthologie de la nouvelle littérature nègre et malgache de langue française.* 1948. Paris: Le Livre Contemporain, 1992.

Sudarkasa, Niara. "The "Status of Women" in Indigenous African Societies." *Women in Africa and the African Diaspora.* Ed. Rosalyn Terborg-Penn, Sharon Harley & Andrea Benton Rushing. Washington, D.C.: Howard UP, 1987: 25-41.

Whyte, Martin K. *The Status of Women in Preindustrial Societies.* Princeton, N.J.: Princeton UP, 1978.

African Women: Educational Opportunities and the Dynamics of Change

Bill Gaudelli
University of Central Florida

The persistence of a gender gap with regard to the educational opportunities offered to girls and boys globally has been well established. The 1996 UNDP Human Development Report and the Fourth World Conference on Women in Beijing asserted that the disparity between educational access for girls and boys is widespread and intertwined with the tenacity of poverty around the world. The lack of opportunities for girls as contrasted with boys is significant and has taken on an alarmingly universal character.

This problem is a troubling yet dynamic phenomenon. The exploratory ethnographic inquiry presented herein raises questions regarding changes that are currently occurring with regard to the education of young women in Africa, but particularly in Kenya. These changes are most evident in the following categories: family obligations and expectations, educational gender stereotypes and intra-group tensions among women. Each of these patterns will be examined in greater depth throughout this paper, while concentrating on Kenyan society as a mirror that will reflect some of the most vivid challenges that young women are facing in modern African societies in general.

Kenya, as is the case in most sub-Saharan countries and societies, is truly a youthful nation. With a population exceeding 28 million, a 3.2% rate of population increase and an astounding 45% of its population under the age of 25, Kenya is among the fastest growing nations in the world (United Nations 1998: 1). Children in Kenya, as in all societies, represent the challenge, change, and promise of the future. Education, formal and otherwise, is a social institution dedicated to the promotion of that promise.

Until the mid-1980s, the Kenyan educational system was premised on the British system. The system was reformed over a decade ago, from a British-styled system, to a Canadian model referred to as 8+4+4, because it includes eight years of primary education, four years of secondary education and four years to the first degree in college. There are approximately 15,500 primary schools in Kenya, each responsible for administering the nationwide Kenya Certificate of Primary Education (K.C.P.E.) (Education 1998:1). The exam is highly competitive and only 40% of primary students progress to secondary education (Kaunjuga 1998:1). After secondary school, students are required to take a secondary exam, known as the Kenya Certificate of Secondary Education (K.C.S.E.). Approximately 150,000 students graduate from secondary school each year and prepare to take the exam. However, "...there is an acute shortage of higher education places," so many qualified students are denied access to a college-level education (Kaunjuga 1998: 2). The future prosperity of Kenyan society, regardless of gender, is threatened by the lack of educational opportunities for large and increasing numbers of its youth.

The Gender Gap

In family life as well as in education, boys and girls do not equally share the promise and possibilities of youth. In African societies, young, pre-adolescent girls are often expected to play a significant part in maintenance of homes. They are viewed as assisting the mother(s) in her (their) myriad tasks about the home, including cooking, cleaning, gathering firewood, raising children, and working in the garden (Kilbride & Kilbride: 89). These duties vary among ethnic groups throughout sub-Saharan Africa, but generally, girls have a greater burden to bear in maintenance of the family when compared to their brothers. Girl children are socialized from a very young age to work with their mothers, which perpetuates and strengthens the traditional female role in African societies (Kayongo-Male & Onyango 1984: 42).

Traditional adolescence for girls is seen as a preparation for marriage and adulthood (Kilbride & Kilbride 1990: 91). Young women are either expected to maintain the family line in matrilineal communities or it is anticipated that women will leave the family, in patrilineal communities. Regardless of the context, there is pervasive social pressure for women to prepare for motherhood. Young women generally do not view being single as an option in a traditional African context. It is assumed that women will marry and bear children. Those who cannot reproduce are considered "barren" and may lose status in their community.

Teenage girls must also cope, often alone and with great societal and family pressure, with early, unplanned pregnancies. Teenage girls suffer the moral indignation of bearing a child out of wedlock along with the anticipated economic challenge of not completing school. It was required in Kenya, until the mid-1980s, that young women who became pregnant had to leave school (Kilbride & Kilbride 1990: 178). Although the legal sanctions have been altered, girls still encounter the social stigmatization of pregnancy, that forces many to abort secretly and/or leave school of their own accord (Pjua and Kassimoto 1990: 64-65).

The gender gap evident in family life and adolescence is compounded by the fact that previous curricula in Kenya paid little attention to practical learning as compared to traditional academic subjects, such as mathematics, sciences, and languages (Puja and Kassimoto 1994: 59). These subjects were not designed to prepare women for motherhood and family life, and therefore, education in general was viewed as a "luxury" which many rural, poor families could not indulge. Academic education beyond standard eight is viewed by some as superfluous to maternity preparation, especially when resources for school fees are limited.

Girl children are reared in a setting that places a high value on their current economic productivity and the future establishment of their family role as mother and caretaker, rather than their educational promise. Young girls in poor families between the ages of 5 and 14 are often called upon to support the family through direct labor. This economic pressure further contributes to the notion that education is a "luxury" that cannot be afforded.

One of the most important resources which women have to draw on in meeting these demands is the help of their children. Children look after each other, run messages, take care of small livestock, fetch water, wash dishes, and later take part in more difficult work which contributes to income more directly (than education). Luo women in western Kenya, who also combine farming with small-scale trade, depend heavily upon children to cover many of their duties (Geyer 1995: 24)

Mothers rely mainly upon their young girls to assist in maintaining the domicile. Since these young girls cannot afford the "luxury" of education, they will remain in poverty, thus perpetuating the cyclical gender gap in families.

Educational resources among African families tend to go to boys rather than girls, an unfortunate phenomenon found in many parts of the world. "Voluminous evidence of different sex ratios throughout the world testifies to the fact that equal access to education has been achieved in few countries (Tomasevski 1993: 26)." Kenya and other African societies are no exception to this reality. Boys are widely considered a "better educational investment," since patterns of discrimination against women in career opportunities persist. Although many girls do attend school, there is still a widespread feeling that "education is for boys" and that women are best suited to perform domestic duties (Kilbride & Kilbride 1990: 91).

Among patrilineal groups, it is understood that the young women will eventually leave the family and join a different family. Thus, women will not be part of the family of origin to provide security to parents in their old age. Families, when "losing" their daughters are usually given a bridewealth, which can be "paid" in a number of different ways, from property, such as cattle, to consumer goods, such as beer. Beyond the bridewealth, there is relative certainty that girls will not be present to provide financially for their elderly parents. Parents have an interest, therefore, in investing in their sons' education since they will eventually reap the security of their economic success.[1]

The value of education for young women is at least an economic consideration if not also a matter of personal fulfillment. Surprisingly, for most Africans, and Kenyans in particular, education is now assumed to be the most effective means available to end poverty. In a recent study conducted on the phenomenon of street children in Nairobi, "...most of the parents (of street children) suggested the provision of free and compulsory basic education for the children" as the number one priority in dealing with this crisis (Suda 1993: 73). Over 50% of the children in this study dropped out of school, but 38% of those interviewed believed education was the key to their economic future, the most frequent response of all those given. This finding suggests that even among the most destitute of society, there is a widespread belief in the economic value of education in providing a "good life."[2]

As Mengara shows in the preceding essay, African women, in the context of colonial history, have generally not had equal access to modern education, which has further contributed to the feminization of poverty in sub-Saharan Africa. The persistence of this inequality has contributed to African women lacking the very basic skills for participation in modern community life, such as literacy. A majority of Kenyan women over the age of 25 (54%) are functionally illiterate, as compared to 37% of males (Kaunjuga 1998: 1). The younger generation of Kenyans has a lower incidence of illiteracy as compared to the older generations, suggesting a positive trend in the extension of primary education to more people. The gender gap persists even in the younger generation, however, with 13.9% of women being illiterate as compared to 8.1% of illiterate males between the ages of 15 and 24 (United Nations 1998: 1). An important correlation between female illiteracy and the lack of education for young girls exists in Kenya. Bradley found that:

> Gender equity at the secondary school level in Kenya is less encouraging. In 1987, national level statistics show a ratio of 107 boys attending primary school for every 100 girls. At the secondary school level, this ratio is dropped, with 144 boys attending for every 100 girls. (1997: 239-40)

Bradley also found, however, an aberration in this pattern among the Lagoli of western Kenya. She identified a dynamic situation where girls and boys had similar absentee rates and parents expected both boys and girls to attend school. As one 25 year old man said, "It's better to go to school first before doing anything because education is the most important key to life (239)." Bradley noted that the emerging pattern of educational gender equality is at odds with much of the previous research conducted related to the education of girls (Bradley 1993). She contended that the distribution of educational resources according to gender in Kenya is dynamic and fluid, a finding in accordance with the arguments presented in this paper.

However, behind the statistics of illiteracy and school enrollment lies the experience of young women in Kenya today. The challenge of discrimination against women in Kenya, particularly as it relates to access to education, makes their future even more daunting. Their situation, however, is not hopeless. The young girls and women that I interviewed looked optimistically towards the future, despite their social status. This study attempts to present exploratory insights into the social reality of selected young women in Kenya to illustrate the nature of the gender inequity and how the roles of young women in Kenya are changing.

The research analyzed herein was collected over the course of one month in Nairobi, Kenya, during the summer of 1997. Working with a research assistant who is a former teacher and lives in Nairobi, I was able to gain access to a variety of informants. Thirteen young women were interviewed in the study, ranging in age from 13 to 26. Four of these women were raised in rural areas throughout Kenya, from communities as distant as Mombassa and Eldoret, and attended a religious boarding school at the time of this investigation. Eight of the interviewees lived in the Mathare Valley slum and attended primary school there. Another young woman was a recent graduate from a neighborhood high school in Nairobi, awaiting admission to college.[3]

The informants are certainly not representative of all women in Kenya; rather, they are illustrative of the group and the society in which they are situated.[4] This study is not intended to be a comprehensive cataloguing of all the different perspectives on gender. Rather, it is intended to be an exploration into the changing nature of young women's place in the educational landscape of Kenya in particular, and Africa in general. I also queried teachers and parents as to their views about the education of young girls. I interviewed a rural teacher of religion and a retired public primary school teacher from the same village. In Nairobi, I interviewed 3 male high school teachers between the ages of 38-42 and 2 female high school teachers, aged 23 and 30, respectively. Finally, I conducted multiple classroom observations at a middle class high school and a slum school. Observations and interviews lasted from 45 minutes to 2 hours, depending upon the responsiveness of the various informants. All names used herein to identify interviewees are pseudonyms. Questions were kept to a minimum during the interviews and were open-ended in nature, such as: Describe your experience in school.[5]

The interviews were conducted without the aid of a tape recording device. I took notes during each interview to avoid any discomfort associated with informants being tape-recorded. The field notes were then formatted and typed. My research assistant carefully read all field notes for accuracy and completeness, and adjustments were made accordingly. This was especially necessary in interviews that required translation from Kiswahili and Luo. After the interview process was completed, the field notes were coded.[6] The following themes emerged as explanations for the disparity in education for Kenyan girls and the dynamics of change:

1) Family obligations and expectations
2) Educational gender stereotypes
3) Tensions among women

Family Obligations and Expectations

Families represent the primary socializing force in any society. I, therefore, made a conscious choice to seek information about the upbringing of children in the study. Thomas Mikwana, an elderly retired teacher living a subsistence life in the village of Kajula near Lake Victoria, asserted that the family roles of men and women were and continue to be fairly distinct. As a child, he said that men were required to do the "...hard work of raising cattle and fixing housing structures, while women were responsible for working around the house, cooking, cleaning, and child-rearing." He said that this had changed in the context of his current family where boys and girls do things equally. This assertion, however, was not confirmed by actions I observed during a stay at his home. The women and girls prepared all of the food, cleaned the compound, harvested maize, and awoke at 5:00am to prepare hot bath water for the men.

This rural cultural pattern also seemed to resonate in urban Nairobi. Boys and girls interviewed in the slum school said that the girls do the bulk of the work around the house. The reasons cited for this varied from "My brother is bigger and he refuses to do work" to "My brother has to go to school so I need to work to give him time to study," an ironic response from a school-age girl. The burden of chores has a direct and profound impact on the education of these young girls. Assuming that each child must prioritize time for home chores and schoolwork, female children as a group have less time to commit to studies as compared to males. This leads to a higher incidence of girls dropping out of school throughout Kenya, particularly after standard eight, due to significant lapses in their learning. If girls do make it to residential secondary schools, they are more likely to break out of the traditional female family roles. Female children in poverty, however, are much less likely than their middle class cohorts to have these educational opportunities. Alteration of role expectations does not generally occur among poor girls since they are not afforded boarding school socialization like some middle class girls and are quickly socialized into the role of mother and domicile caretaker.

A group of young women who attended a middle class boarding school confirmed the home chore pattern asserted by the younger children. Edy Nakuru said "The boys think housework is not for them and are not expected by parents to contribute as much to the home as the girls." The importance of young women's work in the home seems to have a bearing on this group's failure to continue their education. Since women are so crucial to the functioning of the family, the potential loss of female family labor to secondary school may serve as a barrier to young girls leaving home. As Catherine Martori noted, her brother was currently studying in India at the post-graduate level, but she needed to stay close to home for college. She said that her younger siblings required supervision, which her parents' schedule prohibited them from providing. While I conducted an interview in her home, both parents were out and the children were noisily playing in another room of the apartment. Parents also reinforced the idea that sons should act in a traditionally masculine way and daughters should be feminine. John Gadanga, a schoolteacher, said, "If I find my son playing with a doll, you can be sure I'll be mad. I don't want him 'playing lunch'!" illustrating the fixed nature of male roles.[7]

The rigidity of family gender differentiation seems to be fading, however. Single-sex, residential secondary schools are increasingly common in Kenya, although coeducational secondary schools remain the norm. This has created an entirely new socializing agent in Kenya which was not nearly as prevalent 30 years ago (Kilbride & Kilbride 1990:91). The women in the Catholic boarding school noted significant changes since they were children in the rural areas. While Christine Malum echoed the sentiment of others that "The boys don't think housework is for them... ", she also suggested that this is no longer true in the urban areas. She said that the parents who moved to the cities in Kenya were generally better educated and did not need the social security of male children as those who live in rural areas require. She asserted that the "old ways" of "African men just looking out for themselves" were changing since urban women did not need to marry.

Edy Nakuru, who attends a single-sex secondary boarding school, declared that she was not going to get married since she did not want to have to constantly worry about her husband hanging around the pub. She emphatically stated, "Times have changed! It is now acceptable for a woman to ask a man to marry in Nairobi!" These differences are even more apparent when one examines divorce rates. Brigitte Lomobos, who attends the same school as Edy, said that women are much more likely to divorce in Nairobi as compared to the rural areas. The divorce rates in Kenya are approximately 30%, an estimated statistic since many Kenyan spouses live separate lives and avoid the costly, time-consuming process of civil divorce.

While middle-class and poor girls generally are expected to be responsible for the home, some are counter-socialized by boarding schools to accept values of independence and opportunity that promote a career path, strongly influenced by the requirements of modern, urban life.

Gender Stereotypes in Education

The traditionally strict division of gender roles in families may also contribute to the formation of negative gender stereotypes in the society as a whole. The tendency to view women as "less able" than men academically was, up until recently, built into the analysis of the national exams. Catherine Martori recalled when her brother took the K.C.S.E. exam a few years ago; the scores were normed for boys and girls separately. The passing grade for girls was three points lower in that particular year, which may be seen as an effort to raise the level of female achievement. A result of norming the standardized national exam was to increase female eligibility college slots that are highly prized and scarce. Martori reported that the national exam scores are no longer normed by gender, making entrance into post-secondary education more challenging. This challenge is aggravated by the lack of space available in higher education for all students, regardless of gender.

The stereotype that women are intellectually less capable is strongly held in reference to the study of math and science. Catherine Martori said that math was her favorite subject, which she said was an oddity for Kenyan girls since it is generally viewed as a "male subject." She did not perform well enough to gain entry into the medical field, even with her proclivity for math, so she seemed resigned to be a teacher. When I raised this issue with the group of young women who were currently enrolled in a single-sex secondary boarding school, they suggested that boys received more attention by teachers, especially in those classes that were viewed as "male" areas, such as math, science, and athletic instruction. Rosalyn Lobo asserted that if a girl protested the undue attention given to boys, the girl would be told to "Go do home science!"

The attitude that men perform better in math and science because, as Vance Argundo said, "That is where the man belongs," seems to contribute to the idea that women should be academically subordinate to men. Vance reinforced this attitude, relating a personal anecdote: "I took my child to see the doctor and a woman walked in the room and I asked where the doctor was. The woman said she was the doctor and I was shocked!" When asked about his views on the trend towards more women in traditionally male careers, he said "A man is stronger...the Bible says that women should be subject to their husbands."

The assumption that there are jobs best suited for men and women respectively was a consistent pattern throughout the interviews, although informants struggled to provide a rationale for holding such beliefs. John Gadanga provided an interesting response saying, "Textbooks are always biased in the direction of portraying men as pilots, engineers, and doctors, and ignoring women in these higher status careers." This assertion was confirmed by a form 3 textbook that I encountered. The textbook, entitled *Form 3-Mathematics*, illustrated a man teaching three male students on the cover. The text used men and boys as characters in all of the word problems, in many cases portraying them as individuals who need to solve a problem and were able to do so using mathematics.

I was surprised to see, while casually watching Kenyan Television Network one day, a commercial related to young women and science. The setting was a classroom with a female teacher and a mixture of boys and girls. The girls were shown responding to questions and performing science experiments. The closing message of the advertisement was "Girls...become scientists!" There seems to be a growing awareness in Kenyan society, if not acceptance, that women can do traditionally male jobs. This was an encouraging advertisement that demonstrates, again, a change in career expectations vis-à-vis education.

The younger children interviewed seemed less wedded to the notion that there are male and female careers, lending more credence to the idea that a social change is underway. The young girls hoped for careers that were generally not in accordance with prevailing gender stereotypes. The young girls in standards six and seven, ranging in age from 13 to 14, hoped to become a business person, publisher, engineer, and scientist. Jill Amakove wanted to be a scientist so she can "...predict the weather." She was excited about the chance to "Do something which no one else in my community had done." Their optimism about careers and the future is tempered, however, by the reality of growing up a young woman in Kenya. Opportunities for uneducated women are scarce and these young girls were clearly aware of this danger. Geneva Wavura said, "My parents don't want me to become a prostitute so they stress education."

The children also seem to realize the precarious nature of their economic situation. Patricia Autuoro's mother told her that she hoped Patricia would pursue a great career. Her mother promised to assist in the task of "getting out" of the slum. Patricia said, "If I work hard in school and she is still alive, she will help pay for secondary education." Imbedded in this comment is a realization that slum dwellers do not have as long a life span as other Kenyans and that secondary schooling is crucial to the educational advancement of young women. It is interesting to note that although these children lived in the slum, their low economic status did not dampen their dreams for the future. In some ways they were more optimistic than the other young women in the study were. They were also more fatalistic about what the future holds, however, consistently making reference to the possibility of the death of a parent, inability to find work, or the anticipation of not being able to pay school fees.

None of the parents interviewed claimed to discourage girls from pursuing non-traditional careers. They all said they encouraged their children to achieve to their maximum potential, but interestingly, most of the ultimate career choices fit the larger societal patterns for men and women (e.g. teaching and nursing for women). The importance of the dynamic between careers and gender is demonstrated in at least economic terms. Women are involved in careers that tend to be lower paying and having lesser social status than male-dominated professions (e.g. teaching vs. engineering). This seems to be a cyclical pattern as there are fewer female role models in non-traditional careers, children continue to view female doctors as unusual.

The under-representation of women in traditionally male careers is a self-perpetuating phenomenon, but again, a dynamic situation. Girls and young women generally lack the role models in those careers, but women and men are crossing the boundaries to hold non-traditional careers in growing numbers throughout Kenya. As Vance Argundo noted with surprise, there are now three men in his primary teacher-training program, which he claimed would never have happened ten years ago. Mary Kinyotta recalled her father saying, "...because of my culture, I cannot give you inheritance, so I can only give you education." Mary went on to pursue a career teaching high school science as a result of her father's encouragement and financial support.

Tensions Among Women

The idea that secondary and higher education is a masculine pursuit, and thus, not available to women, seemed to be a source of tension among women. A competitive tension appeared most pronounced in the interactions between the female students and their female teachers, but also existed among female students. Edy Nakuru asserted that female teachers "...show off by wearing fancy clothes, rather than serving as an intellectual role model for their students." Edy seemed to be uncomfortable with the femininity of a woman in an institution essentially for men. She noted that this tension was greatest in coeducational secondary schools, which are very few in Nairobi, but still common in rural areas. Mary Kinyotta confirmed female competition from "the other side of the desk". She once taught in a coeducational high school, but preferred to work with boys because "...girls look down on other women," and "The girls were too worried about how their teachers looked rather than what they taught."

I observed two classrooms in Moi High School, a coeducational secondary school, with the intent of examining this gender dynamic. Two English classes led by pre-service teachers, one male and the other female, were observed. I focused upon the patterns of classroom gender interactions, since this issue appeared so prominently in previous interviews. The results of these observations shed more light on the notion of competition among women. The girls were more actively engaged in the male teacher's class, and the boys were more active in the female teacher's class. In Mr. Burt Morugo's class, 15 of the 25 total student responses in class were offered by girls while in Mrs. Elizabeth Aroyo's class, 8 of the 9 total responses given were made by boys. Eva posed a question, seeking student volunteers. Two girls seated in the back of the class raised their hands, but Mrs. Ayou called upon a boy seated in the middle of the center row who had not raised his hand.

Of all the findings in this study, these data appear to be the most idiosyncratic. They are not void of meaning, however. There was a previous study that demonstrated African teachers' tendency to favor boys unconsciously by paying more attention to boys in classrooms (Puja & Kassimoto 1994: 46). Why would such a pattern persist if indeed changes were occurring regarding gender roles? The explanation for this trend might be that women's roles in Kenyan society are rapidly being transformed and there is limited access to careers like medicine that were otherwise the exclusive domain of men. Women may internalize this competition at an early age and carry it into their careers as teachers. Further, the young women students, recognizing the improbability of many women making it into a male-dominated career, may feel the need to push out the weaker female students among them. The girls also noted competition amongst themselves and a tendency to ask boys for help on assignments rather than girls. Brigitte Lomobos asserted, "Boys will help you get the right answers whereas girls will purposely mislead you so they can get ahead of you in the class."

The finding of intra-group tension in the data also suggests that a change is underway with regard to educational achievement and gender in Kenya. It is not unusual for a social group that has historically been marginalized to experience intense intra-group strife as their roles vis-a-vis the dominant group change. Kenyan women have more opportunity for educational and career parity with men than ever before. The number of places available for all high school graduates in Kenyan colleges is severely limited. This creates fierce competition for limited resources. This competition seems to be exacerbated for women. The intra-group tensions evident in the data suggest that the status of women is changing, as more opportunities for education become available.

Conclusion

The gender gap with regard to educational access is all too common around the globe. Kenya is no exception to this phenomenon, and may be one of the more extreme cases illustrating the limitations of education for girls. Through a series of interviews and observations in various parts of Kenya, some explanations as to why the statistical disparities persist seem evident. Girls are socialized from a very young age to take on a traditionally female role, which is further enhanced by socially diffused stereotypes disparaging women's academic capabilities. Specifically, women are seen as incompetent in areas related to math and science, which has perpetuated certain high status careers being occupied almost exclusively by men. This perception becomes a self-fulfilling prophecy. Girls are either discouraged by parents from pursuing "male careers" or lack appropriate female role models in these occupations. The limited number of places for women in "male careers" may propagate increased competition among women, eventually leading to a weeding out process of otherwise qualified women from higher education and higher income jobs.

The lack of educational opportunities for women in Kenya is a phenomenon in flux. Traditional families in Kenya are being transformed as some girls leave their rural homes at the end of elementary education and are socialized in single sex schools that espouse values such as equality, opportunity and independence. This cultural change has begun to surface in attitudes towards women. Young girls are still viewed as "less competent" in math and science subjects, and yet many of the young women wanted to pursue careers in these areas. As women do approach greater parity in non-traditional careers, however, there is growing tension between women for access to occupations previously "off-limits."

The implications of this study are many. It is my sincere hope that people interested in this issue continue and extend upon this research. I assume there are many other factors that contribute to the inequality in educational access, but it will require more extended, reflective inquiry to further illuminate this phenomenon. Ultimately, the goal of this research is to enhance the lives of those being directly affected. Research related to social problems of this enormity deserves an audience in the realm of policy-makers. Through informed debate about these social phenomenon and other related issues, access to education can be made available to more women, a change that will uplift the dignity of all people.

As we conclude this study, there is one thing that must be kept in mind. The inequalities described herein are not to be viewed as resulting from inherent unequal gender standards that would be rampant within African societies. Rather, as Mengara as shown previously, one must keep in mind that a lot has happened in Africa since the Arabs and the Europeans colonized the continent. The imbalances observed in this paper must therefore be thought of as coming from a variety of sociohistorical and sociocultural processes that, when combined, have not always looked at women favorably when it comes to modern-time educational requirements. In other words, African nations in general, and Kenyan society in particular, have simply continued to use educational systems that, for the most part, are legacies of the missionary models left in place by the Europeans as the educational frameworks of reference. African nations have basically continued to evolve within educational frameworks that, for centuries in Europe itself, tended to consistently deny education to women.

This is why African policy-makers must take a harder look at their educational systems, and seek to incorporate therein values that, with the proper investment, would open the door to egalitarian, unrestricted instruction for both young boys and young girls as the best way of eliminating poverty and enhancing their citizens' overall standards of living.

Notes

[1] Buchi Emecheta, *The Bride Price* (New York: G. Braziller, 1976) offers a provocative fictional look at the issue of bride wealth through the eyes of a young woman living in Nigeria.

[2] Collette Suda, "Child Welfare Society of Kenya" (Nairobi: Kenya Bureau of Information, 1993) provides an in-depth analysis of the multifaceted lives of street children through interviews and observations conducted in Nairobi.

[3] The issue of how many informants is "enough" is a primary concern in ethnographic research. Steiner Kvale, *InterViews* (London: SAGE Publications, 1996) recommends 15 + 10 as a guideline. The key criteria, however, is interviewing until you do not learn new ideas from informants.

[4] Anselm Strauss and Juliet Corbin, *Basics of Qualitative Research: Grounded Theory Procedures and Techniques* (London: SAGE Publications, 1990), 191. states "...we are not attempting to generalize as such but to specify. We specify the conditions under which our phenomena exist, the action/interaction that pertains to them, and the associated outcomes or consequences."

[5] See Steiner Kvale *Interviews* (London: SAGE Publications, 1996), 157-8, for further description of the open-ended interview.

[6] See Anselm Strauss and Juliet Corbin, *Basics of Qualitative Research: Grounded Theory Procedures and Techniques* (London: SAGE Publications, 1990), 61-141 for a thorough explanation of coding procedures.

[7] See Jomo Kenyatta's *Facing Mount Kenya* (New York: Vintage Books, 1965), 52-67 and Tepilit Ole Saitoti's *The Worlds of a Masaai Warrior* (Berkeley: University of California Press, 1988), 56-65, for more discussion of the differentiation between male and female roles among two ethnic groups in Kenya.

Acknowledgements

The author wishes to thank Dr. Michael Kirwen of the Maryknoll Institute for African Studies for introducing him to Africa and Kenyan society. "Make Africanists of them all!" Erokomano, Mike!

Works Cited

Bradley, Candice. "Why Fertility is Going Down in Maragoli." Ed. Weisner, Thomas S., Bradley, Candice & Kilbride, Philip L. *African Families and the Crisis of Social Change.* London: Bergin and Garvey, 1997, 227-252.
Education in Kenya. http.brit.coun.org/kenya/keneduc.htm.The

British Council. 9-24-99.

Geyer, Jane I. "Women in the Rural Economy: Contemporary Variations." Ed. Hay, Margaret Jean & Stichter, Sharon. African Women South of the Sahara. New York: John Wiley and Son Publishing, 1995, 19-32.

Kaunjuga, Margaret. (1998). "The Education System of Kenya." The British Council. *http://www.britcoun.org/kenya/kenedue.htm* 9/24/98.

Kayongo-Male, Diane & Onyango, Philista. *The Sociology of the African Family.* London: Longmans Press, 1984.

Kilbride, Philip Leroy & Kilbride, Janet Capriotti. *Changing Family Life in East Africa: Women and Children at Risk.* Nairobi, Kenya: Gideon S. Were Press, 1990.

Puja, Grace K & Kassimoto, Tuli. "Girls in Education and Pregrancy at School." Ed. Tumbo-Masabo, Zubeida & Liljestrom, Rita. *Chelewa, Chelewa: The Dilemma of Teenage Girls.* London: Zed Books Limited, 1994, 54-75.

Singh, Malkiat & Dhillon, Simi. *Form 3 Mathematics.* Nairobi, Kenya : Sama Group Limited Publishing, 1987.

Suda, Collette. "Child Welfare Society of Kenya: Report of a Baseline Survey on Street Children in Nairobi." Kenyan Bureau of Information, 1993.

Tomasevski, Katarina. *Women and Human Rights.* London: Zed Books, Ltd 1993.

United Nations Home Page. *http://www.un.org/Depts/unsd/.* 2-27-98.

PART VII

African Literatures: Text and Pretext

Once Upon A Time...
Representations, Misrepresentations
and Rehabilitation in African
Literatures

Augustine Okereke
Universität Bielefeld, Germany

Introduction

"**O**nce upon a time...", in those days, stories were told of our people, stories of orderliness, of heroes and ordinary people, of cultured societies, of a well-organized system of government with popular leaders who came to power through a well established hierarchy of succession; but there were also stories told of imperfections, of sickness, of wars and killings, of famine and natural disasters. Since those days, other stories have been told that were neither spoken nor performed, but written and read. The times of African oral literature have now been replaced by those of the written text.

Literature, in general, is known to be mostly a reflection of the society in which the particular literature emanates. Therefore, directly or indirectly, the actions of the society, its values, norms, politics, strengths and weaknesses provide themes and inspiration for writers. Obiechina notes this when he tells us that:

> The way the writer arranges his subject matter and the ideas and concepts which he presents to his readers, the social habits and customs and the modes of thought and

action which he takes for granted in his writings all give a distinctive quality and tone to his work which can be related to the culture to which the author belongs (Obiechina 1975: 3).

In traditional oral performance, the relationship between the storyteller and his society is even more pronounced. This relationship makes it necessary for any formulation of the tale to take into account the social and historic context of the society from which it emanates. What this means is that African oral literature is largely a communal literature. It is the people's literature handed down to them from generation to generation, a literature that discusses their various social, historical and political backgrounds. Ruth Finnegan, in her study of oral literature in Africa, says that "a full examination of any one African literature would have to include a detailed discussion of the particularities of that single literature and historical period, and the same in turn of each other instance" (1970: 48). In effect, what the storyteller tells is what he experiences and what the society experiences too, in addition, to his creative imagination. His portrayal of characters falls within the societal experiences and expectations. It is in the same vein that Buchbinder (1991) explains that the literary work takes its existence, first within the history of the author's life, and second, within the culture and its history.

The point that is being stressed here is that what writers or performers write or perform is somewhat of a recreation of the ways of life of the community which they describe. That is to say that the writer or performer represents his characters and actions in a way that is consistent with the social behaviors and norms of the referent community. Even if imaginative creation is taken into consideration, imagination plays itself out within the total experiences of the referent society. To be authentic, the writer or performer does not, and cannot afford to, go out of his way to manufacture false, unrealistic experiences in the name of creative imagination.

Representations & Misrepresentations

In traditional African societies, oral performers have often held the function of chroniclers of the history and cultural legacy of their societies. "Once upon a time,"--the timeframe in which oral performers set their tales--tells of wholesome societies with appropriate behaviors as well as sanctions for inappropriate behaviors. In those good, old days when oral narrators had no cause to exaggerate either in the positive or negative, they narrated what they saw in their societies or what had been handed down from earlier generations. They narrated and exaggerated only to educate and be educated, transmit and remember. In brief, they told stories that maintained the various sociocultural equilibria needed for society to remain stable and keep a sense of purpose and history.

However, the cultural clash of Africa with Europe, and the various dislocations and misconstructions that ensued have revealed a clear inadequation between the modes of functioning and thinking of Europe and those of Africa. For instance, Sakaana, writing on myth and the European concept of myth as it relates to Africa has this to say:

> Myth is a system of storing history by a concise method which involves tales, symbolism and gestures. This symbolism, constituting a language, can be represented by animals or beings in unusual postures, positions and acts. These were not meant to be arbitrarily interpreted, nor to be available to the general public, but to be symbolically understood as an explanation of something to those who are initiated to a higher level of education. These means that mythology differed in the use of symbolism from culture to culture, and implies a thorough grounding in the culture of a particular society in order to 'decode' the message/memory. However, with the advent of Europe's exploitation of human resources, and the concomitant decreasing status of previously ascendant societies, particular derogatory meanings were placed on the myths and meanings of the latter societies (Sakaara 1996: 16).

Obviously, such distortions are deliberate. Deliberate because European explorers, missionaries and writers wanted to prove that there are low and high cultures, superior and inferior civilizations, superior and inferior myths. Consequently, they created stories, situations and characters that would match their prejudiced view of Africa--characters that are stupid, unimaginative, unartistic-- and societies that are portrayed as condoning and tolerating such personalities.

Thus, without prejudice to whatever artistic qualities are exhibited by Joyce Cary in *Mister Johnson* (1952), it is clear to me that the novel misrepresents and distorts African culture, personality, norms and values. This assertion may appear to be overstressed but given the experiences encountered by Africans contemporaneously, one cannot help but redefine the novel and the issues arising therefrom. It may be necessary to take Echeruo's definition of the foreign novel of Africa as a backdrop for explaining the idea of creating an African scene for a particular purpose:

> What is the 'foreign novel of Africa' and in what sense is it a special kind of novel? For many readers, the first business of a foreign novel–a novel with an alien setting–is to record, evoke and interpret the life and situation of a foreign people for the education and entertainment of the author's native readers. In this sense, a foreign novel is like a letter home from abroad. The reader is disposed to believe that the facts presented to him are true or essentially so, and that the interpretations based on them are consistent with all the evidence available to the author. In putting so much faith in the authenticity and truth of a foreign novel, the native reader is trying to reassure himself that he has a reliable basis for the responses which are demanded of him by the new and often exotic experiences of the novel (Echeruo 1973: 1-2).

If Echeruo's definition is applied to Cary's portrayal of the African setting in *Mister Johnson,* two things can be deduced. First, Cary interpreted an African situation he does not have in-depth knowledge of. Second, he portrays an African scene that will suit the perception his readers at home have of Africa. The Africans as portrayed in the person of Mister Johnson will be highly entertaining to Cary's home audience. It is necessary for him to portray an African continent that is exotic and weird. Indeed, letters written home from abroad tell stories which are most often exaggerated and embellished both to promote the image of the letter writer and to satisfy the home audience. Exaggeration and embellishment of facts are common features in the novels of Africa by foreigners. In a reference to Conrad's *Heart of Darkness*, Achebe says that:

> "When a writer while pretending to record scenes, incidents and their impact is in reality engaged in inducing hypnotic stupor in his readers through a bombardment of emotive words and other forms of trickery, much more has to be at stake than stylistic felicity" (1988: 3).

Misplaced and misguided imaginations are very important in the discussion of the portrayal of Mister Johnson, the chief character in Cary's *Mister Johnson*. Critics have assigned to Johnson the power of creative imagination. Echeruo says that Johnson is imaginative "enough to seek to break away from both the constrictions of the native lethargy and the mechanical routine of administrative life" (1973: 123), and Cook opines that "Cary has made the imaginative, innovative, ever-hopeful Johnson a triumphant exemplar of the creative power inherent in human nature" (1981: 70). But Johnson's imagination is not only misplaced and misguided, it is also a stupid one. His imagination is used to devise ways of turning his failures into things of joy. Johnson fails to go to work on time but how does he translate this failure?

> But his legs, translating the panic into leaps and springs, exaggerate it on their account. They are full of energy and enjoy cutting capers, until Johnson, feeling their mood of exuberance, begins to enjoy it himself and improve upon it. He performs several extraordinary new and original leaps and springs over roots and holes, in a style very pleasing to himself (Cary 1952: 19).

After this emotional outburst of happiness, Johnson, still transforming his lateness into happiness, moves into singing one of his spontaneous poetic composition–'I got a lil girl, she round like the worl. / She smooth like the water, she shine like the sky' (Cary 1952: 19). This is a 'typical' African in the imagination of Cary and his home audience. An African who never shows remorse in wrongful actions. Here also is "creative African poet" Johnson exploding, rejoicing, and spontaneously composing beautiful love lyrics. But to what end? I think that assigning to Johnson this great creative ability at this point in time and in this context is a deliberate attempt at ridiculing him. This thinking may have informed Christian's (1988: 2) analysis when he writes that Cary's African novels "show both how creative imagination works in primitive society and the effect of development on the formation of new ideas about life." It is pertinent to inform Christian that this is not how African creative imagination works. What is referred to as Johnson's creative imagination is a creation of Cary which is informed by his ignorance of African values or a deliberate attempt at distorting events and culture to suit his home audience.

Picture this: the stupid, debtor boy sees a beautiful girl and there and then decides to marry her against all cultural norms, values and social behaviors. He even goes further to discuss the bride price immediately: "'I want to marry her, of course. I'm clerk Johnson. I'm an important man and rich. I'll pay you a large sum of money....' 'Fifteen pounds!' Johnson cries. 'She's worth it. I never saw such a girl'" (Cary 1952: 12-13). With this idea of marrying a beautiful a girl in his mind and the fact of his lateness, he came to work and his creditors confronted him. Again, at this time, Cary put into his African hero the creative, clever ability to outwit and to outmaneuver. He first of all came to the realization of himself rolling up "(...) his eyes to the roof and [muttering], 'Oh, Gawd! Oh Jesus! I done finish – I finish now – I finish now – Mister Johnson done finish – Oh, Gawd, you no fit do nutting – Mister Johnson too big dam' fool – he fool Chile – oh, my Gawd'" (Cary 1952: 20). Of course, this realization is to be short-lived because he immediately falls back into the stupidity of thinking about his favorite writing past time--to make a perfect capital 'S'. Thereafter, Johnson manifests one of his so called 'cleverness' by spontaneously asking Blore: "If you kindly would advance me a little small portion of next month's pay" (Cary 1952: 22).

Not only is Johnson a debtor, he also steals in order to satisfy his insatiable appetite for throwing parties. Characters develop in novels to maturity, to a realization and awareness of their environment, but Johnson is created to develop into crime. At times, he steals, not for any calculated purposeful end but for the joy the process will give him. He is not calculating enough to check the final consequences of his intended actions, rather he glorifies in the joy the process of the action gives him. That image which Cary creates--the image of a young African, half-educated, torn between "civilized" European values and "primitive" African values--is now made to steal not because he wants to solve his problems with the money, but because stealing is a way of life for him. Somehow, I think that the character Johnson is one who has the determination to break out of his limited environment to a more mixed, open and novel environment. But such a character will be out of tune with the perceptions Cary's home audience have of Africa and will also be out of place for the tag--a "typical African." He is made to steal, because stealing is a way of life for the African. The description of the process of stealing Gollup's gin to Ajali and Benjamin is a pointer to this. One finds Johnson even enjoying the story and process he is narrating:

> Johnson laughs, delighting in Ajali's wonder. 'I go to store – I look – I wait behind door' – drawing himself up to tiptoe – 'till I see Sargy light cigarette – it shine for his eyes.' 'I go down.' Johnson suddenly sinks down on his haunches. 'I go past quick, quick.' He moves along the ground on his heels with a waddling gait, like the second figure of a hornpipe; but with surpassing rapidity and silence. 'I go for store, take my money. But I bump my head against de shelf – all de tins fall down, plank, plunkety. Sargy shout, "Whossat comes for store?" I go down' – crouching down with his hands over his head – 'by de counter. Sargy lookum store – because he so dark – I go out – see his room empty – se dem gin under bed – so I tink – Ajali and Benjamin like some gin' (Cary 1952: 194).

What is remarkable about Johnson's behaviors is that society watches with complacency, at times with admiration, as he acts and performs these anti-social acts. Benjamin and Ajali in a way admire Johnson's courage. Ajali's reaction to Johnson's narration of one of his robbery exploits is described as "amazed, exited, sweating with the thrill of Johnson's deeds, and grinning with condescension for Johnson" (Cary 1952: 196).

Now if we may go back to the society of oral narratives, of humans and animals, we would see that the whole of Africa's orature body is about a didactism aimed at the socialization of the individual. It concentrates heavily on the need for the rule of law, the oppositions between good and evil, and sociocultural behaviour. In other words, society before the Europeans came had a well entrenched system of not only sanctioning deviancies, but also of preventing them through the use of cultural socialization strategies, the core of which was in storytelling. In Johnson's own African society, this was not so. As described by Cary, the African society Johnson is evolving in is all about crime for the sake of crime, the joy and relsih of it, and has no local system of checking deviant behaviours.

Johnson and Rudbeck's relationship in the novel is an interesting one. Mamood (1966: 177) writes that the "center of interest in *Mister Johnson* is not, however, the relationship of the married couples, but the relationship between Johnson and Rudbeck." They both have a common sympathy for each other, and they both have a common goal. The completion of the road that will link Fada to other parts of the country is Rudbeck's passion. It is equally Johnson's passion. Therefore, both men throw in whatever they have in order to have the work completed. Even though they have a common goal, they have different reasons for wanting the goal to be accomplished. To Rudbeck, the road will open up Fada for trade and consequently develop it; to Johnson, the process of building the road gives him pleasure and offers him the opportunity to continue in his stupid antics and self-pride. The one has a noble objective, the other a fickle reason. When the sources of funds for the project dried out, Johnson encouraged his assumed friend Rudbeck to misappropriate funds to complete the road. He even went further to impose and enforce a certain form of taxation on the people to raise money which is then used to buy beer for the laborers to raise their moral. Without Johnson's help, the road would not have been completed, but for him it is all for pleasure. This could be seen in one of the conversations between him and Rudbeck:

'You seem to get a lot of work out of your gang, Johnson.'

'Dey good men – very good gang. Dey wanna make road.'
Johnson has no idea why his gang does more work than
the others (Cary 1952: 148).

As reward, Rudbeck promotes him and this encourages him
to want to satisfy his personal mundane pleasures. Cary writes:

> Rudbeck promotes him headmen of all gangs, except the
> bridge men under Tasuki. Johnson at once engages twenty
> more drummers, not apparently to improve the rate of
> work, but simply to please himself. As he says to
> Rudbeck, 'I like to hear dose drum when we work. De men
> like to sing too much' (Cary 1952: 148).

Johnson regards himself as a friend of Rudbeck and
therefore would go any length to help him accomplish their
common objective. He also takes certain privileges like asking
the workers to take time off from the office. Most
interestingly, he thinks that being Rudbeck's friend will save
him from execution after killing Gollup. Rudbeck too was
confused on how to handle the matter because he could not
come to an appropriate conclusion on how to execute
Johnson. This relationship between Johnson the ordinary
clerk on the one hand, and Rudbeck the District Officer on
the other, highlights the portrayal of Africans by foreign
novelists to suit their home audience. Rudbeck's relationship
with Johnson is that of a master and his dog. He kills him out
of sympathy so as to lessen his sufferings.

Some critics argue that *Mister Johnson* should not be read
as one of the novels that deal with the relationship between
the colonizers and the colonized. In the opinion of Mahood:

> *Mister Johnson,* like almost every masterpiece, has been
> misunderstood from the day of its publication. Its African
> setting is largely responsible. With *The African Witch*
> fresh in their memories, reviewers decided to treat the
> new novel as a portrayal of the Negro mind, whatever
> that abstraction may be. A *Times Literary Supplement*
> comment is typical: 'Mr. Cary has personified the
> maladjustment of races and civilization in *Mr Johnson.*'
> And the mid-centuries obsession with race relations still
> distorts the book for black and white readers alike. One

African admirer of Joyce Cary classes the work (though with his tongue a little in his cheek) among those European novels that have to end by either shooting or hanging the African hero because the writer doesn't know what else to do with him, And I have seen sensitive English readers protest that *Mister Johnson* is a 'patronizing' book, since Rudbeck's feelings for Johnson correspond to those of a man for a favorite dog that he is compelled to shoot (Mahood 1964: 170).

The question one might ask Mahood is: in what context then should *Mister Johnson* be discussed? The fact that the author sets the novel in Africa with African characters portrayed during the period of transition from a traditional culture to a colonized society is enough for the novel to evoke such criticisms. It may interest us to read Larsen's view that:

The first three African novels explore with incisiveness the problems posed by a pagan culture emerging from darkness into the light of civilization. Their merit lies precisely in their analysis of the forces that stimulate and the forces that inhibit the development of the mind and the exercise of the imagination. The question is not, how much will it take? Rather it is, how do the primitives and civilized people connect? And even more important, how do they connect without the explosiveness of revolution and anarchy? The success or failure of the enterprise depends upon providing the proper historical perspective, or, in other words, upon cultivating a sufficient degree of emotional and intellectual sophistication so that the native will be able to handle the immensely potent concepts of civilization (Larsen 1965: 23).

Even though the above statement is a problem in itself, it at least agrees with the intention of Cary in writing *Mister Johnson*--the exploration of the problems posed by a pagan culture emerging from darkness into the light of civilization. And there is no better way of portraying a people emerging from darkness than to show them as stupid, fickle, unreflecting, rogues, lazy and eventually murderers! In addition, it is a factual statement that the best way of "showing light to the pagan culture" is to provide the proper historical perspective so that the natives could grasp meaningfully the concept of civilization. It is, however, this proper historical perspective that Joyce Cary fails to provide. His failure to provide it, therefore, triggers off a spate of refutations from the natives who have been "civilized" against their will.

Rehabilitation

Most of what is modern African literature written by Africans is an attempt at refuting the assumptions and the distortions of African ways of life and people by the European writers who have used Africa as their literary or anthropological setting. Consequently, their writings become a kind of recreation and re-enactment of traditional African life. By doing this, they try to achieve two aims: firstly, to make African life more respectable to both Europeans and themselves, and secondly, to restore the confidence of the Africans in their culture and teach them that they had a past which was also glorious, orderly and dignifying in its own way and right.[1] A confidence that was eroded by colonialism and the subsequent denigration of their ways of life in the novels of writers such as Cary, Greene and Conrad. As a reaction to these distortions and misrepresentations, African writers set themselves the great task of correcting the anomalies and at the same time rehabilitating the minds of their people. In the words of Achebe:

> This theme–put quite simply–is that African people did not hear of culture for the first time from Europeans; that their societies were not mindless but frequently had a philosophy of great depth and beauty, that they had poetry and, above all, they had dignity. It is this dignity that many African people all but lost during the colonial period and it is this that they must now regain (1973: 8).

Achebe goes on to achieve his theme in practical terms. His response to Cary's *Mister Johnson* is *Things Fall Apart* where he shows the culture of the people before the advent of colonialism. According to Maja-Pearce (1992: 18) "Achebe's response is to suggest that there are more ways than one of measuring the worth of a society, and that the spiritual values of pre-colonial Africa were in no way inferior to those of Europe, merely different." *Things Fall Apart* chronicles the life of a harmonious African society before European civilization came. The people live at peace with each other, and are guided by rules and order; principles which are influenced by the belief in the existence of supernatural powers. There are acknowledged patterns of resolving conflicts within the society. In this society, there are heroes; heroes who have flaws and make mistakes. But because the society does not condone evil, the heroes are subsequently punished for their misdeeds. Also in this society, there are the weak ones and the lazy ones like Unoka and Nwoye; and there are the strong ones like Okonkwo, Maduka. There are also the clever and calculating ones like Obierika and Ezeudu. Okonkwo the hero of *Things Fall Apart* could be likened to the hero of oral tradition, who rises and falls victim to his own ambitions. These comparable qualities highlight the fact that Achebe is trying to follow a tradition of writing. A tradition that is developed out of the people's experiences as embodied in Africa's oral culture itself.

In some of Achebe's (1975) essays and interviews, he pointedly outlines the task that faces him as a writer. As far as he is concerned, he "would be quite satisfied if [his] novels (especially the ones [he] set in the past) did no more than teach my readers that their past—with all its imperfections—was not one long night of savagery from which the first Europeans acting on God's behalf delivered them."

Conclusion

Most of what is known as modern African writing is, directly or indirectly, an attempt to correct the misrepresentation and the distortion of the African continent and its people by foreign writers. And in doing this they had to consciously or unconsciously follow a pattern that builds on each other. Be it a literature of refutation such as Achebe's, Emecheta's or Nwapa's, of political disillusionment such as Armah's, Soyinka's or Ngugi's, or even of violence and social injustice such as can be found in the writings of Iyayi, Okpewho, Omotosho, among others, they are all trying to show that despite all the problems brought about by colonialism, Africans can still survive and stand on their own feet.

Obviously, literature does not and cannot exist in a vacuum. This means, in effect, that it draws its themes from the society of the writer or from his experiences in that society. The implication of this is that the events and changes that happen in any society are, to a large extent, mirrored in literature. Furthermore, literature develops and grows by building on itself from generation to generation. As society passes through different stages of development and grows as a result of the experiences acquired, so also does its literature. That is why there are periods in literature, because each period builds upon the foundations laid by the previous ones and thus helps the referent society develop a specific and cultural personality. Therefore, there is a certain kind of continuity that is necessary for literature to be considered a living cultural act. Any deviation from this pattern is necessarily an indication of a breakage in the link. Missing cultural and literary links can, for instance, be reflected in the case of a foreign intervention that has imposed or artificially forced itself upon the developmental process of both society and literature in colonial contexts.

With this in mind, I regard the period in which Cary and his foreign contemporaries appeared on the African literary scene as the "dark ages" of African literatures and cultures. As has been said earlier, literature builds upon itself as it develops, but the writings of Cary did not build on any known African tradition or sources. There is no denying the fact that the hero Okonkwo is a creative imagination of Achebe, but it is an imagination that is shaped by the past and present events in Achebe's society and culture. In other words, Achebe had to go back and dig deep into the historical mind of his own tradition in order to create a hero that transcends both the past and the present. Therefore, in Achebe's *Things Fall Apart* (1958), Okonkwo becomes a character identifiable by and within African society, that is a champion of the people, created out of a preceding culture and aspiring to take his people to the present in his own way. Cary's Johnson character is like a creation dropped from nowhere, and that cannot be identified within, or traced back to, the society in which he is set to evolve. The portrayal of Johnson does not fall back on any preceding pattern nor does it mirror the personality of the people that the novel purports to describe. He is simply a character created to satisfy certain assumptions from outside the society. That is why *Mister Johnson* can be said to have been written to satisfy a specific purpose—that of giving a stamp of approval to the stereotypical view of Africa as a "dark continent" in urgent need of European enlightenment.

Notes

[1] Kenneth Harrow makes a re-invigorated, renewed and insightful discussion on the old theme of change in African literature in his *Thresholds of Change in African Literature: The Emergence of a Tradition* (Portsmount: Heinemann, 1994).

Works Cited

Achebe, Chinua. *Things Fall Apart*. London: Heinemann, 1958.
_____. "An Image of Africa: Racism in *Conrad's Heart of Darkness*" in *Hopes and Impediments: Selected Essays 1965-1987*. London: Heinemann, 1988.
_____. *Morning Yet on Creation Day*. London: Heinemann, 1975.
_____. "The Role of the Writer in a New Nation" in G. D. Killam ed. *African Writers on African Writing*. London: Heinemann, 1973.
Cary, Joyce. *Mister Johnson*. London: Michael Joseph, Carfax Edition, 1952.
Christian, Edwin Ernest. *Joyce Cary's Creative Imagination*. New York: Peter Lang, 1988.
Cook, Cornelia. *Joyce Cary: Liberal Principles*. London: Vision Press, 1981.
Echeruo, Michael. *Joyce Cary and the Novel of Africa*. London: Longman, 1973.
Emenyonu, Ernest. *The Rise of the Igbo Novel*. Oxford: Oxford University Press, 1978.
Finnegan, Ruth. *Oral Literature in Africa*. Nairobi: Oxford University Press, 1970.

Harrow, Kenneth. *Thresholds of Change in African Literature: The Emergence of a Tradition*. Portsmount: Heinemann, 1994.

Larsen, Golden. *The Dark Descent: Social Change and Moral Responsibility in the Novels of Joyce Cary*. London: Michael Joseph, 1965.

Maja-Pearce. Adewale. *A Mask Dancing: Nigerian Novelists of the Eighties*. London: Hans Zell, 1992.

Mahood, M. M. *Joyce Cary's Africa*. London: Methuen, 1964.

Obiechina, Emmanuel. *Culture, Tradition and Society in the West African Novel*. Cambridge: Cambridge University Press, 1975.

Preiswerk, Roy and Perrot, Dominic. *Ethnocentrism and History*. New York and Lagos: Nok Publishers, 1978.

Sakaara, Amon Saba. *Colonialism and the Deconstruction of the Mind*. London: Karnak House, 1996.

"Oxford, Black Oxford": Dambudzo Marechera and the Last Colony in Africa

David Pattison
University of Lincolnshire and Humberside, United Kingdom

There is an assumption in the expression "Zimbabwean literary canon" that should be explained. Among others, Kahari (1980), Zimunya (1982), McLoughlin (1984a, 1991), Riemenschneider (1989), Veit-Wild (1992a, 1992b) and Pattison (1999) have presented powerful arguments recognising the existence of a discrete and recognisable Zimbabwean literature. Although considerable work has been published in the indigenous languages of Shona and Ndebele, this essay, rather, will concentrate on black writing in English. The principal reason for this is that Shona and Ndebele writing in the 1960s and 1970s was encouraged and subsidised by the Rhodesian Literature Bureau. However, the Bureau acted as censors to ensure that a depoliticised, romantic and folkloric literature emerged that bore little resemblance to the life endured by black Zimbabweans, but was supportive of the white minority government. The Bureau still exists (as the Zimbabwean Literature Bureau of course) but now concentrates on "how-to" works of a practical nature rather than works of fiction (Veit-Wild 1992b, Pattison 1999).

Recent years have, however, seen an imbalance in the study of "African literature" as it has been dominated by the likes of Soyinka, Achebe, Ngugi and Armah and the established literary fields of East and West Africa (Lindfors 1995). Inevitably, these authors have confronted issues of colonialism and neo-colonialism as experienced by particular ethnic groups. Chapman (1996) argues that it is now more appropriate to consider literatures defined by the nation-state rather than by linguistic ethnic units. Admittedly, colonially-imposed borders that encompassed different groups of people with different cultural assumptions and expectations have presented, and will continue to present, massive problems in the emergence of a national identity. But if a national identity is to be assured the emergence of a literature that captures and reflects the national experience is a key agent. South Africa itself has, for example, a wealth of literatures in the form of English literature, Afrikaans literature, Zulu literature, Xhosa literature, and Sotho literature, among others. No doubt these literatures will contribute to the eventual emergence of a meta-literature that is heterogeneous and recognisably South African. Because a culture is not static, it is necessarily dynamic and evolutionary in its development, and a national literary canon will reflect that.

Zimbabwe is indeed part of a region that has undergone cataclysmic change although, as I discuss later, it was isolated from developments outside its borders. As far as Zimbabwe's literary relationship with its neighbours in Southern Africa is concerned Chapman argues that:

South Africa... in terms of its literary interests, publication outlets and relatively large readership, has virtually subsumed any literary identity there might once have been in the neighbouring states of Botswana, Lesotho and Swaziland. The next most viable culture is to be found in Zimbabwe. Malawi and Zambia have more modest outputs while Namibia is still finding its feet as an independent country. An impressive literature by Angolans and Mozambicans, which was mostly published abroad, characterised the years leading up to the freedom struggles in the late 1950s and 1960s. Undoubtedly, the output has not been sustained during the lengthy civil wars that in the post-independence period have sapped the energies of two countries (1996: xvii).

This is not the place for a detailed comparison of writers from the various Southern African countries. Neither is it the place to speculate why different literary cultures have advanced at different rates other than to emphasise the effect of alternative reactions to internal and external environmental conditions. Suffice it to say that such issues of, *inter alia*, oppression and racism, gender discrimination, colonialism and neo-colonialism, loss of identity and psychological trauma are common to literatures throughout the region. For example, comparisons can be made between Marechera and the Botswanan writer Bessie Head in their treatment of mental illness brought about by living under a colonial system. Or between the Soweto novels of Mbulelo Mzamane, Mtutzeli Matshoba, and the Hararean urban literature of Chencherai Hove, Marechera and Charles Mungoshi.

Despite enormous difficulties, it is apparent that a relatively strong literary culture has emerged in Zimbabwe.[1] The double alienation suffered by black Zimbabweans in the 1960s and 1970s may well have prevented the emergence of a literary culture comparable to those of East and West Africa. Clearly, the structures of decades of colonisation were exacerbated by the actions of the illegal Smith regime, actions that oppressed and further disadvantaged black Africans in Zimbabwe. Then, the imposition of comprehensive sanctions by the British Government, which was supported by newly independent African countries,[2] not only had a serious material effect, but also precluded black Zimbabweans from any sort of socio-cultural and intellectual interchange with other rapidly developing societies (Birmingham and Martin 1983, Wills 1985, Grace and Laffin 1991). As a result, from November 1965 until December 1979, black artists and writers, as well as intellectuals and academics, were under colonial Rhodesia denied the opportunity to share in the rapidly developing creativity that newly acquired freedom inspired in freshly independent African countries. When Southern Rhodesia, the last colony in Africa[3], became the independent republic of Zimbabwe in April 1980, this independence signalled the end of colonial rule in Africa.

The process of recapturing an "African identity," begun many years earlier elsewhere in Africa, was only beginning to gather force in Rhodesia/Zimbabwe. These differences, therefore, must be considered when drawing comparisons between Zimbabwean literary development and literary developments elsewhere in Africa.

With the possible exception of Charles Mungoshi, Dambudzo Marechera is probably the most well known black writer from Zimbabwe. During his lifetime Marechera was undoubtedly better known for his occasionally outrageous behaviour and his lifestyle of the writer-tramp than for his writing. The stereotype of the "tortured genius"[4] or "two minds in one body" kind has been readily attached to Marechera. And it is tempting to avoid the limiting tendency of this stereotype by refusing to cast him in the role of the outcast, the loner, the young and very sensitive artist, at odds with the brutality and horror of the townships and the desperate predicament of his family, the grinding poverty and extreme hardship. But, in actual fact, this *was* his inevitable role. For the adolescent Marechera the effect of his immediate environment, which owed much to the cumulative effect of seventy years of white minority rule, was devastating[5]. The effect of his wider environment--the illegal Smith Government declared the Unilateral Declaration of Independence (UDI) in 1966, further worsening conditions for black Zimbabweans --was no less so.

Dambudzo Marechera was born on the 4th of June 1952 in Vengere Township in what was then Rhodesia. He died on August 18th, 1987 in Harare, Zimbabwe. His short but eventful life encompassed, *inter alia*, the ill-fated Central African Federation, UDI and the years of the Smith Government, the Second Chimurenga, Independence and the early years of the Mugabe administration. Expelled from the University of Rhodesia in July 1973 he went up to New College Oxford in October 1974 to read English. He lasted less than 18 months as he was sent down in March 1976. He then lived variously in Oxford, Cardiff and London, often homeless and destitute, before returning to Zimbabwe in February 1982 to cooperate in a documentary based on his best known work, *The House of Hunger.*

During his life Marechera published a collection of short stories, The *House of Hunger* (1978), which won for the writer the 1979 Guardian Fiction Prize, a novella, *Black Sunlight* (1980), and *Mindblast* (1984), an eclectic mixture of prose, plays and poetry. After his death the Dambudzo Marechera Trust was established with two main aims: to collect the unpublished work of Marechera so as to promote its publication, and to honour Marechera's memory by encouraging young writers[6]. By August 1994 the first phase had been completed but the second phase, that of assisting young writers, was still in the very early stages of development. Since its formation in 1988 the Trust has published a novella (written in 1979), *The Black Insider* (1990) the collected poetry, *Cemetery of Mind* (1992) and finally to complete the canon of published work, a miscellany of short stories, children's stories and plays under the title *Scrapiron Blues* (1994). The launch of *Scrapiron Blues* (in Harare, July 1994) was greeted enthusiastically by young Zimbabweans to whom Marechera has become something of a cult figure.[7] Such indications of a sustained and growing interest, not only in the work but also in the life of the writer, suggests that Dambudzo Marechera will eventually enjoy a more permanent place in Zimbabwean and African literature, and possibly on a wider, international scale, than looked likely in the barren years that followed his return in 1982.

In January 1999 the first collection of critical essays on the work of Dambudzo Marechera was published by Africa World Press in their Emerging Perspectives Series. *Emerging Perspectives on Dambudzo Marechera* was edited by Flora Veit-Wild and Anthony Chennells and includes contributions from an international array of writers and scholars including Wole Soyinka. Veit-Wild (1992a) produced a valuable volume, full of biographical material and a very comprehensive bibliography of primary and secondary sources. It is fair to claim that most comment has concentrated on the longer works with the exception of my own work (1999 and forthcoming[8]) which redresses the balance by examining the poems, the plays, the criticism, and the short stories as well as the novellas.

A Perspective on Marechera and His Fellow Zimbabwean Writers

The initial wave of black Zimbabweans writing in English produced fiction as a secondary occupation. For example, Samkange was first and foremost a historian and university lecturer, Vambe a teacher and journalist, Mutswairo a teacher and university lecturer and Sithole a politician. Their genre was historical fiction, or more accurately half fiction, a mixture of truths and part truths, folk stories and historical "facts". Presented in realistic, if sometimes idealistic, style, the works were authoritative in tone and didactic in intent. Samkange admits when interviewed for the film *After the Hunger and the Drought*,[9] "I wanted to reach people who wouldn't be caught dead reading history books, so I wrote fiction by sugar coating my history." This approach occasionally left his work uncomfortably between fact and fiction and thereby open to adverse criticism. As Michael Chapman (1996: 162) observes: "A mythologising tendency in his [Samkange's] work ...undermines historical causality." This is a good point, but one that may well have been lost on an unsophisticated audience who, unable to differentiate between myth and historical fact, would not have questioned the authenticity of the work.

Vambe and Samkange in particular took much of their information from Terence Ranger's book, *Revolt in Southern Rhodesia 1896-1897*, which was subsequently discredited by Beach (1979) and Cobbing (1977)[10]. By endorsing the version of a great and glorious past (the First Chimurenga), Vambe, Samkange and Mutswairo encouraged the perception of the liberation struggle as a Second Chimurenga by presenting a utopian vision of the restoration of the empire that apparently had existed before the whites had arrived. As McLoughlin (1984: 105) points out these earlier writers, particularly Samkange, wrote novels with "...a veneer of historical accuracy" but with the emphasis on "...historical processes rather than historicity."

Of course those most directly involved in the struggle were

largely illiterate and those who could read had little access to books[11] and would have been presented with a world purporting to be theirs but unrecognisable and of little relevance. So, at what audience were Samkange and his contemporaries directing themselves? It seems that they were aiming at a small intellectual elite within Zimbabwe, but mainly for consumption by a growing number of readers of "African literature" in Europe and the United States. Apart from the very unspecific "writing about Zimbabwe", this may be the only point of reference between Marechera and his predecessors, that is, writing for an audience outside of Zimbabwe.

However, it was against this literature of false historicity and extravagant ideas about nationhood and national identity that Marechera attempted to express his own experiences of growing up in a country isolated from the rest of Africa by the activities of the Smith government, and a country in which power, wealth and status was firmly in the grasp of the white minority. Little wonder perhaps that he did not share the rosy view of the earlier writers who only began to write, often from self-imposed exile, when their own positions protected them from the dreadful hardships experienced by the vast majority of black Zimbabweans. Unlike his predecessors and his contemporaries Marechera was a full-time writer. However, he never managed to earn a living from his writing and survived solely due to the support of friends and fellow writers.

In a study of the black Zimbabweans who were writing in the years around Independence, Ranga Zinyemba (1983: 7-10) observes "... to move from Nyamfukudza to Marechera is to move from cynicism to oblivion, from sickness to death, to nothingness." In the same vein, Zimunya (1982: 97) observed "From Mungoshi to Marechera is a season away", whereas McLoughlin (1991: 152) commented "[Marechera] has long been regarded as the iconoclastic outsider in Zimbabwean writing. The posthumous publication of his novella *The Black Insider* may well add to the case for keeping him on the fringes."

Marechera's own view of his fellow writers was unequivocal, as he remarked to the Dutch journalist Alle Lansu: "Zimbabwean writers--my own contemporaries--will never dare to write something like *Mindblast,* precisely because there is this heavy emphasis on developing our traditional values" (Veit-Wild 1992b: 38). Whether he meant the same "traditional values" as those espoused by the Literature Bureau or something different is not clear, but other writers did tackle similar themes to Marechera's, albeit in vastly different styles. For example, in *Going to Heaven,* the sequel to *Son of the Soil,* Wilson Katiyo explores the difficulties of a Zimbabwean exile adjusting to life in London after escaping from pre-independence Zimbabwe.

Writing at the same time as *The Black Insider* Katiyo uses a straightforward linear structure unified by the perspective of the third-person omniscient narrator to examine the inner conflict of Alexio Shonga as he encounters the culture shock of leaving his homeland and of becoming a student in London. Although *Going to Heaven* raises the same basic issues--the problems facing the terrorist sympathiser in Rhodesia, and subsequently, the black exile in London--as *The Black Insider,* comparisons are difficult to draw. *Going to Heaven,* with its accessibility, simple and direct narrative, its detached tone, the absence of the author's voice and the complete lack of existential angst, is fundamentally different from *The Black Insider.* On reading *Going to Heaven* one gets the sense of Katiyo consulting his *London A-Z* in order to locate his characters whereas with Marechera the reader is left in no doubt that he had actually walked the streets of "that vast and anonymous London" (1992: 94).

Although Marechera often reacted to his experiences and recorded them in a way that was unique to him, the experiences themselves were not unique. For example, at least two of his contemporaries shared his experience of expulsion from the University of Rhodesia in 1973; Nyamfukudza and Zimunya were also expelled, and also gained scholarships to read English at Oxford (Nyamfukudza) and English and History at Canterbury (Zimunya). Both completed their degree courses, and Zimunya went on to study for an MA in modern literature. Zimunya's MA thesis became *Those Years of Drought and Hunger,* and although his poetry has been distributed quite widely, he has not published any prose fiction, apart from the occasional short story. Nyamfukudza has published works of fiction but none makes reference to his experiences in England. His first, and to date, only full length novel, *The Non-Believer's Journey* is firmly grounded in Zimbabwe and set in the final years of the war. His other published work is a collection of short stories (*If God was a Woman*, College Press, 1991) about the struggles of the individual to adjust to the new life after Independence.

Charles Mungoshi has not attracted the fervent personal following of Marechera. However his achievements in both Shona and in English--in 1976 he won the top prizes in two sections of the PEN International Book Centre Award for the best work in an African language and in English with his novels *Ndiko kupindana kwamazuva* (*How Time Passes*) and *Waiting for the Rain*--suggests he is a better role model than Marechera for the would-be writer. That apart the consistently high quality of his prose fiction and poetry assures his central position in any assessment of Zimbabwean literature. Writing steadily throughout the 1970s and 1980s, Mungoshi published ten books between 1970 and 1989. He met with international recognition when a collection of the stories from *Coming of the Dry Season* and *Some Kinds of Wounds* published as *The Setting Sun and the Rolling World*, won the Commonwealth Literature Prize in 1988. In comparing the two writers, McLoughlin (1984: 112) observed that "with the independence of Zimbabwe in 1980 and the conclusion of the war, fiction is less likely to take Marechera as an example than Mungoshi whose work offers a more feasible mode of analysing the one area of experience that has so closely touched millions of lives in Zimbabwe for so long, the war". In spite of his eminence as a Zimbabwean writer Mungoshi, in common with Marechera, saw his experience as redolent of the human condition on the grand scale, as he remarked to an interviewer in 1988: "What I had to say was universal. There is no English fire or African fire, human experience is human experience" (Veit-Wild 1992b: 297).

Wilson Katiyo, whose novel *Son of the Soil* closes with the stereotypical metaphor of the birth of a healthy child and the implication that the struggle was worthwhile and productive, offers a view that is not shared by Mungoshi, Marechera or Nyamfukudza. Instead they confront the socio-psychological traumas left by both colonialism and the struggle for independence: recognising the reconstruction of the lost pre-colonial society to be an impossible dream they search instead for the location of the inner self, the key characters are strangers in their own land. The writers who preceded them, notably, Samkange, Vambe and Mutswairo fused historical matter with fiction, looking back to and beyond the first meeting with white settlers, in an attempt to recover an ethnic identity and to create a national image with which to greet a hopeful future. This line is also followed to some extent by Katiyo but rejected by his contemporaries who concerned themselves with the "here and now" cataclysmic effect on the individual of past and recent history. Of those contemporaries none explored that direction with greater determination and dramatic effect than Marechera.

The utopianism of Samkange and his contemporaries was replaced by the existential angst of Mungoshi, Marechera and Nyamfukudza, which in its turn has given way to the dystopian view of their successors. In his article "Land War and Literature in Zimbabwe," ldred Jones (1993) argues that "for these Zimbabwean writers,[12] victory and liberation have a hollow ring. The war has not solved even the problem of the land; it remains to be divided up, fought over, worked and suffered with, all over again."

Jones points to a consistency in the development of a Zimbabwean literature written in English. The themes and issues remain the same as thirty years ago and it is possible to discern a line linking the historical realism of Samkange *et al* through the social realism of Mungoshi and Nyamfukudza to a similar approach adopted by the more recent writers such as Hove, Chinodya, Dangarembga and Vera. Chapman (1996: 301) comments:

> In replying to a concern that writers should look to the civil society rather than back to the destruction, Chinodya says he believes that "writers shouldn't rush to deal with current affairs, but let time give perspective to their vision."

That particular sentiment has a certain Marecheran

resonance about it. However it is difficult to maintain that he had anything other than an implicit influence on other writers, and that probably owes more to the man, his lifestyle and his reputation, rather than to the writer, in that, without exception, the standard conventions of form and content are observed by his contemporaries.

Chinodya's *Harvest of Thorns* explores the pre- and post-liberation period subjectively rather than in a quasi-historical fashion and includes biographical material, but there the similarities end. Of Marechera's "experimentation,"[13] there is no trace. This complete absence of any sense of experimentation is common to the work of all the other Zimbabwean writers with the minor exceptions perhaps of Hove's mystical, almost surreal, evocation of the First Chimurenga in *Bones* or Tsitsi Dangarembga's exploration of new grounds in *Nervous Conditions* in which she discusses such issues as anorexia and the exploitation of Zimbabwean women.[14] Referred to as "one of the most consistent and inspired of writers to emerge during this decade,"[15] Yvonne Vera has produced a volume of short stories *Why don't you carve other animals?* (1992), and two novels *Nehanda* (1993) and *Without a Name* (1994). Born in Bulawayo Vera writes of the experience of women in the war of liberation but also evokes a sense of history by confronting the issues aroused by opposing cultures; for example, of a treaty offered by the white men, Ibwe, a chief and a central character in *Nehanda* has this to say:

Our people know the power of words. It is because of this that they desire to have words continuously spoken and kept alive. We do not believe that words can become independent of the speech that bore them, of the humans who controlled and gave birth to them. Can words exchanged today on this clearing surrounded by waving grass become like a child brought up by strangers? Words surrendered to the stranger, like the abandoned child, will become alien - a stranger to our tongues. (1993: 39-40)

There is a similarity here with Marechera's work in that he

too was fascinated by language and what he saw as its traps ("You can bind a man with long ropes of words" (1980: 3) for example). It seems the similarity is not accidental. In our conversation,[16] Vera spoke of Marechera "luxuriating in language". On Marechera's current relevance, Vera said, "Marechera is still very trendy among the young. I don't think people write because of him. I think it is fair to say that he inspired an attitude to literature, which was more a love of reading, rather than the practise of writing." A less sanguine view was expressed by Nyamfukudza who, although he agreed that young Zimbabweans still admire Marechera, argued that it is an admiration "based on the figure [Marechera] presented rather than on his writing. Zimbabweans," he added, "are not great readers of books."[17]

Dambudzo Marechera and "Oxford, Black Oxford"

Although it is his novels that have attracted most attention I will, in this paper, examine two short stories. In the main concentrating on "Oxford, Black Oxford", in which the writer faces up to the difficulties of a black Zimbabwean in the 1970s Oxford, but also looking briefly at "First Street Tumult" which very cleverly exposes the exploitative nature of neo-colonialism in Zimbabwe. By doing this I will be able to indicate that even after his return from exile in London and Oxford the writer remained in exile on his return to Zimbabwe due to his iconoclastic nature and his inability to become reconciled to the demands of the nation builders. In his writing Marechera engaged with the major issues of colonialism and neo-colonialism, class and race, among others, but in a highly individual way that humanised the sometimes depersonalising effect of such global terms. His was the struggle, his was the nightmare.

Despairing of the many and various attempts to create an "African image" Marechera was particularly scathing in his attack on the Government of the newly independent Zimbabwe dismissing it as a "machine like state" with a desire to "...give the citizen a prefabricated identity and consciousness made up of the rouge and lipstick of the struggle and the revolution" (1980: 142). Not that he had any answers himself as he immediately follows that particular attack with the bemused "Had we lost the African image or had the African image lost us?"

Perhaps better known for his uncompromising "If you are a writer for a specific nation or a specific race, then fuck you" (Veit-Wild 1988: 3), Marechera could also use a cruelly incisive humour. For example, "Writing has made me the worst kind of hypocrite--an honest one" and his disparaging reference to the African exiles as "those dogs in London" (1980: 179) and their talk of "cabbages and kings of racist phenomena and the onions and inkwells of the African image in the diaspora" (1980: 171). As for nationalism, "National culture," he scoffed "...seems to mean a lot of fat women dressed in the Leader's colours and a crowd of half-naked traditional dancers leaping in clouds of dust" (1994: 26).

The tragic irony is that Marechera was pointing a way forward. One of the idiosyncratic aspects of Zimbabwe (and elsewhere, of course) is that "forward" is the direction indicated by the Government, there is no space for alternative voices.

Opinions on the quality of his work have polarised between "potential genius" and "pretentious rubbish"[18]. One of the secondary aims of this paper is to offer an alternative reading, revealing that although Marechera's "fiction" is often autobiographical, he is an accomplished writer in a variety of genres. As well as a highly talented novelist Marechera was also a fine short story writer, a very effective dramatist, and a perceptive and moving lyric poet. The primary aim of this paper is to engage with the text in order to demonstrate how the expectations of others bedevilled the artistic and personal development of this uniquely gifted, extraordinary, if ultimately tragic, figure.

Of course a major factor in the "failure" of his ambitions at university was his sending down from New College, an issue that is central to "Oxford, Black Oxford", a compact piece which very effectively demonstrates Marechera's considerable talent as a short story writer. "Oxford, Black Oxford" presents a central character, clearly Marechera himself, as a diligent and gifted student but one whose very survival as a student is placed at risk by his alternative existence as a violent drunk. The disjunction within the characterisation, gifted student or drunk, is matched by a disjunction in the story as, with dramatic effect, the portraits of Oxford and Africa presented in the opening paragraphs are superseded by a foregrounding of the protagonist and a shift in narrative style and tone.

The story was probably written shortly after he had left New College in 1978, and the title "Oxford, Black Oxford" contains several nuances. With the obvious echoes of William Henley's "England, my England"[19] it can be read as a bitterly ironic comment on Marechera's experience of exclusion at Oxford. Such a reading suggests that Marechera may have felt an enormous sense of loss at leaving Oxford. "Oxford, Black Oxford" is also black in the sense that Marechera was black and a mocking acknowledgement that although Oxford accepts black students it is, the story suggests, underpinned by white values. The title can also be seen as a direct reference to the bouts of depression and paranoia that caused the writer such grave problems during his time at New College. In this instance black has the same correlation with mental illness as it has when applied to Churchill's "black dog" or Kristeva's "black sun" [20].

The opening paragraph concludes with the sentence "My mind an essay in itself." and the first two paragraphs can be read as a typical student essay with Marechera as the ideal student. The first paragraph presenting a collage of Oxford images and the second a collage of African images juxtaposed to draw vivid comparisons. The imaginative link connecting the paragraphs of the "slow calm walk to a tutorial in All Souls" reflecting Marechera's actual journey from Africa to Oxford.

A few rusty spears of sunlight had pierced through the overhead drizzling clouds. Behind the gloom of rain and mist, I could see a wizened but fearfully blood-shot sun. And everywhere, the sweet clangour of bells pushed in clear tones what secret rites had evolved with this city. Narrow cobbled streets, ancient warren of diverse architecture all backed up into itself, with here there and everywhere the massive masonry of college after college (1992a: 158).

With its colourful combination of a stereotypical African icon (a spear) and a stereotypical English icon (rain) the opening sentences--"A few rusty spears of sunlight had pierced through the overhead drizzling clouds. Behind the gloom of rain and mist, I could see a wizened but fearfully blood-shot sun."--offer a memorable image. In view of what ensues it is worthy of note that the spear (the African?) has been damaged by the action of the rain (the English?). The "wizened but fearfully blood-shot sun" can be seen as a vision of the future under threat but more reasonably represents Africa, and the "spears of sunlight" represents Africans leaving Africa. Thus, it can be argued that "spears of sunlight" is an implicit metaphor for the black Africans at Oxford and the "drizzling clouds... the gloom of rain and mist" likewise a metaphor for the hostile environment that greeted them.

In the opening paragraph the language teems with images of exclusion: "secret rites" and "ancient warren"; the almost incestuous "backed up into itself;" "close-packed little shops;" "crowded pavements"; leading us to the agencies which had directed Marechera to Oxford, agencies of faith, hope and charity, given cynical expression here as "Myth, illusion, reality." It is perhaps not too far-fetched to see the faith he had placed in the education system destroyed because it was based on the myth of equality for all, his hopes therefore an illusion and his dependence on charity a reality. Of course Marechera rejected any notion of charity but, that rejection apart, the reality is that his very existence became dependent on the charitable actions of diverse others, his presence at New College the result of a Junior Common Room Scholarship partly funded by the fees of other undergraduates. [21]

"Myth, illusion, reality were all consumed by the dull gold, inwardness, narrowness". That "Myth, illusion, reality" should be consumed by an "inwardness," a "narrowness," is in keeping with the tone of the paragraph, but why "dull gold"? An oxymoron, "dull gold" signifies the welcome and unwelcome experienced by Marechera at Oxford. It also represents a tarnishing of the prize he had "won" with his scholarship to Oxford. The "sheer and brilliant" extent of his achievement and its potential seem now an "impossibility... as the raindrops splashed and the castanets of stray sunlight beams clapped against the slate roofs, walls and doorways". Notably the raindrops act together but the sunlight acts in "stray" beams and is denied access at all points as the psychological and cultural barriers opposing the black African are given physical, if metaphorical, form.

The reference to Zuleika Dobson--"...did Zuleika Dobson ride past, her carriage horses striking up sparks from the flint of the road?"--is more than a mere example of wide reading. By implication it inserts the black narrator, intertextually, into the earlier work by Max Beerbohm.

> As the landau rolled into "the Corn", another youth - a pedestrian, and very different - saluted the Warden. He wore a black jacket, rusty and amorphous. His trousers were too short: almost a dwarf. His face was as plain as his gait was undistinguished. He squinted behind spectacles.
>
> "And who is that?" asked Zuleika.
>
> A deep flush overspread the cheek of the Warden. "That," he said, "is also a member of Judas. His name I believe is Noaks."
>
> "Is he dining with us tonight?" asked Zuleika.
>
> "Certainly not," said the Warden. "Most decidedly not."

(1911: 3)

The resemblances to Marechera himself; the unusual appearance, the squint, the spectacles, the implied difficult relationship with the Warden are too strong to have been chosen accidentally. In "Oxford, Black Oxford" Marechera "watches" the carriage pass by, as in *Zuleika Dobson* the passengers in the carriage look out and see his equivalent from the turn of the century. In this way Marechera indicates that his experience of prejudice and exclusion are not unique, they are, he appears to be suggesting, endemic in Oxford.

A key word linking the opening paragraphs is the adjective

sweet, as in "sweet clangour of bells" which pervades Oxford, in contrast with "the evil-sweet fumes of the ever-open beer halls" of the townships. However the main link is between the closing and opening sentences of the respective paragraphs as the "mind" in which the initial essay was written or imagined becomes a vantage point through which various stereotypical images of Africa are presented.

The clear and specific references to Oxford are abandoned here in favour of generalisations aimed not at a locality or even a country but at the continent of Africa itself.

Drawing apart the curtains, opening the windows, to let in... the hail of memories. The reek and ruin of heat and mud-huts through which a people of gnarled and knotty face could not even dream of education, good food, even dignity. Their lifetime was one long day of grim and degrading toil, unappeasable hunger whose child's eyes unflinchingly accused the adults of some gross betrayal (1992a: 158).

Thus the "people of gnarled and knotty face" is, metaphorically speaking, the African nation and "the child's eyes", while probably intentionally reminiscent of the haunting images of starving Biafran children which in themselves became symbolic of Africa in the 1970s. In this context "child's eyes" is a trope for the 1970s generation of Africans whose unattainable dreams and plight of "grim and degrading toil, unappeasable hunger"--intellectual and physical hunger, that is--are blamed on the alleged complicity of earlier generations.

In counterpoint to the "Narrow, cobbled streets, ancient warren of diverse architecture... with here there and everywhere the massive masonry of college after college", township life is described in a single graphic sentence.

The foul smells of the pit latrines and the evil-sweet fumes of the ever-open beer halls, these infiltrated everything, from the smarter whitewashed hovels of the aspirant middle class to the wretched squalor of the tin and mud-huts that slimily coiled and uncoiled together like hideous worms in a bottomless hell. (1992a: 159)

Marechera emphasises the all pervasive extent of horror and filth by using the simile of "hideous worms" to describe the "smells" and "fumes" and stresses the reptilian unpleasantness by describing the fumes as "slimily" coiling and uncoiling in "a bottomless hell", the latter a metaphor not only for the township but also for life in the township. The final sentence returns to images of the African in Oxford before a "sudden downpour" (the hostile environment of Oxford) drives away thoughts of Africa as "the blood-shot mind...[the blood-shot sun of the first paragraph now figuratively the African collective unconscious, saturated with bloodstained memories] was completely shrouded by the heavy clouds".

To a certain extent the opening paragraphs admit their fictionality as the author intrudes to reveal that he is writing an essay. The rest of the story, in contrast, is in realistic mode. The tone shifts, from that of a detached observer to one of intimate involvement as the narrator relates his experiences.. In a series of exchanges with Stephen, a fellow student and a tutor, Dr Martins-Botha, Marechera confronts the issues of class distinction and prejudice, using the different voices to disseminate different points of view and different perspectives. The name, Martins-Botha, is of course a bitter cross-cultural joke. Dr. Martins is the name for the footwear worn almost exclusively (in the 1970s) by National Front skinheads. Pieter Botha was a National Party MP in the Verwoerd government renowned for his extremist support of apartheid and for his views on the purity and supremacy of the Afrikaner. In fairly direct fashion Marechera is, through the made-up name of a college lecturer, linking the supporters of the UK-based National Front and the Afrikaner supporters of apartheid. By placing that link in a position of some authority he is suggesting that racial prejudice can be found in Oxford.

Bakhtin[22] argues that the voice in the novel has an ideological dimension and the various exchanges highlight that Stephen and Dr. Martins-Botha share a value system from which the narrator is excluded. In the following extract the tutor has asked the narrator a question but before waiting for an answer turns to address Stephen:

> 'Had a good shoot?'
> Stephen actually blushed with pride as he said, 'I bagged seven. Two are on the way to your house right now.'
> 'Ah, a decent meal for once' (1992a: 161).

In addition to the idiomatic "Englishness" of the language, for example, "good shoot" and "bagged seven", the exclusive intimacy implied in this exchange by the revelations that Dr. Botha knew Stephen had been shooting, Stephen knew Dr. Botha's address and that he would accept a gift, is confirmed when the narrator observes "Dr. Martins-Botha's right hand was between Stephen's thighs" (1992a: 162). This homosexual encounter could be hallucinatory. It certainly has a surreal air, and shockingly emphasises the narrator's isolation. On the other hand it could be realistic and a comment on the impotence of the black student in that he is of so little significance that he is allowed to witness behaviour that, if reported, could have severe consequences for the perpetrators. The narrator is of course unable to make such a report because, apart from the obvious barriers of class and status, his own reputation is such that it is unlikely that anyone would give credibility to his complaints about the "bad" behaviour of others.

In the following example the themes of drinking--the reason for his precarious situation--and exclusion are combined and when he says he is "dying for a drink" and Stephen "produced his hip flask, a silver and leather thing" (1992a: 160) in response, drink is clearly in the text and exclusion, equally clearly, in the sub-text. Earlier the "sweet clangour of bells" (1992a: 158) in Oxford was contrasted with the "evil-sweet fumes of the ever-open beer halls" (1992a: 159) of the unnamed township. The gulf between the students is again driven home. The taking of alcohol, in the case of the white student, involves a silver and leather flask and in the case of the black student, it is a stinking experience in a crowded beer hall. In addition, perhaps, as silver is an epithet often used to describe the tone or colour of bells, it is suggested that those who drink from such flasks are more familiar, and therefore have more in common, with an environment ringing with the "sweet clangour of bells" than those who frequent beer halls in a "bottomless hell" (1992a: 159).

In typical contradictory Marecheran fashion the characterisation in this very short story is stronger than in the longer works. Stephen is cast firmly as middle class or even, perhaps, aristocratic. He is on familiar social terms with his tutors, he hunts, he uses a hip flask. When he is first introduced he is presented in the classical pose of the indolent though confident student. "He leaned back against a wall, hands in his pockets, ankle over ankle" (1992a: 159). Marechera's choice of language for Stephen shows him to be patronising, as the following demonstrates:

Always wanted to know where you learned your English, old boy. Excellent. Even better than most of the natives in my own hedge. You know. Wales. (1992a: 160)

At the time of the writing of this story the Welsh Nationalists were deep into their campaign of English-holiday-home-cottage-burning and the restoration of the Welsh language was a major issue. Marechera, who had lived in Wales, would have been aware of those activities and this apparently banal exchange is deep with meaning as he exposes the venal attitude of the coloniser. The exchange continues:

'It's the national lingo in my country.'
'It's not bambazonka like Uganda?'
'Actually yes, your distant cousins are butchering the whole lot of us.'
'Mercenaries, eh. Sorry old man. Money. Nothing personal.' (1992a: 162)

The use of "bambazonka" is confusing--it serves as an arrogant neologism but the absence of a clear meaning obscures the apparent link to genocide made by the author. One possibility is that by using a neologism Marechera was indicating the complete disregard of the European for the African language and by extension, African culture and the African people.

A key phrase here is "Nothing personal" as it is used again when the narrator in an ironic reference to identity confusion cannot distinguish between Stephen and Dr. Martins-Botha:

> I picked up my essay from the floor and began to read. I was halfway through it when Dr. Martins-Botha laughed quite scornfully. I stopped. I did not look up. I waited until he had finished. I was about to resume when he suddenly - or was it Stephen's voice? - said, 'Nothing personal. You know.' (1992a: 162)

There is of course a heavy irony in Marechera's use of the phrase "Nothing personal". The action of the coloniser had disastrous effects on the individual, the scorn of the tutor is clearly aimed at the narrator--by linking the two denials Marechera suggests that such acts are justified by the perpetrator by the simple expedient of denying the individuality of the other. Significantly, Marechera closes his story with a reference to "something intensely personal [which] was flying towards me" (1992a: 163).

Of particular interest in this short piece is Marechera's reference to "the language of power". Although apparently aimed at the mocking "Language, dear boy. Language" (1992a: 160), it actually refers to the summons from the Warden and appears to acknowledge that power is inevitably associated with status. The exchange that precedes this bleak statement is notable for two things. One is the carefully affected tone of the students dialogue, in which both observe a student's script in playing their parts. The other is the contrast between the narrator's utterances and his thoughts.

> Shit. I had forgotten to check my mail. There was probably a summons to the dean in it. Not again, for Chrissake. But I said in an off-hand way, "Bloody uppity these porters, if you ask me. When a bloke is quietly sneaking back into his

rooms, they make a fuss." (1992a: 159)

Here, perhaps, is the nub of the story. The desperation of the unspoken thoughts is very evident in the appeal "Not again. for Chrissake." but his observable reaction is very different. The character created by Marechera cannot show concern for such matters (both in this story and in his own life, it could be argued.) and responds "Bloody uppity, these porters...". His use of "uppity" to describe the porters may hint at its common association with "uppity nigger" deliberately reversing the stereotype. In this way, by contrasting the content of the spoken with the unspoken, Marechera is able to highlight the dilemma of his narrator who apparently cares deeply about an issue but, because it would contradict the image of the hard-drinking, anarchic student, is unable to admit that is the case. His reaction confirms the image he has presented, and the result is another step away from his role as "ideal student".

Almost inevitably the story closes with the narrator drinking triple whiskies as he contemplates an uncertain future. "At last something--not much--but something intensely personal was flying towards me like the flight of a burning sparrow" (1992a: 162). "Intensely personal" is a repudiation of the earlier "Nothing personal" protestations of Stephen and Dr Martins-Botha and the "burning sparrow" a nightmare vision, or , perhaps, a deliberate Spoonerism of spear and arrow? As so often happens with Marechera's work the reader is left with uncertainty--is the ending a carefully crafted surreal image, or a flashy meaningless gesture of a writer suddenly bored with the exercise? Unfortunately for the reader looking for certainty, the complexity of the man and the writer is such that either alternative could be true.

"First Street Tumult" was first published in *The Sunday Mail* of 29 May 1983 and is notable for its detached tone and complete absence of authorial intrusion as the author maintains a third person narrative voice. This aesthetically appealing story is a "multicoloured sketch of the cityscape of Harare" (1994: pxi). The opening paragraph captures a moment when:

Sunlight stencilled her image in the big gleaming shop-front window. Like a photograph negative held up to the light, her image lingered among the pink harlequins dressed in velvet, silks, corduroy, lingered long and longingly among the latest fashions from London and Paris, a hazy gold-shot silhouette of a tall graceful Afro-crowned single woman, a teacher at Blake High School in Fourth Street, Harare' (1994: 108).

The narrator lightly plays with the obvious Fanonesque postcolonial moralism of the richly clad "pink harlequins" (Europeans) contrasted with the "negative" image of the African in favour of a more subtle dialectic between illusion and reality. The writer, in cinematic fashion, then pans around the First Street Mall, describing the scene in order to locate the woman and the moment before he finally returns to her and closes to reveal why he was writing about the woman. But the answer contains a mystery "And the fierce pulsing rays of the sun could not penetrate to the glittering secret tears coursing one by one down her cheeks" (1994: 111). In a curiously jarring shift to the language of an inferior love story--"In just such a way she had thrown all of herself at Dan" (1994: 109)--, part of the secret is revealed. Her lover has left her, she is no longer a virgin "The freshly mown grass would be the small print on her living contact", and is pregnant: "Green seedlings, suddenly the matter of the morrow" (1994:110). Her flat, to which she is reluctant to return, is now a place of "too many silent and invisible things" (1994: 109).

A recurring motif in "First Street Tumult" is a captured image as the writer engages in a debate on the nature of the relationship between illusion and reality. In addition to the "photograph negative" of the opening paragraph Marechera uses as tropes "the sharp watercolour strokes of pastel-shade people" (1994: 108); "A still photograph from a film"; "A hastily scrawled drawing"; "a painting by Monet" (1994: 109): "a portrait on the wall" (1994: 110). Pursuing the same motif in the actions of his characters he introduces "A young Swede [who] was calmly taking pictures" (1994: 110) and "two Norwegian girls [who] carried five canvas paintings" (1994: 110/111).

Linking the woman psychologically to his use of artistic terms Marechera reveals she is a teacher, who "taught art: drawing, painting and sculpture" (1994: 109). Perhaps for her the illusion of love has become the reality of an unwanted pregnancy.

The closing mystery of the story, the "secret glittering tears" (1994: 111), suggests that the image cannot be penetrated. A casual observer will see that the woman is crying but does not know the reason for her tears. As observer he (or she) can only interpret subjectively what he (or she) sees.

The theme is made clear in surreal fashion by "A group of young university students, dressed in white chef's uniforms cycled into the Mall on a six-seater bicycle; cycled slowly round and round, ringing a Holy communion bell", who read a poem:

I am what you see, said the cat,
What you see is in your head.
Am I in your head, or am I me (1994: 111).

The theme is the familiar Marecheran conundrum of the nature of identity as dialectic between illusion and reality. The images, which are captured in various ways throughout the story, exist in an alternative non-literary medium. But, the writer is asking, how does the captured image relate to the thing itself? Which is the real "I", the one that exists in the minds of others or the "I" that I believe myself to be? In addition to that riddle there is a subtle allegorical link on the nature of illusion, as Zimbabwe moves from the distortions of colonialism to a socialism that is no less distorted. A very clever and appropriate allegory that captures the art teacher's unwanted pregnancy and connects it with the notion of the "new" Zimbabwe being little more than the bastard child of colonialism.

In this vividly illustrated and, considering its shortness, powerful and psychologically complex story the central message of "First Street Tumult" is very simple, if not correspondingly clear. The message is: whoever is in power, ultimately the people are exploited, and suffer.

Conclusion

When Marechera wrote the plaintive "I have been an outsider in my own biography" (1987a: 102), he was lamenting the implacable historical and ideological influences which inevitably informed his writing. By standing outside his biography Marechera was able to comment on it in such a way that the forces that dominated his life are clearly exposed. His lasting achievement is that having lived through the most turbulent years of Zimbabwe's history he left behind a body of work which is a rich source of invaluable information on those years.

Reference is made above to McLoughlin's suggestion that Marechera was "on the fringes" of Zimbabwean writing; there is a pejorative implication to this that is inappropriate for a writer who has international status.[23] Marechera was on the fringes only in the sense that his treatment of his subject matter was different to that of any other Zimbabwean writer. One contribution to Zimbabwean literature is then clear--Marechera's work has promoted the notion of a Zimbabwean literature to a worldwide audience. His "experimental" style, whether it is classed as 'intellectual anarchism" (Veit-Wild 1992a: 185) "pretentious rubbish" (see above) or somewhere in between, continues to attract comment and to polarise views. Another contribution is not yet quite so clear. Dambudzo Marechera was a very charismatic figure and even after his death he has a large following in Zimbabwe. Whether that will lead to an increase in reading and eventually to an increase in writing is difficult to determine and dependent, in no small degree, on the activities of the Mugabe Government and a much increased investment in the education system throughout Zimbabwe, from the primary sector through to the universities.

Dambudzo Marechera may or may not inspire others to write; to an extent, investment in education apart, that fate will be decided by the whim of what is in vogue. What is certain is that his corpus of work will grow in stature as time allows memories of the man and the myth to fade and those who would know Marechera and want to understand him, or quite simply want to know what it was like to be "black in a too white world",[24] turn to his novels, his plays and his poems.

Notes

[1] For a comprehensive examination of the background to literary development in Zimbabwe see Flora Veit-Wild (1992b).

[2] The ban was in fact observed worldwide. Inevitably perhaps, South Africa was the only country to maintain relations with the illegal Smith regime. The overall effect of the British Government-led sanctions was to further widen the gap between the affluent whites and the impoverished blacks (Stoneman 1998).

[3] *The Last Colony in Africa* is the title of a book by Michael Charlton (Oxford: Blackwell, 1990) in which he interviews the key players in the lead up to independence.

[4] Dr. Robert Fraser, writer and academic, befriended Marechera during his time in London. During a conversation with me in July 1997 he used this expression and compared Marechera to the likes of, among others, Patrick Kavanagh, Dylan Thomas and Van Gogh.

[5] Marechera suffered from, at times, quite severe mental health problems. I argue that this illness was directly related to the actions of the coloniser (Pattison, 1994; 1999)--in doing so I am supporting many of the arguments advanced by Franz Fanon's seminal work *The Wretched of the Earth* (1961) (London: Penguin, 1967).

[6] The Dambudzo Marechera Trust was established in 1988 with Michael Marechera (the late writer's brother), Flora Veit-Wild and Hugh Lewin as founder trustees. The Trust can be contacted at Box 6387, Harare, Zimbabwe. However as Michael Marechera died in 1995, Veit-Wild accepted a permanent post in Germany in the same year and Hugh Lewin has also left Zimbabwe, the Trust has an uncertain future.

[7] See *'"An Outsider in my own Biography" - From Public Voice to Fragmented Self in Zimbabwean Autobiographical Fiction'*, an unpublished paper by Flora Veit-Wild. Veit-Wild refers to Marechera as 'the mouthpiece of the "lost generation" of Zimbabwean intellectuals [in] the 1970s and a cult figure amongst young Zimbabweans after his death in 1987'. See also Veit-Wild (1992a: 310, 382 and 392).

[8] A detailed study of Marechera's work has been completed by David Pattison and is to be published as *No Room for Cowardice* by the Africa World Press of Trenton, New Jersey, forthcoming.

[9] *After the Hunger and the Drought* (1988) is a film made by Moonlight Productions of Harare in which several Zimbabwean writers (including Marechera) discuss developments in Zimbabwean literature.

[10] David Beach, 'The Politics of Collaboration', University of Rhodesia, History Seminar Paper, No 9, 1969, and 'The Rising in South Western Mashonaland, 1896-7', doctoral thesis, University of London, 1971. Julian Cobbing *The Ndebele under the Khumalos, 1820-1896*, doctoral thesis, University of Lancaster, 1976. Additionally, 'The Absent Priesthood: Another look at the Rhodesian Risings of 1896-97', *Journal of African History*, Vol 28, No 1, 1977.

[11] This is a situation that has changed very little. In an interview for the *Herald* (Harare Saturday August 5th 1995 'Read more books, urges minister.') the Minister of Higher Education, Dr Ignatius Chombo, said, 'If writing is a form of communication, then the communication circuit can only be complete when there is a readership. One of our greatest problems lies in the dearth of a readership. As a nation, we are not doing enough to nurture the readers who are to read what we write.'. Supporting this view an unnamed Southern African publisher reported in The Zimbabwe International Book Fair Bulletin (Number 16 March/April 1998) "For me, the greatest benefit at ZIBF was meeting and sharing problems with other small publishers from Africa. Discussion revealed that most of us are struggling in the face of tremendous odds. All of us faced the desperate poverty of our audience and the absence of a reading culture." Unfortunately the current (writing this in early 2000) parlous economic condition of Zimbabwe offers very little hope of improvement.

[12] Jones's article referred specifically to Chencherai Hove, *Bones* (London: Heinemann, 1988), Alexander Kangengoni, *Effortless Tears* (Harare: Baobab Books, 1993), Nevanji Madanhire, *Goatsmell* (Harare: Anvil Press, 1992) and Yvonne Vera, *Nehanda* (Harare: Baobab Books, 1993).

[13] An examination of Marechera's works reveals that he wrote in a number of styles, including social realism, magical realism, surrealism, farce, comic, tragic, tragi-comic. This mixture sometimes leaves his work open to accusations of inconsistency and of being difficult or obscure. I see his 'experimentation' as a tribute to his versatility but more importantly as a search for his true voice.

[14] Because of her stance Dangarembga has attracted a great deal of attention although it should be pointed out that Hove's *Bones* deals very powerfully with the plight of Zimbabwean women as does Barbara Makhalisa whose collection of short stories, *The Underdog*, was published in 1984 and whose first work (in Ndebele) was published in 1969.

[15] A comment made by Davison Maruziva in his column 'Book Fair File' in the Harare *Herald* dated Saturday August 5th 1995.

[16] Telephone interview with David Pattison, 28th May 1998.

[17] Telephone interview with David Pattison, 3rd June 1998.

[18] Examination of the Heinemann files reveals a lack of consensus among the readers of Marechera's works. Many were ambivalent and suggested editing and rewriting. Some such as Ann Godfrey were condemnatory ('pretentious

rubbish') and others John Wylie and Heinemann African Writers Series Editor, James Currey, talked openly of 'potential genius' and, as the Heinemann files make clear, regarded Marechera as a possible Zimbabwean Achebe or Soyinka.

[19] William Henley, *For England's Sake*: 'What have I done for you, England, my England? / What is there I would not do, England, my own?'

[20] Sir Winston Churchill was British Prime Minister during World War II. He suffered from chronic depression which he likened to being followed everywhere by a 'large black dog'. A 'black sun' is, of course, a symbol for mental illness, particularly depression as Kristeva explored in her work on depression and melancholia, *Black Sun*. Her despairing 'Where does this black sun come from? Out of what eerie galaxy do its invisible, lethargic rays reach me, pinning me down to the ground...', is a cry from the heart which Marechera would certainly have recognised (Julia Kristeva, *Black Sun* (New York: Columbia University Press, 1986), p3).

[21] Professor Anne Barton, one of Marechera's tutors at New College, in a letter to me dated 5th July 1997, cast an interesting light on Marechera's relationships with his fellow students:

> Charles was a small man, but he could and did inflict a good deal
> of physical damage on the other undergraduates when (as was
> pretty often the case) he was drunk and spoiling for a fight. They
> were sympathetic to him, but understandably found it hard to be
> regularly beaten up by someone they had themselves brought to
> the college and wanted – without any condescension whatever –
> to make friends with.

Marechera's behaviour had dire implications for other would-be students as Barton accurately points out, "The JCR experiment, I believe, has never in consequence been repeated."

[22] Quoted by Jeremy Hawthorn in *Studying The Novel* (London: Edward Arnold, 1992), pp. 109-110.

[23] All the work published by Heinemann, *House of Hunger, Black Sunlight* and *The Black Insider*, is on current worldwide distribution. *Mindblast, Cemetery of Mind* and *Scrapiron Blues* were in print in Zimbabwe only until Africa World Press made new editions available internationally in June 1999.

[24] Heinemann reader John Wyllie commented on Marechera's '...tragic circumstances of being black in a too white world' (Veit-Wild 1992a: 204).

Works Cited

Beerbohm, Max. *Zuleika Dobson*. 1911 London: Heinemann, 1947.

Birmingham, David and Terence Ranger. 'Settlers and liberators in the south, 1953-1980', *History of Central Africa*, Volume Two, David Birmingham and Phyllis Martin Eds. Harlow: Longman, 1983.

Chapman, Michael. *Southern African Literatures.* London: Longman, 1996.

Chennells, Anthony and Flora Veit-Wild Eds. *Emerging Perspectives on Dambudzo Marechera.* New Jersey: Africa World Press, 1999.

Chinodya, Shimmer. *Dew in the Morning.* Gweru: Mambo, 1982.

----. *Harvest of Thorns.* 1989. London: Heinemann, 1990.

Dangarembga, Tsitsi.. *Nervous Conditions.* London: The Women's Press, 1988.

Fanon, Franz. *The Wretched of the Earth,* 1961. London: Penguin, 1990.

Grace, John and John Laffin. *Africa since 1960.* London: Fontana, 1991.

Holst Petersen, Kirsten. *An Articulate Anger Dambudzo Marechera: 1952-87* Sydney: Dangaroo Press, 1988.

Hove, Chencherai. *Bones.* London: Heinemann, 1988.

----. *Shadows.* London: Heinemann, 1991.

----. *Shebeen Tales* London: Serif, 1994.

Jones, Eldred D. 'Land, War & Literature in Zimbabwe: A Sampling' *African Literature,* Vol 20. London: James Currey, 1996.

Kahari, George. *The Search for Zimbabwean Identity.* Gwelo: Mambo Press, 1980.

Kangengoni, Alexander. *Effortless Tears.* Harare: Baobab Books, 1993.

Katiyo, Wilson. *A Son of the Soil* 1976. Harlow: Longman, 1988.

----. *Going to Heaven.* London: Rex Collings, 1979.

Kristeva, Julia *Black Sun* New York: Columbia University Press, 1989.

Lindfors, Bernth. *Long Drums and Canons* New Jersey: Africa World Press, 1995.

Makhalisa, Barbara C. *The Underdog and Other Stories* Gweru: Mambo, 1984.

Maja-Pearce, Adewale. 'Humbug hater', *New Statesman &*

Society. London: *31st* January 1992.

----. 'In Pursuit of Excellence', *Research in African Literatures,* Vol 23, No 4 Austin: University of Texas Press, 1992.

Marechera, Dambudzo. *The House of Hunger.* London: Heinemann, 1978.

----. *Black Sunlight.* London: Heinemann, 1980.

----. *Mindblast.* Harare: College Press, 1984.

----. *The Black Insider.* Harare: Baobab Books, 1990 and London: Lawrence and Wishart, 1992. References taken from the 1992 edition.

----. *Cemetery of Mind* Harare: Baobab Books, 1992.

----. *Scrapiron Blues* Harare: Baobab Books, 1994.

----. 'The African Writer's Experience of European Literature', *Zambezia,* XIV (ii) Harare: University of Zimbabwe, 1987a.

----. 'Soyinka, Dostoevsky: The Writer on Trial for his Time', *Zambezia,* XIV (ii) Harare: University of Zimbabwe, 1987b.

Maruziva, Davison. 'Another prize for Vera', The *Herald.* Harare: August 5th 1995.

McLoughlin, T. O. 'Black Writing in English from Zimbabwe'. *The Writing of East and Central Africa,* G.D. Killam ed. London: Heinemann, 1984a.

----. 'Men at War: Writers and Fighters in Recent Zimbabwean Fiction', *Current Writing,* No 3. Natal: University of Natal Press, 1991.

----. 'The Past and The Present in African Literature: Examples from Contemporary Zimbabwean Fiction', Presence *Africaine,* Vol 132 Paris: Societe Nouvelle Presence Africaine, 1984b.

Mungoshi, Charles. *Coming of the Dry Season* Harare: Zimbabwe Publishing House, 1972.

----. *Waiting for the Rain* London: Heinemann, 1975.

----. *Some Kinds of Wounds* Harare: Mambo Press, 1980.

----. *The Setting Sun and the Rolling World.* London: Heinemann, 1989.

Mutswairo, Solomon. *Mapondera: Soldier of Zimbabwe.* Washington: Three Continents Press, 1978.

----. *Chaminuka: Prophet of Zimbabwe* Washington: Three Continents Press, 1983.

Nyamfukudza, Stanley. *The Non-Believer's Journey.* London: Heinemann, 1980.

----. *Aftermaths.* Harare: College Press, 1983.

----. *If God Was a Woman.* Harare: College Press, 1991.

Pattison, David. 'Call No Man Happy: Inside *The Black Insider*: Marechera's Journey to Become a Writer? *Journal of Southern African Studies*, Vol 20, No 2 Abingdon: Carfax Publishing, 1994.

----. *From Rhodesia to Zimbabwe via Oxford and London* PhD Thesis unpublished, University of Hull, England, 1999.

----. *No Room for Cowardice* New Jersey: Africa World Press, forthcoming.

Ranger, Terence. *Revolt in Southern Rhodesia 1896-1897*, 1967. London: Heinemann, Second Edition, 1979.

Riemenschneider, Dieter. 'Short Fiction from Zimbabwe', *Research in African Literature*, Vol 20, No 3 Austin: University of Texas Press, 1989.

Samkange, Stanlake On *Trial for My Country.* London: Heinemann, 1966.

The Mourned One. London: Heinemann, 1975.

Year of the Uprising. London: Heinemann, 1978.

Sithole, Ndabaningi. *The Polygamist.* New York: Third World Press, 1972.

Roots of a Revolution Oxford: Oxford University Press, 1977.

Stoneman, Colin. Editor, Zimbabwe's *Prospects.* London: Macmillan, 1988.

Veit-Wild, Flora.

----. *Dambudzo Marechera 1952-1987.* Harare: Baobab Books, 1988.

----. *Dambudzo Marechera: A Source Book on his Life and Work* London: Hans Zell, 1992a.

----. *Teachers, Preachers, Non-Believers* London: Hans Zell, 1992b.

Vera, Yvonne. *Nehanda.* Harare: Baobab Books, 1993.

----. *Why Don't You Carve Other Animals?.* Harare: Baobab Books, 1994.

----. *Without A Name.* Harare: Baobab Books, 1994.

Zimunya, Musaemura. *Those Years of Drought and Hunger.*

Gwelo: Mambo Press, 1982.
Zinyemba, Ranga. 'Zimbabwe's lost novelists in search of direction', *Moto*, August 1983.

Playing Africa:
The Fictions of Ferdinand Oyono

Sharmila Sen
Harvard University

In October, 1959, Jean Genet's *Les Nègres* opened in Paris with tremendous success. Genet's meta-theatrical work placed an all-black cast in front of a white audience forcing issues of performance and spectatorship to be viewed under the glare of French colonialism in Africa. Was this presentation of the African colonial subject for the European gaze a sophisticated reprisal of the 1931 Paris Exposition? Did Africa remain the spectacle--even though Genet provocatively displayed the spectacle-ness of Africa--for the white audience in 1959? During the second half of the twentieth century, the eyes which critically viewed the theatricality of Africa were not only European ones: African writers of the period were also increasingly interested in Africa as a spectacle. Ferdinand Oyono's two novels, *The Old Man and the Medal* (1956) and *The Road to Europe* (1960), focus on the theatricality of African life and employ that theatricality as a mode of resistance in colonial Cameroon.

I. Setting the Stage

Scholars such as John Conteh-Morgan have argued that the popularity of theater in Africa is largely based on the ritualistic aspect of kinship and communal relationships of the area (Conteh-Morgan, 1994). Lee Warren (1975), for instance, also draws connections between the importance of ritualized ceremonies such as the I-Njoku elephant ceremony of the Bakwerri in Cameroon and the popularity of African theater. Roles and rituals, it seems, are more important than personalities in Francophone Africa. Of course, role-theory sociologists (and common sense) points out that performance is an aspect of all human life. In this case, an unequivocal case for the particularity of Africa vis-à-vis the importance of role-playing can only be made at the cost of exoticizing the continent. Oyono's novels do indeed support some of these assertions about the importance of ritual in Cameroonian society, while complicating the whole notion of staged identities in a colonial setting. His work does not propose a world where theatricality is solely the domain of the black African. Both the whites and the blacks are involved in producing choreographed images of themselves. Oyono captures the explosive moments when the two dramas, the European and the African, collide into each other within the larger stage of colonialism. The medal ceremony in *Old Man* provides us with a seminal moment where the two theaters collapse onto each other upon the figure of Meka. I will return to discuss this scene in greater detail later in this essay. At this point, I propose that the medal scene serve us as a symbol of the hostile colonial stage upon which two dramas cannot exist in a state of mutual coexistence but must enter into combat to gain the greater advantage.

In the carnival of cultures--German, French, and Greek on the Western side, as well as numerous indigenous ones--of colonial Cameroon in the fifties the atmosphere is obviously not one of a joyous coalition. Within the power structures those who can manipulate both the shifting European and African identities dexterously emerge as winners. In Oyono's novels this manipulation of multiple identities for a desired outcome marks the use of theatricality as resistance. Cultural hybridity, in this reading, is the realm of the stage. And Africa or the vision of Africa as produced in literature becomes that stage where the drama is performed. Under Oyono's pen theatricality is not only the domain of the textual narrative, it is also the domain of Africanist literary discourse.

This reading of theatricality within the shifting colonial setting of French Cameroon attempts to answer the following questions: Does theatricality empower the African figures or are they further disempowered by being forced to assume degraded roles? Do the gender implications of the spectacle-spectator relationship help us to understand the role of women and femininity within a political movement (particularly in its incarnation as Negritude) with masculinist tones? Finally, can the playfulness, the opaque artifice of theatricality, rescue our reading of Oyono from the politically fixed polemical?

Much of the critical discourse surrounding Oyono's novels tends to fall alongside Richard Bjornson's assertion in *The African Quest for Freedom and Identity* that Toundi, Meka, and Barnabas are characters made pathetic by their assimilationist delusions.[1]

All of Oyono's protagonists suffer because of their "false dreams." The mask of the obedient houseboy, of the good Christian, and of the budding colonial scholar are all detrimental ones. Only upon removal of these masks can the characters gain "the intellectual penetration that Oyono regards as essential in coping with a world of illusory appearances" (Bjornson 80). According to this line of critical thought, Africans have little to gain by staging a drama about themselves. Bjornson's argument presupposes a true-false dichotomy in which there exists a mythical state of "true" African-ness outside the boundaries of "false" colonialism. Such thinking assumes that within their own communities Africans are anything but artificial. On the contrary, Oyono's village gatherings render the indigenous community to be as steeped in ritual artifice as the protocol-ridden French.

II. Staged Literary Resistance

When Meka returns from his night in jail in *Old Man* his wife, Kelara, and the other women treat the villagers to the spectacular:

> Kelara went into the hut supported by Amalia. Some of the visitors made room so that she could roll on the ground, which she lost no time in doing. As quick as a flash she was down on the floor. She rolled from the dresser to the head of Meka's bed and from there to the back of the hut where the chickens slept. She waved her arms and legs about, crawled, knelt, lay down again, panted, spat, tore her dress, and uncovered her aged body, shrieking as loud as she could, and

only getting to her feet so that she could throw herself down onto the floor with renewed violence. Amalia followed her example and so did the other women. The men watched this performance with gleaming eyes, and called feebly for silence. All eyes were on the wife of Essomba whose dress had come right off. As she rolled on the ground she was kicking her legs violently up into the air (Oyono 1956: 149).

The parodic tone of this passage marks it as distinctly wavering from the amateur ethnographer mode of African literature. Olatubosun Ogunsanwo has made the astute observation that the "narrative tone of *The Old Man and the Medal* creates a 'shock therapy' that achieves an 'alienation effect' in the Brechtian sense--the inhibition of the author's identification with the characters on the stage and its replacement by a detached, critical attitude" (Ogunsanwo 111). The ironic narrative voice which breathlessly notes Kelara's repertoire of aerobic movements and adds that she stands up only to hurl herself down on the floor creates a distance between the reader and the characters in the scene. While we are critically aware of the humorous bawdiness of the women's action, the speechless male spectators are engaged without self-consciousness. The double-voiced narrative presents the reader with a traditional mourning scene while slyly questioning the propriety of the way Essomba's wife displays her sorrow. Is her behavior "natural" to the situation? Or is it as culturally choreographed as Madame Décazy's polite afternoon chat with the doctor's wife in *Houseboy*?

This passage is emblematic of Oyono's multi-layered discourse in the novel. His representation of Cameroonian life is rarely to educate the cultural outsider. He uses multiple voices within one narrative to engage readers, Cameroonian or not, to understand and question indigenous rituals. The scene in Meka's house is on one level a depiction of how rural Africa copes with community misfortune. On another level, it is a commentary on the artifice, the theatricality, of such a response. In "Discourse in the Novel," Bakhtin has described double-voicedness of the novel as the conscious hybridization of literary language. It is "an artistically organized system for bringing different languages in contact with one another, a system having as its goal the illumination of one language by means of another, the carving-out of a living image of another language" (Bakhtin 361). Taking our cues from Kenneth Harrow's assertions in *Thresholds of Change in African Literature*, we can critically revise Bakhtin's theories of heteroglossia and make it applicable within a colonial environment (Harrow, 1994). The double-voiced narrative of Oyono contains the inequalities between competing discourses where one discourse (European, politically empowered, scriptocentric) dominates another (African, politically disempowered, oral). Significantly, Francophone African literature occupies a position that is situated liminally between two realms of discourse--European and African. As Meka transcends his whitewash circle to become a player and a spectator within the twin dramas of black and white Doum, Oyono positions the reader both outside and inside the circle of knowledge. He makes it increasingly difficult for the reader to assign labels such as "natural" or "true" to the mourning scene narrated with both insider-knowledge and ironic distance: the text invites the outsider into Meka's hut while intellectually distancing him or her from the circle of villagers. Oyono's novels elude the easy categories of "dream" and "reality" that Bjornson tends to affix.

The theatrical nature of African private life as depicted by Oyono remains problematic when seen in the light of colonial interaction. How are we to understand the nature of role-playing when the audience includes white as well as black members? After all, Oyono's depiction of black characters as actors touches one of the most sensitive racial stereotypes of Africans as feigners, dissemblers, and liars. In "Nationalism as Resistance," Christopher Miller (1993) notes the importance of falseness as a resistant art in *Houseboy*. Playing African, donning the mask of the dissembling, clumsy, childish figure marks the survival skills of Toundi. A return to *Les Nègres* presents us with a grotesque elaboration of black theatricality staged specifically for Western spectators:

> They tell us that we're grown-up children. In that case, what's left for us? The theater! We'll play at being reflected in it, and we'll see ourselves--big black narcissists--slowly disappearing into its waters ... Since they merge us with an

image and drown us in it, let the image set their teeth on edge! (Genet 38-39)

Archibald's call to the black cast members to "play at being reflected" is similar to Oyono's twofold project of using theatricality as a mode of survival within the narrative (l'énoncé) and as a mode of making visible the apparatus of fiction-making-- presenting an image for literary consumption--within the discourse (l'énonciation).

The most powerfully resonant scenes in Oyono are those where the African must "play at being reflected" in front of the white man. Meka who foolishly grins at the medal ceremony, Toundi who stands next to the fridge and refills drinks, and Barnabas who signs his petition to the Governor with an enthusiastic "Long live France," are all playing African. The autobiographical narration of Aki Barnabas' stint as a tour guide takes this theme of playing African to its logical conclusion in the postcolonial arena:

And in a mercenary sort of way, I became their local guardian angel, who enabled them to photograph or film a pygmy, a monkey swinging from its branch, a boa swollen by its painful digestion, a hippopotamus lumbering away from the river bank, and an indigenous marriage in which the bride and bridegroom approach each other while wagging their heads to a balaphon--so many scenes that are "tremendous," "remarkable," and "sensational"! My fellow tribesmen also improvised a ritual for us whenever my explorers were willing to pay the "matabish," usually the price of several demijohns of red wine or palm wine, with which the unemployed, starveling actors drank themselves into a stupor before feverishly staging their production as the spectators smiled at the thought of the next film festival, where they were going to overwhelm the jury and snatch from them the Grand Prize that would consecrate them as Africanists (Oyono 1960: 66).

This passage from Oyono's last novel may be read as a pessimistic vision of the deluded hero. In fact, Bjornson continues to see Barnabas as a character "[l]ess concerned with learning the truth about himself than repressing the sense of shame that undermines his Europeanized self-image" (Bjornson 88). I do not think that Barnabas' "Europeanized" act is anymore repressive than Kelara's traditional mourning act. The very staginess of his narration when seen in context of the final confessional tableau is a form of resistance within the colonial system. Aki Barnabas sells his fictive confession to secure a passage to France. And this act of self-betrayal is what enables him to tell his story in the form of a novel. Selling out and preserving one's selfhood; assuming the role of the performer and retaining the privilege of looking seem, at first, to be mutually exclusive subject positions. However, Oyono's meta-theater clears a space for Africans to occupy both those positions simultaneously.

The "starveling actors" who stage authentic African scenes for the European audience are ridiculed by the narrator for their willingness to perform for a few demijohns of wine. However, the narrator implicitly valorizes them as well for duping the Africanists. Under the colonizers' gaze they enact their Africanness, producing a image which is both "false" and "true." The falseness lies in that the viewers may think they are watching an actual African wedding when in fact it is choreographed. The truth lies in that, unknowingly, the budding Africanists are witnessing a slice-of-life scene. They are witnessing Africans go about their daily lives which, in this case, happens to include tourist-baiting in order to procure a livelihood. Therefore, those consecrated Africanist film-makers at Cannes may have captured a "truer" image of modern Africa than they realize. Oyono valorizes this manipulation of the true/false image as the primary means of survival within colonialism.

The mask of the actor puts Barnabas on the road to Europe. This is Oyono's revision of his earlier novels where the mask proved to be too ill-fitting for both Toundi and Meka to flourish in French Africa. Meka, it should be noted, does make a small move towards realizing his own acting potential when he says that his hands are too "poto-poto" and he does not "want to dirty the white man" as his excuse to not shake Gullet's hands. Meka utilizes his African-ness, his status as the dirty black man, as a means of resistance. This mode of confession of guilt (or dirtiness in Meka's case) is Barnabas' final stage persona. The following poem from Aimé Césaire's *Cahier d'un retour au pays natal*, though responding to and representing a different colonial environment, elaborates the mode of the self-serving confessional:

> I declare my crimes and that there is nothing
> to say in my defense.
> Dances. Idols. An apostate. I too
> I have assasinated God with my laziness
> my words with my gestures
> with my obscene songs
>
> I have worn parrot plumes
> musk cat skins
> I have exhausted the missionaries' patience
> insulted the benefactors of mankind.
> Defied Tyr. Defied Sidon.
> Worshipped the Zambezi.
> The extent of my perversity overwhelms me! (Césaire 51-53)

Césaire's first line, no doubt carefully constructed in its lineation, contains the paradigmatic moment of this poem. In one fell swoop he confesses to European charges against savage Africa *and* challenges those charges by admitting "there is nothing." The confession is really a re-invention of the image of Africa created by Europe. However, the poetic voice appropriates that false charge and shows that the "nothing" is inscribed with a florid fantasy of perversity. Similarly, Barnabas recreates the crowd's images of a sinner's life in the confessional circle. Barnabas decides to "amaze the screaming crowd with [his] story." "What a novel my life," he exclaims and concludes the novel with the final ellipsis: "The first sentence that was going to put me in the road to Europe came into my mind..." Oyono's final novel loops back onto itself as the reader realizes that Aki Barnabas' road to Europe may very well be the book he or she just finished reading. It is a final theatrical removal of the mask to reveal the narrator's identity. Barnabas takes us backstage before he embarks on the performance that will take him to Europe.

However, as in the case of the "starveling actors" who dupe Africanists, the unmasking only serves to confound the spectator/reader further by forcing us to doubt the verity of the narrative we just read. Oyono's characters continue to occupy the position that, borrowing from Henry Louis Gates, Jr., is best signified by the double-faced Esu.

Meta-theater is an especially good vehicle for depicting the multiplicity and contiguity of positions occupied by the African colonial subject. Even that famous African of the Elizabethan stage, Othello, employs meta-theatricality to reconcile his dual roles as the Venetian citizen and the Moor. Othello's meta-theatrical death which attests to the power of drama--even a dying Moor can rise phoenix-like from his grave to play both the avenger-hero and the villainous Turk:

> Oth.   set you down this,
> And say besides, that in Aleppo once,
> Where a malignant and a turban'd Turk
> Beat a Venetian, and traduc'd the state,
> I took by the throat the circumcised dog,
> And smote him thus. [*stabs himself.*]
> (Othello, V, ii, 352-357)[2]

Oyono gives many of his characters the advantage of Othello's classic ploy of theatricality to locate the self and the other within one body. No doubt, reading a Cameroonian novelist by referring to the work of a canonical European author raises many problematic questions. Is African literature always to be read through the telescope of the metropole? Must Western literary references always take refuge in Shakespeare? Ngugi wa Thiong'o might designate this as an enterprise by a "society of bodiless heads and headless bodies"--his formulation of the state of alienation produced by an educational system and a literary culture based on the colonizer's language. Ngugi's critical apparatus might consider a reference to Shakespeare as undermining the "multiplicity of centres... reflected in the new literatures from Asia, Africa, and South America ... [which marks] a pluralism of languages as legitimate vehicles of the human imagination" (Ngugi 6-10). At the surface, then, my Eurocentric reading of

Oyono is on par with Meka's zazou jacket or with Barnabas' French scholarship: vain attempts to Europeanize the African.

Nonetheless, one way of rescuing this line of reading is to argue for the currently vogueish idea of hybridity. *In Morning Yet on Creation Day*, Chinua Achebe has argued the case of hybrid literatures--European languages with African resonances--with exemplary elegance and pragmatism:

> There are not many countries in Africa today where you could abolish the language of the erstwhile colonial powers and still retain the facility for mutual communication. Therefore, those African writers who have chosen English or French are not unpatriotic smart alecs with an eye on the main chance--outside their own countries. They are by-products of the same process that made the new nation states of Africa (Achebe 57).

Achebe's line of thought has a long history of critical precedence. Voices as historically and culturally diverse as Sigmund Freud, Fredric Jameson, Homi Bhabha, Abiola Irele, and Edward Said have argued that the self and the other may be more indistinguishable than we realize. In his most recent book, *Culture and Imperialism*, Said has written that the master and the servant cannot be extricated from each other as London and India or Paris and Algeria cannot be extricated from each other (Said 15).[3] A separation of Oyono's literature from European literature is as feasible as separating Barnabas' French education from his autobiographical narrative. One cannot exist without the other.

I raise the issue of cultural hybridity to clarify the significance of colonial theatricality. Othello's final figurative stance is the diegetic stance of the colonial African. He is both the subject and the object, the spectacle and the spectator. The one who takes advantage of the power to see and of the power of being seen wins the best possible outcome in an otherwise grim political situation. Having the power to see while remaining invisible allows Toundi limited power. He becomes a significant threat to the French only when he crosses over the line of the audience and becomes visible. Conversely, Meka remains an actor for much of the first two sections of *Old Man*. Only when he can cross over to the other side of the stage and have the power to look does he notice the metaphorical and literal similarities between the sow and the Chief of the whites. In Oyono's first two novels the protagonists may come to occupy the dual positions of the spectacle and spectator. But it is too late for them to receive a better fate than an arki-laden death or a reduction to *le vieux nègre*. In his last novel, written before his retirement from a literary career to embark on a diplomatic career, Oyono creates a character who can look and be looked at. It seems only logical, then, that Barnabas' story is written in the first person narrative. Barnabas is both the spectator and the spectacle of the colonial drama.

III. The Player Feminized

As a spectator Barnabas often places women as objects of his gaze. Madame Gruchet, Madame Hébrard, Anantatchia are all paraded through the text as the objects of a male gaze. Do the position of women as spectacles, then, further inform our reading of theatricality within Oyono's work? The prostitutes outside Hôtel de France parade their bodies for sale, inviting the male gaze. These women have adopted European fashion standards as part of their ploy to lure white customers and to deflect the paternalism of black Africa:

> Like the taxis parked nearby, they were tacitly and permanently available until the wee hours of the morning, waiting for the last European, the last possible well-fed customer, to stagger from the hotel and either gratify their daily hope ever so little or dash it completely with a vulgar insult. They constituted a standing affront to the local male population, furious that these lost women had rebelled sexually against them, while cynically introducing eccentricities like straight hair, wigs, lipsticks, cigarette holders, and a predilection for pants as a prelude to their plan for imitating their European rivals and emancipating themselves from the inhuman servitude of the African woman (Oyono 1960: 64).

Critics such as Bjornson have noted the painful similarities between Barnabas and a prostitute such as Anantatchia. The calculated sycophancy of male African characters such as Meka, Barnabas, or Toundi bears unsettling resemblance to the taxi-like availability of the "permit ladies." There is a certain amount of prostitution in Meka's performance as the grinning medal recipient and in Barnabas' performance as the francophile colonial scholar. Yet, this sort of sycophantic performance is often the only slot left open for an African actor on the colonial stage. The "permit ladies" take advantage of their otherwise unenviable role to defy the tyranny of the black men. Theirs is an attempt at emancipation with a very high cost.[4]

Similarly, Oyono's male characters often attain their goal (a passage to France or a medal) at a very high cost (integrity, land, sons). However stained such achievements may be, they are not to be devalued hastily. The "permit ladies" may live a horribly degraded life waiting for well-fed European customers but they do not have to deform their spine carrying the burden of matrimony as Amalia does. The paradoxical nature of the "freedom" attained by the prostitutes parallels much of the "freedom" attained by the men. For the "permit ladies," defiance against one group of men can only be possible through submission to another group of men. For Meka and Barnabas, overcoming barriers erected against blacks can only be achieved through adoption of theatrical black-ness.

Femininity may be the most problematic aspect of conflating colonial African resistance with prostitution. The female body is displayed in Oyono's novels as a powerful magnet for onlookers. Madame Décazy's body creates a spectacular phenomenon in Dangan market. Toundi's desire to look is developed most fully with Madame Décazy's arrival to Africa. Meka's recovery from the night in the jail is partly aided by the invigorating sight of Essomba's wife's body:

Meka was lying on his back like a corpse, his hands folded across his chest, staring up towards the raffia thatch of the roof. When Kelara rolled over to the bed he closed his eyes and opened them again when he heard her wailing under the dresser. But when it was the turn of Essomba's young wife to come twirling over to the bed Meka turned over in a flash gave her a quick glance out of the corner of his eye (Oyono 1956: 149).

The "sirens" in *Old Man* are the ritual symbols of the spectacle. In Oyono's work, both the female and the feminized are marked by their status as the object of gaze.[5]

If one of the crucial stages of resistance in Oyono's novels is to invite the gaze, become the performing African, as I have argued earlier, then how are we to understand the so far unquestioned gender positions of Barnabas and Meka?

In his book, *In Search of an African Theatre*, Scott Kennedy writes that "Africa is a woman." She is natural, naked, not covered with the "artificialities of life." This study, characteristic of its time and its cultural context[6], posits Africa as the primordial female based on anthropological discoveries. Kennedy calls on African-Americans to embrace "Mother Africa." Interestingly, this definition of Africa as female uses exclusively male African figures as examples of modern Africa's worldwide influence: who can forget "Dr. Julius Nyerere, Patrice Lumumba, Jomo Kenyatta, Dr. Kenneth Kuanda, Dr. Kwame Nkrumah, Sékou Touré, Chief Chaka, King Menelik, and Emperor Haile Selassie"? (Kennedy 23). Once again the image of politically active, independent Africa remains masculine, while the so-called organic culture and landscape of the continent remains feminine. We must remember that the rhetoric of African resistance, particularly early Negritude, is marked by its masculinist tone as well.

In this context, Oyono's African men must adopt a role of looked-at-ness even when such a role carries with it implications of femininity--a very sexualized femininity to boot. This is no doubt an ironic commentary on the *hommes murs-hommes circoncis* rhetoric in *Old Man*. The final joke Meka's friends can make about the French is based on African male sexuality. They giggle about the possible repercussions if Meka wore only a bila (slip) to the medal ceremony. The Chief of the whites would have to bend down and pin the medal on Meka's crotch. This childish and vulgar joke contains rhetoric of masculine resistance to colonial authority. It is a final assertion of one's uncircumcised African warrior past. But Engamba and Meka both realize the idealism and futility of such macho shows of power. Engamba finally lets his assegai slip out of his grip and says, "These things are useless now ... [c]ompletely useless" (Oyono 1956: 164). Toundi, too, had made the mistake of underestimating the white man based on traditional African notions of judging masculine power. His glimpse of Décazy's uncircumcised penis had assured him of his boss' limited power. The houseboy, in fact, was mistaken in his assumption. Traditional male symbols of power become inoperative in Oyono's colonial Africa.

On a stage where shaking one's assegai or displaying skulls as trophies can no longer be a practical form of asserting one's independence, what position of resistance is left open for the colonial African? It is not of little significance that the role open to these male protagonists coincide with the role played by African (and European) women. Overt theatricality in social behavior and a constant state of looked-at-ness are part of the lives of figures such as Madame Décazy, Madame Gruchet, Anantatchia, Kelara, and Amalia. In his attempt to use theatricality as a mode of resistance, Barnabas must assume this feminized role--a role perhaps not so different from that of Anantatchia. Oyono manipulates these tensions between assigned and assumed gender roles to crack the monolithic masculine rhetoric of African political resistance. In the multiply-situated theatrical self, Oyono creates a space where women can also take part in political resistance without shaking assegais or beheading white men. Simultaneously, he draws our attention to the hypocrisy and injustice within the male rhetoric of African independence. Neither Meka nor Engamba really treat their wives any better than the white man treats the black man. If critics such as Bjornson and Harrow have argued for the humanity of the black man, it is equally necessary to make a plea for the humanity of the black woman in her own environment. The scope of this paper is not large enough to thoroughly explore the dynamics of gender politics in the home and racial politics outside the home in colonial Cameroonian fiction. However, it cannot be overlooked that Oyono's novels lead us to these questions which complicate the neat true/false, black/white dichotomies of colonialism.

My argument is not one that assumes epistemological impossibility as a blanket statement. It is indeed possible to hold certain individuals responsible for their actions in *Houseboy* and *Old Man*. It is indeed possible to assign blame to Décazy, Moreau, and Gullet. However, *Road* proves to be the most difficult piece in Oyono's trilogy. Complicity marks the novel, as I have tried to argue somewhat differently earlier, both narratologically and discursively. To assign blame, to assign moral responsibility, the reader must be able to ascertain some level of the "reality" of the narrative. However, the final double confessional--the one in which Barnabas confesses his "sins" to the revivalists and the one in which he confesses the basis of the narrative to the reader--de-centers all the preceding chapters. Oyono thwarts the reader's desire for a traditional conclusion which ties up all ends neatly. His final sentence functioning as a *mise-en-abîme* throws all of our previous assumptions into chaos and re-opens the novel. Similarly, the role of women and the role of the resistant protagonists mirror and distort each other. The role played by women serves as explanations or elaborations of the nature of servitude. But as the female characters operate as explanations, they also muddy the villain-victim equations. If Barnabas finds his road to Europe through playing African, and if performance bears connotations of femininity, is Barnabas' authorship a de-masculinized one? Is Meka an unsexed le *vieux nègre* in the end? Before we embark on a traditional mourning of the loss of African masculinity under colonialism, we must recall that Oyono's novels throw plenty of light on the undesirable nature of such traditional masculinity. Finally, if performance may be associated with femaleness, then how are we to account for the absence of significant female protagonists within the literatures of theatrical resistance?

IV. Playing Africa

In Oyono's fiction successful resistance is achieved by a meta-theatricality that places a character such as Meka or Barnabas on both sides of the stage line. This double subjectivity is not a novelistic tool solely. Zakes Mda's Marotholi Travelling Theatre uses rural spectators as actors to present skits for development communication. These villagers of Lesotho perform their own roles for the purposes of the skit.[7]

The critical detachment and self-reflection required to play one's own self are the very qualities that Oyono's characters come to possess through the process of resistance. Playing African becomes the burden and the pleasure within the text. Perhaps if we extend the metaphor of playing to include artistic experimentation and creativity, we can free Oyono from the bounds of polemical literature.

Let me conclude with a slightly different instance of rehearsed African identities within the schoolroom (which itself can be a topic of further critical investigation). The developers of syllabi for the West African Examinations Council (WAEC) and the GCE 'O' Levels who hold Oyono's novels in such high esteem for its anti-colonialism have ironically "colonized" the imaginations of the students by prescribing rote responses to complex questions. Oyono's mission, WAEC prep books such as *Longman Guides to Literature* instill into the minds of the students, is primarily political and not literary.[8]

In a bizarre reiteration of the cliché of life imitating art, WAEC candidates must write strictly rehearsed responses about a trio of novels which seek to manipulate their notions of rehearsed identities and theatricality. In the realm of literature, the postcolonial generation may have to continue playing Africa unless we read fictions such as those by Oyono with greater vigilance.

Notes

[1] See Richard Bjornson, *The African Quest for Freedom and Identity: Cameroonian Writing and the National Experience* (Bloomington: Indiana University Press, 1991). Moreover, Abiola Irele writes that Toundi and Meka are disillusioned characters who experience some sort of illumination of the "real nature of the colonial situation." For more on this argument see, *The African Experience in Literature and Ideology* (London: Heinemann, 1981), 158, by Irele.

[2] I refer to the line numbers according to version of play as published in *The Riverside Shakespeare* (Boston: Houghton Mifflin, 1997), 1288.

[3] My reference to Freud's notion of hybridity is mainly based on his essay, "The Uncanny," where he argues that the *unheimlich* is the *heimlich*. In *The Political Unconscious*, Jameson also makes a point that romance literature culminates in the unmasking of the evil other as the good guy. Bhabha's writings on hybridity are well known enough for me to only point to "Signs Taken

for Wonders" as one of his many essays on the topic. Abiola Irele's "In Praise of Alienation" makes gestures towards hybridity in its assertion that European cultural and technological influence over Africa cannot be shaken off.

[4] I do not mean to suggest that prostitution is a choice these women willingly make to gain freedom from patriarchy. The economic destitution of their community is, no doubt, the primary factor in their so-called choice of making a living.

[5] This analysis is obviously influenced by Freudian formulations of the spectator-spectacle relationship: active, male gaze and passive, female looked-at-ness. I do not propose that Freud's work is as pan-historical and pan-cultural as many psychoanalytical critics tend to think. However, Oyono's novels do follow the Freudian formula to a certain degree.

[6] Afro-centrism of the 1960s and 1970s in the United States.

[7] For further discussion of the travelling theater see, Zakes Mda, When People Play People (Johannesburg: Witwatersrand University Press, 1993).

[8] Also see, 'Biodun Onibonoje's Houseboy: Notes, Q/A (Ibadan: Onibonoje Press & Book Industries, 1975) for another example of such pedagogical strategies.

Works Cited

Achebe, Chinua. *Morning Yet on Creation Day.* London: Heinemann, 1975.

Bakhtin, M.M. *The Dialogic Imagination.* Trans. Caryl Emerson and Michael Holquist.Austin: University of Texas Press, 1981.

Bjornson, Richard. *The African Quest for Freedom and Identity: Cameroonian Writing and the National Experience.* Bloomington: Indiana University Press, 1991.

Césaire, Aimé. *The Collected Poetry.* Trans. Clayton Eshleman and Annette Smith. Berkeley: The University of California Press, 1983.

Conteh-Morgan, John. *Theatre and Drama in Francophone Africa.* Cambridge: Cambridge University Press, 1994.

Genet, Jean. *The Blacks: A Clown Show.* Trans. Bernard Frechtman. New York: Grove Press, 1960.

Harrow, Kenneth. *Thresholds of Change in African Literature: The Emergence of a Tradition.* Portsmount: Heinemann, 1994.

Irele, Abiola. *The African Experience in Literature and Ideology.* London: Heinemann, 1981.

Kennedy, Scott. *In Search of the African Theatre.* New York: Charles Scribner's Sons, 1973.

Miller, Christopher. "Nationalism as Resistance and Resistance to Nationalism in the Literature of Francophone Africa." *Yale French Studies* 82, Post/Colonial Conditions (1993).

Ngugi, wa Thiong'o. *Moving the Center: The Struggle for Cultural Freedoms.* Portsmouth: Heinemann, 1993.

Ogunsanwo, Olatubosun. "The Narrative Voice in Two Novels of Ferdinand Oyono." *English Studies in Africa,* 29:2.

Oyono, Ferdinand. *Road to Europe.* 1960. Trans. Richard Bjornson. Washington, D.C.: Three Continents Press, 1989.

_____.*The Old Man and the Medal.* 1956. Trans. John Reed. Portsmouth: Heinemann, 1967.

Said, Edward. Culture and Imperialism. New York: Random House, 1993.

Shakespeare, William. *The Riverside Shakespeare.* Boston: Houghton Mifflin, 1997.

Warren, Lee. *The Theater of Africa.* Englewood Cliffs: Prentice Hall, 1975.

Index

A

Abba Micah Soudani, 215-216
Abbé Grégoire, 39
ABC Television, 251, 250, 255, 259
Abiola Irele, 385, 391
Abissinia, 36
Abolition, 39, 97
Abraham Lincoln, 216
Abyssinia, 26
Accra, 213
Achebe, 11, 258, 331, 337-339, 344
Addis Ababa, 210-211, 215-217
Adulthood, 309
Adventure, 180, 183, 185
Adversarial, 299, 300
Aesthetics, 365
Africa The Destroyer, 116
Africa World Press, 347
African Americans, 15, 39, 40, 210-
    212, 214-215, 217, 262, 265, 269-
    271, 273, 275, 284, 388
African Ancestry, 265
African Collection, 203
African Consanguinity, 299
African Countries, 345
African Culture, 275, 363, 287, 289,
    291
African Customs, 295
African Demon, 141
African Descent, 217
African Dogs, 109
African Elephant Group, 202
African English, 268
African Environment, 106-107, 109,
    111, 117, 119-120, 122

African Essence, 267
African Expedition Corporation, 199
African Geography, 128
African Hall, 196, 197, 199, 200, 203
African Heat, 134
African Hero, 336
African History, 262, 263, 271
African Identity, 169
African Image, 355
African Infrastructure, 290
African Jungle, 198
African Literature Association, 258
African Literature, 15, 328, 337, 339,
    340, 344, 349
African Maze, 154
African Men, 180, 270, 315
African Mythology, 288, 296
African Narrative, 148, 154
African Novels, 332
African People, 196, 202
African Pigs, 109
African Political Resistance, 389
African Scholars, 258
African Societies, 288, 290, 291, 295,
    297, 300, 309, 332
African Stories, 148
African Tale, 140, 144, 145, 146, 147,
    154, 155
African Universe, 289, 290, 294
African Wildlife, 197, 199
African Women, 259, 269, 284, 298,
    299, 300, 311
African Writers, 337, 376, 385
Africanist Discourse, 224, 377, 382
Africanists, 258, 381, 382, 384
Africanity, 40
African-ness, 382

H

Habäsät, 26
Hadrami, 89
Haggard (H. Rider), 106, 110-111, 113, 115, 119-121, 124-126, 196, 201, 206
Haile Selassie, 211-212, 214-215, 217-218, 388
Hair, 25, 39
Haitian, 273-275
Ham Leugh, 37
Hanley, 116-117, 124, 126
Hannibal, 33
Harar, 34
Harare, 346-347, 365, 368
Haratîn, 31
Harem, 149-150, 176-178, 186
Harlem Renaissance, 12
Harlem, 211, 213-214, 216
Hastings Kamuzu Banda, 16
Heart of Sickness, 245
Hebrew, 244
Hedonism, 92
Hegel, 6, 263
Hegemonic Discourses, 263
Hegemony, 223, 268
Hell, 112
Henry Louis Gates, Jr., 384
Henty, 107-109, 111-112, 115-116, 120, 123-124, 126
Hereros, 220-224, 226-231
Hereros, 222, 227, 229, 231
Hermaphrodite, 295
Hero-Doctor, 247
Herodotus, 3, 24-25, 28-29
Heroes, 329, 338
Hesiod, 24
Heteroglossia, 380
Hexagon, 164, 165
Hierarchies, 90, 329
Hieroglyphs, 270
High School, 312-313, 318-320
Higher Education, 308, 316, 318, 320
Historical Account, 94
Historical Fiction, 348
Historical Inaccuracies, 200
Historical Realism, 352

Historicity, 349
History, 86-87, 91-94, 96, 98-99, 220-225, 230-231
Hitler, 220, 222, 224, 226
HIV Virus, 263
Hobbes, 6
Hollywood, 177, 199, 262, 264-265
Holocene, 31
Holy Land, 26
Homer, 3, 14, 24, 25
Homi Bhabha, 385
Homo Sapiens Sapiens, 107
Homosexuality, 181
Horn of Africa, 34, 41
Hospital, 238-242, 245, 246
Hottentots, 132
Housewives, 298
Housework, 314, 315
Hughes, 210, 212-214, 217
Hugo, 6
Human Condition, 351
Human Experience, 351
Human Sacrifice, 136
Humanitarian, 246
Humans, 284, 288, 334
Hume, 6
Husband, 286, 292, 294, 297, 298
Hyperion, 25

I

Iberian, 37
Ibn Battuta, 2
Idealism, 388
Identification, 211, 215, 379
Identity of the Same, 223
Identity, 3, 4, 11, 12, 16, 160, 164, 168-170, 185, 223, 227, 229, 344-346, 352, 355, 363, 366, 377, 391
Ideological, 361, 367
Idols, 383
Ignorance, 332
Illiteracy, 311, 312
Images, 107, 123, 129, 198, 200-206, 251, 255, 258, 352, 355-357, 359-360, 364-366, 380-383, 388
Imagination, 328, 331, 336, 339, 391
Immigrant Women, 251

Immigration and Naturalization Service, 253
Immorality, 186
Impenetrability, 197, 198
Impenetrable, 108, 111, 113
Imperial Enterprise, 122, 123
Imperial Space, 164
Imperialism, 4, 6-8, 86, 121, 161, 163, 164-165, 167, 171, 176, 182, 187, 211, 220, 224-226, 230, 284
Impersonations, 294
Improvised, 381
Inclusive, 295, 296
Independence, 11, 13, 135, 345-346, 349-352, 368
Independent, 388
India, 87-89, 91, 287, 385
Indian Ocean, 34, 87-89
Indians, 229
Indies, 34, 35
Indigenous Languages, 346
Indigenous, 92, 94, 96, 99, 160, 163, 166, 168, 171, 287, 289, 291, 294-296, 300, 346, 377-379, 381
Indo-European, 32, 33
Inferiority, 223, 285, 286, 329, 338, 340
Infertility, 250, 251
Infibulation, 250, 252, 255-256, 259
Informants, 5
Inheritance, 318
INS, 254
Intellectual Anarchism, 367
Intellectual Sophistication, 336
Intellectual, 336, 345, 368
Interdependent, 298
International Decade for Women, 251
Interpretations, 330
Intertextually, 358
Invasions, 290
Irak, 145
Islam, 24, 26, 30, 34-36, 86, 89, 96, 129, 135, 171, 252, 286, 290-291, 296-298, 300
Islamic Cultures, 296
Islamic Law, 97
Islamic Mesostructure, 290
Islamicized, 291, 297

Italian Takeover, 210, 217
Italians, 24, 40, 169, 215
Italy, 33, 160, 162, 165, 210-211, 213-217
Ituri Peoples, 203
Ituri, 203J

J

Jacobean, 141
Jamaica, 274
Jamaican, 275
James Bruce, 36, 38
James, 12
Japanese, 40, 228-229
Jean-Marie Téno, 273
Jeronimo Lobo, 35, 36
Jersey City, 211
Jerusalem, 34
Jesus, 244, 286, 332
Jewish, 180
Jews, 169, 170, 172
Jews, 34, 95, 180
Jihads, 34
Joe Louis, 213
Johnson, 35, 36
Joinville, 128-129, 136
Jomo Kenyatta, 212, 388
Joseph Conrad, 106, 124, 125
Joyce Cary, 106, 111, 336, 337, 340
Judeo-Christian, 284
Julius Nyerere, 388
Jungle, 111, 119K

K

K.C.S.E., 308, 316
Kant, 238
Kassindja, 253-255
Kebra Nagast, 26
Kenneth Kuanda, 388
Kenya Certificate of Primary Education, 308
Kenya Certificate of Secondary Education, 308
Kenya, 86-88, 90, 93, 96, 98, 111, 254, 308-312, 314-315, 317-318, 320, 322

Maghreb, 28, 30-31, 33, 35, 143, 154
Maghrebi, 36
Mago, 28
Malaria, 90, 245
Malawi, 16, 344
Malcolm X, 228, 231
Male Organ, 251
Male Predominance, 298
Male Rhetoric, 389
Male, 269-270, 282, 284, 286-288, 294-295, 297-298, 300, 379, 386-389
Males, 251, 289, 291, 295
Mali, 37
Malindi Museum Society, 91
Malindi, 86-94, 96, 98-99
Maltese, 169
Man of Mercy, 238, 247
Mangbetu, 203
Manipulation, 377, 382
Mannoni, 112, 126
Mansa Musa, 37
Marcus Garvey, 211
Marechera, 345-358, 360, 362-365, 367, 368
Marginalized, 220, 320
Marriage, 250, 255-256, 291-292, 309, 315, 381
Marseilles, 160
Martin Johnson African Expedition, 199
Martin Johnson, 199
Marx, 225, 226
Marxism, 214, 217
Masculine Weakness, 182
Masculine, 378, 388-390
Mask, 378, 380, 382-383
Massachusetts Magazine, 143, 144, 145, 157-159
Matabele, 122
Maternalist, 284
Mathare Valley, 312
Matrilineal, 309
Matrilinear, 289
Matrimony, 387
Mauresques, 180, 182
Mauritania, 30, 33, 36, 140, 149
Mazrui, 296

Mecca, 89
Medicinal Practice, 297
Medieval, 24, 35-36, 128-129
Mediterranean Man, 170
Mediterranean Sea, 160-161, 163, 165, 169-170, 172
Mediterranean, 24, 32, 128, 130, 146, 148, 151, 272
Memmi (Albert), 112, 127, 223
Memnon, 24
Men, 269-271, 282-283, 286, 297-300, 313, 315-316, 318-320, 379, 387-389
Menelik, 26, 388
Mercenaries, 86, 89, 94
Meroe, 25
Meru People, 200
Messengers, 285
Messiah, 34
Meta-Literature, 344
Metropole, 160-161, 164-165, 384
Metropolis, 227
Metropolitan, 160, 162-165, 171
Middle Ages, 129, 135
Middle East, 251
Middle Eastern, 3, 96, 250-251
Middle Passage, 275
Migrations, 272
Mijikenda, 90, 93, 97, 98
Military Conquests, 176
Minorities, 284
Misconceptions, 129
Misleading, 199
Misrepresentations, 329, 337-338
Mission, 187, 200, 203, 244, 391
Missionaries, 94, 186, 227, 238, 247, 264
Mister Johnson, 330-332, 334-337, 340
Modern, 205, 211, 217, 241, 246, 266-269, 271, 289, 297-299, 337-338, 382, 388
Modernity, 204-205, 267-268, 272
Mogadishu, 255
Mohamedans, 144, 146, 158
Mohammed, 26
Mombasa, 88-89, 97, 312
Monarchical, 9

N

S